ESL学生英语40

附DVD，英语、普通话、粤语三种发音

With complimentary DVD. Pronunciation of Headwords in English, Putonghua and Cantonese is available.

TIMES 4000 WORDS for ESL LEARNERS

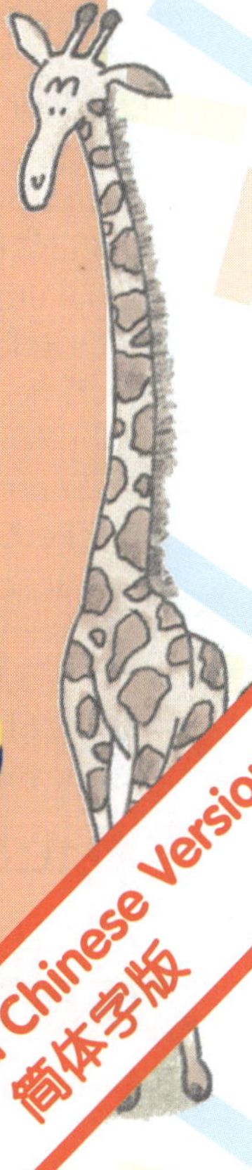

附英语及汉语（普通话）拼音

with phonetic symbols and Hanyu Pinyin

Simplified Chinese Version
简体字版

CONTENTS 目录

TIMES 1000 WORDS IN PICTURES

TIMES 1000 WORDS TO TALK ABOUT

TIMES 1000-WORD DICTIONARY

TIMES 1000 ACTION WORDS

TIMES 1000 WORDS IN PICTURES

Illustrated by

May Kong

A Note to Parents

This section of the book constitutes a picture dictionary designed to introduce students to words in groups, ranging from words about the student's family, body and environment to things in other countries and space. The 1000 vocabulary items include things and concepts within the student's immediate experience, such as **bicycle**, **car** and **van**, as well as more difficult but related words such as **dump truck** and **container lorry**. The related words have been selected not only to introduce young readers to new words but also to new things that will be useful and interesting for them to know.

Every page is attractively laid out, making this section a delightful means for parents to share time with their children. The lively illustrations will provide an opportunity for children to ask and answer questions and so stimulate further interest in learning.

给家长的话

我们在这部分用分类的方式把 **1,000** 个生词介绍给学生。从学生的家庭、身体及周围事物的词汇开始，然后扩大到有关国家及太空的事物。所选的词包括了学生经验范围内的事情和概念，例如 **bicycle**、**car** 和 **van**，以及难度较高、但有关联的词汇，例如 **dump truck** 和 **container lorry**。选择这些词类的目的，不只是给小读者介绍新的词汇，而且是让他们认识既有用又有趣的新事物。

本部分每一页都经过精心设计，让父母与孩子一同快乐阅读。活泼生动的插图给孩子机会发问及回答问题，进一步提高他们的学习兴趣。

Family

家庭

father [ˈfɑːðə]
父亲 [fù qin]
mother [ˈmʌðə]
母亲 [mǔ qin]
baby [ˈbeɪbɪ]
婴儿 [yīng ér]
sister [ˈsɪstə]
姐妹 [jiě mèi]
brother [ˈbrʌðə]
兄弟 [xiōng dì]
grandfather [ˈgrænfɑːðə]
祖父 [zǔ fù]
grandmother [ˈgrænmʌðə]
祖母 [zǔ mǔ]
uncle [ˈʌŋkl]
伯父、叔父、舅父、姑丈、姨丈
[bó fù, shū fù, jiù fù, gū zhàng, yí zhàng]
aunt [ɑːnt]
伯母、婶母、姨母、姑母、舅母
[bó mǔ, shěn mǔ, yí mǔ, gū mǔ, jiù mǔ]
cousins [ˈkʌznz]
堂兄弟、表兄弟、堂姐妹、表姐妹
[táng xiōng dì, biǎo xiōng dì, táng jiě mèi, biǎo jiě mèi]

Body
身体

ear [ɪə]
耳朵 [ěr duo]

arm [ɑːm]
手臂 [shǒu bì]

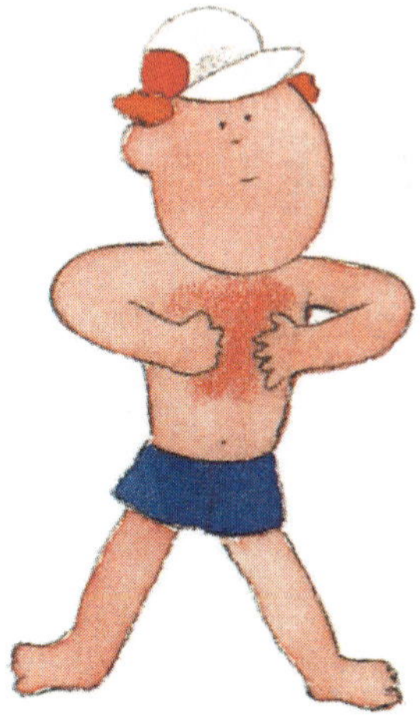

ankle [ˈæŋkl]
踝 [huái]

forehead [ˈfɒrɪd]
前额 [qián é]

chest [tʃest]
胸部 [xiōng bù]

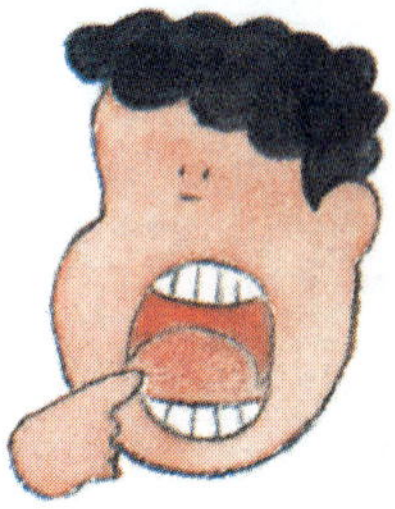

mouth [maʊθ]
口 [kǒu]

face [feɪs]
脸 [liǎn]

hair [heə]
头发 [tóu fà]

cheek [tʃiːk]
面颊 [miàn jiá]

neck [nek]
颈 [jǐng]

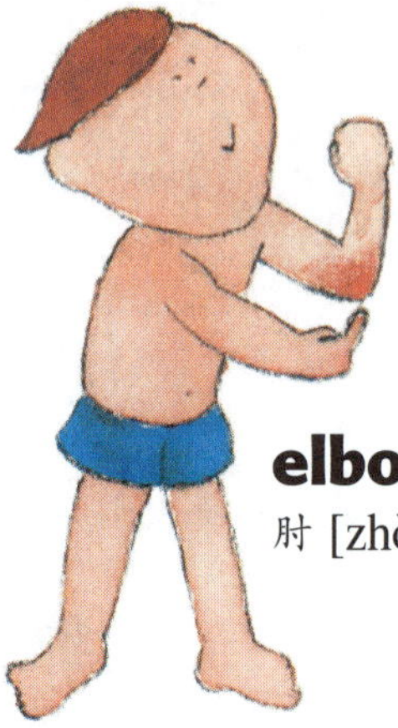

elbow [ˈelbəʊ]
肘 [zhǒu]

foot [fʊt]
脚 [jiǎo]

head [hed]
头 [tóu]

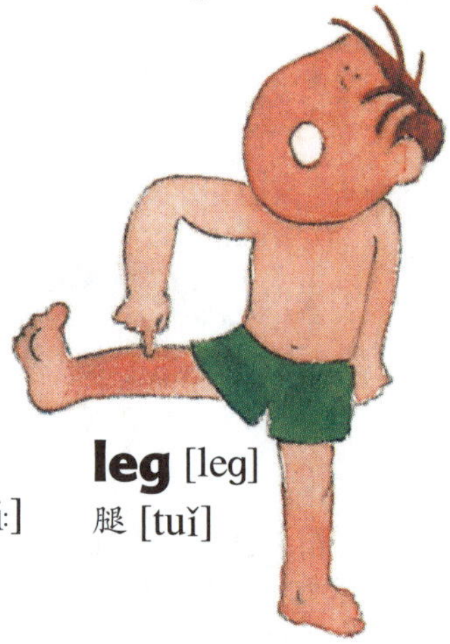

leg [leg]
腿 [tuǐ]

knee [niː]
膝 [xī]

heel [hiːl]
脚后跟 [jiǎo hòu gēn]

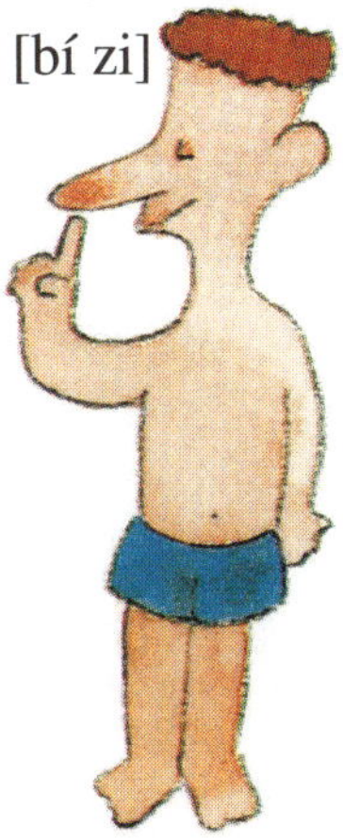

nose [nəʊz]
鼻子 [bí zi]

stomach [ˈstʌmək]
胃 [wèi]

waist [weɪst]
腰部 [yāo bù]

chin [tʃɪn]
下巴 [xià bā]

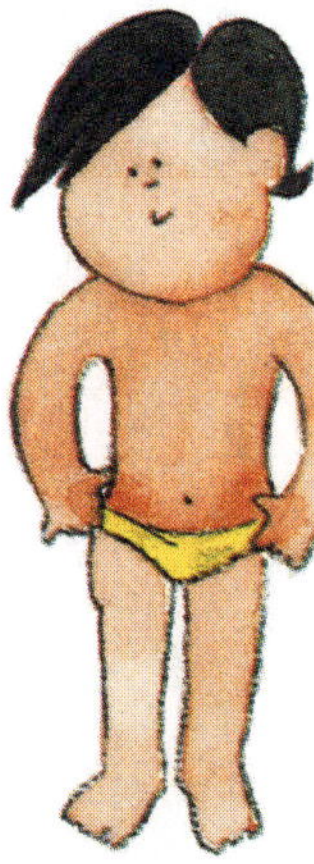

hips [hɪps]
臀部 [tún bù]

wrist [rɪst]
手腕 [shǒu wǎn]

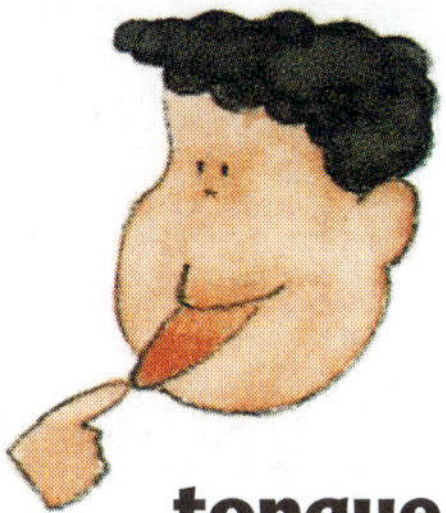

tongue [tʌŋ]
舌头 [shé tou]

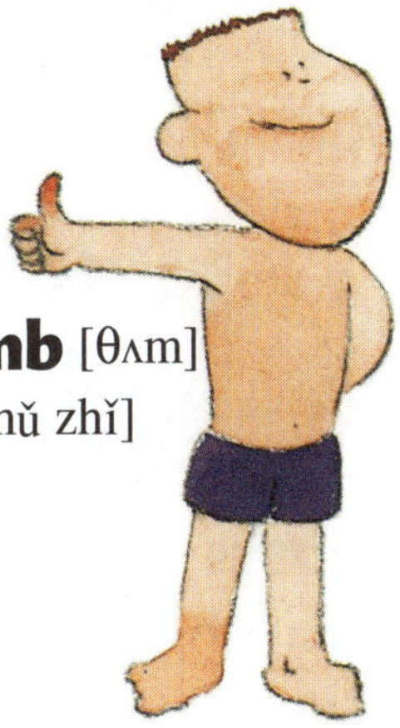

thumb [θʌm]
拇指 [mǔ zhǐ]

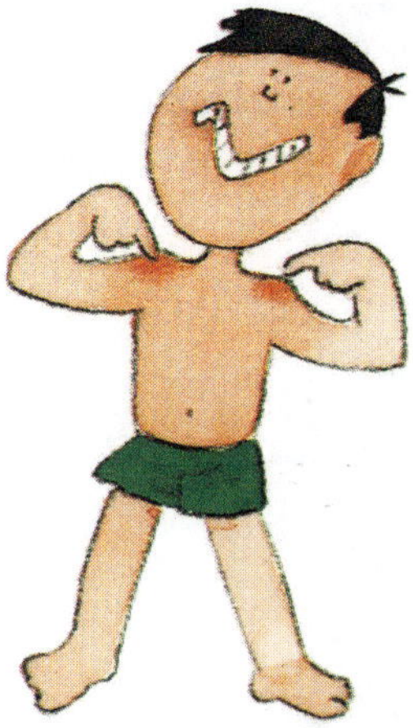

shoulders [ˈʃəʊldəz]
肩膀 [jiān bǎng]

buttocks
[ˈbʌtəks]
屁股 [pì gǔ]

toe [təʊ]
脚趾 [jiǎo zhǐ]

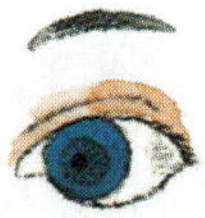

eye [aɪ]
眼睛 [yǎn jing]

lips [lɪps]
唇 [chún]

beard [bɪəd]
胡须[hú xū]

nail [neɪl]
指甲 [zhǐ jiǎ]

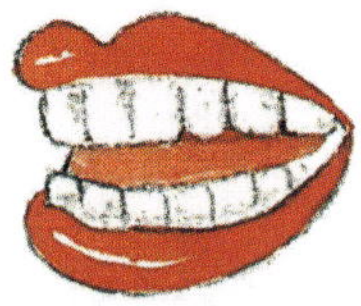

teeth [tiːθ]
牙齿 [yá chǐ]

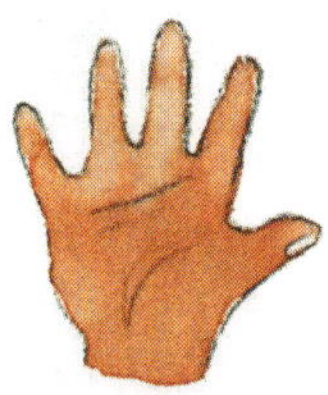

palm [pɑːm]
手掌 [shǒu zhǎng]

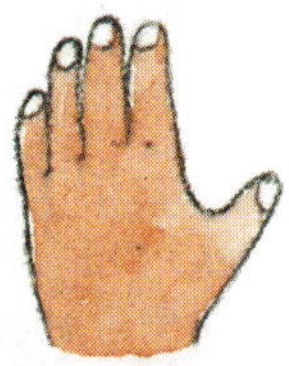

hand
[hænd]
手 [shǒu]

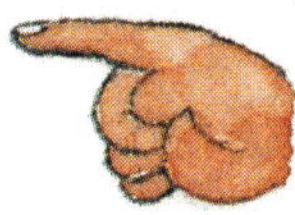

finger [ˈfɪŋgə]
手指 [shǒu zhǐ]

Things We Wear

穿戴衣物

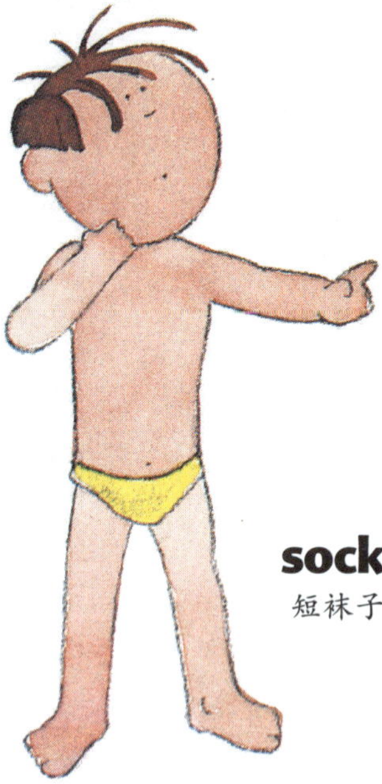

sweater
圆领毛衣 [ˈswetə]
[yuán lǐng máo yī]

trainers [ˈtreɪnəz]
运动鞋 [yùn dòng xié]

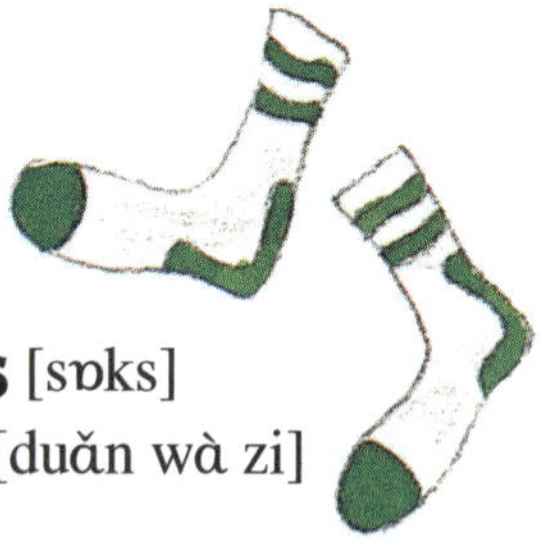

socks [sɒks]
短袜子 [duǎn wà zi]

coat [kəʊt]
大衣 [dà yī]

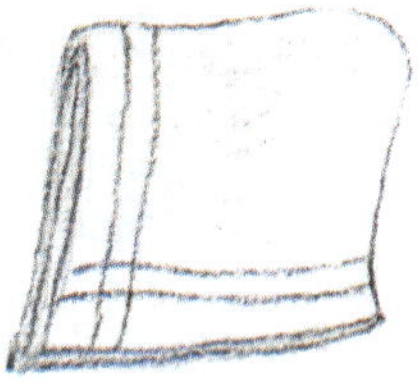

handkerchief
[ˈhæŋkətʃɪf]
手帕 [shǒu pà]

cap [kæp]
便帽、鸭舌帽
[biàn mào, yā shé mào]

badge [bædʒ]
徽章 [huī zhāng]

hat [hæt]
帽子 [mào zi]

shorts [ʃɔːts]
短裤 [duǎn kù]

watch [wɒtʃ]
手表 [shǒu biǎo]

trousers [ˈtraʊzəz]
长裤 [cháng kù]

jeans
[dʒiːnz]
牛仔裤
[niú zǎi kù]

boots [buːts]
长靴 [cháng xuē]

belt [belt]
腰带、皮带
[yāo dài, pí dài]

shirt [ʃɜːt]
衬衫 [chèn shān]

suit [suːt]
西装 [xī zhuāng]

bow tie [ˌbəʊ ˈtaɪ]
蝶形领结
[dié xíng lǐng jié]

T-shirt [tiː ʃɜːt]
汗衫 [hàn shān]

shoes [ʃuːz]
鞋子 [xié zi]

helmet [ˈhelmɪt]
头盔 [tóu kuī]

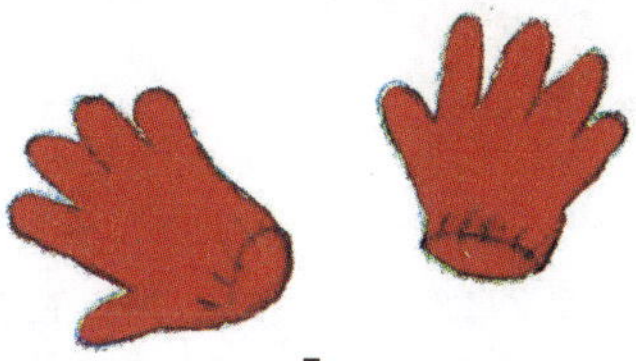

gloves [glʌvz]
手套 [shǒu tào]

jacket [ˈdʒækɪt]
外套 [wài tào]

slippers [ˈslɪpəz]
拖鞋 [tuō xié]

sun visor [ˈsʌn ˌvaɪzə]
太阳帽 [tài yáng mào]

glasses [glɑːsɪz]
眼镜 [yǎn jìng]

swimming trunks[ˈswɪmɪŋ ˌtrʌŋks]
游泳裤 [yóu yǒng kù]

vest [vest]
背心 [bèi xīn]

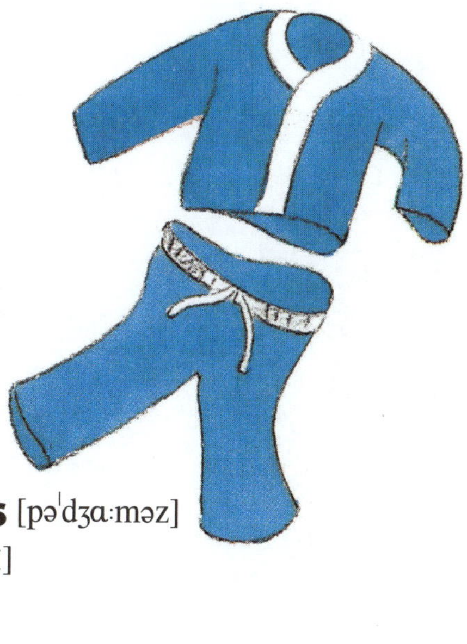

pyjamas [pəˈdʒɑːməz]
睡衣 [shuì yī]

tie [taɪ]
领带 [lǐng dài]

panties [ˈpæntɪz]
女装内裤 [nǔ zhuāng nèi kù]

dress [dres]
裙子 [qún zǐ]

blouse [blaʊz]
女装衬衫
[nǔ zhuāng chèn shān]

hat [hæt]
帽子 [mào zi]

sandals [ˈsændlz]
凉鞋 [liáng xié]

scarf [skɑːf]
围巾 [wéi jīn]

skirt [skɜːt]
短裙 [duǎn qún]

ring [rɪŋ]
戒指、指环
[jiè zhǐ, zhǐ huán]

slip [slɪp]
衬裙 [chèn qún]

stockings [ˈstɒkɪŋz]
长袜 [cháng wà]

raincoat [ˈreɪnˌkəʊt]
雨衣 [yǔ yī]

ribbon [ˈrɪbən]
丝带 [sī dài]

apron [ˈeɪprən]
围裙 [wéi qún]

necklace [ˈneklɪs]
项链 [xiàng liàn]

shoes [ʃuːz]
鞋子 [xié zi]

sunglasses [ˈsʌnglɑːsɪz]
太阳眼镜 [tài yáng yǎn jìng]

button [ˈbʌtn]
钮扣 [niǔ kòu]

collar [ˈkɒlə]
衣领 [yī lǐng]

cuff [kʌf]
袖口 [xiù kǒu]

pocket
[ˈpɒkɪt]
衣袋 [yī dài]

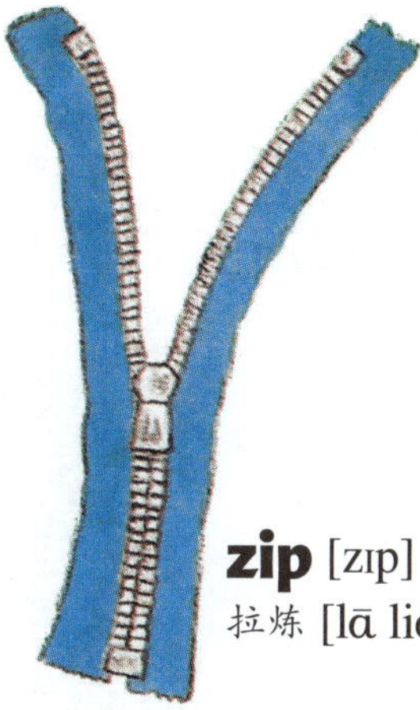

zip [zɪp]
拉炼 [lā liàn]

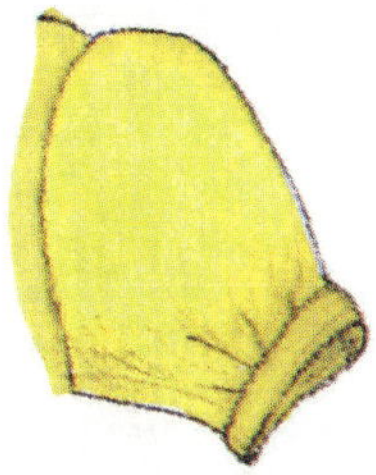

sleeve [sliːv]
袖子 [xiù zi]

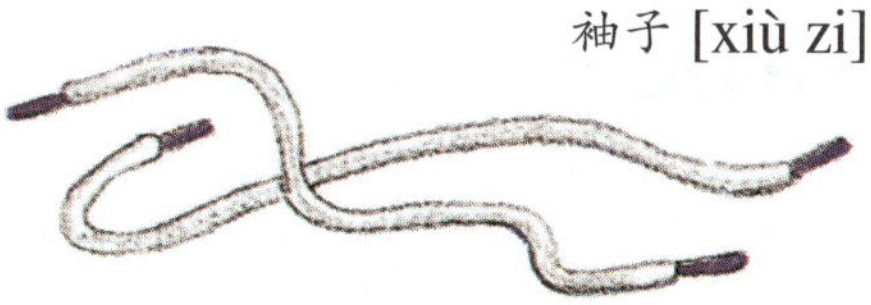

shoelaces [ˈʃuːleɪsz]
鞋带 [xié dài]

nightdress [ˈnaɪtdres]
睡裙 [shuì qún]

swimsuit
[ˈswɪmsuːt]
游泳衣 [yóu yǒng yī]

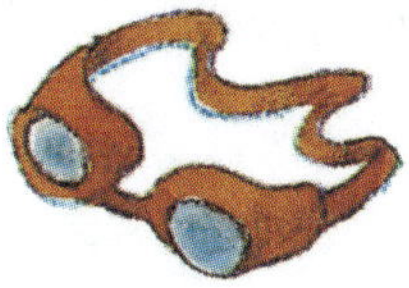

goggles [ˈgɒglz]
游泳镜 [yóu yǒng jìng]

uniform [ˈjnɪʃɔːm]
制服 [zhì fú]

In the House 屋子

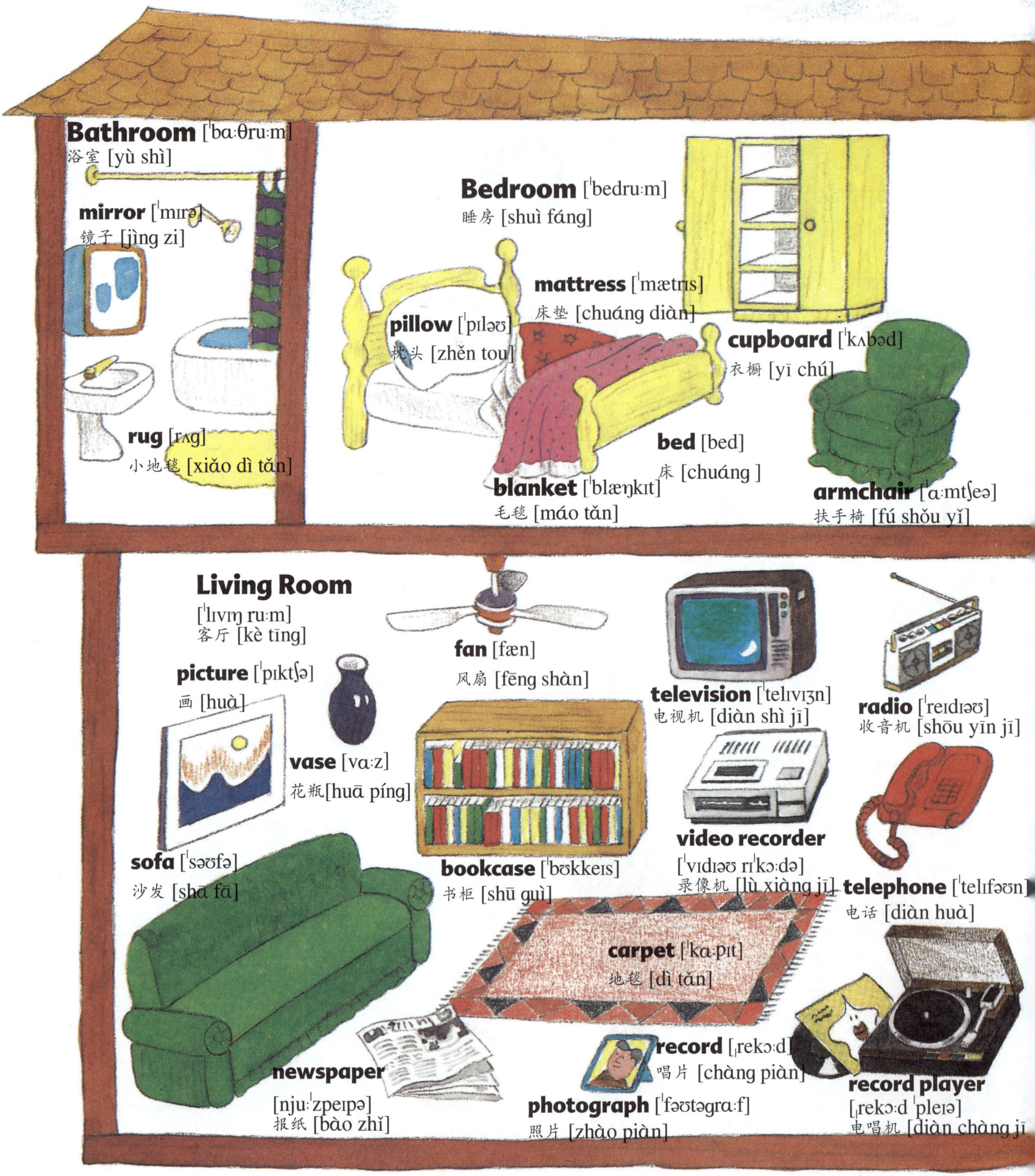

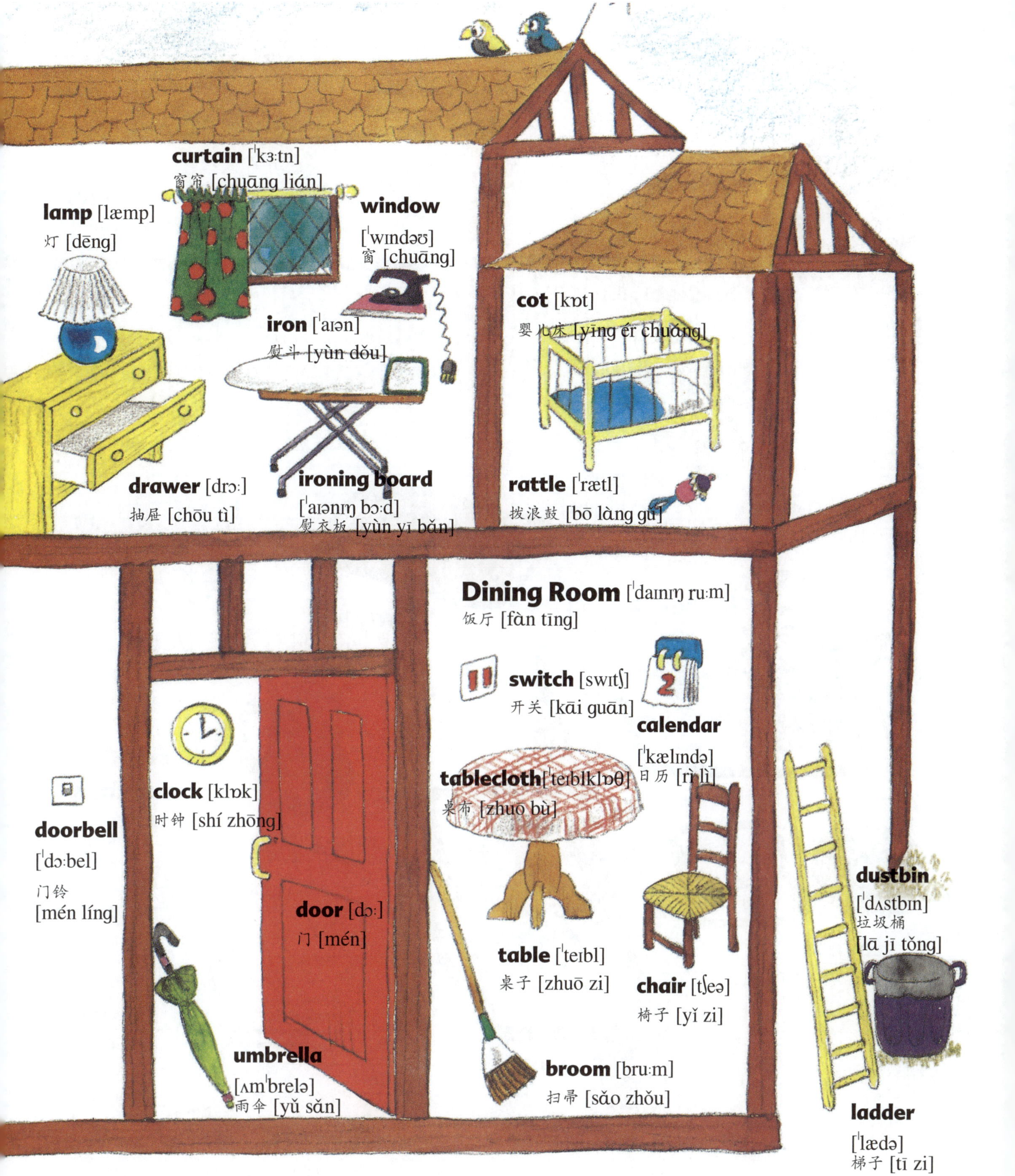
curtain [ˈkɜːtn]
窗帘 [chuāng lián]
lamp [læmp]
灯 [dēng]
window
[ˈwɪndəʊ]
窗 [chuāng]
iron [ˈaɪən]
熨斗 [yùn dǒu]
drawer [drɔː]
抽屉 [chōu tì]
ironing board
[ˈaɪənɪŋ bɔːd]
熨衣板 [yùn yī bǎn]
cot [kɒt]
婴儿床 [yīng ér chuáng]
rattle [ˈrætl]
拨浪鼓 [bō làng gǔ]
Dining Room [ˈdaɪnɪŋ ruːm]
饭厅 [fàn tīng]
switch [swɪtʃ]
开关 [kāi guān]
calendar
[ˈkælɪndə]
日历 [rì lì]
tablecloth[ˈteɪblklɒθ]
桌布 [zhuō bù]
doorbell
[ˈdɔːbel]
门铃
[mén líng]
clock [klɒk]
时钟 [shí zhōng]
door [dɔː]
门 [mén]
table [ˈteɪbl]
桌子 [zhuō zi]
chair [tʃeə]
椅子 [yǐ zi]
dustbin
[ˈdʌstbɪn]
垃圾桶
[lā jī tǒng]
umbrella
[ʌmˈbrelə]
雨伞 [yǔ sǎn]
broom [bruːm]
扫帚 [sǎo zhǒu]
ladder
[ˈlædə]
梯子 [tī zi]

In the Kitchen

厨房

bowl [bəʊl]
碗 [wǎn]

knife [naɪf]
刀子 [dāo zi]

flask [flɑːsk]
暖水瓶 [nuǎn shuǐ píng]

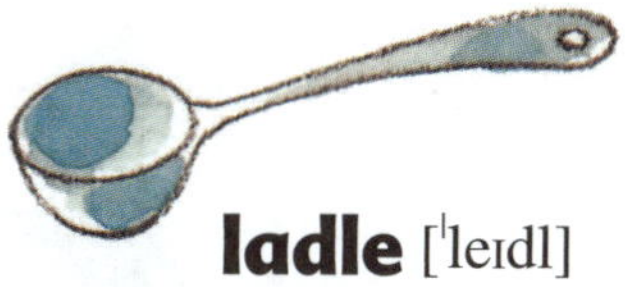

ladle [ˈleɪdl]
长柄勺子
[cháng bǐng sháo zi]

strainer [ˈstreɪnə]
筛网 [shāi wǎng]

sugar [ˈʃʊgə]
糖 [táng]

fork [fɔːk]
叉子 [chā zi]

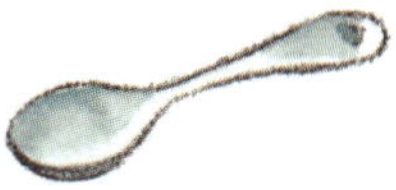

spoon [spuːn]
汤匙 [tāng chí]

glass [glɑːs]
玻璃杯 [bō li bēi]

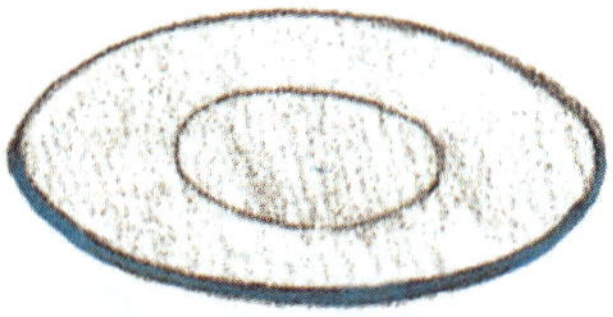

plate [pleɪt]
碟子 [dié zi]

pot [pɒt]
锅子 [guō zi]

saucepan [ˈsɔːspən]
有柄平底锅
[yǒu bǐng píng dǐ guō]

pan [pæn]
煎锅 [jiān guō]

straws [strɔːz]
吸管 [xī guǎn]

cup [kʌp]
有柄茶杯 [yǒu bǐng chá bēi]

saucer [ˈsɔːsə]
浅碟 [qiǎn dié]

mug [mʌg]
大杯、马克杯
[dà bēi, mǎ kè bēi]

In the Bathroom

浴室

In the Classroom

教室

chalk [tʃɔːk]
粉笔 [fěn bǐ]

duster [ˈdʌstə]
板擦儿 [bǎn cār]

blackboard [ˈblækbɔːd] 黑板 [hēi bǎn]

map [mæp]
地图 [dì tú]

pupils [ˈpjuːpɪlz]
学生 [xué sheng]

book [bʊk]
书 [shū]

desk [desk]
书桌 [shū zhuō]

eraser [ɪˈreɪzə]
橡皮 [xiàng pí]

pencil [ˈpensl]
铅笔 [qiān bǐ]

sharpener [ˈʃɑːpnə]
铅笔削具 [qiān bǐ xuē jù]

pen [pen]
笔 [bǐ]

glue [gluː]
胶水 [jiāo shuǐ]

dictionary
[ˈdɪkʃənˈərɪ]
字典 [zì diǎn]

felt-tip pen [ˈfeltɪp ˈpen]
水笔 [shuǐ bǐ]

ruler [ˈruːlə]
直尺 [zhí chǐ]

crayon [ˈkreɪən]
颜色笔、蜡笔 [yán sè bǐ, là bǐ]

wastepaper basket
[ˈweɪstpeɪpə ˈbɑːskɪt]
废纸篓 [fèi zhǐ lǒu]

In the Playground
游乐场

tricycle [ˈtraɪsɪkl]
三轮车 [sān lún chē]

climbing frame [ˈklaɪmɪŋ freɪm]
攀玩架 [pān wán jià]

skipping rope [ˈskɪpɪŋ rəʊp]
跳绳 [tiào shéng]

skateboard [ˈskeɪtbɔːd]
滑板 [huá bǎn]

seesaw [ˈsiːsɔː]
跷跷板 [qiāo qiāo bǎn]

slide [slaɪd]

滑梯 [huá tī]

kite [kaɪt]

风筝 [fēng zheng]

bat [bæt]

球棒 [qiú bàng]

swing [swɪŋ]

秋千 [qiū qiān]

merry-go-round

[ˈmerɪ-gəʊ-raʊnd]

旋转盘 [xuán zhuàn pán]

football [ˈfʊtbɔːl]

足球 [zú qiú]

In the Hospital

医院

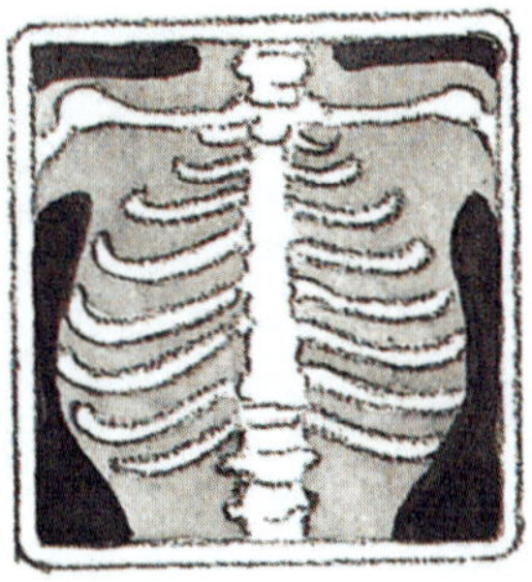

X-ray [ˈeks reɪ]
X射线照片
[X shè xiàn zhào piàn]

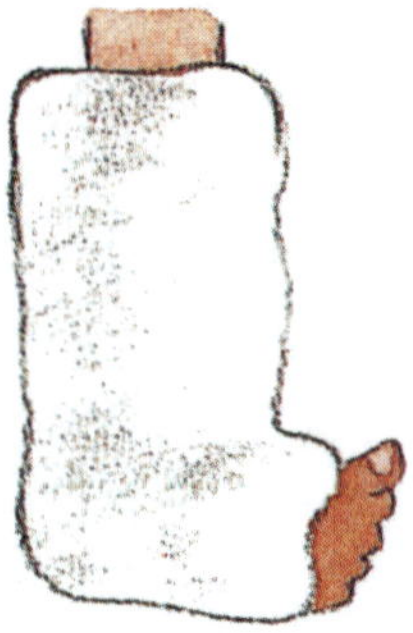

plaster cast
[ˈplɑːstə kɑːst]
石膏绷带 [shí gāo bēng dài]

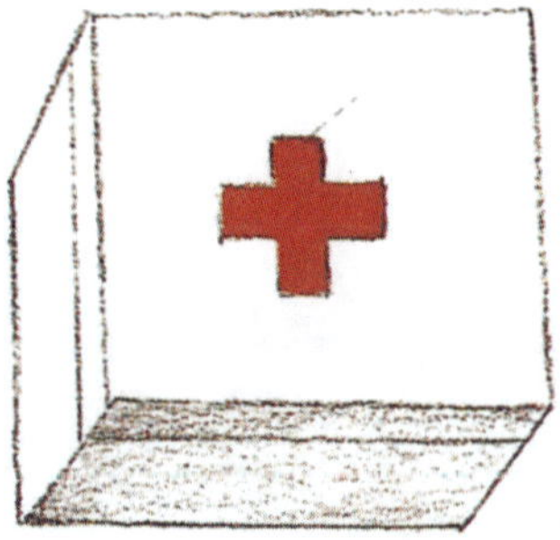

first-aid kit [ˈfɜːsteɪd kIt]
急救药箱 [jí jiù yào xiāng]

thermometer
[θəˈmɒmɪtə]
探热计 [tàn rè jì]

tablets [ˈtæblɪts]
药片 [yào piàn]

medicine
[ˈmedsn]
药 [yào]

capsules
[ˈkæpsjuːlz]
胶囊药丸
[jiāo náng yào wán]

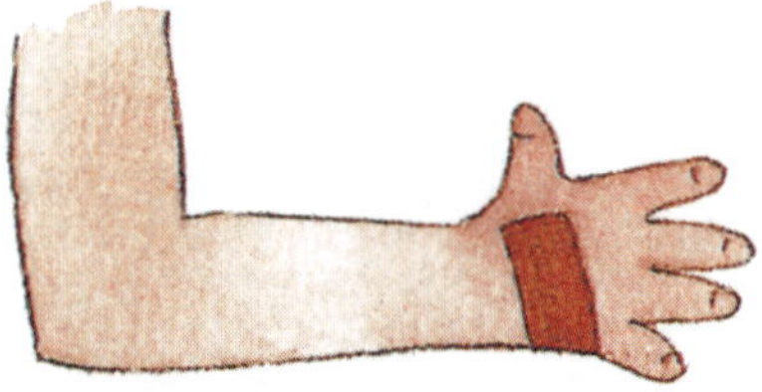

plaster [ˈplɑːstə]
胶布 [jiāo bù]

cotton wool
[ˈkɒtn wʊl]
药棉 [yào mián]

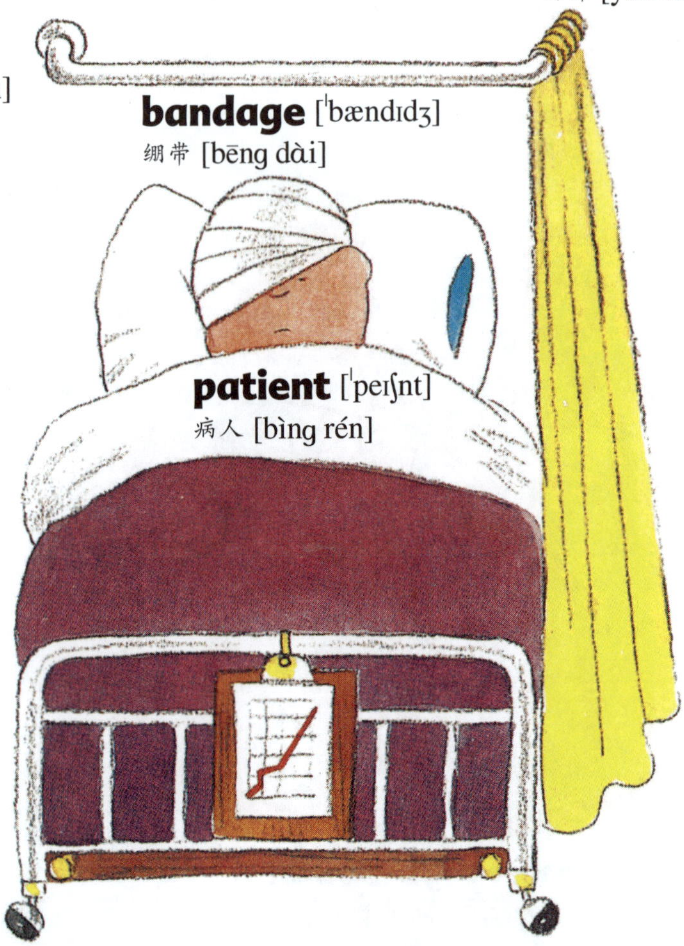

bandage [ˈbændɪdʒ]
绷带 [bēng dài]

patient [ˈpeɪʃnt]
病人 [bìng rén]

nurse [nɜːs]
护士 [hù shì]

wheelchair [ˈwiːltʃeə]
轮椅 [lún yǐ]

injection [ɪnˈdʒekʃn]
注射 [zhù shè]

surgeon [ˈsɜːdʒən]
外科医生
[wài kē yī shēng]

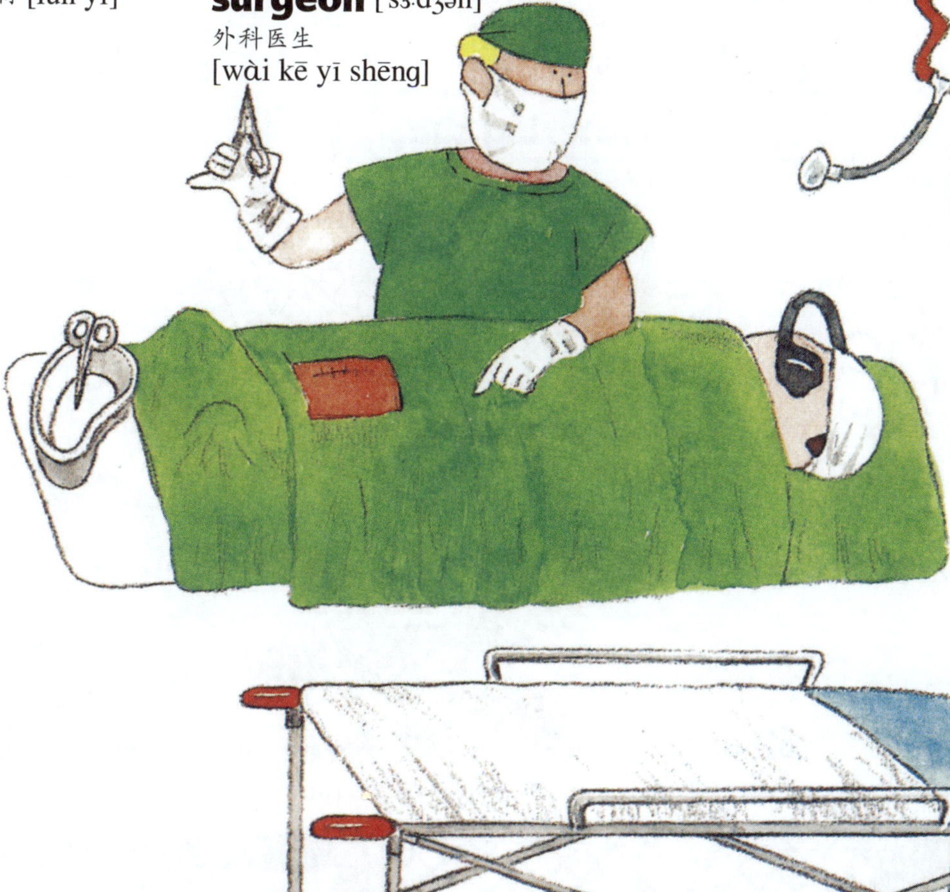

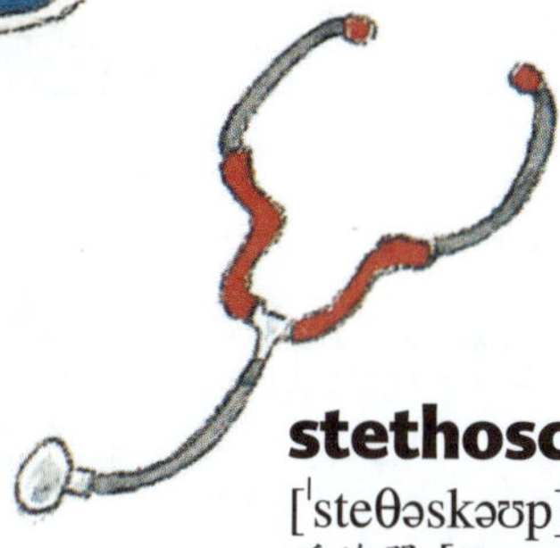

stethoscope
[ˈsteθəskəʊp]
听诊器 [tīng zhěn qì]

stretcher [ˈstretʃə]
担架 [dān jià]

In the Garden

花园

bench [bentʃ]
长椅 [cháng yǐ]

grass [grɑːs]
草 [cǎo]

nest [nest]
巢 [cháo]

trunk [trʌŋk]
树干 [shù gàn]

branch [brɑːntʃ]
树枝 [shù zhī]

tree [triː]
树 [shù]

stick [stɪk]
枝 [zhī]

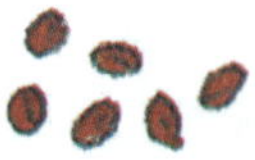

seeds [siːdz]
种子 [zhǒng zi]

watering can [ˈwɔːtərɪŋ kən]
洒水壶 [sǎ shuǐ hú]

weeds [wiːdz]
杂草 [zá cǎo]

plants [plɑːnt]
植物 [zhí wù]

fountain [ˈfaʊntɪn]
喷水池 [pēn shuǐ chí]

stone [stəʊn]
石头 [shí tou]

soil [sɔɪl]
泥土 [ní tǔ]

fern [fɜːn]
蕨 [jué]

bushes [bʊʃɪz]
灌木丛 [guàn mù cóng]

fence [fens]
篱笆 [lí bā]

gate [geɪt]
闸门 [zhá mén]

Flowers
花

carnation [kɑːˈneɪʃn]
康乃馨 [kāng nǎi xīn]

daffodil [ˈdæfədɪl]
水仙花 [shuǐ xiān huā]

daisy [ˈdeɪzɪ]
雏菊 [chú jú]

tulip [ˈtjuːlɪp]
郁金香 [yù jīn xiāng]

lily [ˈlɪli]
百合花 [bǎi hé huā]

hibiscus [hɪˈbɪskəs]
大红花 [dà hóng huā]

orchid [ˈɔːkɪd]
兰花 [lán huā]

rose [ˈrəʊz]
玫瑰花 [méi guì huā]

morning glory [ˈmɔːnɪŋ ˈglɔːrɪ]
牵牛花 [qiān niú huā]

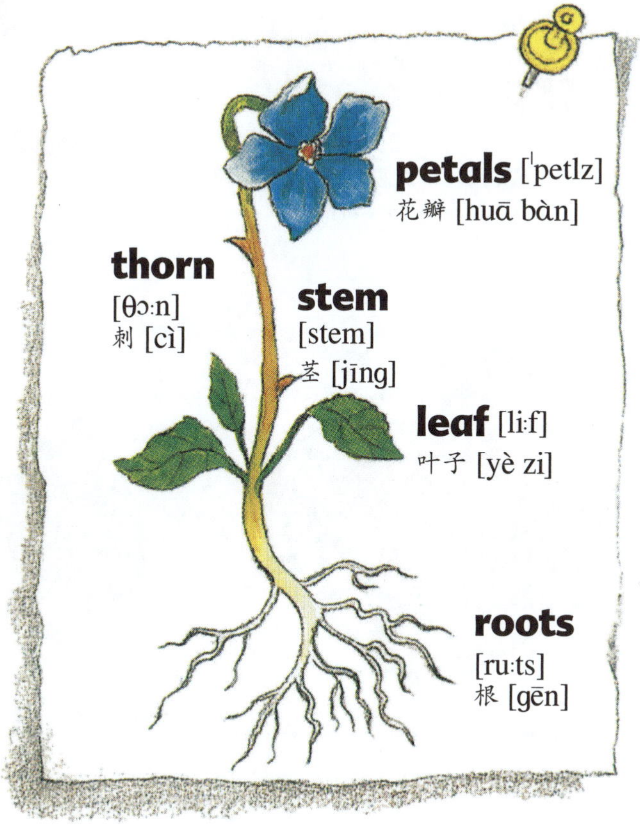

petals [ˈpetlz]
花瓣 [huā bàn]

thorn
[θɔːn]
刺 [cì]

stem
[stem]
茎 [jīng]

leaf [liːf]
叶子 [yè zi]

roots
[ruːts]
根 [gēn]

Fruit
水果

peach [piːtʃ]
桃子 [táo zi]

honeydew melon
[ˈhʌnɪdjuː ˈmelən]
香蜜瓜 [xiāng mì guā]

blackberries
[ˈblækbərɪz]
黑莓[hēi méi]

bananas [bəˈnɑːnəz]
香蕉 [xiāng jiāo]

grapefruit [ˈgreɪpfruːt]
葡萄柚 [pú táo yòu]

cherries [ˈtʃerɪz]
樱桃 [yīng táo]

orange [ˈɒrIndʒ]
橙 [chéng]

plums [plʌmz]
李子 [lǐ zi]

strawberries [ˈstrɔːbərɪz]
草莓 [cǎo méi]

avocados
[ˈævəˈkɑːdəʊz]
鳄梨 [è lí]

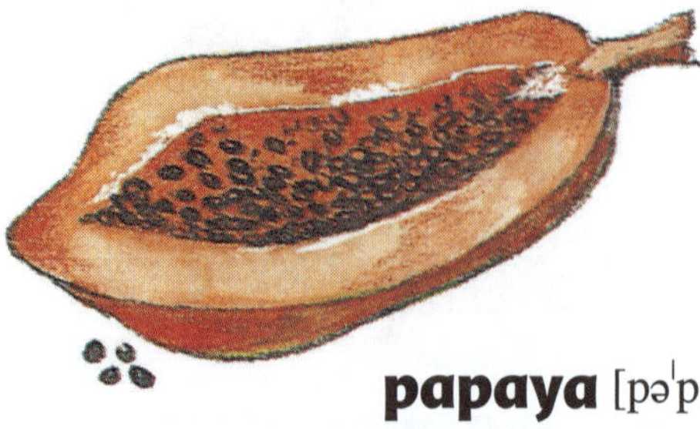

papaya [pəˈpaɪə]
木瓜 [mù guā]

raspberry [ˈrɑːzbrɪ]
蓝莓 [lán méi]

coconuts [ˈkəʊkənʌts]
椰子 [yē zi]

pineapple [ˈpaɪnæpl]
菠萝 [bō luó]

cantaloupes
[ˈkæntəluːps]
甜瓜 [tián guā]

apple [ˈæpl]
苹果 [píng guǒ]

pear [peə]
梨 [lí]

mango [ˈmæŋgəʊ]
芒果 [máng guǒ]

grapes [greɪps]
葡萄 [pú táo]

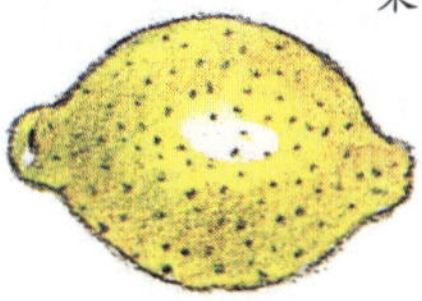

lemon [ˈlemən]
柠檬 [níng méng]

tomato [təˈmɑːtəʊ]
番茄 [fān qié]

kiwi fruit [ˈkiːwiː fruːt]
奇异果 [qí yì guǒ]

watermelon
[ˈwɔːtəmelən]
西瓜 [xī guā]

Vegetables
蔬菜

celery [ˈselərɪ]
芹菜 [qín cài]

cabbage [ˈkæbɪdʒ]
卷心菜 [juǎn xīn cài]

eggplant [ˈegplɑːnt]
茄子 [qié zi]

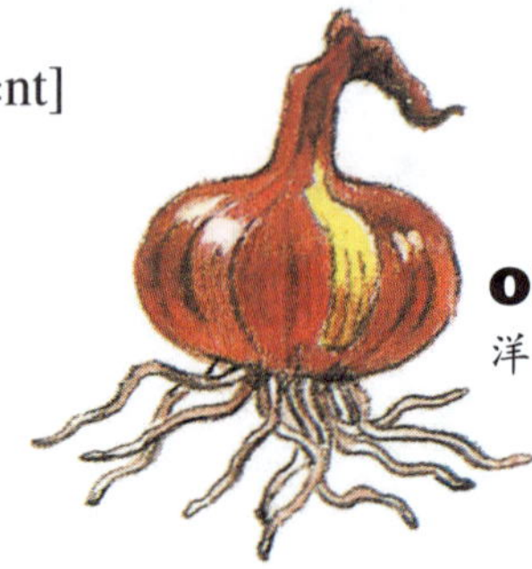

onion [ˈʌnjən]
洋葱 [yáng cōng]

carrots
[ˈkærəts]
胡萝卜 [hú luó bo]

cauliflower
[ˈkɒlɪʃlaʊə]
花椰菜 [huā yē cài]

pumpkin [ˈpʌmpkɪn]
南瓜 [nán guā]

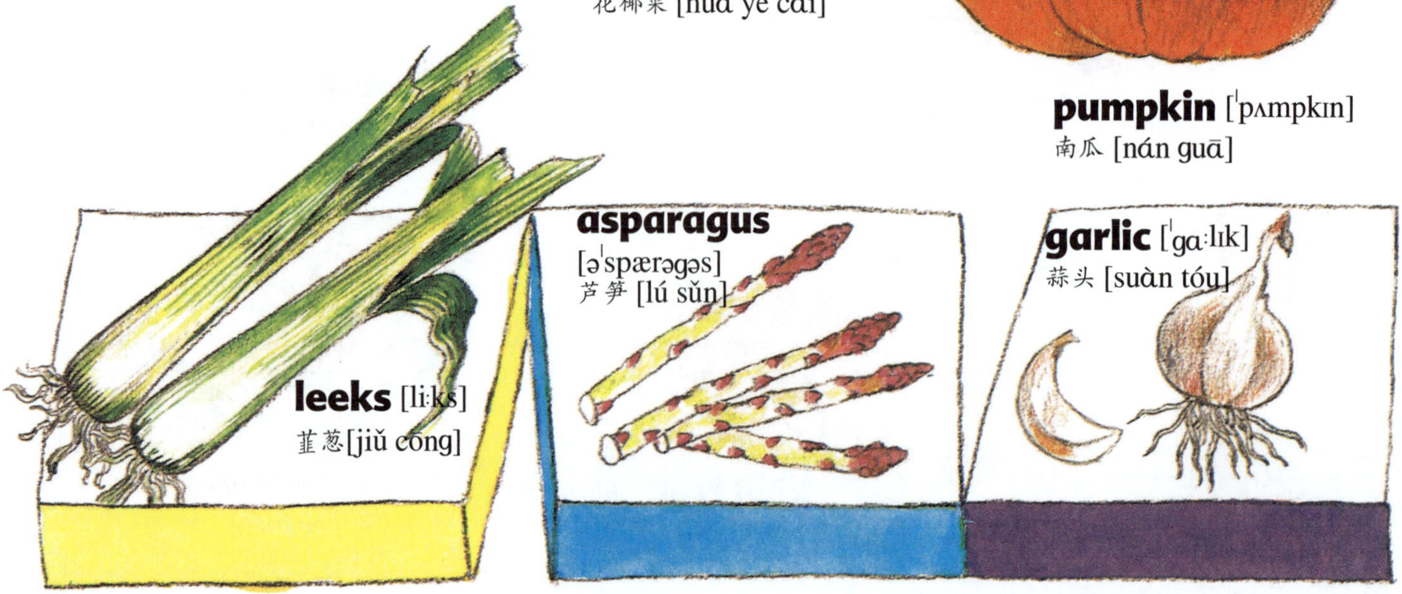

leeks [liːks]
韭葱[jiǔ cōng]

asparagus
[əˈspærəgəs]
芦笋 [lú sǔn]

garlic [ˈgɑːlɪk]
蒜头 [suàn tóu]

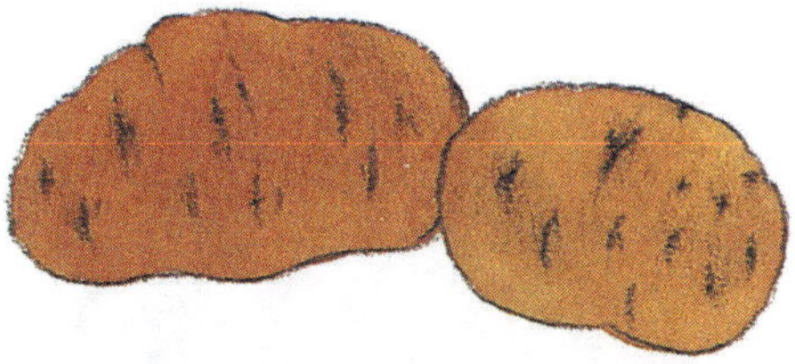

potatoes [pəˈteɪtəʊz]
马铃薯 [mǎ líng shǔ]

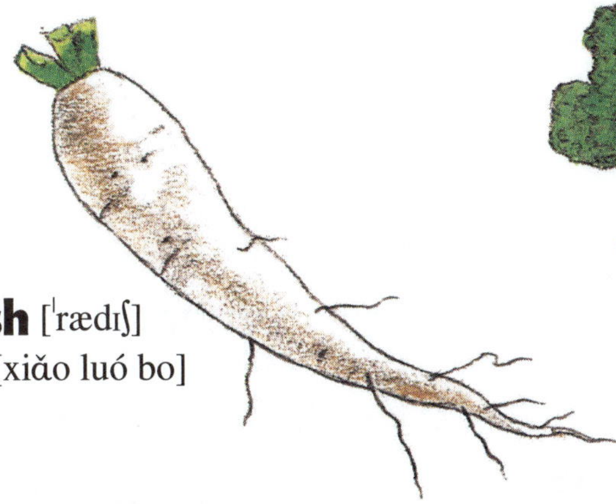

radish [ˈrædɪʃ]
小萝卜 [xiǎo luó bo]

broccoli [ˈbrɒkəli]
绿色花椰菜
[lǜ sè huā yē cài]

green peppers
[griːn pepəz]
青椒 [qīng jiāo]

turnip [ˈtɜːnɪp]
芜菁 [wú jīng]

cucumber [ˈkjuːkʌmbə]
黄瓜 [huáng guɑ]

lettuce [ˈletɪs]
生菜 [shēng cài]

spinach [ˈspɪnɪdʒ]
菠菜 [bō cài]

chillies [ˈtʃɪlɪz]
辣椒 [là jiāo]

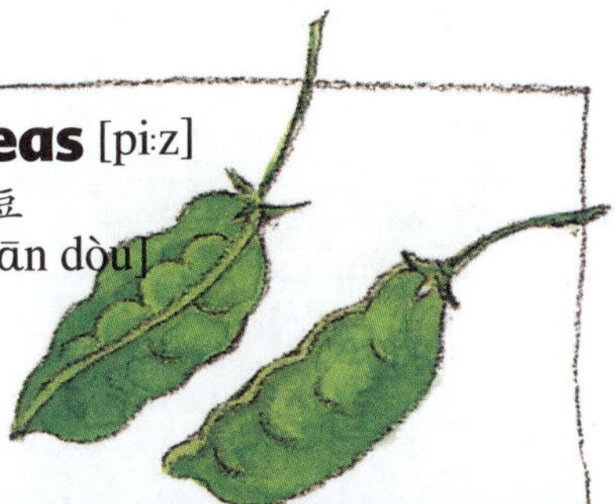

peas [piːz]
豌豆
[wān dòu]

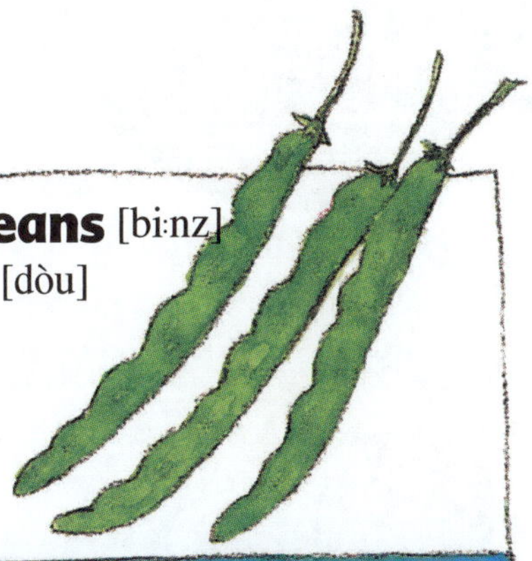

beans [biːnz]
豆 [dòu]

Food and Drink
食物和饮品

soup [suːp]
汤 [tāng]

pizza [ˈpiːtsə]
意大利薄饼
[yì dà lì bó bǐng]

pancakes [ˈpæŋkeɪks]
烙饼 [lào bǐng]

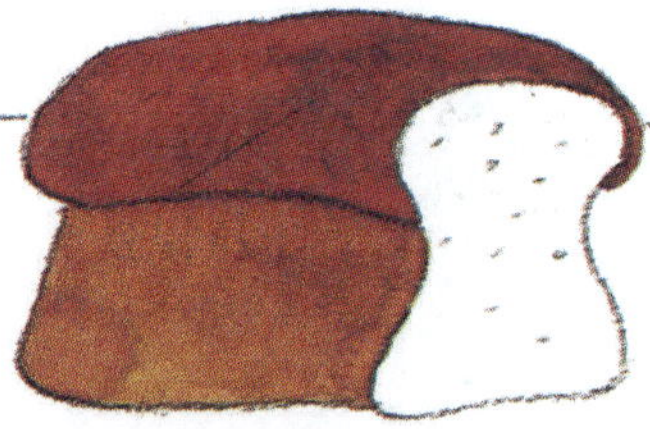

bread [bred]
面包 [miàn bāo]

hot dog [hɒt dɒg]
热狗 [rè gǒu]

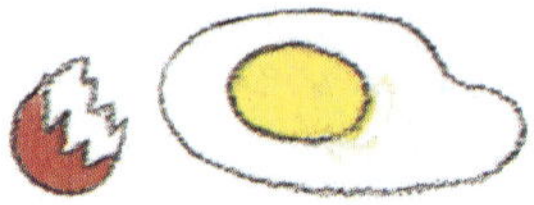

egg [eg]
鸡蛋 [jī dàn]

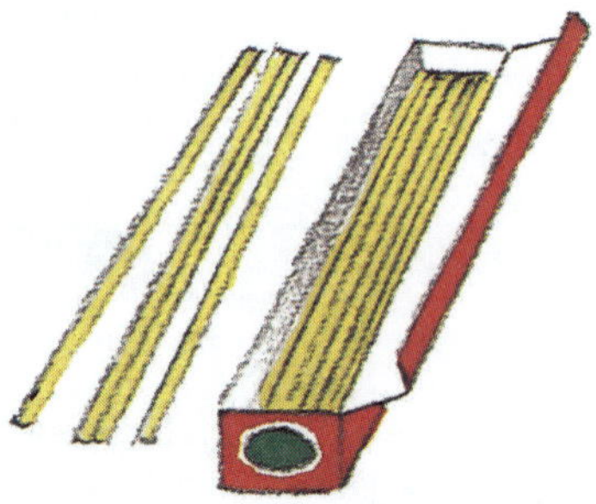

spaghetti [spəˈgetɪ]
意大利 [yì dà lì miàn]

cookies [ˈkʊkɪz]
饼干 [bǐng gān]

salad [ˈsæləd]
沙拉 [shā lā]

milk [mɪlk]
牛奶 [niú nǎi]

fruit juice
[fruːt dʒuːs]
果汁 [guǒ zhī]

coffee [ˈkɒfɪ]
咖啡 [kā fēi]

tea [tiː]
茶 [chá]

toast [təʊst]
吐司、烤面包
[tǔ sī, kǎo miàn bāo]

bun [bʌn]
小圆面包
[xiǎo yuán miàn bāo]

margarine [ˈmɑːdʒəˈriːn]
人造牛油 [rén zào niú yóu]

meat [miːt]
肉 [ròu]

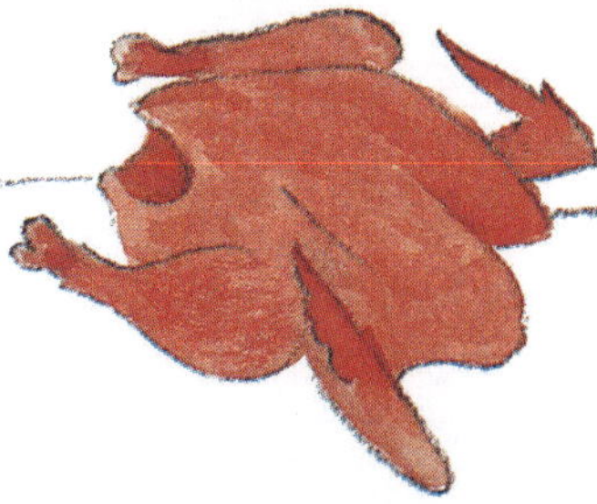

chicken [ˈtʃɪkɪn]
鸡肉 [jī ròu]

chocolate [ˈtʃɒklət]
巧克力 [qiǎo kè lì]

cheese [tʃiːz]
干酪 [gān lào]

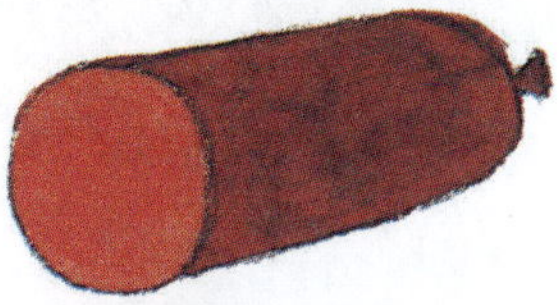

sausage [ˈsɒsɪdʒ]
香肠 [xiāng cháng]

sardines [sɑːˈdiːnz]
沙丁鱼 [shā dīng yú]

honey [ˈhʌnɪ]
蜂蜜 [fēng mì]

hamburger [ˈhæmbɜːgə]
汉堡包 [hàn bǎo bāo]

cake [keɪk]
蛋糕 [dàn gāo]

jam [dʒæm]
果酱 [guǒ jiàng]

ice cream [aɪskriːm]
冰淇淋、冰激凌
[bīng qí lín, bīng ji líng]

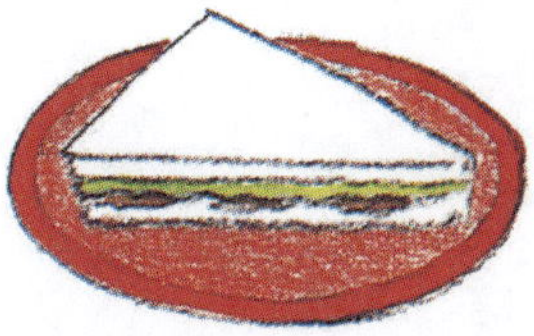

sandwich [ˈsænwɪdʒ]
三明治 [sān míng zhì]

doughnut [ˈdəʊnʌt]
甜圈 [tián quān]

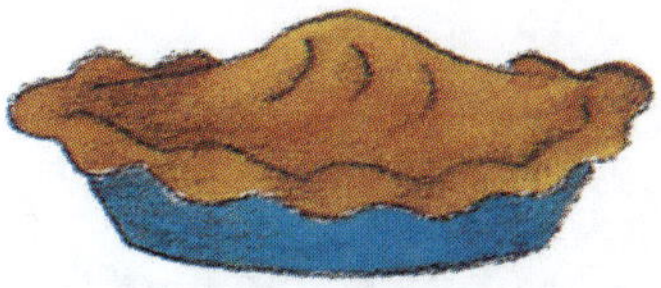

pie [paɪ]
饼 [bǐng]

butter [ˈbʌtə]
牛油 [niú yóu]

peanut butter
[ˈpiːnʌt ˈbʌtə]
花生酱 [huā shēng jiàng]

croissant [ˈkwæsɒŋ]
新月形面包
[xīn yuè xíng miàn bāo]

Animals
动物

bat [bæt]
蝙蝠 [biān fú]

spider [ˈspaɪdə]
蜘蛛 [zhī zhū]

orangutan
[ɔːˌræŋuːˈtæn]
猩猩 [xīng xīng]

elephant [ˈelɪfənt]
象 [xiàng]

lamb [læm]
小羊 [xiǎo yáng]

sheep [ʃiːp]
羊 [yáng]

tiger [ˈtaɪɡə]
老虎 [lǎo hǔ]

monkey [ˈmʌŋkɪ]
猴子 [hóu zi]

panda [ˈpændə]
熊猫 [xióng māo]

tortoise [ˈtɔːtəs]
乌龟 [wū guī]

frog [frɒg]
青蛙 [qīng wā]

giraffes [dʒɪˈrɑːfs]
长颈鹿 [cháng jǐng lù]

porcupine
[ˈpɔːkjʊpaɪn]
箭猪 [jiàn zhū]

kangaroos [ˌkæŋgəˈruːz]
袋鼠 [dài shǔ]

chimpanzee [ˈtʃɪmpænˈziː]
黑猩猩 [hēi xīng xīng]

cub [kʌb]
小狮子 [xiǎo shī zi]

lion [ˈlaɪən]
狮子 [shī zi]

leopard [ˈlepəd]
豹 [bào]

wolf [wʊlf]
狼 [láng]

lizard
[ˈlɪzəd]
蜥蜴 [xī yì]

fox [fɒks]
狐狸 [hú li]

polar bear [ˈpəʊlə beə]
北极熊 [běi jí xióng]

reindeer [ˈreɪndɪə]
驯鹿 [xún lù]

gorillas [gəˈrɪləs]
大猩猩 [dà xīng xīng]

horse [hɔːs]
马 [mǎ]

foal [fəʊl]
小马 [xiǎo mǎ]

hippopotamus
[ˈhɪpəˈpɒtəməs]
河马 [hé mǎ]

mouse [maʊs]
鼠 [shǔ]

rhinoceros [raɪˈnɒsərəs]
犀牛 [xī niú]

squirrel
[ˈskwɪrəl]
松鼠 [sōng shǔ]

cow [kaʊ]
母牛 [mǔ niú]

rabbit [ˈræbɪt]
兔子 [tù zi]

calf [kɑːf]
小牛 [xiǎo niú]

bear [beə]
熊 [xióng]

donkey [ˈdɒŋkɪ]
驴子 [lǘ zi]

deer [dɪə]
鹿 [lù]

crocodile
[ˈkrɒkədaɪl]
鳄鱼 [è yú]

cat [kæt]
猫 [māo]

kitten [ˈkɪtn]
小猫 [xiǎo māo]

goat [gəʊt]
山羊 [shān yáng]

kid [kɪd]
小山羊 [xiǎo shān yáng]

koalas [kəʊˈɑːləz]
树熊 [shù xióng]

camel [ˈkæml]
骆驼 [luò tuó]

snail [sneɪl]
蜗牛 [wō niú]

rat [ræt]
大鼠 [dà shǔ]

dog [dɒg]
狗 [gǒu]

puppy [ˈpʌpɪ]
小狗 [xiǎo gǒu]

chipmunk [ˈtʃɪpmʌŋk]
金花鼠 [jīn huā shǔ]

bison [ˈbaɪsn]
野牛 [yě niú]

piglet [ˈpɪglət]
小猪 [xiǎo zhū]

pig [pɪg]
猪 [zhū]

moose [mu:s]
麋鹿 [mí lù]

hoof [hu:f]
蹄 [tí]

horns [hɔ:nz]
角 [jiǎo]

paw [pɔ:]
爪 [zhǎo]

tail [teɪl]
尾 [wěi]

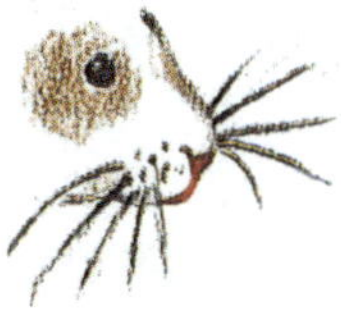

whiskers [ˈwɪskəz]
须 [xū]

hamster [ˈhæmstə]
仓鼠 [cāng shǔ]

zebra [ˈzebrə]
斑马 [bān mǎ]

guinea pig [ˈgɪnɪ pɪg]
豚鼠、天竺鼠 [tún shǔ, tiān zhú shǔ]

water buffalo [ˈwɔ:tə ˈbʌfələʊ]
水牛 [shuǐ niú]

caterpillar [ˈkætəpilə]
毛虫 [máo chóng]

Insects
昆虫

beetle [ˈbiːtl]
甲虫 [jiǎ chóng]

ant [ænt]
蚂蚁 [mǎ yǐ]

ladybird [ˈleɪdɪbɜːd]
瓢虫 [piáo chóng]

fly [flaɪ]
苍蝇 [cāng yíng]

bee [biː]
蜜蜂 [mì fēng]

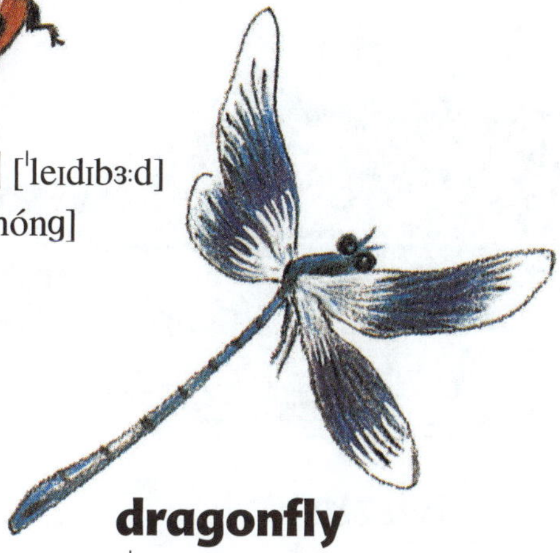

dragonfly
[ˈdræɡənflaɪ]
蜻蜓 [qīng tíng]

butterfly [ˈbʌtəflaɪ]
蝴蝶 [hú dié]

cockroach [ˈkɒkrəʊtʃ]
蟑螂 [zhāng láng]

mosquito [məˈskiːtəʊ]
蚊子 [wén zi]

termite
[ˈtɜːmaɪt]
白蚁 [bái yǐ]

grasshopper [ˈɡrɑːshɒpə]
蚱蜢 [zhà měng]

flea [fliː]
跳蚤 [tiào zǎo]

cricket [ˈkrɪkɪt]
蟋蟀 [xī shuài]

Water Animals

水生动物

turtle [ˈtɜːtl]
海龟 [hǎi guī]

whale [weɪl]
鲸鱼 [jīng yú]

crab [kræb]
蟹 [xiè]

fish [fɪʃ]
鱼 [yú]

prawn [prɔːn]
虾 [xiā]

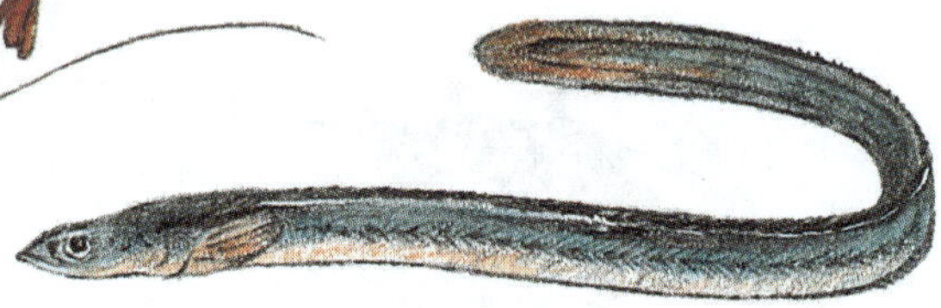

eel [iːl]
鳝 [shàn]

dolphin [ˈdɒlfɪn]
海豚 [hǎi tún]

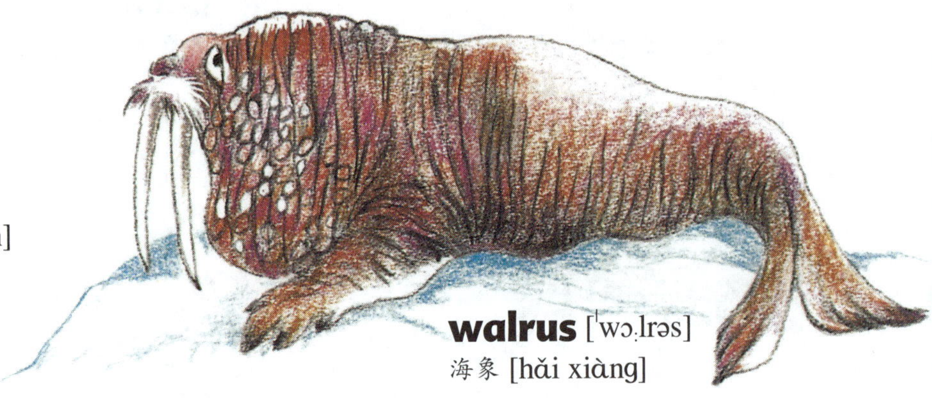

walrus [ˈwɔːlrəs]
海象 [hǎi xiàng]

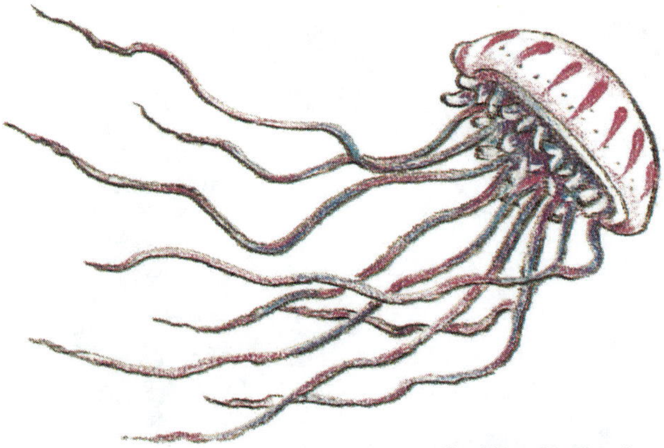

jellyfish [ˈdʒelɪfɪʃ]
水母 [shuǐ mǔ]

fin [fɪn]
鳍 [qí]

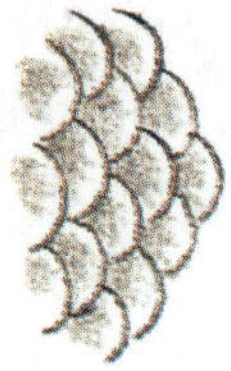

scales [skeɪlz]
鱼鳞 [yú lín]

shark [ʃɑːk]
鲨鱼 [shā yú]

octopus [ˈɒktəpəs]
章鱼 [zhāng yú]

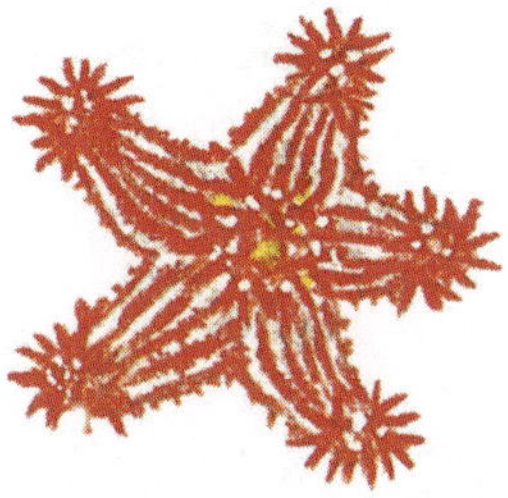

starfish [ˈstɑːfɪʃ]
海星 [hǎi xīng]

squid [skwɪd]
鱿鱼 [yóu yú]

lobster [ˈlɒbstə]
龙虾 [lóng xiā]

seal [siːl]
海豹 [hǎi bào]

Birds
鸟类

kiwi [ˈkiːwiː]
鹬鸵 [yù tuó]

toucan [ˈtuːkæn]
巨嘴鸟 [jù zuǐ niǎo]

canary [kəˈneərɪ]
金丝雀 [jīn sī què]

pigeon [ˈpɪdʒɪn]
鸽子 [gē zi]

dove [dʌv]
鸽 [gē]

seagull [ˈsiːgʌl]
海鸥 [hǎi ōu]

parrot [ˈpærət]
鹦鹉 [yīng wǔ]

kookaburra [ˈkʊkəbʌrə]
笑翠鸟 [xiào cuì niǎo]

turkey
[ˈtɜːkɪ]
火鸡 [huǒ jī]

owl [aʊl]
猫头鹰 [māo tóu yīng]
swallow [ˈswɒləʊ]
燕子 [yàn zi]
hummingbird
[ˈhʌmɪŋbɜːd]
蜂鸟 [fēng niǎo]
nightingale
[ˈnaɪtɪŋgeɪl]
夜莺 [yè yīng]
robin [ˈrɒbɪn]
知更鸟 [zhī gēng niǎo]
mynah [ˈmaɪnə]
燕八哥 [yàn bā gē]
pelican [ˈpelɪkən]
鹈鹕、塘鹅 [tí hú, táng é]
peacock [ˈpiːkɒk]
孔雀 [kǒng què]
kingfisher [ˈkɪŋfɪʃə]
鱼狗 [yú gǒu]

woodpecker [ˈwʊdpekə]
啄木鸟 [zhuó mù niǎo]

puffin [ˈpʌfɪn]
海鹦 [hǎi yīng]

penguin [ˈpeŋgwɪn]
企鹅 [qǐ é]

goose [guːs]
鹅 [é]

gosling [ˈgɒzlɪŋ]
小鹅 [xiǎo é]

flamingo
[fləˈmɪŋgəʊ]
红鹤 [hóng hè]

swan [swɒn]
天鹅 [tiān é]

cock [kɒk]
公鸡 [gōng jī]

chick [tʃɪk]
小鸡 [xiǎo jī]

hen [hen]
母鸡 [mǔ jī]

duck [dʌk]
鸭 [yā]

duckling [ˈdʌklɪŋ]
小鸭 [xiǎo yā]

hawk [hɔ:k]
隼 [sǔn]
beak [bi:k]
鸟嘴 [niǎo zuǐ]
claw[klɔ:]
爪 [zhǎo]
feathers [ˈfeðəz]
羽毛 [yǔ máo]
wing [wɪŋ]
翅膀 [chì bǎng]
eagle [ˈi:gl]
鹰 [yīng]
sparrow [ˈspærəʊ]
麻雀 [má què]
crow [krəʊ]
乌鸦 [wū yā]
stork [stɔ:k]
鹳 [guàn]
ostrich [ˈɒstrɪtʃ]
鸵鸟 [tuó niǎo]

Colours
颜色

brown [braʊn]
褐色 [hè sè]

yellow [ˈjeləʊ]
黄色 [huáng sè]

red [red]
红色 [hóng sè]

pink [pɪŋk]
粉红色 [fěn hóng sè]

orange [ˈɒrɪndʒ]
橙色 [chéng sè]

grey [greɪ]
灰色 [huī sè]

green [griːn]
绿色 [lǜ sè]

blue [bluː]
蓝色 [lán sè]

purple [ˈpɜːpl]
紫色 [zǐ sè]

white [waɪt]
白色 [bái sè]

black [blæk]
黑色 [hēi sè]

Musical Instruments

乐器

piano [pɪˈænəʊ]
钢琴 [gāng qín]

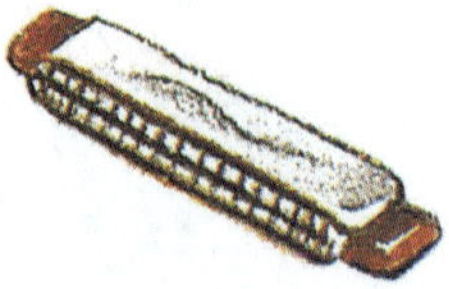

harmonica
[hɑːˈmɒnɪkə]
口琴 [kǒu qín]

tuba [ˈtjuːbə]
低音号
[dī yīn hào]

drum [drʌm]
鼓 [gǔ]

trumpet
[ˈtrʌmpɪt]
喇叭 [lǎ bā]

guitar [ɡɪˈtɑː]
吉他 [jí tā]

violin [ˌvaɪəˈlɪn]
小提琴 [xiǎo tí qín]

banjo [ˈbændʒəʊ]
班鸠琴 [bān jiū qín]

tambourine
[ˌtæmbəˈriːn]
铃鼓 [líng gǔ]

electric guitar
[ɪˈlektrɪk gɪˈtɑː]
电吉他 [diàn jí tā]

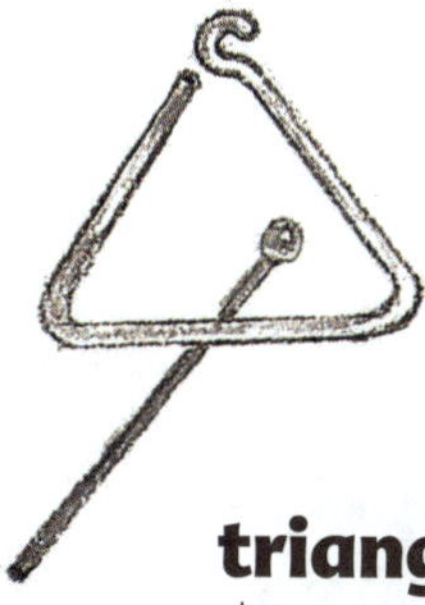

triangle
[ˈtraɪæŋgl]
三角铁 [sān jiǎo tiě]

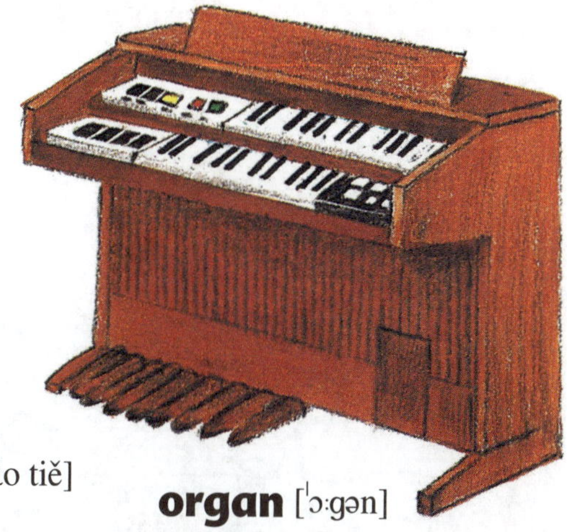

organ [ˈɔːgən]
风琴 [fēng qín]

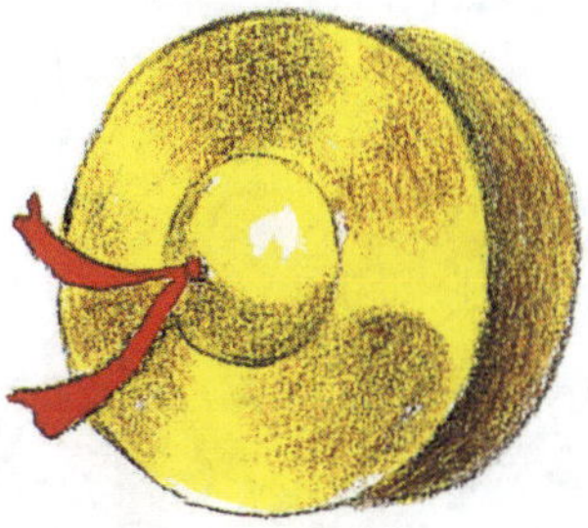

cymbals [ˈsɪmblz]
铙钹 [náo bó]

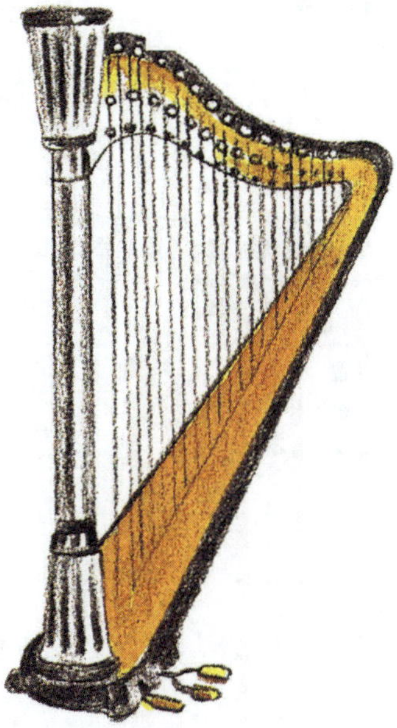

harp [hɑːp]
竖琴 [shù qín]

trombone
[trɒmˈbəʊn]
长号 [cháng hào]

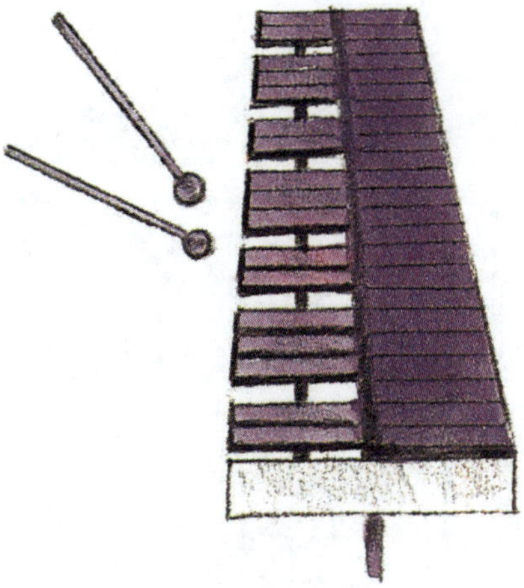

xylophone
[ˈzaɪləfəʊn]
木琴 [mù qín]

flute [fluːt]
长笛 [cháng dí]

cello [ˈtʃeləʊ]
大提琴 [dà tí qín]

Buildings and Places
建筑物及场所

school [skuːl]
学校 [xué xiào]

airport [ˈeəpɔːt]
飞机场 [fēi jī chǎng]

windmill
[ˈwɪndmɪl]
风车 [fēng chē]

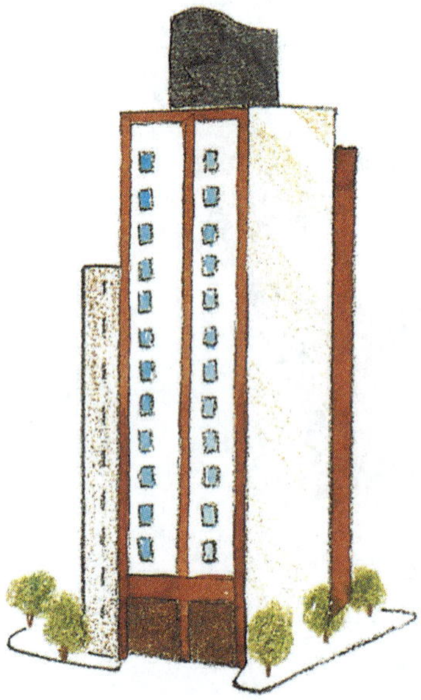

apartments
[əˈpɑːtmənts]
住宅大厦 [zhù zhái dà shà]

house [haʊs]
房子 [fáng zi]

castle [ˈkɑːsl]
城堡 [chéng bǎo]

library [ˈlaɪbrərɪ]
图书馆 [tú shū guǎn]

mosque [mɒsk]
清真寺 [qīng zhēn sì]

temple [ˈtempl]
庙宇 [miào yǔ]

factory [ˈfæktərɪ]
工厂 [gōng chǎng]

church [tʃɜːtʃ]
教堂 [jiào táng]

synagogue [ˈsɪnəgɒg]
犹太教堂 [yóu tài jiào táng]

cinema [ˈsɪnəmɑː]
影院 [yǐng yuàn]

fire station [ˌfaɪə ˈsteɪʃn]
消防局 [xiāo fáng jú]

cafeteria [kæfiˈtɪərɪə]
自助餐馆 [zì zhù cān guǎn]

police station [pəˈliːs steɪʃn]
警察局 [jǐng chá jú]

post office [pəʊst ˈɒfɪs]
邮政局 [yóu zhèng jú]

hospital [ˈhɒspɪtl]
医院 [yī yuàn]

train station [treɪn ˈsteɪʃn]
火车站 [huǒ chē zhàn]

park [pɑːk]
公园 [gōng yuán]

beach [biːtʃ]
沙滩 [shā tān]

harbour [ˈhɑːbə]
海港 [hǎi gǎng]

office [ˈɒfɪs]
办公室 [bàn gōng shì]

department store [dɪˈpɑːtmənt stɔː]
百货公司 [bǎi huò gōng sī]

pier [pɪə]
码头 [mǎ tou]

swimming pool [ˈswɪmɪŋ puːl]
游泳池 [yóu yǒng chí]

restaurant [ˈrestrɒnt]
餐厅 [cān tīng]

zoo [zuː]
动物园 [dòng wù yuán]

supermarket
[ˈsuːpəmɑːkɪt]
超级市场 [chāo jí shì chǎng]

bank [bæŋk]
银行 [yín háng]

hotel [həʊˈtel]
酒店 [jiǔ diàn]

museum [mjuːˈziəm]
博物馆 [bó wù guǎn]

elevator [ˈelɪveɪtə]
升降机 [shēng jiàng jī]

escalator [ˈeskəleɪtə]
电动楼梯 [diàn dòng lóu tī]

stairs [steəz]
楼梯 [lóu tī]

roof [ruːf]
屋顶 [wū dǐng]

balcony [ˈbælkənɪ]
露台 [lòu tái]

corridor [ˈkɒrɪdɔː]
走廊 [zǒu láng]

Transport

交通工具

bicycle [ˈbaɪsɪkl]
自行车 [zì xíng chē]

fire engine [ˈfaɪə endʒɪn]
救火车 [jiù huǒ chē]

motorcycle [ˈməʊtəsaɪkl]
摩托车 [mó tuō chē]

car [kɑː]
汽车 [qì chē]

container lorry [kənˈteɪnə lɒrɪ]
货柜车 [huò guì chē]

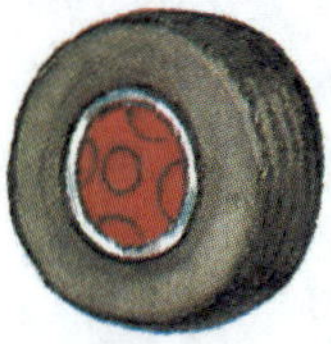

tyre [ˈtaɪə]
轮胎 [lún tāi]

wheel [wiːl]
车轮 [chē lún]

railway [ˈreɪlweɪ]
铁路 [tiě lù]

van [væn]
客货车 [kè huò chē]

taxi [ˈtæksɪ]
计程车 [jì chéng chē]

train [treɪn]
火车 [huǒ chē]

dump truck [dʌmp trʌk]
卸货卡车 [xiè huò kǎ chē]

truck [trʌk]
货车 [huò chē]

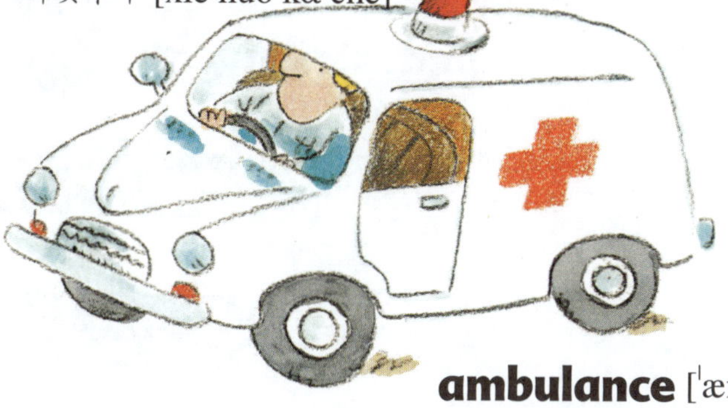

ambulance [ˈæmbjʊləns]
救护车 [jiù hù chē]

jeep [dʒiːp]
吉普车 [jí pǔ chē]

bus [bʌs]
公共汽车 [gōng gòng qì chē]

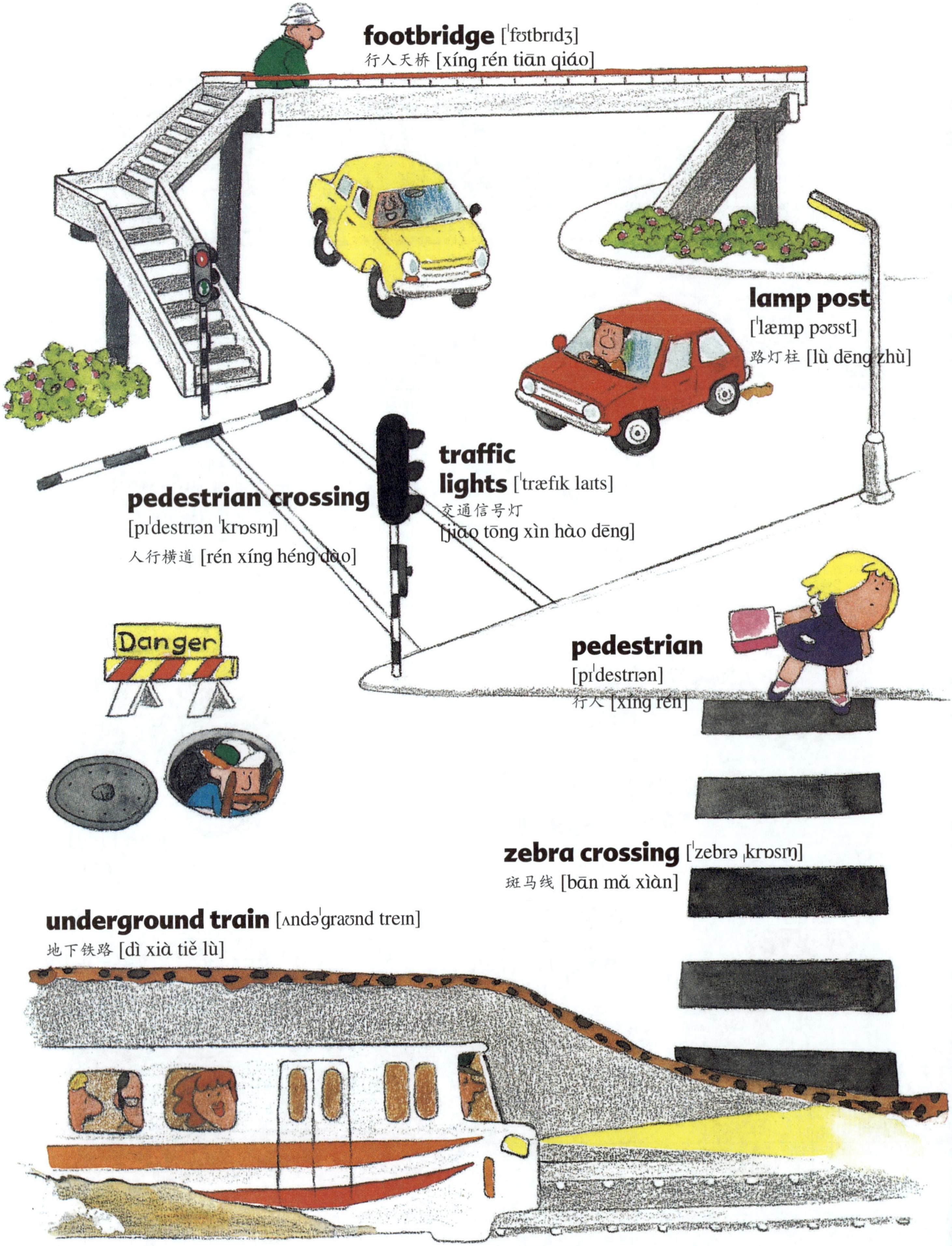

footbridge [ˈfʊtbrɪdʒ]
行人天桥 [xíng rén tiān qiáo]
lamp post [ˈlæmp pəʊst]
路灯柱 [lù dēng zhù]
traffic lights [ˈtræfɪk laɪts]
交通信号灯 [jiāo tōng xìn hào dēng]
pedestrian crossing [pɪˈdestrɪən ˈkrɒsɪŋ]
人行横道 [rén xíng héng dào]
Danger
pedestrian [pɪˈdestrɪən]
行人 [xíng rén]
zebra crossing [ˈzebrə ˌkrɒsɪŋ]
斑马线 [bān mǎ xiàn]
underground train [ʌndəˈgraʊnd treɪn]
地下铁路 [dì xià tiě lù]

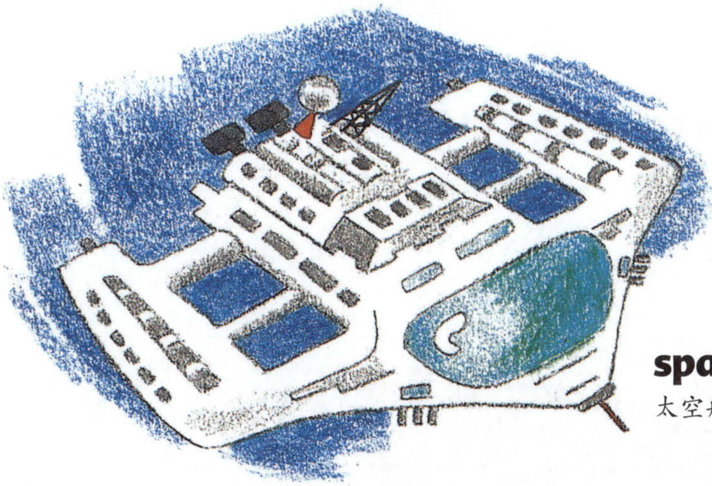

spaceship [ˈspeɪsʃɪp]
太空船 [tài kōng chuán]

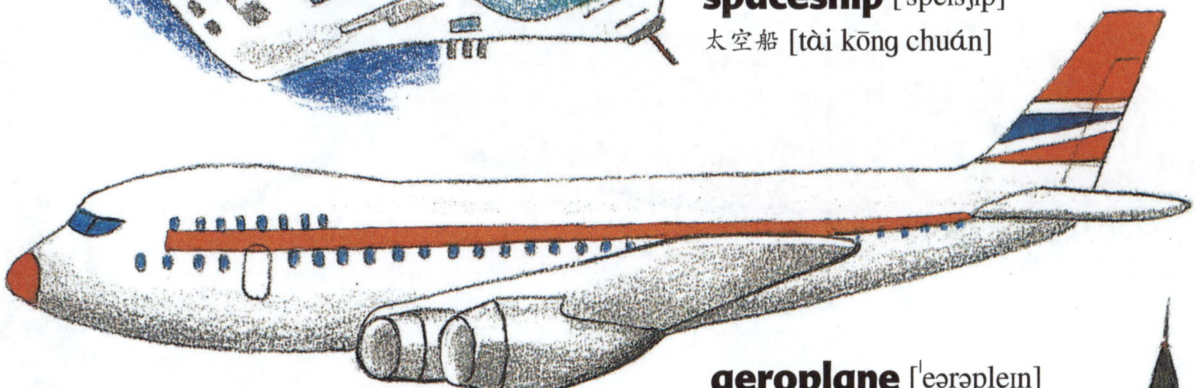

aeroplane [ˈeərəpleɪn]
飞机 [fēi jī]

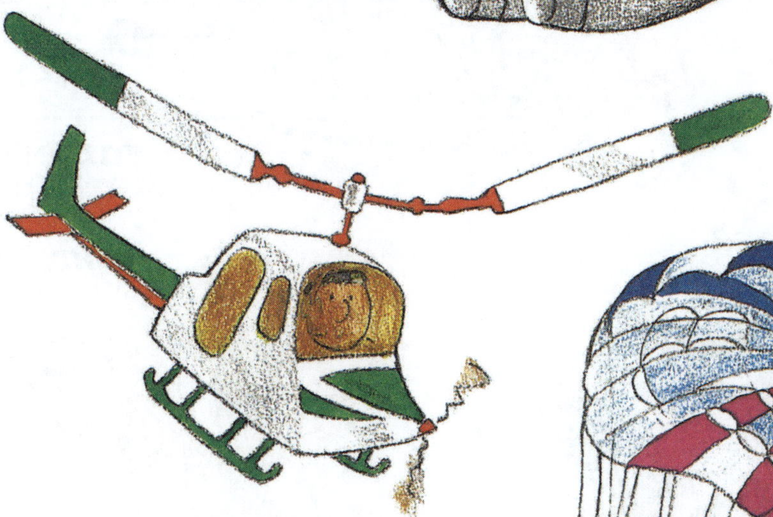

helicopter [ˈhelɪkɒptə]
直升机 [zhí shēng jī]

parachute [ˈpærəʃuːt]
降落伞 [jiàng luò sǎn]

balloon [bəˈluːn]
热气球 [rè qì qiú]

rocket [ˈrɒkɪt]
火箭 [huǒ jiàn]

ferry [ˈferɪ]
渡轮 [dù lún]

yacht [jɒt]
游艇 [yóu tǐng]

boat [bəʊt]
小船、艇
[xiǎo chuán, tǐng]

oar [ɔː]
划桨 [huá jiǎng]

hovercraft [ˈhɒvəkrɑːft]
气垫船 [qì diàn chuán]

buoy [bɔɪ]
浮标 [fú biāo]

submarine [ˌsʌbməˈriːn]
潜水艇 [qián shuǐ tǐng]

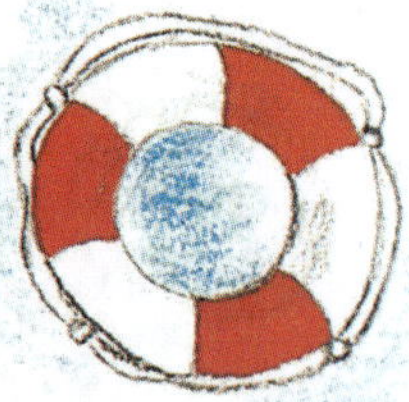

lifesaver [ˈlaɪfseɪvə]
救生圈 [jiù shēng quān]

bridge [brɪdʒ]
桥 [qiáo]

ship [ʃɪp]
船 [chuán]

gondola [ˈgɒndələ]
平底船 [píng dǐ chuán]

tugboat [ˈtʌgbəʊt]
拖船 [tuō chuán]

anchor [ˈæŋkə]
锚 [máo]

paddle [ˈpædl]
桨 [jiǎng]

canoe [kəˈnuː]
独木舟 [dú mù zhōu]

speedboat [ˈspiːdbəʊt]
快艇 [kuài tǐng]

Things We Do

动作

beat [biːt]
敲、打 [qiāo, dǎ]

blow [bləʊ]
吹 [chuī]

break [breɪk]
打破 [dǎ pò]

scrub [skrʌb]
擦洗 [cā xǐ]

clap [klæp]
拍手 [pāi shǒu]

catch [kætʃ]
接 [jiē]

chase [tʃeɪs]
追 [zhuī]

cook [kʊk]
煮 [zhǔ]

close [kləʊs]
关 [guān]

climb [klaɪm]
攀爬 [pān pá]

cry [kraɪ]
哭 [kū]

dance [dɑːns]
跳舞 [tiào wǔ]

dig [dɪg]
挖掘 [wā jué]

dive [daɪv]
跳水 [tiào shuǐ]

draw [drɔː]
绘画 [huì huà]

drink [drɪŋk]
喝 [hē]

dream [driːm]
做梦 [zuò mèng]

drive [draɪv]
驾驶 [jià shǐ]

exercise [ˈeksəsaɪz]
做运动 [zuò yùn dòng]

eat [iːt]
吃 [chī]

fall [fɔːl]
跌 [diē]

feed [fiːd]
喂 [wèi]

fight [faɪt]
打架 [dǎ jià]

float [fləʊt]
漂浮 [piāo fú]

fly [flaɪ]
飞行 [feī xíng]

hide [haɪd]
躲藏 [duǒ cáng]

hop [hɒp]
单足跳 [dān zú tiào]

jog [dʒɒg]
缓步跑 [huǎn bù pǎo]

jump [dʒʌmp]
跳 [tiào]

kick [kɪk]
踢 [tī]

kiss [kɪs]
吻 [wěn]

knock [nɒk]
敲 [qiāo]

laugh [lɑːf]
笑 [xiào]

march [mɑːtʃ]
步操走 [bù cāo zǒu]

open [ˈəʊpən]
打开 [dǎ kāi]

paint [peɪnt]
涂上颜色 [tú shàng yán sè]

peel [piːl]

剥 [bō]

point [pɔɪnt]

指向 [zhǐ xiàng]

pour [pɔː]

灌 [guàn]

pull [pʊl]

拉 [lā]

push [pʊʃ]

推 [tuī]

read [riːd]

阅读 [yuè dú]

ride [raɪd]

骑 [qí]

roll [rəʊl]

辗薄 [zhǎn bó]

run [rʌn]

跑 [pǎo]

sew [səʊ]

缝纫 [féng rèn]

shoot [ʃuːt]

射击 [shè jī]

sing [sɪŋ]

唱歌 [chàng gē]

sit [sɪt]
坐 [zuò]

skate [skeɪt]
溜冰 [liū bīng]

skip [skɪp]
跳绳 [tiào shéng]

slide [slaɪd]
滑行 [huá xíng]

smell [smel]
闻、嗅 [wén, xiù]

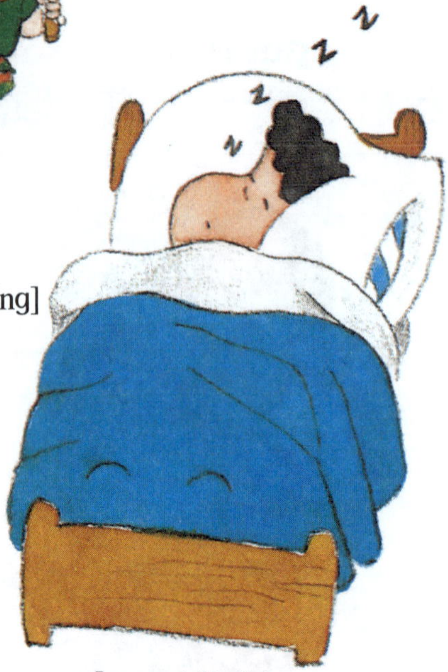

sleep [sli:p]
睡觉 [shuì jiào]

smile [smaɪl]
微笑 [wēi xiào]

squeeze [skwi:z]
挤、榨 [jǐ, zhà]

sweep [swi:p]
扫 [sǎo]

swing [swɪŋ]
荡 [dàng]

stand [stænd]
站立 [zhàn lì]

swim [swɪm]
游泳 [yóu yǒng]

tear [tɛɪ]
撕开 [sī kāi]

walk [wɔːk]
行走 [xíng zǒu]

throw [θrəʊ]
抛 [pāo]

tie [taɪ]
结领带 [jiē lǐng dài]

whistle [ˈwɪsl]
吹口哨
[chuī kǒu shào]

wash [wɒʃ]
洗 [xǐ]

wave [weɪv]
挥手 [huī shǒu]

yawn [jɔːn]
打呵欠 [dǎ hē qiàn]

wrap [ræp]
包裹 [bāo guǒ]

write [raɪt]
写 [xiě]

Positions
位置

behind
[bɪˈhaɪnd]
在后面、
在 ...... 之后
[zài hòu mian,
zài ...... zhī hòu]

in front of
[ɪn frʌnt əv]
在前面、在 ...... 之前
[zài qián mian,
zài ...... zhī qián]

upside down
[ˈʌpsaɪd daʊn]
倒置 [dǎo zhì]

over [ˈəʊvə]
在 ...... 上面
[zài ......
shàng mian]

under [ˈʌndə]
在 ...... 下面
[zài ...... xià mian]

beside [bɪˈsaɪd]
在 ...... 旁边
[zài ...... páng biān]

between [bɪˈtwiːn]
在 ...... 中间
[zài ...... zhōng jiān]

in [ɪn]
在 ...... 里
[zài ...... lǐ]

out [aʊt]
在 ...... 外
[zài ...... wài]

above [əˈbʌv]
在上面、在 ...... 之上
[zài shàng mian, zài ...... zhī shàng]

after [ˈɑːftə]
在后面、在 ...... 之后
[zài hòu mian, zài ...... zhī hòu]

before [bɪˈfɔː]
在前面、在 ...... 之前
[zài qián mian, zài ...... zhī qián]

below [bɪˈləʊ]
在下面、在 ..... 之下
[zài xià mian, zài ...... zhī xià]

top [tɒp]
顶 [dǐng]

up [ʌp]
向上
[xiàng shàng]

on [ɒn]
在上面、在 ...... 之上
[zài shàng mian, zài ...... zhī shàng]

down [daʊn]
向下 [xiàng xià]

bottom [ˈbɒtəm]
底 [dǐ]

Describing Words

形容词

big [bɪg]
大的 [dà de]

small [smɔːl]
小的 [xiǎo de]

thick [θɪk]
粗的 [cū de]

thin [θɪn]
细的 [xì de]

high [haɪ]
高的 [gāo de]

low [ləʊ]
低的 [dī de]

clean [kliːn]
清洁的 [qīng jié de]

dirty [ˈdɜːtɪ]
肮脏的 [kāng zāng de]

new [njuː]
新的 [xīn de]

old [əʊld]
旧的 [jiù de]

cold [kəʊld]
冷的 [lěng de]

hot [hɒt]
热的 [rè de]

long [lɒŋ]
长的 [cháng de]

short [ʃɔːt]
短的 [duǎn de]

fat [fæt]
胖的 [pàng de]

thin [θɪn]
瘦的 [shòu de]

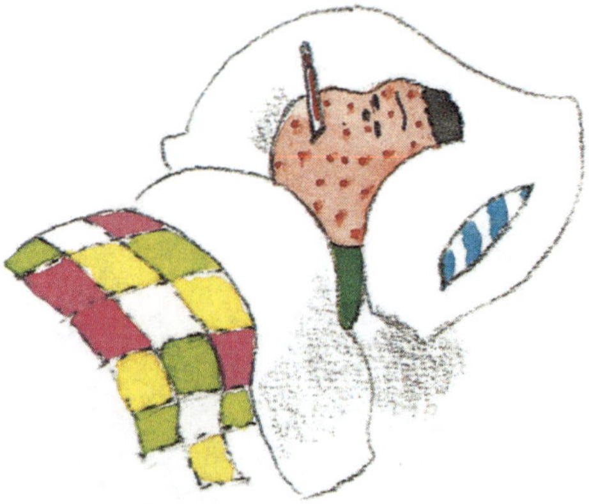

sick [sɪk]
有病的 [yǒu bìng de]

well [wel]
健康的 [jiàn kāng de]

loud [laʊd]
响亮的 [xiǎng liàng de]

quiet
[ˈkwaɪət]
轻声的 [qīng shēng de]

tall [tɔːl]
高的 [gāo de]

short [ʃɔːt]
矮的 [ǎi de]

dark [dɑːk]
黑暗的 [hēi àn de]

bright [braɪt]
明亮的 [míng liàng de]

left [left]
左 [zuǒ]

right
[raɪt]
右 [yòu]

near [nɪə]
近的 [jìn de]

far [fɑː]
远的 [yuǎn de]

shallow [ˈʃæləʊ]
浅的 [qiǎn de]

deep [diːp]
深的 [shēn de]

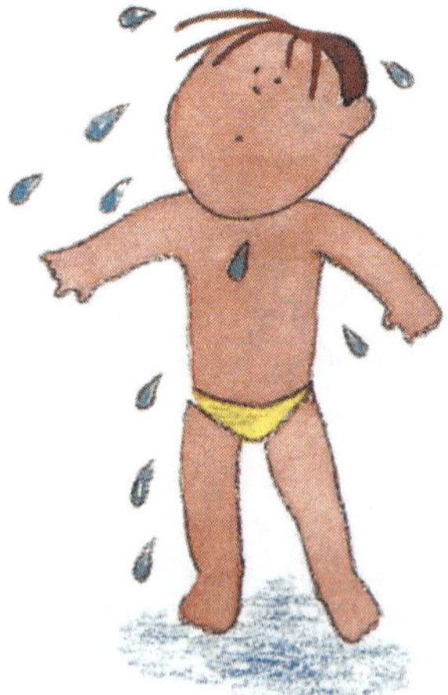

wet [wet]
湿的 [shī de]

dry [draɪ]
干的 [gān de]

heavy [ˈhevɪ]
重的 [zhòng de]

light [laɪt]
轻的 [qīng de]

young [jʌŋ]
年青的 [nián qīng de]

old [əʊld]
年老的 [nián lǎo de]

wide [waɪd]
宽阔的 [kuān kuò de]

narrow [ˈnærəʊ]
狭窄的 [xiá zhǎi de]

open [ˈəʊpən]
开了的 [kāi le de]

shut [ʃʌt]
关闭的 [guān bì de]

slow [sləʊ]
慢的 [màn de]

fast [fɑːst]
快的 [kuài de]

alive [əˈlaɪv]
活着的
[huó zhuó de]

dead [ded]
死掉的
[sǐ diào de]

Shapes
形状

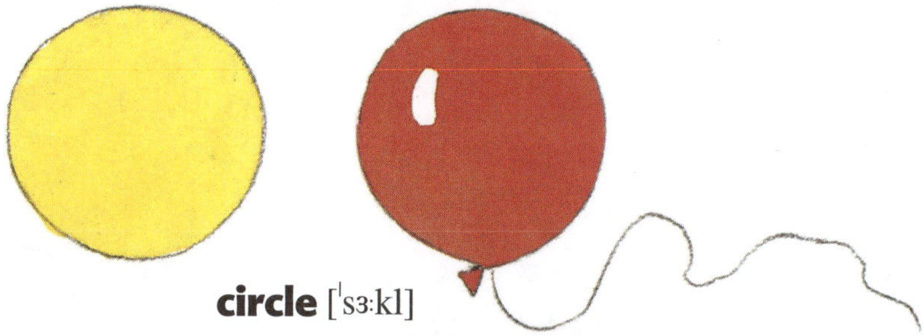

circle [ˈsɜːkl]
圆形 [yuán xíng]

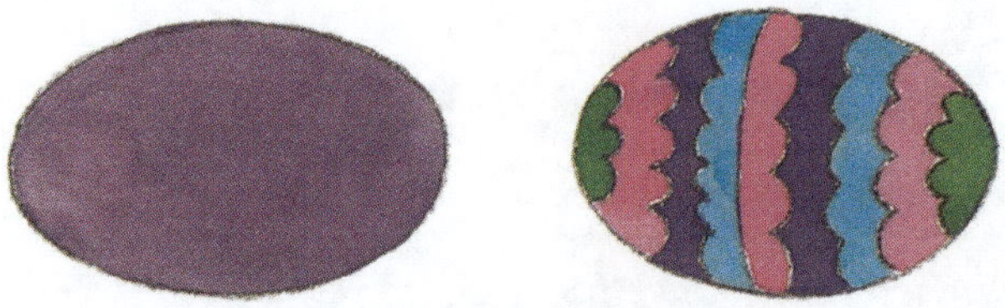

oval [ˈəʊvl]
椭圆形 [tuǒ yuán xíng]

heart [hɑːt]
心形 [xīn xíng]

cone [kəʊn]
椎体 [chuí tī]

rectangle [ˈrektæŋgl]
长方形 [cháng fāng xíng]

diamond
[ˈdaɪəmənd]
菱形 [líng xíng]

square [skweə]
正方形 [zhèng fāng xíng]

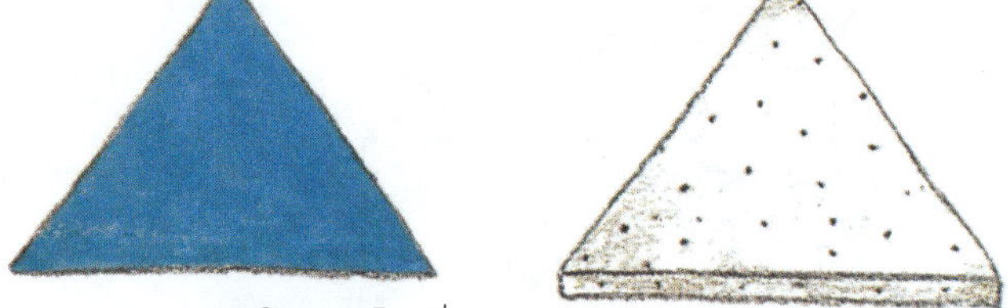

triangle [ˈtraɪæŋgl]
三角形 [sān jiǎo xíng]

Machines and Tools

机器及工具

wheelbarrow
[ˈwiːlbærəʊ]
独轮手推车
[dú lún shǒu tuī chē]

bulldozer [ˈbʊldəʊzə]
推土机 [tuī tǔ jī]

crane [kreɪn]
起重机 [qǐ zhòng jī]

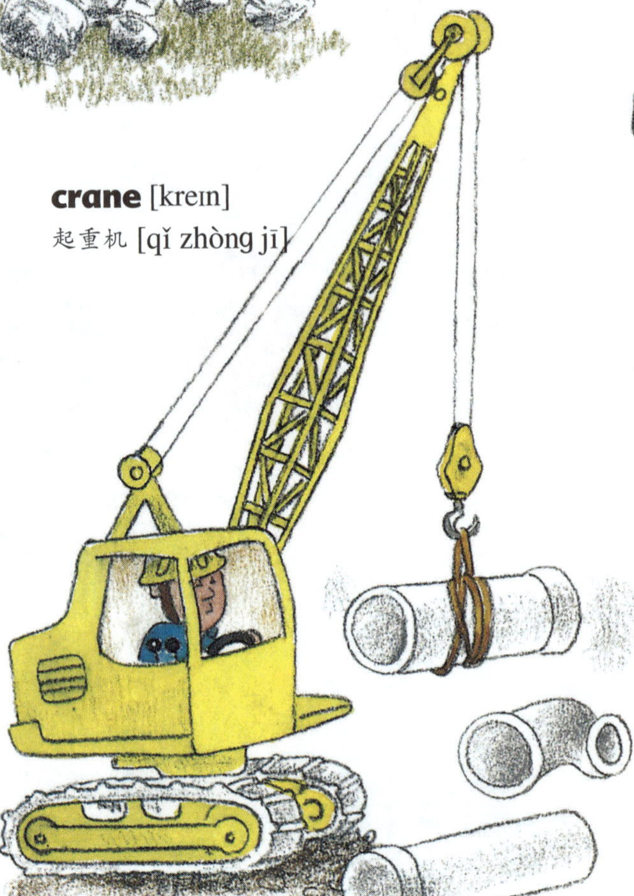

cement mixer [sɪˈment mɪksə]
混凝土车 [hùn níng tǔ chē]

tractor [ˈtræktə]
拖拉机 [tuō lā jī]

axe [æks]
斧头 [fǔ tóu]

penknife [ˈpennaɪf]
小刀 [xiǎo dāo]

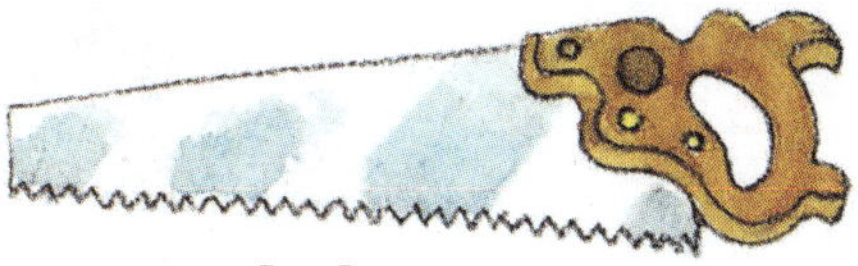

saw [sɔː]
锯 [jù]

scissors [ˈsɪzəz]
剪刀 [jiǎn dāo]

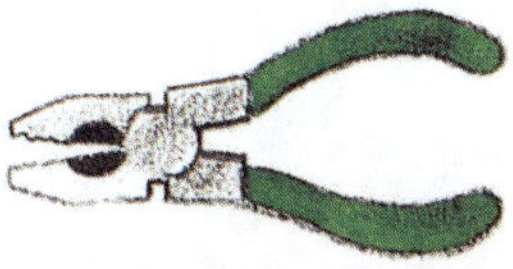

pliers [ˈplaɪəz]
钳 [qián]

screwdriver [ˈskruːdraɪvə]
螺丝起子 [luó sī qǐ zi]

spanner [ˈspænə]
扳钳 [bān qián]

hammer [ˈhæmə]
铁锤 [tiě chuí]

drill [drɪl]
钻 [zuān]

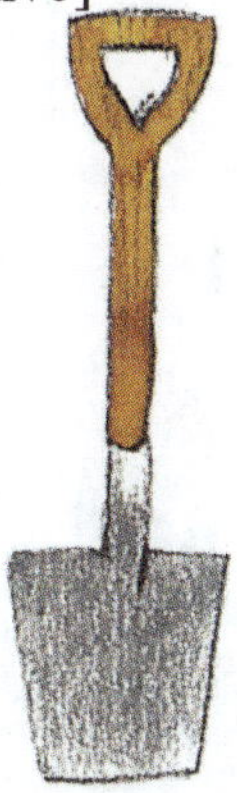

spade [speɪd]
铲 [chǎn]

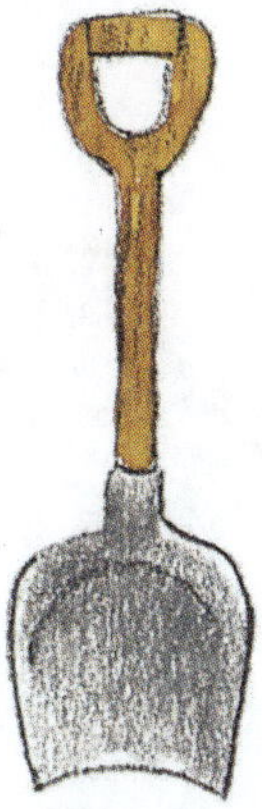

shovel [ˈʃʌvl]
锨 [xiān]

nail [neɪl]
钉 [dīng]

screw [skruː]
螺钉 [luó dīng]

compass
[ˈkʌmpəs]
圆规 [yuán guī]

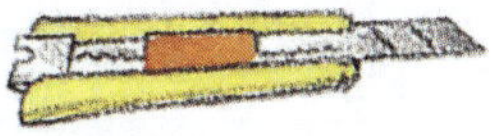

cutter [ˈkʌtə]
切割刀 [qiē gē dāo]

computer [kəmˈpjuːtə]
电脑 [diàn nǎo]

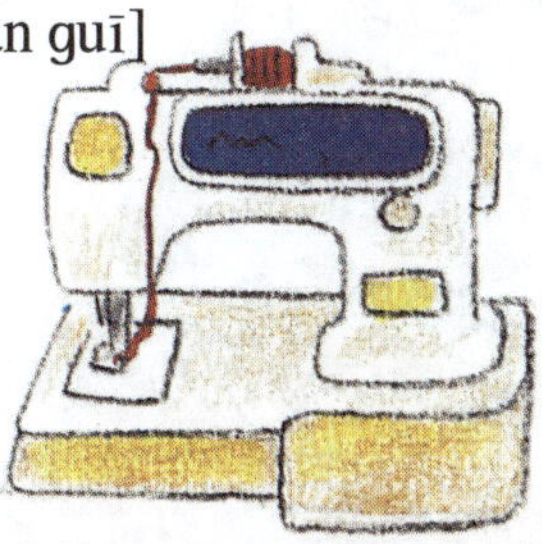

sewing machine [ˈsəʊɪŋ məˈʃiːn]
缝纫机 [féng rèn jī]

typewriter [ˈtaɪpraɪtə]
打字机 [dǎ zì jī]

camera [ˈkæmərə]
照相机 [zhào xiàng jī]

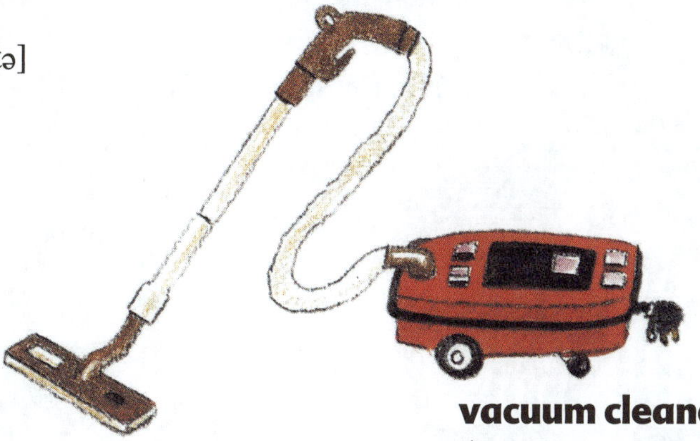

vacuum cleaner
[ˈvækjʊəm ˌkliːnə]
吸尘机 [xī chén jī]

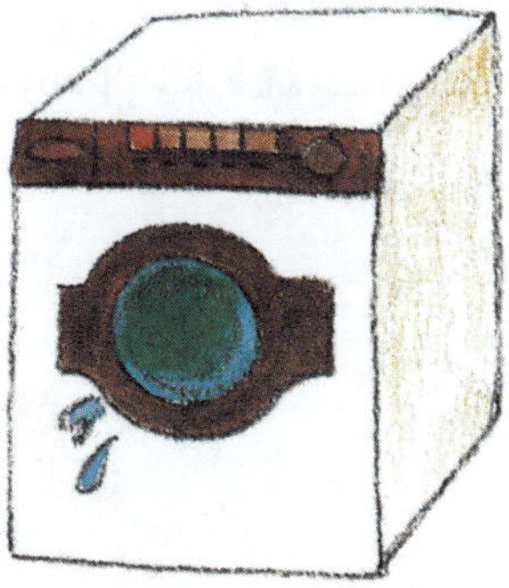

washing machine
[ˈwɒʃɪŋ məˈʃiːn]
洗衣机 [xǐ yī jī]

Jobs
职业

actor [ˈæktə]
男演员 [nán yǎn yuán]

actress [ˈæktrɪs]
女演员 [nǚ yǎn yuán]

artist [ˈɑːtɪst]
画家 [huà jiā]

astronaut [ˈæstrənɔːt]
太空人 [tài kōng rén]

baker [ˈbeɪkə]
面包师傅 [miàn bāo shī fu]

bus driver
[ˈbʌs draɪvə]
公共汽车司机 [gōng gòng qì chē sī jī]

carpenter [ˈkɑːpəntə]
木匠 [mù jiàng]

butcher [ˈbʊtʃə]
屠夫、肉商
[tú fū, ròu shāng]

cashier [kæˈʃɪə]
出纳员 [chū nà yuán]

clown [klaʊn]
小丑 [xiǎo chǒu]

shoemaker
[ˌʃuːˈmeɪkə]
鞋匠 [xié jiàng]

bus conductor
[bʌs kənˈdʌktə]
公共汽车售票员
[gōng gòng qì chē shòu piào yuán]

conductor
[kənˈdʌktə]
指挥 [zhǐ huī]

cook [kʊk]
厨师 [chú shī]

cowboy
[ˈkaʊbɔɪ]
牧童 [mù tóng]

dentist [ˈdentɪst]
牙医 [yá yī]

doctor [ˈdɒktə]
医生 [yī shēng]

farmer [ˈfɑːmə]
农夫 [nóng fū]

fire officer
[ˈfaɪə ɒfɪsə]
消防队员
[xiāo fáng duì yuán]

florist [ˈflɒrɪst]
花店主人 [huā diàn zhǔ rén]

gardener [ˈgɑːdnə]
园丁 [yuán dīng]

hairdresser
[ˈheədresə]
理发师 [lǐ fà shī]

magician [məˈdʒɪʃn]
魔术师 [mó shù shī]

nurse [nɜːs]
护士 [hù shì]

pilot [ˈpaɪlət]
飞行员
[fēi xíng yuán]

police officer [pəˈliːs ɒfɪsə]
警察 [jǐng chá]

porter [ˈpɔːtə]
行理搬运员 [xíng lǐ bān yùn yuán]

postman [ˈpəʊstmən]
邮差 [yóu chāi]

sailor [ˈseɪlə]
水手 [shuǐ shǒu]

saleswoman
[ˈseɪlzwʊmən]
女售货员
[nǚ shòu huò yuán]

salesman
[ˈseɪlzmən]
男售货员
[nán shòu huò yuán]

tailor [ˈteɪlə]
裁缝 [cái féng]

teacher [ˈtiːtʃə]
教师 [jiào shī]

waiter [ˈweɪtə]
男侍应生
[nán shì yìng shēng]

waitress
[ˈweɪtrɪs]
女侍应生
[nǚ shì yìng shēng]

Storybook People
童话人物

witch [wɪtʃ]
女巫 [nǚ wū]

monster [ˈmɒnstə]
妖怪 [yāo guài]

pirate [ˈpaɪrət]
海盗 [hǎi dào]

elf [elf]
淘气小鬼
[táo qì xiǎo guǐ]

fairy [ˈfeərɪ]
仙女 [xiān nǚ]

king [kɪŋ]
国王 [guó wáng]

queen [kwiːn]
王后 [wáng hòu]

princess [prɪnˈses]
公主 [gōng zhǔ]

prince [prɪns]
王子 [wáng zǐ]

dwarf [dwɔːf]
矮子、侏儒 [ǎi zi, zhū rú]

giant [ˈdʒaɪənt]
巨人 [jù rén]

Occasions

活动

barbecue

[ˈbɑːbɪkjuː]

烧烤[shāo kǎo]

birthday party

[ˌbɜːθdeɪ ˈpɑːtɪ]

生日会 [shēng rì huì]

camping

[ˈkæmpɪŋ]

露营 [lù yíng]

picnic [ˈpɪknɪk]

野餐 [yě cān]

wedding [ˈwedɪŋ]

婚礼 [hūn lǐ]

Weather
天气

rain [reɪn]
雨 [yǔ]

lightning [ˈlaɪtnɪŋ]
闪电 [shǎn diàn]

snow [snəʊ]
雪 [xuě]

wind [wɪnd]
风 [fēng]

fog [fɒg]
雾 [wù]

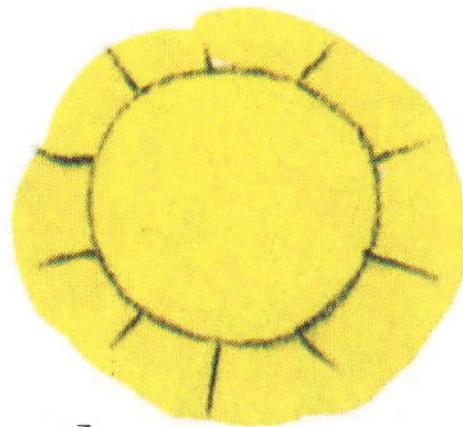

sun [sʌn]
太阳 [tài yáng]

cloud [klaʊd]
云 [yún]

Nature

自然

sky [skaɪ]
天空 [tiān kōng]

rainbow
[ˈreɪnbəʊ]
彩虹 [cǎi hóng]

mountain
[ˈmaʊntɪn]
山 [shān]

hill [hɪl]
小山 [xiǎo shān]

river [ˈrɪvə]
河 [hé]

forest [ˈfɒrɪst]
森林 [sēn lín]

waterfall [ˈwɔːtəfɔːl]
瀑布 [pù bù]

jungle [ˈdʒʌŋgl]
丛林 [cóng lín]

star [stɑː]
星星 [xīng xīng]

moon [muːn]
月亮 [yuè liang]

sea [siː]
海 [hǎi]

island [ˈaɪlənd]
島 [dǎo]

waves [weɪvz]
浪 [làng]

lake [leɪk]
湖 [hú]

volcano [vɒlˈkeɪnəʊ]
火山 [huǒ shān]

pond [pɒnd]
池塘 [chí táng]

Toys
玩具

teddy bear [ˈtedɪ beə]
玩具熊 [wán jù xióng]

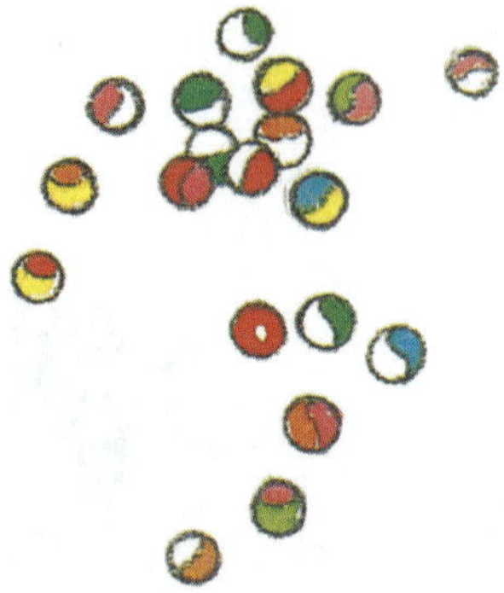

marbles [ˈmɑːblz]
弹珠 [dàn zhū]

balloons [bəˈluːnz]
气球 [qì qiú]

puppet [ˈpʌpɪt]
木偶 [mù ǒu]

mask [mɑːsk]
面具 [miàn jù]

blocks [blɒks]
积木 [jī mù]

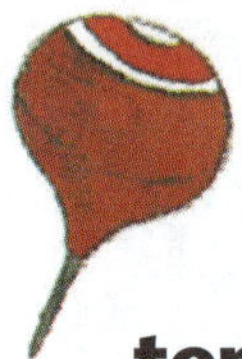

top [tɒp]
陀螺 [tuó luó]

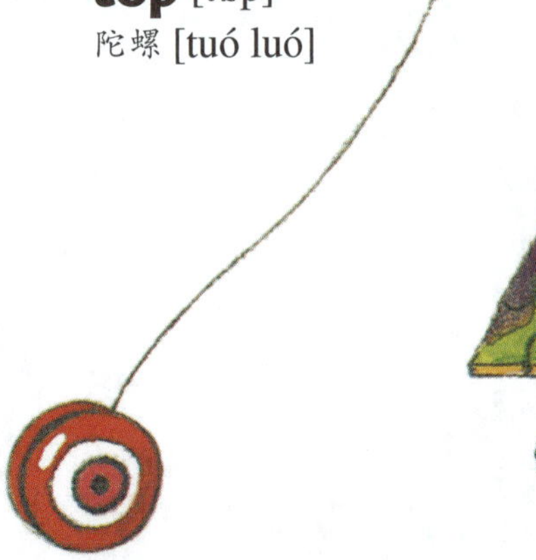

doll [dɒl]
洋娃娃 [yáng wá wa]

yo-yo [ˈjəʊjəʊ]
摇摇 [yáo yao]

jigsaw puzzle [ˈdʒɪgsɔː pʌzl]
拼图游戏 [pīn tú yóu xì]

Feelings

心情、态度

jealous [ˈdʒeləs]
妒忌的 [dù jì de]

proud [praʊd]
骄傲的 [jiāo ào de]

selfish [ˈselfɪʃ]
自私的 [zì sī de]

generous [ˈdʒenərəs]
慷慨的 [kāng kǎi de]

happy [ˈhæpɪ]
快乐的 [kuài lè de]

frightened [ˈfraɪtnd]
受惊的 [shòu jīng de]

sad [sæd]
悲伤的 [bēi shāng de]

angry [ˈæŋgrɪ]
愤怒的 [fèn nù de]

Numbers
数目

one thumb [wʌn θʌm]
一根拇指 [yī gēn mǔ zhǐ]

two flags [tuː flægz]
两面旗 [liǎng miàn qí]

three heads [θriː hedz]
三个头 [sān gè tóu]

four legs [fɔː legz]
四条腿 [sì tiáo tuǐ]

five candles [faɪv ˈkændlz]
五支蜡烛 [wǔ zhī là zhú]

six legs [sɪks legz]
六条腿 [liù tiáo tuǐ]

seven posts [ˈsevn pəʊsts]
七根柱子 [qī gēn zhù zi]

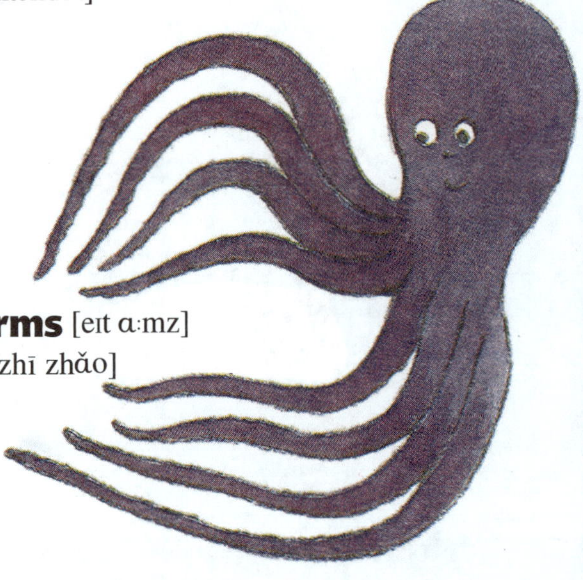

eight arms [eɪt ɑːmz]
八只爪 [bā zhī zhǎo]

nine apples [naɪn ˈæplz]
九个苹果 [jiǔ gè píng guǒ]

ten fingers [ten ˈfɪŋgəz]
十根手指 [shí gēn shǒu zhǐ]

eleven flowers [ɪˌlevn ˈflaʊəz]
十一朵花 [shí yī duǒ huā]

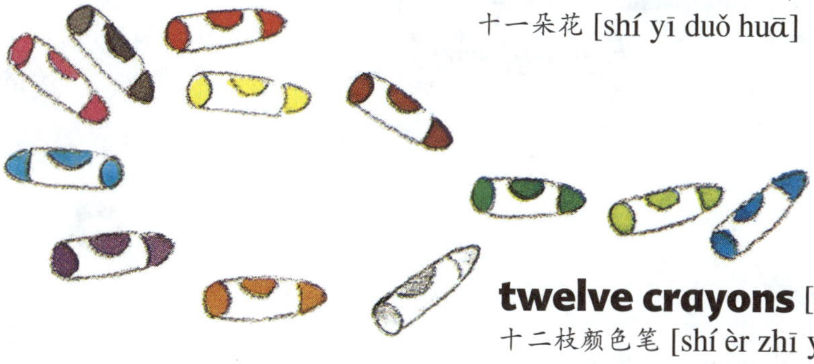

twelve crayons [twelv ˈkreɪənz]
十二枝颜色笔 [shí èr zhī yán sè bǐ]

thirteen ladybugs
[ˌθɜːˈtiːn ˈleɪdɪbʌgz]
十三只瓢虫
[shí sān zhī piáo chóng]

fourteen cans [ˌfɔːˈtiːn kænz]
十四个罐 [shí sì gè guàn]

fifteen footprints [ˌfɪfˈtiːn ˈfʊtprɪnts] 十五个脚印 [shí wǔ gè jiǎo yìn]

sixteen beads
[ˌsɪksˈtiːn biːdz]
十六粒珠子
[shí liù lì zhū zi]

seventeen butterflies
[ˌsevənˈtiːn ˈbʌtəflaɪz]
十七只蝴蝶 [shí qī zhī hú dié]

nineteen nails
[ˌnaɪnˈtiːn neɪlz]
十九口钉子 [shí jiǔ kǒu dīng zi]

eighteen cookies[ˌeɪˈtiːn ˈkʊkɪz]
十八块饼干 [shí bā kuài bǐng gān]

twenty eggs
[ˈtwentɪ egz]
二十个鸡蛋
[èr shí gè jī dàn]

In Space
太空

satellite [ˈsætəlaɪt]
人造卫星 [rén zào wèi xīng]

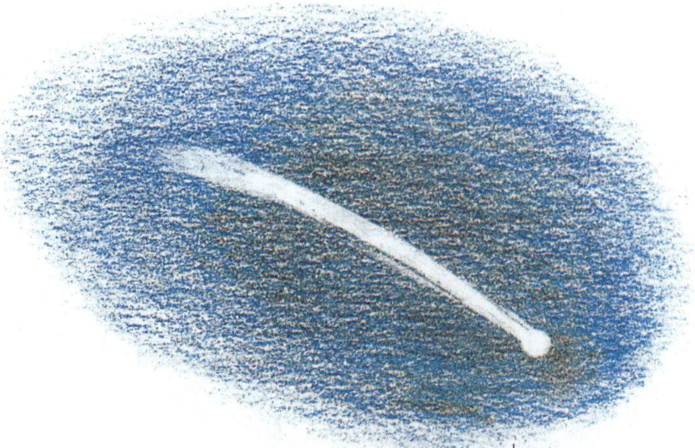

meteor [ˈmiːtɪɔː]
流星 [liú xīng]

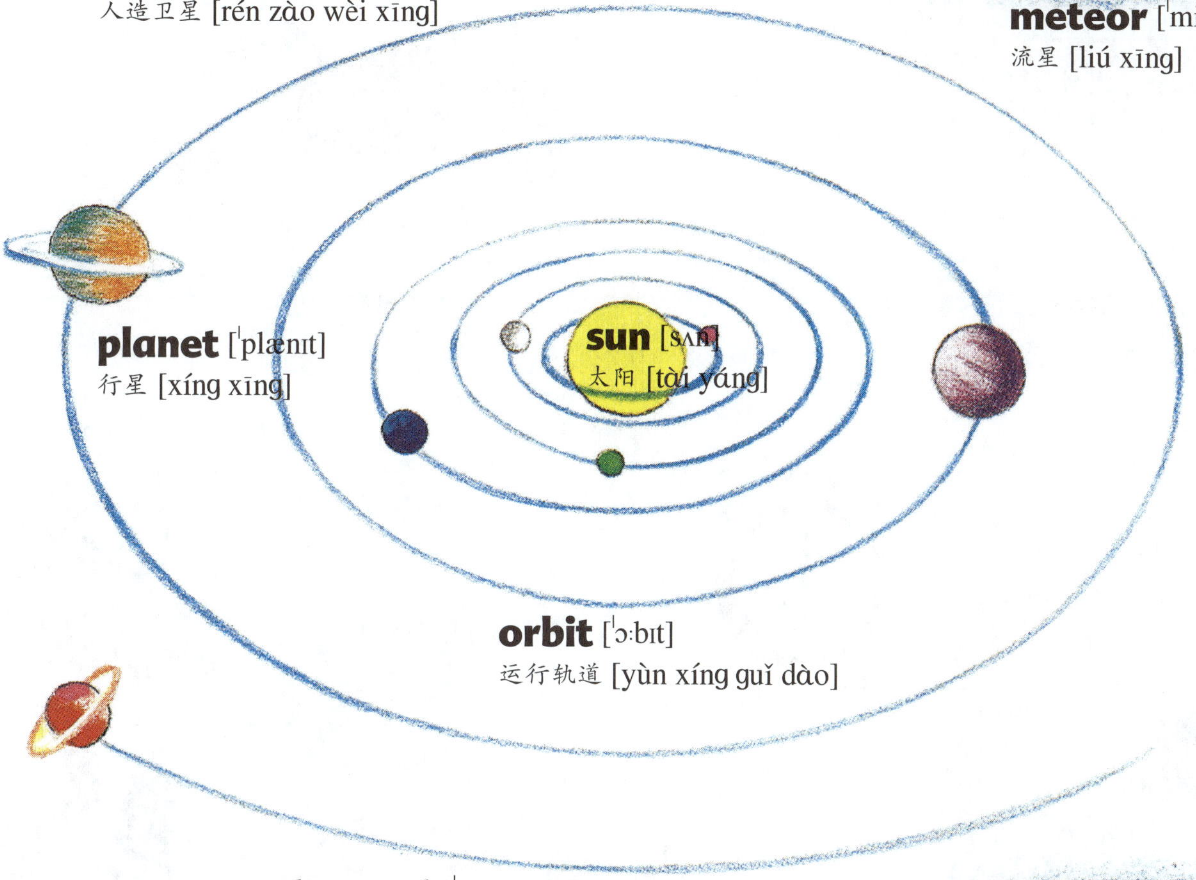

planet [ˈplænɪt]
行星 [xíng xīng]

sun [sʌn]
太阳 [tài yáng]

orbit [ˈɔːbɪt]
运行轨道 [yùn xíng guǐ dào]

astronaut [ˈæstrənɔːt]
太空人 [tài kōng rén]

Milky Way [ˈmɪlkɪ weɪ]
银河 [yín hé]

Times of the Day
一日内的时间

morning [ˈmɔːnɪŋ]
上午 [shàng wǔ]

breakfast [ˈbrekfəst]
早餐 [zǎo cān]

afternoon
[ˌɑːftəˈnuːn]
下午 [xià wǔ]

lunch [lʌntʃ]
午餐 [wǔ cān]

evening [ˈiːvnɪŋ]
黄昏 [huáng hūn]

dinner [ˈdɪnə]
晚餐 [wǎn cān]

night [naɪt]
晚上 [wǎn shang]

bedtime [bedtaɪm]
就寝时间 [jiù qǐn shí jiān]

Days of the Week

星期

Sports and Games
体育项目及竞赛

racket [ˈrækɪt]
网球拍 [wǎng qiú pāi]

tennis [ˈtenɪs]
网球 [wǎng qiú]

American football
[əˈmerɪkən ˈfʊtbɔːl]
美式足球 [měi shì zú qiú]

finishing line [ˈfɪnɪʃɪŋ laɪn]
终点 [zhōng diǎn]

running [ˈrʌnɪŋ]
赛跑[sài pǎo]

goalpost [ˈgəʊlpəʊst]
门柱 [mén zhù]

football [ˈfʊtbɔːl]
足球 [zú qiú]

volleyball [ˈvɒlibɔːl]
排球 [pái qiú]

basketball [ˈbɑːskɪtbɔːl]
篮球 [lán qiú]

baseball
[ˈbeɪsbɔːl]
棒球 [bàng qiú]

high jump
[haɪ dʒʌmp]
跳高 [tiào gāo]

squash [skwɒʃ]
壁球 [bì qiú]

hurdles [ˈhɜːdlz]
跨栏 [kuà lán]

surfing [sɜːfɪŋ]
冲浪 [chōng làng]

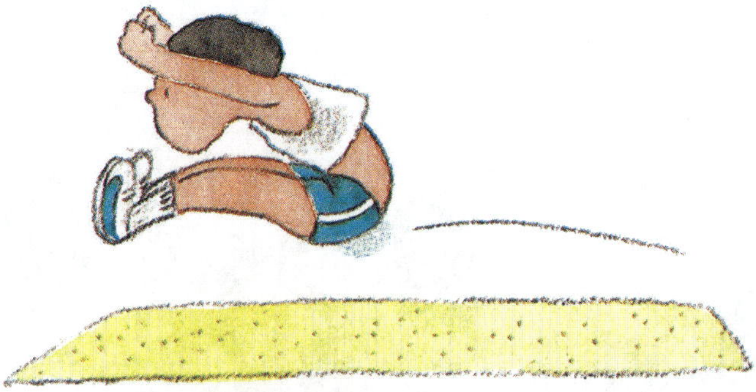

long jump [lɒŋ dʒʌmp]
跳远 [tiào yuǎn]

boxing ring
[ˈbɒksɪŋ rɪŋ]
拳击台
[quán jī tái]

boxing [ˈbɒksɪŋ]
拳击 [quán jī]

bat [bæt]
球棒 [qiú bàng]

cricket [ˈkrɪkɪt]
板球 [bǎn qiú]

ice hockey [aɪs ˈhɒkɪ]
冰球 [bīng qiú]

swimming [ˈswɪmɪŋ]
游泳 [yóu yǒng]

golf club
[gɒlf klʌb]
高尔夫球棒
[gāo ěr fū qiú bàng]

golf [gɒlf]
高尔夫球 [gāo ěr fū qiú]

rugby ball [ˈrʌgbɪ ˈbɔ:l]
橄榄球 [gǎn lǎn qiú]

judo [ˈdʒu:dəʊ]
柔道 [róu dào]

water polo [ˈwɔ:tə pəʊləʊ]
水球 [shuǐ qiú]

rugby [ˈrʌgbɪ]
橄榄球运动
[gǎn lǎn qiú yùn dòng]

roller skates
[ˈrəʊlə skeɪtz]
滚轴溜冰鞋
[gǔn zhóu liū bīng xié]

roller skating
[ˌrəʊlə ˈskeɪtɪŋ]
速度滑行 [sù dù huá xíng]

table tennis [ˌteɪbl ˈtenɪs]
乒乓球 [pīng pāng qiú]

weight lifting
[weɪt lɪftɪŋ]
举重 [jǔ zhòng]

netball [ˈnetbɔ:l]
无挡板篮球 [wú dǎng bǎn lán qiú]

ice skates
[aɪs skeɪtz]
溜冰鞋
[liū bīng xié]

ice skating
[aɪs ˈskeɪtɪŋ]
溜冰 [liū bīng]

cycling [ˈsaɪklɪŋ]
骑自行车 [qí zì xíng chē]

rowing [rəʊɪŋ]
划船 [huá chuán]

fishing rod
[ˈfɪʃɪŋ rɒd]
钓竿 [diào gān]

fishing [ˈfɪʃɪŋ]
钓鱼 [diào yú]

shuttlecock [ˈʃʌtlkɒk]
羽毛球 [yǔ máo qiú]

badminton [ˈbædmɪntən]
羽毛球运动 [yǔ máo qiú yùn dòng]

gymnastics
[dʒɪmˈnæstɪks]
体操 [tǐ cāo]

bowling pins
[ˈbəʊlɪŋ pɪns]
保龄球瓶
[bǎo líng qiú píng]

bowling [ˈbəʊlɪŋ]
保龄球 [bǎo líng qiú]

hockey stick [ˈhɒkɪ stɪk]
曲棍球棒
[qū gùn qiú bàng]

hockey [ˈhɒkɪ]
曲棍球 [qū gùn qiú]

wrestling
[ˈreslɪŋ]
摔跤 [shuāi jiāo]

skis [ski:z]
雪橇 [xuě qiāo]

skiing [ski:ɪŋ]
滑雪 [huá xuě]

People of the World

世界各国人民

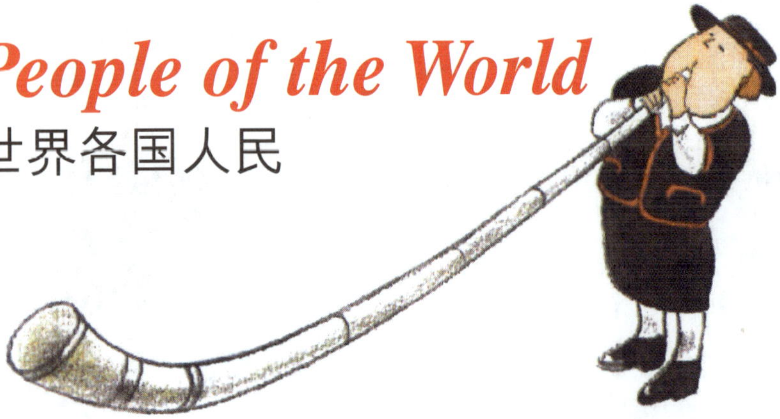

Swiss [swɪs]
瑞士人 [ruì shì rén]

Dutchman [ˈdʌtʃmən]
荷兰人 [hé lán rén]

German [ˈdʒʌɜːmən
德国人 [dé guó rén]

Indian
[ˈɪndɪən]
印度人
[yìn dù rén]

Eskimo [ˈeskɪməʊ]
爱斯基摩人[ài sī jī mó rén]

Russian
[ˈrʌʃn]
俄罗斯人
[é luó sī rén]

Frenchman
[ˈfrentʃmən]
法国人 [fǎ guó rén]

Englishman
[ˈɪŋglɪʃmən]
英国人
[yīng guó rén]

Scot [skɒt]
苏格兰人
[sū gé lán rén]

Nigerian
[naɪˈdʒɪərɪən]
尼日利亚人
[ní rì lì yà rén]

Thai [taɪ]
泰国人 [tài guó rén]

Austrian [ˈɒstrɪən]
奥地利人 [ào dì lì rén]

Korean [kəˈriːən]
韩国人 [hán guó rén]

Italian [ɪˈtælɪən]
意大利人 [yì dà lì ré]

Greek [griːk]
希腊人 [xī là rén]

American [əˈmerɪkən]
美国人 [měi guó rén]

Native American
[ˈneɪtɪv əˈmerɪkən]
印第安人 [yìn dì ān rén]

Spanish
[ˈspænɪʃ]
西班牙人 [xī bān yá rén]

Filipino [ˈfɪlɪˈpiːnəʊ]
菲律宾人 [fēi lǜ bīn rén]

Vietnamese
[ˌvjetnəˈmiːz]
越南人 [yuè nán rén]

Malay[məˈleɪ]
马来人 [mǎ lái rén]

Hawaiian [həˈwaɪən]
夏威夷人 [xià wēi yí rén]

Pakistani [pɑːkɪˈstɑːnɪ]
巴基斯坦人 [bā jī sī tǎn rén]

Indonesian
[ɪndəˈniːzɪən]
印尼人 [yìn ní rén]

Maori
[ˈmaʊrɪ]
毛利人
[máo lì rén]

Burmese
[bəɪˈmiːz]
缅甸人
[miǎn diàn rén]

Afghan
[ˈæfgæn]
阿富汗人
[ā fù hàn rén]

Arab [ˈærəb]
阿拉伯人 [ā lā bó rén]

Japanese
[ˌdʒæpəˈniːz]
日本人 [rì běn rén]

Chinese [ˌtʃaɪˈniːz]
中国人 [zhōng guó rén]

Mexican [ˈmeksɪkən]
墨西哥人 [mò xī gē rén]

Weapons
武器

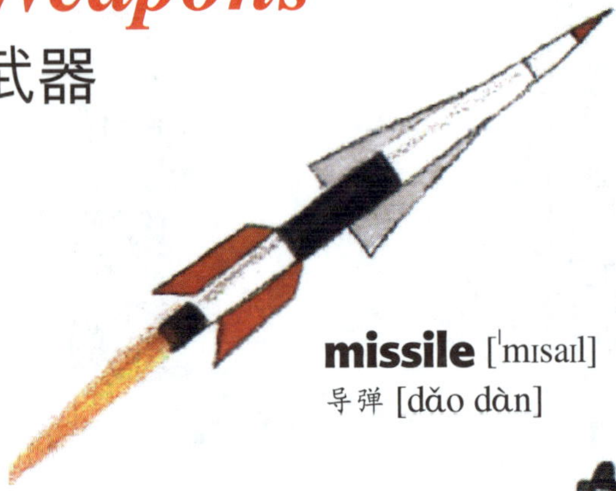

missile [ˈmɪsaɪl]
导弹 [dǎo dàn]

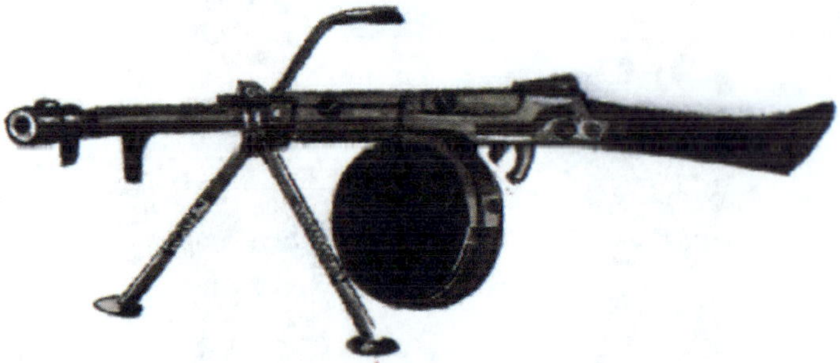

machine gun [məˈʃiːn gʌn]
机关枪 [jī guān qiāng]

gun [gʌn]
枪 [qiāng]

rifle [ˈraɪfl]
来福枪 [lái fú qiāng]

spear [spɪə]
矛 [máo]

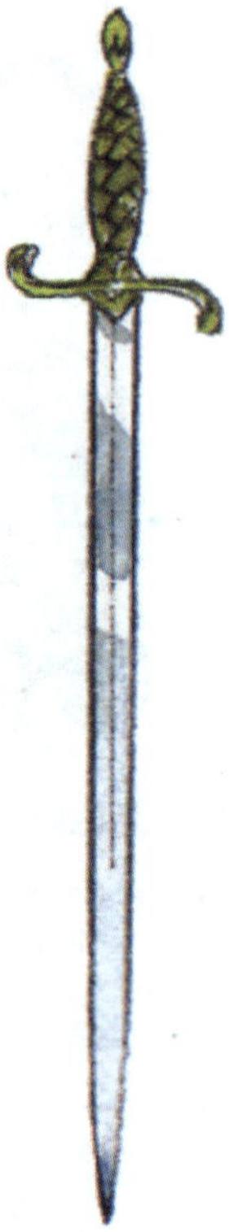

sword [sɔːd]
剑 [jiàn]

bow and arrow
[bəʊ ənd ˈærəʊ]
弓箭 [gōng jiàn]

cannon
[ˈkænən]
大炮 [dà pào]

TO TALK ABOUT

Kathleen Lloyd
Illustrated by Paul Yong

A Note to Parents

This section of the book has been designed as a 'talk-about book'. The main pictures on each spread have therefore been conceptualised to stimulate students to talk freely about the situations, people and objects shown.

Why a 'talk-about book'?
Children enjoy seeing other children involved in the same activities that occupy their everyday life. So, this section with its detailed and colourful pictures of people in familiar situations can provide them with many hours of pleasure. They can trace the 'story' of the members of a family, their relatives and friends through the pictures, and play the game of finding the named objects around the main picture in the picture itself.

By talking about the different situations in the pictures, students will acquire a large and varied spoken vocabulary, and they will also develop their ability to interpret pictures.

Asking questions
The questions given on each spread in this section invite students to talk about the main picture. Some of the questions have a suitable, but not exclusively correct, answer printed on the picture at the appropriate place. Others are marked with a red bullet. These questions require students to use their imagination to reason and make predictions — an important reading skill — and no answers are suggested for them.

Please note that the questions and answers are given as guidelines only, so avoid using them as a test or reading drill. Try to make this 'talk-about book' an enjoyable experience for children. If you do, you will find that their interest will be stimulated, their vocabulary extended and their ability to express themselves greatly enhanced.

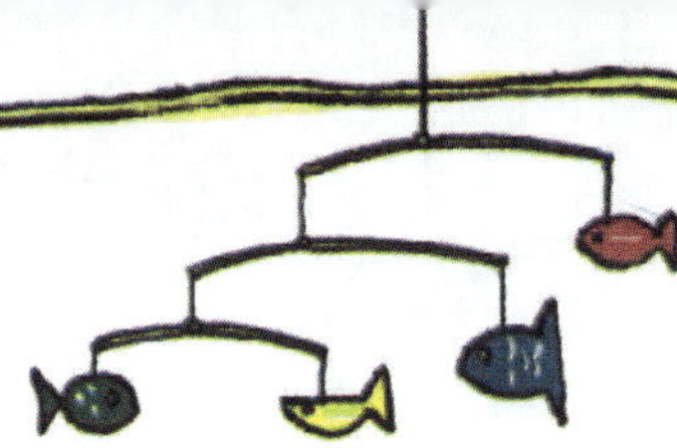

给家长的话

本部分主要提供会话词汇。那横跨两页的大幅插图，用以激发学生自由讨论其中的情况、人物和事情。

为甚么需要提供会话词汇?

对于其他小朋友跟自己日常生活一般无异的活 ，孩子总看得津津有味。本部分能为孩子提供长时间的娱乐，这是由于书中有多采多姿的图画，而书中人物的情况都是他们所熟稔的。他们可以透过图画的脉络，探究出那一家人及其亲友的「经历」，又可以在主图中找出指定的事物。

讲述不同的情况需用大量的词汇，学生得以发展理解图画的能力。

提出问题

本部分所列出的问题，都要求学生就主图发表意见。部分问题的答案印在画中恰当的位置上，但答案非唯一正确的。有些问题不设答案，以红点为记，需要学生发挥其阅读技巧，即需要学生运用其想像力去判断和作出揣测。

请注意，问题和答案只是指引，避免采用这些问答作为测验或阅读练习。尝试让孩子觉得阅读本部分乃赏心乐事，如此，你们将发现他们越看越有兴趣，其词汇得以充实，而其坦然表达自己的能力亦有所提高。

The family 家庭

- What is the family doing?
- Who is Grandfather holding?
- Whose teddy bear is Grandmother holding?
- Why is the dog barking?
- What do you think the cat will do next?

Father [ˈfɑːðə]
父亲 [fù qin]
Mother [ˈmʌðə]
母亲 [mǔ qin]
Baby
[ˈbeɪbɪ]
婴儿
[yīng ér]
Susan [ˈsuːzn]
苏珊 [sū shān]
Grandmother [grænmʌðə]
祖母 [zǔ mǔ]
Grandfather [grænfɑːðə]
祖父 [zǔ fù]

It's time to wake up
是时候起床了

- Where is Father?
- What is Mother doing?
- Is Susan awake? What is she doing?
- What does Baby want to do?
- Where is David?
- What do you think the children will do next?

beads [bi:dz]
珠串 [zhū chuàn]

curtain [ˈkɜ:tn]
窗帘 [chuāng lián]

cot [kɒt]
婴儿床 [yīng ér chuáng]

alarm clock [əˈlɑ:m klɒk]
闹钟 [nào zhōng]

blanket [ˈblæŋkɪt]
毛毯 [máo tǎn]

lamp [læmp]
灯 [dēng]

pillow [ˈpɪləʊ]
枕头 [zhěn tou]

vase of flowers [vɑ:z əv ˈflaʊə]
一瓶花 [yī píng huā]

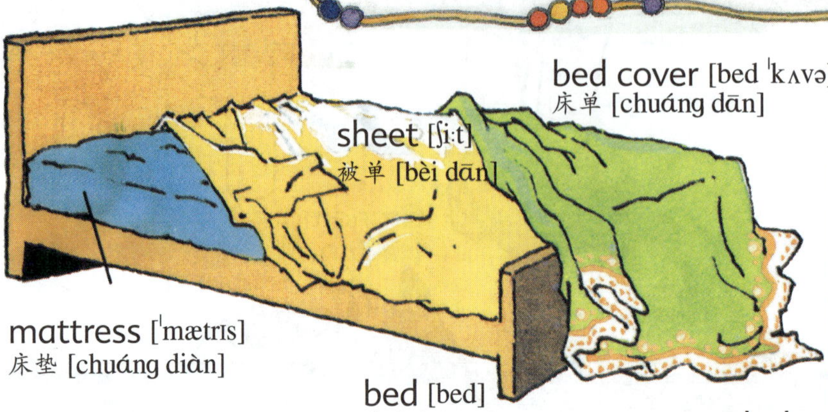

bed cover [bed ˈkʌvə]
床单 [chuáng dān]

sheet [ʃi:t]
被单 [bèi dān]

mattress [ˈmætrɪs]
床垫 [chuáng diàn]

bed [bed]
床 [chuáng]

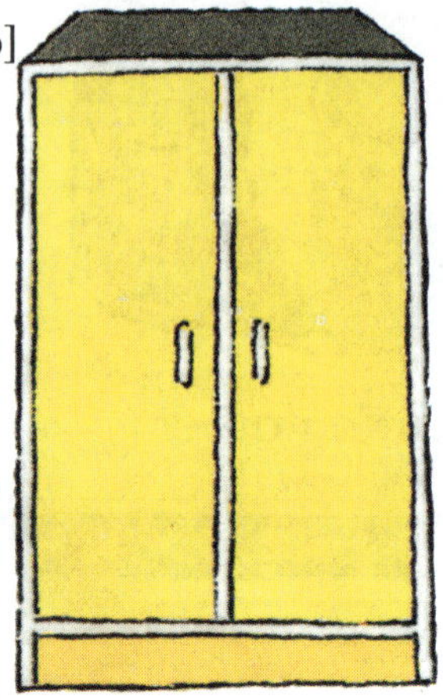

wardrobe [ˈwɔ:drəʊb]
衣柜 [yī guì]

drawer [drɔː]
抽屉 [chōu ti]

fan [fæn]
风扇 [fēng shàn]

picture [ˈpɪktʃə]
画 [huà]

pyjamas [pəˈdʒaːməz]
睡衣裤 [shuì yī kù]

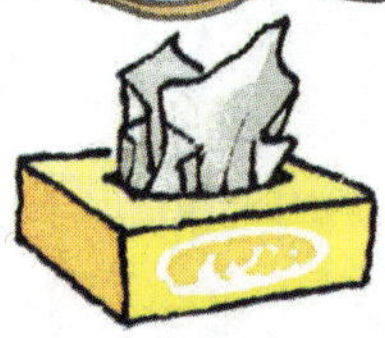

tissues [ˈtɪʃuːz]
纸巾 [zhǐ jīn]

rug [rʌg]
小地毯 [xiǎo dì tǎn]

nightgown [ˈnaɪtgaʊn]
睡袍 [shuì páo]

stretch [stretʃ]
伸懒腰 [shēn lǎn yāo]

Let's get dressed

穿好衣服

- Who is combing her hair?
- What is David thinking about?
- Who is taking off his pyjamas?
- What is Mother doing?
- Who do you think will be the last to get dressed?

jacket [ˈdʒækɪt]
外套 [wài tào]

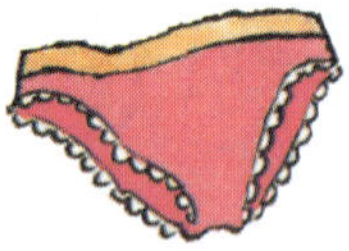

panties [ˈpæntɪz]
女装内裤 [nǚ zhuāng nèi kù]

shirt [ʃɜːt]
衬衫 [chèn shān]

jeans [dʒiːnz]
牛仔裤
[niú zǎi kù]

tie [taɪ]
领带 [lǐng dài]

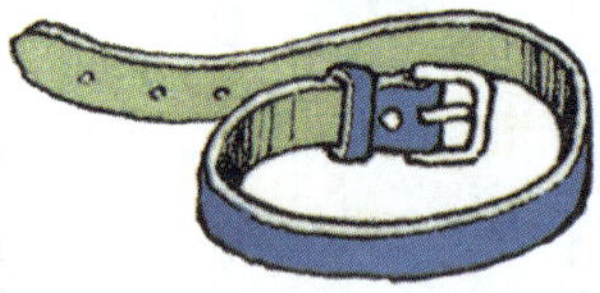

belt [belt]
皮带 [pí dài]

cap [kæp]
便帽 [biàn mào]

pants [pænts]
裤子 [kù zi]

dress [dres]
裙子 [qún zi]

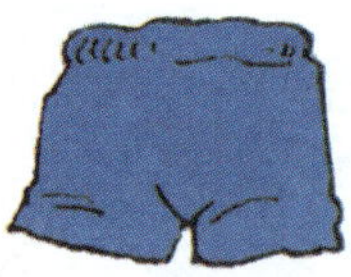

shorts [ʃɔːts]
短裤 [duǎn kù]

blouse [blaʊz]
女装衬衫
[nǚ zhuāng chèn shān]

skirt [skɜːt]
短裙 [duǎn qún]

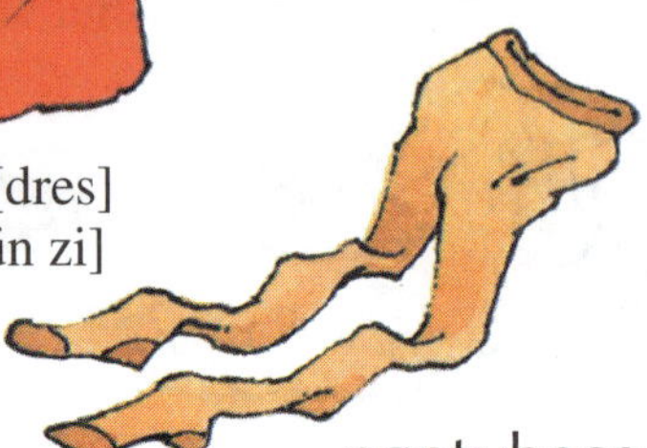

pantyhose [ˈpæntɪhəʊz]
裤袜 [kù wà]

T-shirt
[tiː ʃɜːt]
汗衫 [hàn shān]

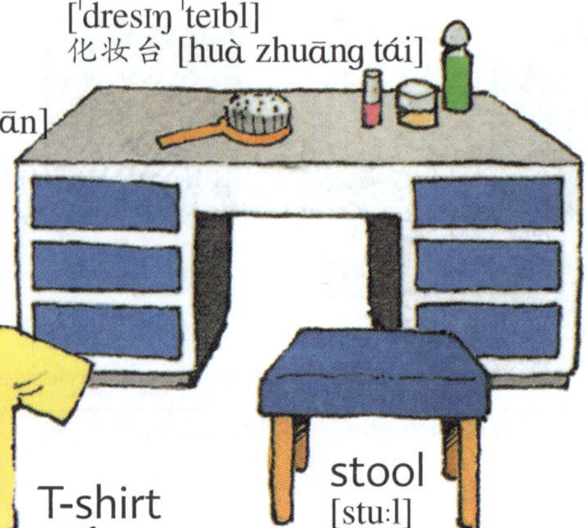

dressing table
[ˈdresɪŋ ˈteɪbl]
化妆台 [huà zhuāng tái]

stool
[stuːl]
凳子
[dèng zi]

shoes [ʃuːz]
鞋子 [xié zi]

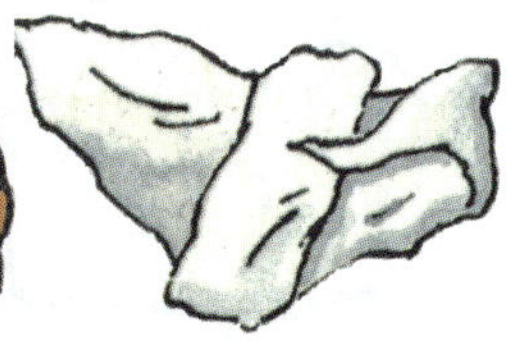

diaper [ˈdaɪəpə]
尿布 [niào bù]

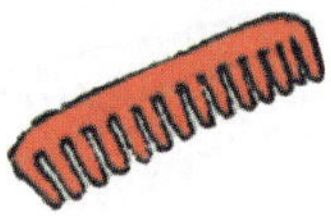

comb [kəʊm]
梳子 [shū zi]

hairbrush [ˈheəbrʌʃ]
发刷 [fà shuā]

put on [pʊt ɒn]
穿上 [chuān shang]

trainers [ˈtreɪnəz]
运动鞋 [yùn dòng xié]

socks [sɒks]
短袜子 [duǎn wà zi]

slippers [ˈslɪpəz]
拖鞋 [tuō xié]

mirror [ˈmɪrə]
镜子[jìng zi]

take off [teɪk ɒf]
脱去 [tuō qù]

Breakfast 早餐时间

- Who is late for breakfast?
- What is Susan eating?
- Who is drinking coffee?
- What is Mother pouring?
- Oh dear! What has Baby done?
- What do you think the cat will do?

jug of juice [dʒʌg əv dʒuːs]
一壶果汁 [yī hú guǒ zhī]

glass [glaːs]
玻璃杯 [bō li bēi]

mug [mʌg]
大杯 [dà bēi]

milk [mɪlk]
奶 [nǎi]

kettle [ˈketl]
水壶 [shuǐ hú]

teapot [ˈtiːpɒt]
茶壶 [chá hú]

toast [təʊst]
烤面包 [kǎo miàn bāo]

coffee pot [ˈkɒfɪ pɒt]
咖啡壶 [kā fēi hú]

toaster [təʊstə]
烤面包机 [kǎo miàn bāo jī]

cereal [ˈsɪərɪəl]
谷类食物
[gǔ lèi shí wù]

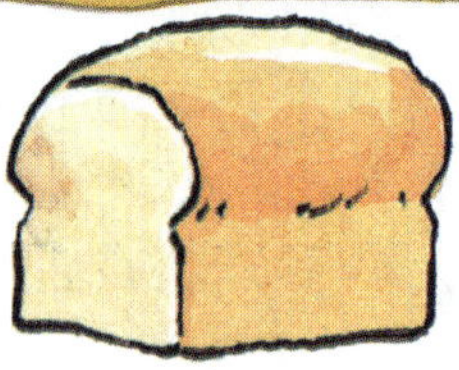

bread [bred]
面包 [miàn bāo]

sugar [ˈʃʊgə]
糖 [táng]

egg [eg]
鸡蛋 [jī dàn]

fruit [fruːt]
水果 [shuǐ guǒ]

jar of jam
[dʒɑː əv dʒæm]
一瓶果酱
[yī píng guǒ jiàng]

saucepan [ˈsɔːspən]
有柄平底锅
[yǒu bǐng píng dǐ guō]

honey [ˈhʌnɪ]
蜂蜜 [fēng mì]

eat [iːt]
吃 [chī]

spill [spɪl]
溢出 [yì chū]

butter [ˈbʌtə]
牛油 [niú yóu]

doormat [ˈdɔːmæt]
蹭鞋垫 [cèng xié diàn]

drink [drɪŋk]
喝 [hē]

pour [pɔː]
倒出 [dào chū]

Going to school 上学去

- Who is Susan waving to?
- Can you see Aziz? What is he doing?
- How does David come to school?
- How do some children come to school?
- What do you think Mother is saying to David and Susan?

friend [frend]
朋友 [péng yǒu]

school bag [sku:l bæg]
书包 [shū bāo]

broom
[bru:m]
扫帚
[sào zhǒu]

street sweeper
[stri:t ˈswiːpə]
清道夫 [qīng dào fū]

water bottle
[ˌwɔ:tə ˈbɒtl]
水壶 [shuǐ hú]

car [kɑ:]
汽车 [qì chē]

hump [hʌmp]
路墩 [lù dūn]

pushchair [ˈpʊʃtʃeə]
婴儿车
[yīng ér chē]

bicycle [ˈbaɪsɪkl]
自行车 [zì xíng chē]

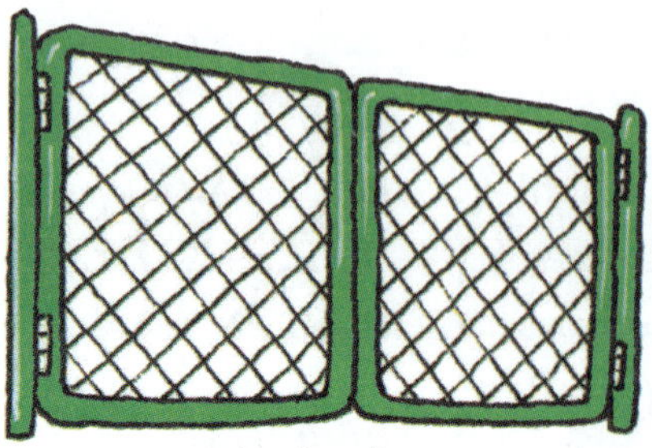

gate [geɪt]
大门 [dà mén]

zebra crossing
[ˌzebrə ˈkrɒsɪŋ]
斑马线 [bān mǎ xiàn]

Some children come to school by bus.
Susan is waving to Carol.

walk [wɔːk]
步行 [bù xíng]
wave [weɪv]
挥手 [huī shǒu]
sweep [swiːp]
扫 [sǎo]
run [rʌn]
跑 [pǎo]
cycle [ˈsaɪkl]
骑自行车
[qí zì xíng chē]
wait [weɪt]
等候 [děng hòu]
school bus
[skuːl bʌs]
校车 [xiào chē]
sidewalk [ˈsaɪdˌwɔk]
人行道 [rén xíng dào]
kerb [kɜːb]
边石 [biān shí]

In the classroom
上课时间

- What is the teacher doing?
- What is David doing?
- Who is colouring shapes?
- Who is not listening to the story?
- Who is sitting next to Susan?
- What do you think the teacher will say to Aziz?

Gita is sitting next to Susan.

Susan is colouring shapes.

book [bʊk]
书 [shū]

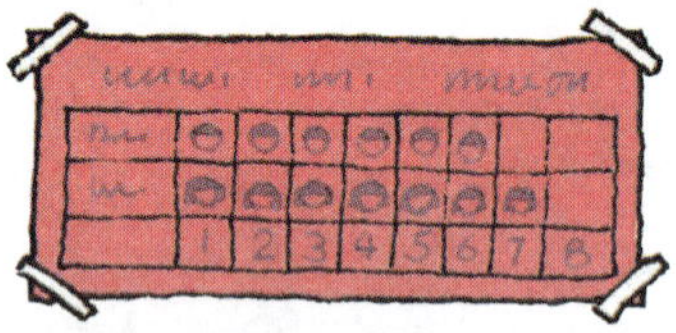

chart [tʃɑːt]
图表 [tú biǎo]

teacher [ˈtiːtʃə]
教师 [jiào shī]

pencil [ˈpensl]
铅笔 [qiān bǐ]

paper [ˈpeɪpə]
纸张 [zhǐ zhāng]

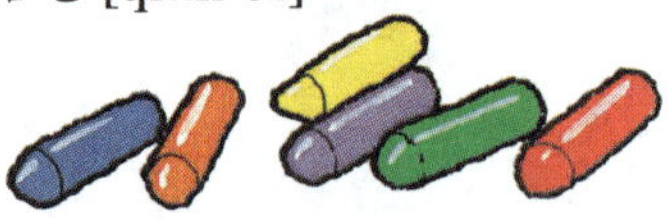

crayons [ˈkreɪənz]
蜡笔 [là bǐ]

wastepaper basket
[ˈweɪstˌpeɪpə bɑːskɪt]
废纸篓 [fèi zhǐ lǒu]

numbers [ˈnʌmbəz]
数字 [shù zì]

table [ˈteɪbl]
桌子 [zhuō zi]

glue [gluː]
胶水 [jiāo shuǐ]

scissors [ˈsɪzəz]
剪刀 [jiǎn dāo]

letters [ˈletəz]
字母 [zì mǔ]

label [ˈleɪbl]
标签 [biāo qiān]

chair [tʃeə]
椅子 [yǐ zi]

door [dɔː]
门 [mén]

window [ˈwɪndəʊ]
窗 [chuāng]

shapes [ʃeɪps]
形状 [xíng zhuàng]

write [raɪt]
写 [xiě]

colour [ˈkʌlə]
着色 [zhuó sè]

fish tank [fɪʃ tæŋk]
鱼缸 [yú gāng]

read [riːd]
阅读 [yuè dú]

paste [peɪst]
粘贴 [zhān tiē]

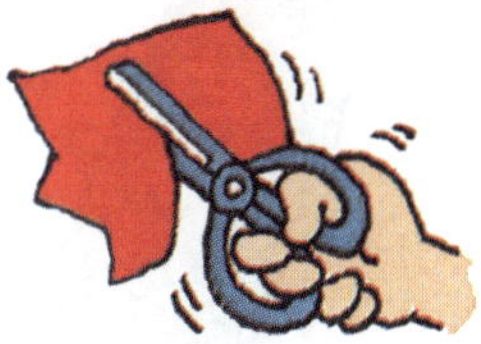

cut [kʌt]
剪 [jiǎn]

Indoor playtime 室内游戏时间

- What is David doing?
- What are the children at the table doing?
- Carol is in the home corner. What is she doing?
- Can you see Aziz? What is he doing?
- Susan has finished her jigsaw puzzle. What is she doing now?

Carol is ironing in the home corner.

blocks [blɒks]
积木 [jī mù]

jigsaw puzzle [ˈdʒɪgsɔː pʌzl]
拼图游戏 [pīn tú yóu xì]

shape [ʃeɪp]
模子 [mú zi]

play dough [pleɪ dəʊ]
生面团 [shēng miàn tuán]

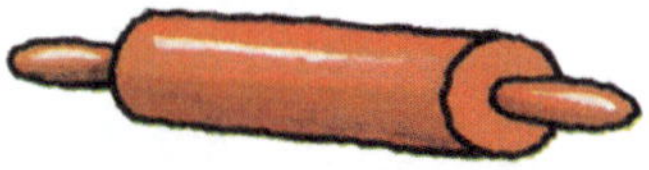

rolling pin [ˈrəʊlɪŋ pɪn]
擀面杖 [gǎn miàn zhàng]

knife [naɪf]
刀子 [dāo zi]

painting [peɪntɪŋ]
水彩画 [shuǐ cǎi huà]

paints [peɪnt]
颜料 [yán liào]

easel [ˈiːzl]
画架 [huà jià]

brush [brʌʃ]
画笔 [huà bǐ]

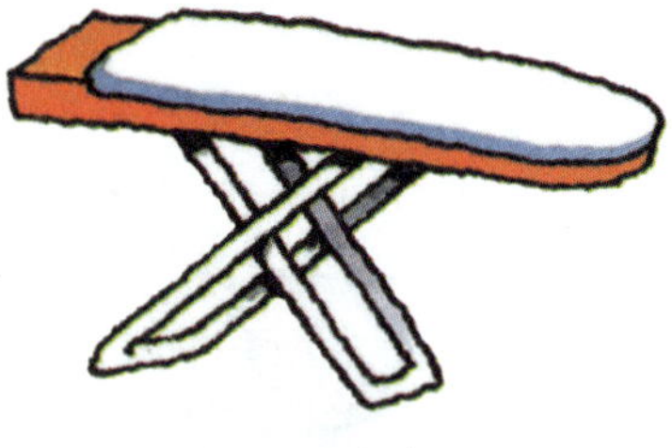

ironing board [ˈaɪənɪŋ bɔːd]
熨衣板 [yùn yī bǎn]

iron [ˈaɪən]
熨斗 [yùn dǒu]

doll [dɒl]
洋娃娃 [yáng wá wa]

puppet [ˈpʌpɪt]
木偶 [mù ǒu]

box [bɒks]
箱子 [xiāng zi]

toy car [tɔɪ kɑː]
玩具车 [wán jù chē]

tea set [tiː set]
茶具 [chá jù]

paint [peɪnt]
给…… 上颜色 [gěi …… shàng yán sè]

build [bɪld]
筑盖 [zhù gài]

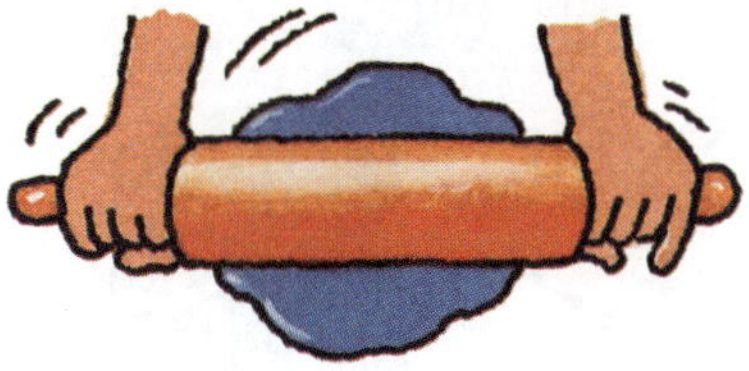

roll [rəʊl]
碾薄 [niǎn bó]

Outdoor playtime

户外游戏时间

- Who is playing ball?
- What is Carol doing?
- Can you see Gita? What is she looking at?
- What is Aziz going to do?
- Who is blowing bubbles?
- What was Gita playing with before she saw the worm?

football [ˈfʊtbɔːl]
足球 [zú qiú]

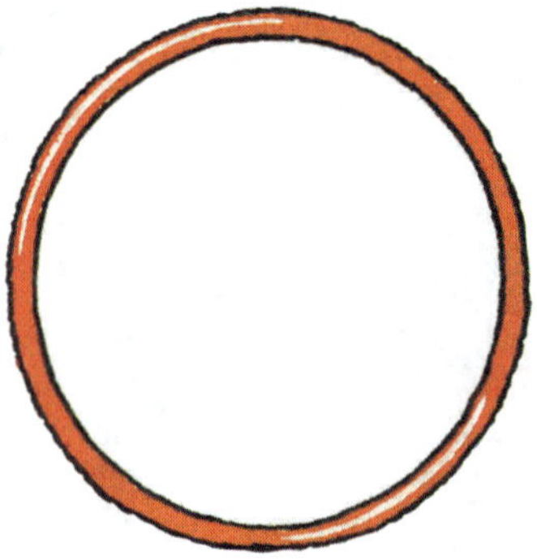

hoop [huːp]
大圈 [dà quān]

tricycle [ˈtraɪsɪkəl]
三轮车 [sān lún chē]

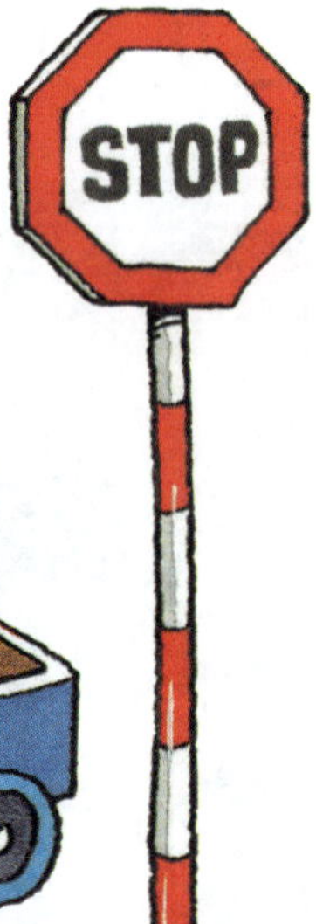

cart [kaːt]
手推车
[shǒu tuī chē]

stop sign
[stɒp saɪn]
停车标志 [tíng chē biāo zhì]

scooter [ˈskuːtə]
踏板车 [tà bǎn chē]

spade [speɪd]
铲子 [chǎn zi]

bucket [ˈbʌkɪt]
桶子 [tǒng zi]

sieve [sɪv]
筛 [shāi]

boat [bəʊt]
小船 [xiǎo chuán]

funnel [ˈfʌnl]
漏斗 [lòu dǒu]

sand [sænd]
沙 [shā]

worm [wɜːm]
虫 [chóng]

dig [dɪg]
挖掘 [wā jué]

blow [bləʊ]
吹 [chuī]

crawl [krɔːl]
爬行 [pá xíng]

swing [swɪŋ]
荡 [dàng]

ride [raɪd]
骑 [qí]

climb [klaɪm]
爬 [pá]

wall [wɔːl]
墙 [qiáng]

tunnel [ˈtʌnl]
管道 [guǎn dào]

kick [kɪk]
踢 [tī]

jump [dʒʌmp]
跳 [tiào]

Snacktime 茶点时间

- What is the teacher doing?
- Who is serving the drinks?
- Where is Susan? What is she doing?
- Who are the helpers today?
- Who is helping to wipe the table?
- What did the children have to eat and drink for snacktime?

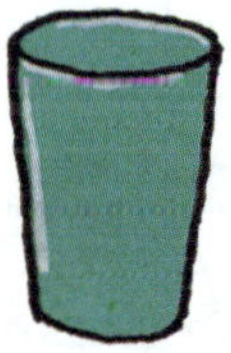

glass [glɑ:s]
玻璃杯 [bō li bēi]

cookies [ˈkʊkɪ]
饼乾 [bǐng gān]

apple [ˈæpl]
苹果 [píng guǒ]

banana [bəˈnɑ:nə]
香蕉 [xiāng jiāo]

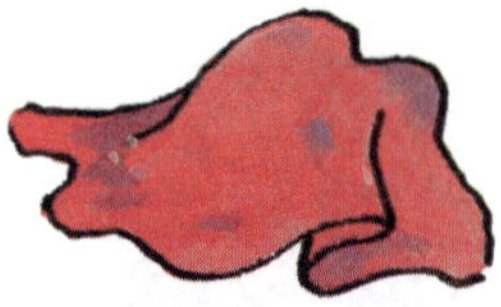

cloth [klɒθ]
擦布 [cā bù]

badge [bædʒ]
徽章 [huī zhāng]

hand towel
[hænd ˈtaʊəl]
手巾 [shǒu jīn]

apron [ˈeɪprən]
围裙 [wéi qún]

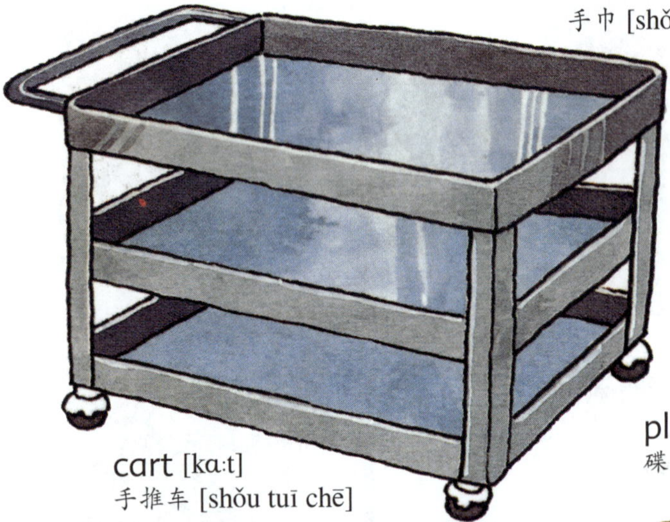

cart [kɑ:t]
手推车 [shǒu tuī chē]

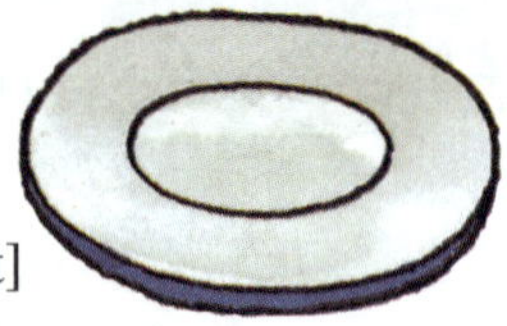

plate [pleɪt]
碟子 [dié zi]

apple core [ˈæpəl kɔ:]
苹果心 [píng guǒ xīn]

full [fʊl]
装满的 [zhuāng mǎn de]

empty [ˈemptɪ]
空的 [kōng de]

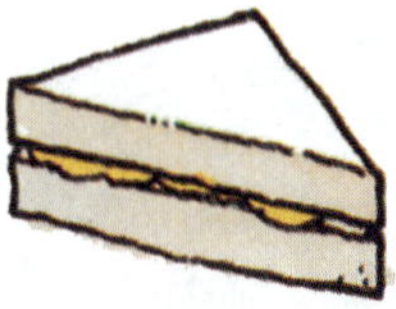

sandwich
[ˈsænwɪdʒ]
三明治 [sān míng zhì]

banana skin
[bəˈnɑ:nə skɪn]
香蕉皮 [xiāng jiāo pí]

push in [pʊʃ ɪn]
推进去 [tuī jìn qù]

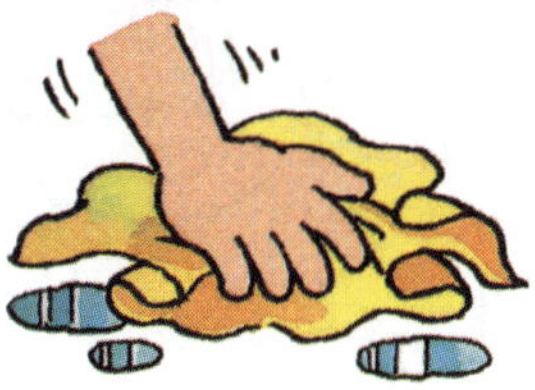

wipe [waɪp]
擦拭 [cā shì]

wash [wɒʃ]
洗 [xǐ]

bite [baɪt]
咬 [yǎo]

stack up [stæk ʌp]
摞起 [luò qǐ]

refrigerator
[rɪˈfrɪdʒəreɪtə]
冰箱 [bīng xiāng]

sink [sɪŋk]
洗涤槽 [xǐ dí cáo]

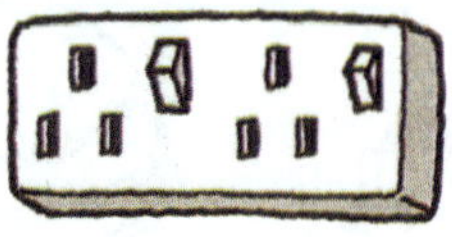

socket [ˈsɒkɪt]
插座 [chā zuò]

plug [plʌg]
插头 [chā tóu]

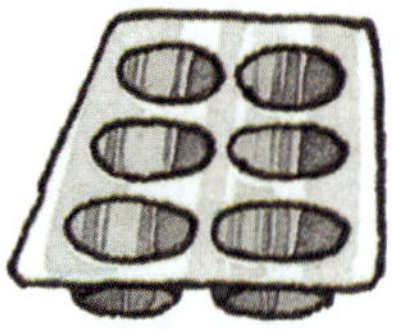

cupcake tray
[kʌpkeɪk treɪ]
杯形蛋糕盘
[bēi xíng dàn gāo pán]

wooden spoon
[ˈwʊdn spuːn]
木杓 [mù sháo]

dish rack / drying rack
[dɪʃ rak] / [drʌɪn rak]
碗碟架 [wǎn dié jià]

tin [tɪn]
罐头 [guàn tou]

cake mixer
[keɪk ˈmɪksə]
面粉搅拌器
[miàn fěn jiǎo bàn qì]

In the kitchen 在厨房

- What is Baby watching?
- Who is cooking?
- What are David and Grandfather doing?
- What are Mother and Susan doing?
- Why is David standing on a stool?
- What do you like to do in the kitchen?

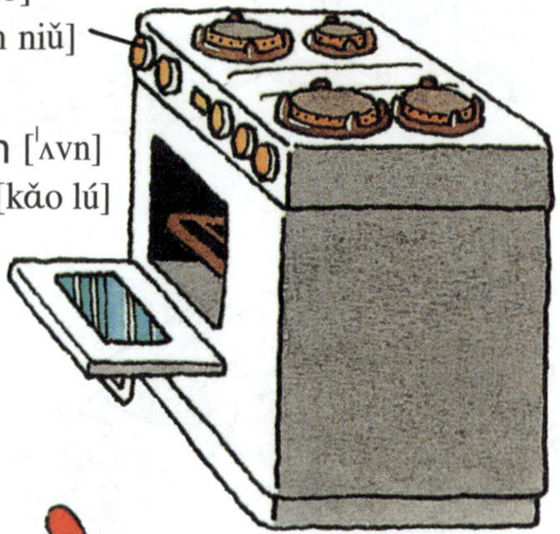

knob [nɒb]
旋钮 [xuán niǔ]

oven [ˈʌvn]
烤炉 [kǎo lú]

cooker [ˈkʊkə]
炉具 [lú jù]

mop [mɒp]
拖把 [tuō bǎ]

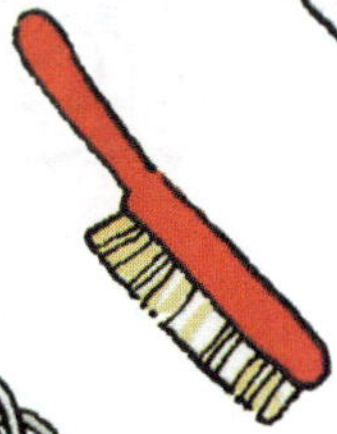

brush [brʌʃ]
刷子 [shuā zi]

dustpan
[ˈdʌstpæn]
畚箕 [běn jī]

cherries [ˈtʃerɪz]
樱桃 [yīng táo]

flour [flaʊə]
面粉 [miàn fěn]

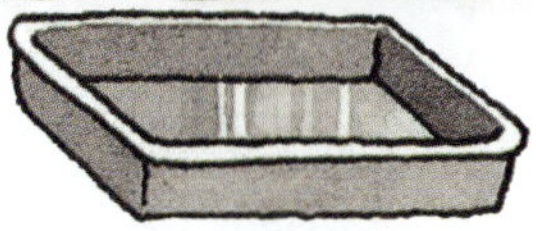

baking tray
[beɪkɪŋ treɪ]
烘烤盘 [hōng kǎo pán]

margarine
[ˈmaːdʒəˈriːn]
人造牛油 [rén zào niú yóu]

laundry basket
[ˈlɔːndrɪ ˌbaːskɪt]
洗衣篮 [xǐ yī lán]

mixing bowl
[mɪksɪŋ bəʊl]
搅拌钵 [jiǎo bàn bō]

cupcake
[kʌpkeɪk]
杯形蛋糕
[bēi xíng dàn gāo]

wok [wɒk]
锅子 [guō zi]

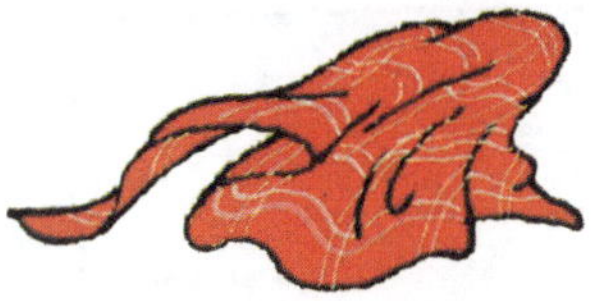

kitchen cloth [ˈkɪtʃɪn klɒθ]
擦布 [cā bù]

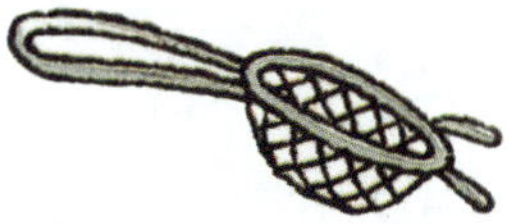

strainer [ˈstreɪnə]
滤网 [lǜ wǎng]

Dinner time 晚餐时间

- Who is feeding Baby?
- Why is David unhappy?
- What is Susan doing?
- Who is carrying the fruit salad?
- What is Gita carrying?
- What do you think the family had to eat first?

vegetables [ˈvedʒtəbəlz]
蔬菜 [shū cài]

noodles [ˈnuːdlz]
面条 [miàn tiáo]

meatballs [ˈmiːtbɔːlz]
肉丸 [ròu wán]

fruit salad [fruːt ˈsæləd]
杂果沙拉 [zá guǒ shā lā]

ice cream [aɪs kriːm]
冰激凌、冰淇淋
[bīng ji líng], [bīng qí lín]

spoon [spuːn]
汤匙 [tāng chí]

mat [mæt]
地垫 [dì diàn]

fork [fɔːk]
叉子 [chā zi]

bowl [bəʊl]
碗 [wǎn]

cup [kʌp]
茶杯 [chá bēi]

saucer [ˈsɔːsə]
茶托 [chá tuō]

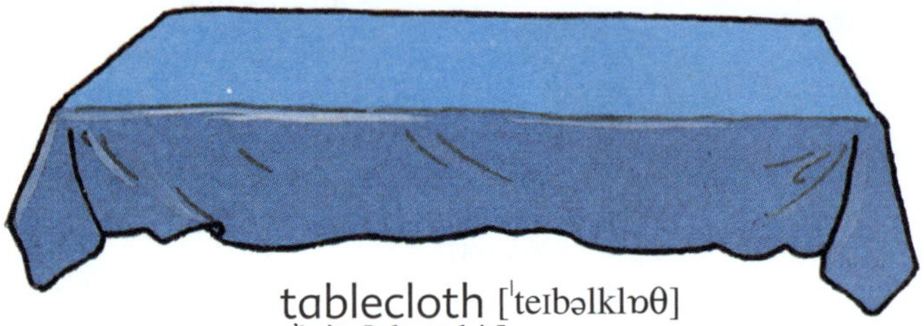
tablecloth [ˈteɪbəlklɒθ]
桌布 [zhuō bù]

tray [treɪ]
托盘 [tuō pán]

napkin [ˈnæpkɪn]
餐布 [cān bù]

cushion [ˈkʊʃn]
椅垫 [yǐ diàn]

sideboard [ˈsaɪdbɔːd]
餐具柜 [cān jù guì]

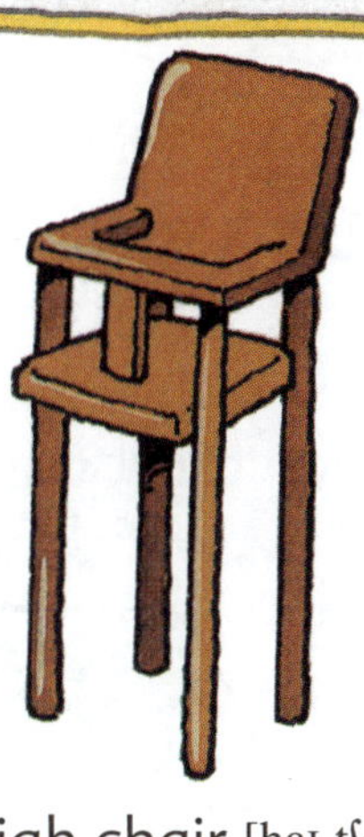

high chair [haɪ tʃeə]
婴儿高椅 [yīng ér gāo yǐ]

set the table
[set ðə ˈteɪbl]
分发餐具 [fēn fā cān jù]

feed [fiːd]
喂 [wèi]

carry [ˈkærɪ]
搬运 [bān yùn]

In the bathroom
在浴室

- What is David doing?
- Who is shaving?
- Where is Baby?
- What is Susan doing?
- Who do you think will wash Baby?
- Do you wash yourself?

towel [ˈtaʊəl]
毛巾 [máo jīn]

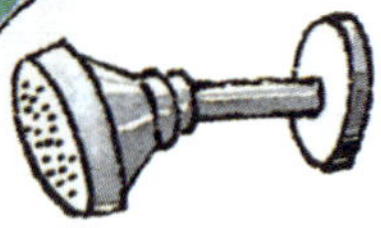

shower [ˈʃaʊə]
淋浴器 [lín yù qì]

Father is shaving.

washcloth
[ˈwɒʃklɒθ]
面巾 [miàn jīn]

basin [ˈbeɪsn]
洗脸盆 [xǐ liǎn pén]

shower curtain
[ˈʃaʊə ˈkɜːtn]
淋浴帘 [lín yù lián]

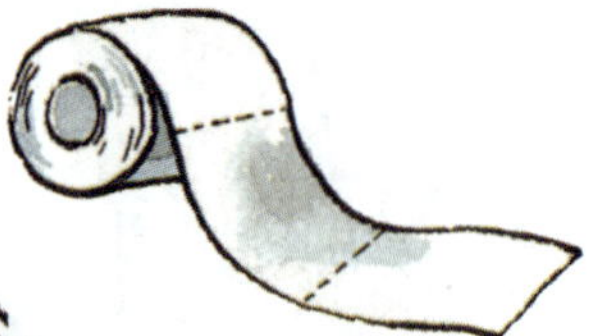

potty [ˈpɒtɪ]
便盆 [biàn pén]

toilet paper [ˈtɔɪlɪt peɪpə]
卫生纸 [wèi shēng zhǐ]

bath tub [ˈbɑːθ tʌb]
浴缸 [yù gāng]

bath mat [ˈbɑːθ mæt]
浴室脚垫 [yù shì jiǎo diàn]

toilet [ˈtɔɪlɪt]
厕所 [cè suǒ]

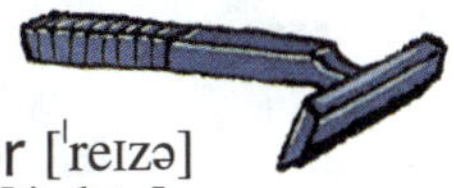

razor [ˈreɪzə]
剃刀 [tì dāo]

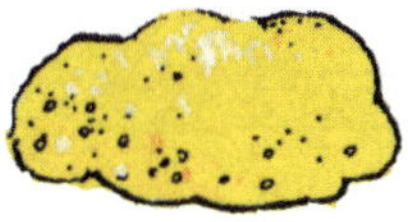

sponge [spʌndʒ]
海棉 [hǎi mián]

nailbrush [neɪlbrʌʃ]
甲刷 [jiǎ shuā]

plug [plʌg]
塞子 [sāi zi]

tap [tæp]
水龙头 [shuǐ lóng tóu]

powder [ˈpaʊdə]
爽身粉 [shuǎng shēn fěn]

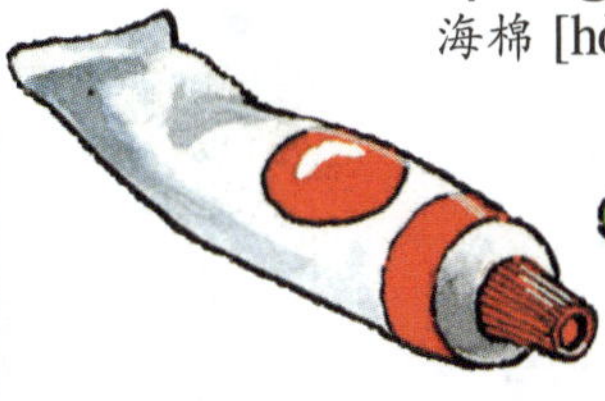

toothpaste [ˈtu:θpeɪst]
牙膏 [yá gāo]

toothbrush [ˈtu:θbrʌʃ]
牙刷 [yá shuā]

soap [səʊp]
肥皂 [féi zào]

bathroom scale
[ˈbɑ:θru:m skeɪl]
浴室磅秤 [yù shì bàng chèng]

shave [ʃeɪv]
刮胡子 [guā hú zi]

Let's relax 轻松一下

- Who is watching television?
- What are the girls playing?
- Where is Baby? What is he doing?
- What are Mother and Father doing?
- What time is it? How do you know?

television [ˈtelɪvɪʒn]
电视机 [diàn shì jī]

blinds [blaɪndz]
窗帘 [chuāng lián]

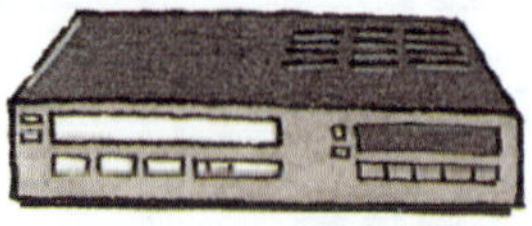

video recorder
[ˌvɪdɪəʊ rɪˈkɔːdə]
录像机 [lù xiàng jī]

telephone [ˈtelɪfəʊn]
电话 [diàn huà]

radio-cassette player
[ˌreɪdɪəʊ kəˈset pleɪə]
收音录音机 [shōu yīn lù yīn jī]

calendar [ˈkælɪndə]
月历 [yuè lì]

plant [plɑːnt]
植物
[zhí wù]

board game [bɔːd geɪm]
棋类游戏 [qí lèi yóu xì]

dice [daɪs]
骰子 [tóu zi]

videotape
[ˈvɪdɪəʊteɪp]
录像带 [lù xiàng dài]

cassette [kəˈset]
盒式录音带
[hé shì lù yīn dài]

toy [tɔɪ]
玩具 [wán jù]

armchair [ɑːmˈtʃeə]
扶手椅 [fú shǒu yǐ]

sofa [ˈsəʊfə]
沙发 [shā fā]

carpet [ˈkɑːpɪt]
地毯 [dì tǎn]

newspaper [ˈnjuːspeɪpə]
报纸 [bào zhǐ]

magazine [ˌmægəˈziːn]
杂志 [zá zhì]

clock [klɒk]
时钟 [shí zhōng]

glasses [glaːsɪz]
眼镜 [yǎn jìng]

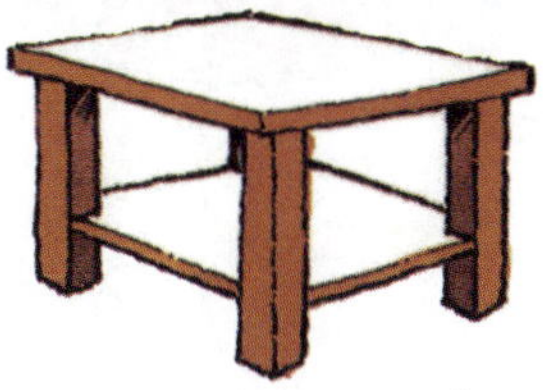
side table [saɪd ˈteɪbl]
靠墙小几 [kào qiáng xiǎo jī]

watch [wɒtʃ]
观看 [guān kàn]

roll [rəʊl]
滚动 [gǔn dòng]

Bedtime 睡觉时间

- Where is Baby?
- Who is reading to David?
- What is Susan doing?
- Who is spending the night with Susan?
- Where do you think Susan and Gita will sleep?

stars [stɑːz]
星星 [xīng xing]

moon [muːn]
月亮 [yuè liang]

comic [ˈkɒmɪk]
漫画 [màn huà]

milk bottle
[mɪlk ˈbɒtl]
奶瓶 [nǎi píng]

stickers [ˈstɪkəz]
贴纸 [tiē zhǐ]

piggy bank
[pɪgɪ bæŋk]
钱箱 [qián xiāng]

bookcase [bʊkkeɪs]
书柜 [shū guì]

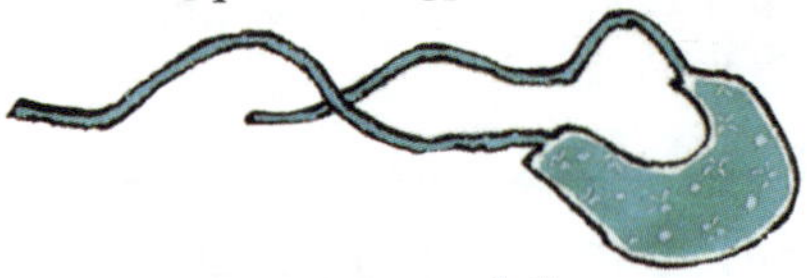

bib [bɪb]
围嘴 [wéi zuǐ]

photograph [ˈfəʊtəgrɑːf]
照片 [zhào piàn]

switch [swɪtʃ]
开关 [kāi guān]

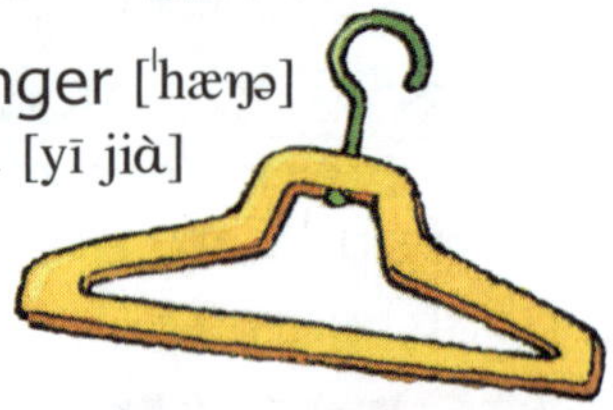

hanger [ˈhæŋə]
衣架 [yī jià]

light [laɪt]
灯光 [dēng guāng]

hair clip
[ˈheə klɪp]
发夹 [fà jiā]

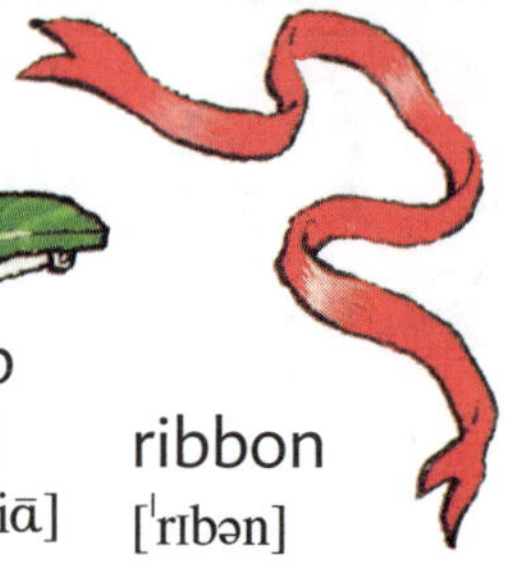

ribbon
[ˈrɪbən]
丝带 [sī dài]

mobile [ˈməʊbaɪl]
可动挂饰 [kě dòng guà shì]

suitcase [ˈsuːtkeɪs]
手提箱 [shǒu tí xiāng]

kiss [kɪs]
吻 [wěn]

yawn [jɔːn]
打呵欠
[dǎ hē qiàn]

clothes [kləʊðz]
衣服 [yī fu]

sleep [sliːp]
睡觉 [shuì jiào]

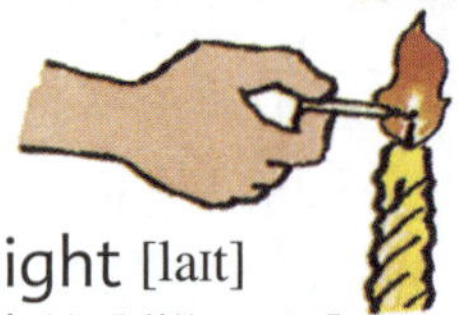

light [laɪt]
点燃 [diǎn rán]

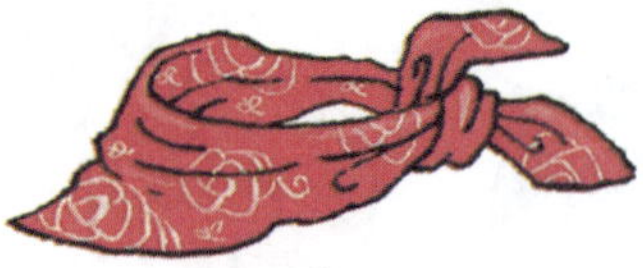

scarf [skɑːf]
围巾 [wēi jīn]

streamers
[ˈstriːməz]
彩色饰带
[cǎi sè shì dài]

kneel [niːl]
跪下 [guì xià]

smile [smaɪl]
微笑 [wēi xiào]

presents [ˈpreznts]
礼物 [lǐ wù]

party game [pɑːtɪ geɪm]
派对游戏 [pài duì yóu xì]

Happy Birthday, David! 生日快乐!

- Whose birthday is it?
- How old is he?
- What is Mother doing?
- What are the children doing?
- What do you think the children will do next?

sausages [ˈsɒsɪdʒz]
香肠 [xiāng cháng]

nuts [nʌts]
果仁 [guǒ rén]

chocolate [ˈtʃɒklət]
巧克力 [qiǎo kè lì]

jelly [ˈdʒelɪ]
果冻 [guǒ dòng]

fruit pie [fruːt paɪ]
水果馅饼
[shuǐ guǒ xiàn bǐng]

pudding [ˈpʊdɪŋ]
布丁 [bù dīng]

party hat [ˈpɑːtɪ hæt]
派对帽子
[pài duì mào zi]

box of matches
[bɒks əv mætʃz]
一盒火柴 [yī hé huǒ chái]

cards [kɑːdz]
卡 [kǎ]

candle [ˈkændl]
蜡烛 [là zhú]

birthday cake [ˈbɜːθdeɪ keɪk]
生日蛋糕 [shēng rì dàn gāo]

balloon [bəˈluːn]
气球 [qì qiú]

candies
[ˈkændɪz]
糖果 [táng guǒ]

It's sunny today!

今日阳光普照

- What is Mother doing?
- Where is David?
- What is Grandfather doing?
- Who is mowing the lawn?
- Who do you think has been painting the fence?
- What weather do you like?

washing [wɒʃɪŋ]
洗好的衣服 [xǐ hǎo de yī fu]

clothes pin [kləʊðz pɪn]
衣夹 [yī jiā]

branch [brɑːntʃ]
树枝 [shù zhī]

trunk [trʌŋk]
树干 [shù gàn]

tree [triː]
树 [shù]

mower [ˈməʊə]
割草机 [gē cǎo jī]

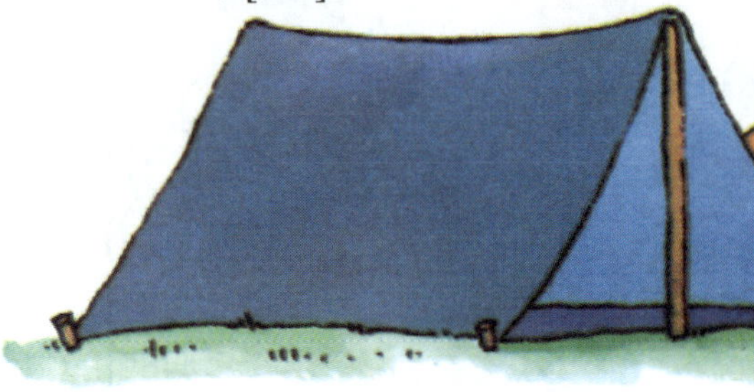

fence [fens] 篱笆 [lí ba]

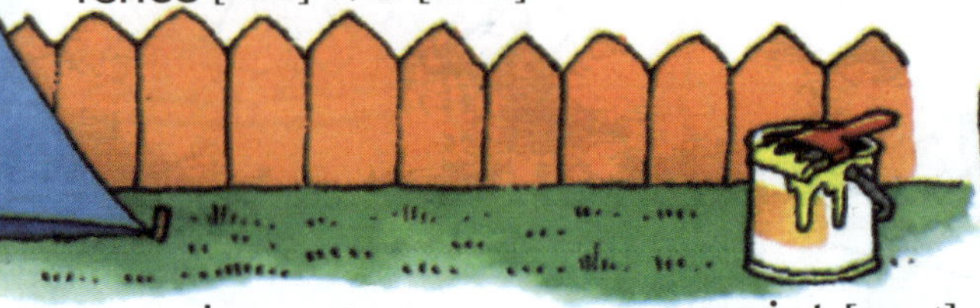

tent [tent]
帐篷 [zhàng péng]

lawn [lɔːn]
草坪 [cǎo píng]

paint [peɪnt]
油漆 [yóu qī]

pool [puːl]
儿童玩水池
[ér tóng wán shuǐ chí]

water [ˈwɔːtə]
浇水
[jiāo shuǐ]

mow [məʊ]
割草 [gē cǎo]

smoke [sməʊk]
烟 [yān]

barbecue [ˈbɑːbɪkjuː]
烧烤 [shāo kǎo]

sun hat [sʌn hæt]
太阳帽 [tài yáng mào]

ot
ɒt]
盆 [huā pén]

seeds [siːdz]
种子 [zhǒng zi]

soil [sɔɪl]
泥土 [ní tǔ]

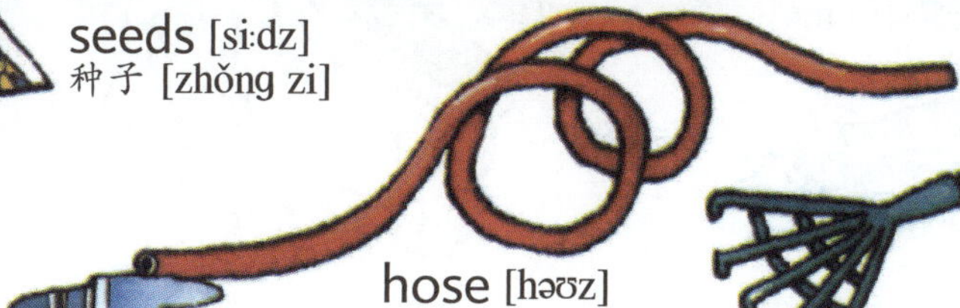

hose [həʊz]
塑胶管 [sù jiāo guǎn]

rake [reɪk]
耙 [pá]

leaves [liːvz]
树叶 [shù yè]

chirp [tʃɜːp]
啁啾地叫 [zhōu jiū de jiào]

pet [pæt]
抚摸 [fǔ mō]

leash [liːʃ]
牵引带 [qiān yǐn dài]

collar [ˈkɒlə]
项圈 [xiàng quān]

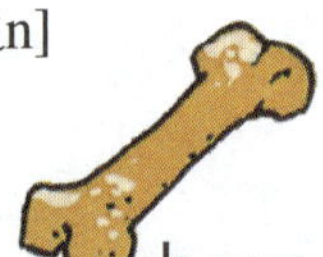

bone [bəʊn]
骨头 [gǔ tou]

whistle [ˈwɪsl]
吹口哨 [chuī kǒu shào]

peck [pek]
啄 [zhuó]

brush [brʌʃ]
刷 [shuā]

nibble [ˈnɪbl]
一点点地咬
[yī diǎn diǎn de yǎo]

Our pet show 宠物展览会

- What is David doing?
- Who is whistling to his bird?
- What is Sam crawling after?
- How many white mice does Jack have?
- What is Susan doing?
- Which pet do you think will win first prize?
- Which pet would you like?

fishbowl [ˈfɪʃbəʊl]
金鱼缸
[jīn yú gāng]

goldfish [ˈgəʊldfɪʃ]
金鱼 [jīn yú]

tortoise [ˈtɔːtəs]
乌龟 [wū guī]

terrapin [ˈterəpɪn]
泥龟 [ní guī]

bird [bɜːd]
鸟 [niǎo]

perch [pɜːtʃ]
栖木 [qī mù]

white mouse
[waɪt maʊs]
白老鼠 [bái lǎo shǔ]

cage [keɪdʒ]
鸟笼 [niǎo lóng]

basket [ˈbɑːskɪt]
篮子 [lán zi]

prize [praɪz]
奖品 [jiǎng pǐn]

rabbit [ˈræbɪt]
兔子 [tù zi]

white mice
[waɪt maɪs]
白老鼠 [bái lǎo shǔ]

carrot [ˈkærət]
胡萝卜 [hú luó bo]

Our school concert 学校音乐会

- What are Susan and David doing?
- What instrument are Carol and Aziz playing?
- Where is the teacher?
- Can you see Grandfather? What is he doing?
- What is Gita doing?
- What part do you think Gita is acting?

keys [ki:z]
琴键 [qín jiàn]

piano [pɪˈænəʊ]
钢琴 [gāng qín]

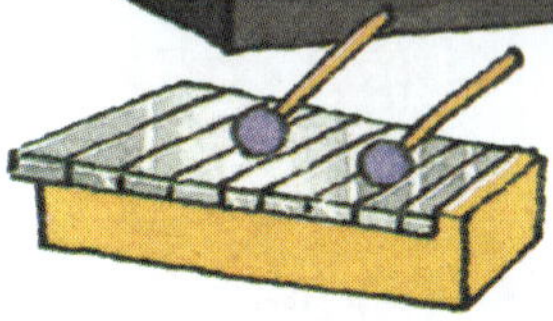

xylophone [ˈzaɪləfəʊn]
木琴 [mù qín]

soldier [ˈsəʊldʒə]
士兵 [shì bīng]

fairy [ˈfeərɪ]
仙女
[xiān nǚ]

prince
[prɪns]
王子
[wáng zǐ]

princess [prɪnˈses]
公主 [gōng zhǔ]

Humpty Dumpty
[ˈhʌmptɪ ˈdʌmptɪ]
矮胖子 [ǎi pàng zi]

stage [steɪdʒ] 舞台 [wǔ tái]

audience [ˈɔ:dɪəns]
观众 [guān zhòng]

drumsticks
[ˈdrʌmstɪks]
鼓槌
[gǔ chuí]

drum [drʌm]
鼓 [gǔ]

tambourine
[ˌtæmbəˈri:n]
铃鼓 [líng gǔ]

triangle
[ˈtraɪæŋgl]
三角铁
[sān jiǎo tiě]

scores [skɔːz]
乐谱 [yuè pǔ]

bow [baʊ]
鞠躬 [jū gōng]

curtsy [ˈkɜːtsɪ]
行屈膝礼
[xíng qū xī lǐ]

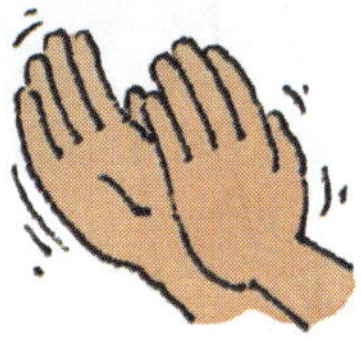

clap [ˈklæp]
鼓掌 [gǔ zhǎng]

peep [piːp]
偷看 [tōu kàn]

cry [kraɪ]
哭 [kū]

At the fast-food restaurant 在快餐店里

- What is the waitress doing?
- Who has a takeaway meal?
- Where do David and Aziz want to eat?
- What are the girls having?
- Who is eating a cheeseburger?
- What do you think Father and Mother are talking about?
- What do you think Baby wants?

waiter [ˈweɪtə]
男侍应生
[nán shì yìng shēng]

waitress
[ˈweɪtrɪs]
女侍应生
[nǚ shì yìng shēng]

chocolate sauce
[ˈtʃɒklət sɔ:s]
巧克力酱
[qiǎo kè lì jiàng]

mustard
[ˈmʌstəd]
芥末 [jiè mo]

tomato ketchup
[təˈma:təʊ ˈketʃʌp]
茄汁 [qié zhī]

sundae
[ˈsʌndeɪ]
新地 [xīn dì]

French fries
[frentʃ fraɪz]
炸土豆条
[zhà tǔ dòu tiáo]

strawberry topping
[ˌstrɔ:brɪ ˈtɒpɪŋ]
草莓酱
[cǎo méi jiàng]

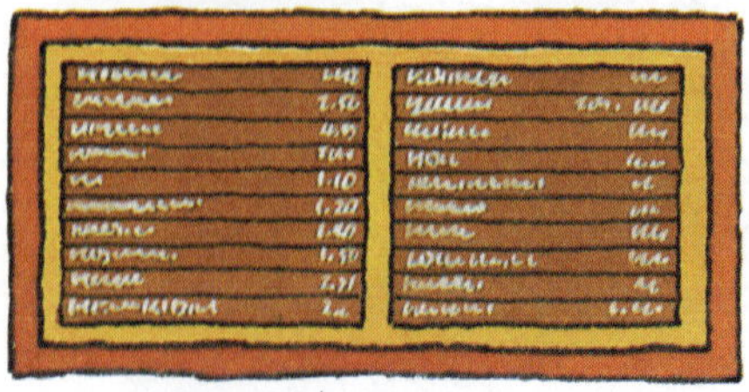

menu [ˈmenju:]
菜单 [cài dān]

milkshake
[mɪlkʃeɪk]
奶昔 [nǎi xī]

sweet corn
[swi:t kɔ:n]
甜玉米
[tián yù mǐ]

hamburger
[ˈhæmbɜ:gə]
汉堡包 [hàn bǎo bāo]

cheeseburger
[ˈtʃi:zbɜ:gə]
乾酪汉堡包
[gān lào hàn bǎo bāo]

staircase [ˌsteəkeɪs]
楼梯 [lóu tī]

wallet [ˈwɒlɪt]
钱包 [qián bāo]

ice cube
[aɪs kjuːb]
冰块 [bīng kuài]

straw [strɔː]
吸管 [xī guǎn]

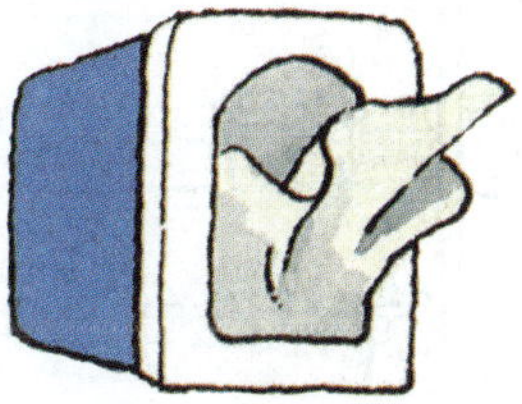

napkin
[ˈnæpkɪn]
餐巾 [cān jīn]

apple pie [ˈæpl paɪ]
苹果馅饼
[píng guǒ xiàn bǐng]

onion rings
[ˈʌnjən rɪŋz]
洋葱圈
[yáng cōng quān]

hot dog
[hɒt dɒg]
热狗 [rè gǒu]

pancakes [ˈpæŋkeɪks]
烙饼 [lào bǐng]

takeaway
[teɪkəˈweɪ]
外卖 [wài mài]

At the supermarket
在超级市场里

- Where is Father?
- Who has Mother met?
- What are Grandfather and Grandmother doing?
- What is the checkout assistant doing?
- What do you think Sam wants to buy?
- Who do you think Gita is waiting for?

Grandfather and Grandmother are still shopping.

shopping trolley [ˈʃɒpɪŋ ˈtrɒli]
手推车 [shǒu tuī chē]

basket [ˈbɑːskɪt]
篮子 [lán zi]

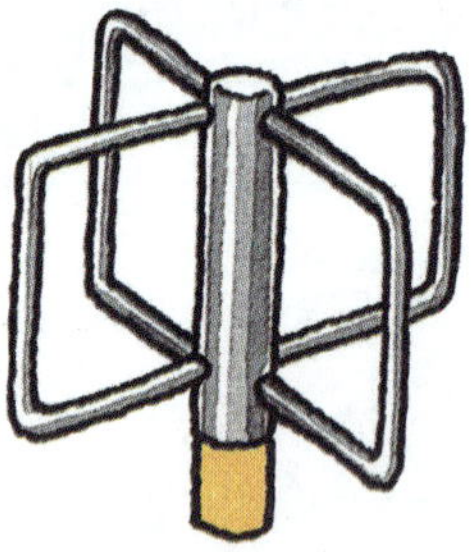

turnstile [ˈtɜːnstaɪl]
旋转门
[xuán zhuǎn mén]

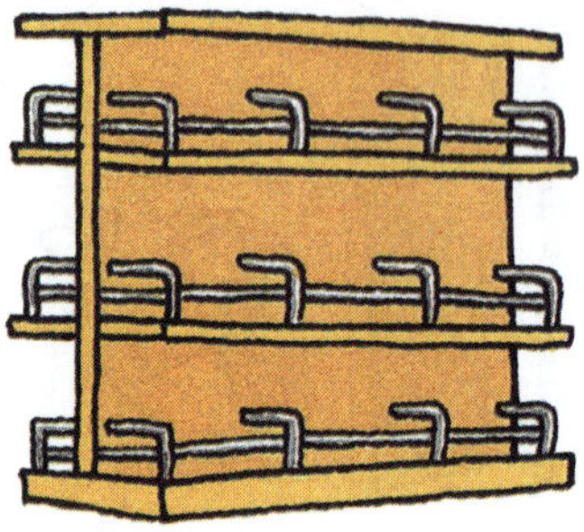

shelves [ˈʃelvz]
搁架 [gē jià]

pack of cookies
[pæk əv ˈkʊkɪz]
一包饼乾 [yī bāo bǐng gān]

freezer [ˈfriːzə]
冰箱 [bīng xiāng]

customer
[ˈkʌstəmə]
顾客 [gù kè]

cashier [kæˈʃɪə]
出纳员 [chū nà yuán]

assistant
[əˈsɪstənt]
店员
[diàn yuán]

checkout counter [ˌtʃekaʊt ˈkaʊntə]
柜台 [guì tái]

bottles of juice
[ˈbɒtl əv dʒuːs]
几瓶果汁
[jǐ píng guǒ zhī]

bag of rice
[bæg əv raɪs]
一袋米 [yī dài mǐ]

washing powder
[ˌwɒʃɪŋ ˈpaʊdə]
洗衣粉 [xǐ yī fěn]

pie [paɪ]
馅饼 [xiàn bǐng]

cat food [kæt fuːd]
猫食 [māo shí]

cash register
[kæʃ ˈredʒɪstə]
现金出纳机
[xiàn jīn chū nà jī]

money [ˈmʌnɪ]
钱 [qián]

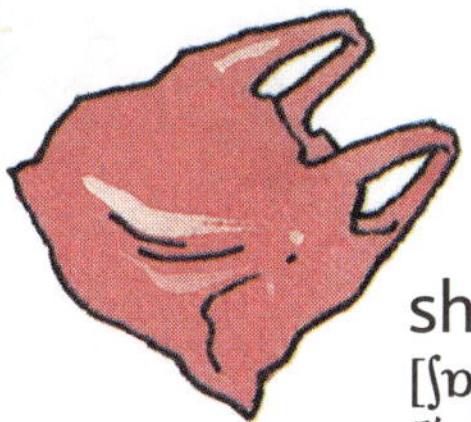

shopping bag
[ʃɒpɪŋ bæg]
购物袋 [gòu wù dài]

chicken [ˈtʃɪkɪn]
鸡肉 [jī ròu]

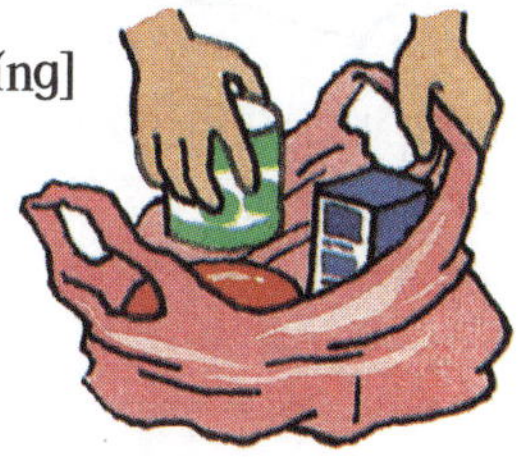

pack [pæk]
把...... 装进
[bǎ ...... zhuāng jìn]

At the shopping centre 购物中心里

- What is Mother buying?
- Where is Father going?
- What are David and Ben doing?
- Who can you see in the elevator?
- Is Susan in the shopping centre? What is she doing?
- What do you think Mrs. Lee is doing? Do you think she will buy the blue shoes?

shop [ʃɒp]
商店 [shāng diàn]

elevator [ˈelɪveɪtə]
升降机 [shēng jiàng jī]

watch [wɒtʃ]
手表 [shǒu biǎo]

racket [ˈrækɪt]
球拍 [qiú pāi]

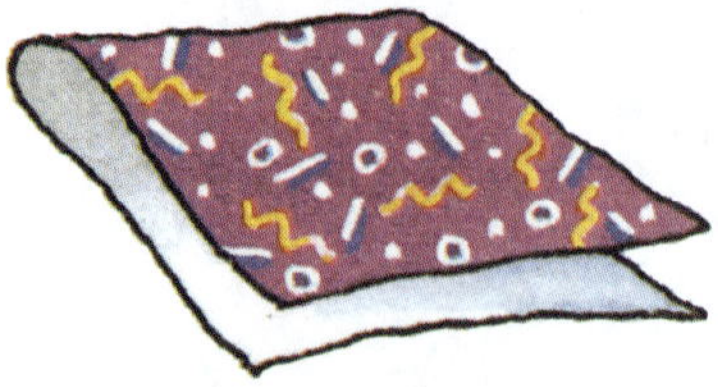

wrapping paper [ræpɪŋ ˈpeɪpə]
包装纸 [bāo zhuāng zhǐ]

salesman [ˈseɪlzmən]
男店员 [nán diàn yuán]

saleswoman [ˈseɪlzwʊmən]
女店员 [nǚ diàn yuán]

postcards [ˈpəʊstkɑːdz]
明信片 [míng xìn piān]

remote-controlled car [ˈrɪˌməʊt-kənˈtrəʊld kɑː]
无线电遥控车
[wú xiàn diàn yáo kòng chē]

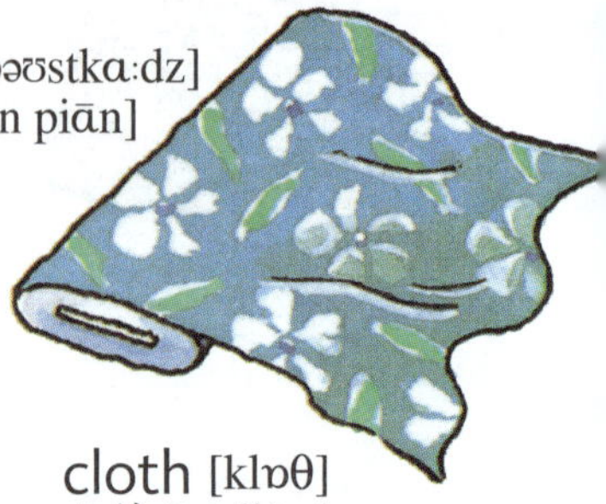

cloth [klɒθ]
衣料 [yī liào]

pen [pen]
笔 [bǐ]

earrings
[ˈɪərɪŋz]
耳环 [ěr huán]

necklace
[ˈneklɪs]
项链
[xiàng liàn]

look at
[lʊk ət]
注视 [zhù shì]

washing machine
[ˈwɒʃɪŋ məˈʃiːn]
洗衣机 [xǐ yī jī]

camera
[ˈkæmərə]
照相机 [zhào xiàng jī]

robot [ˈrəʊbɒt]
机器人 [jī qì rén]

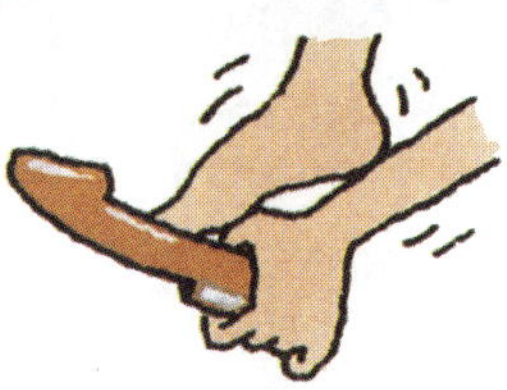

try on [traɪ ɒn]
试穿 [shì chuān]

down [daʊn]
降 [jiàng]

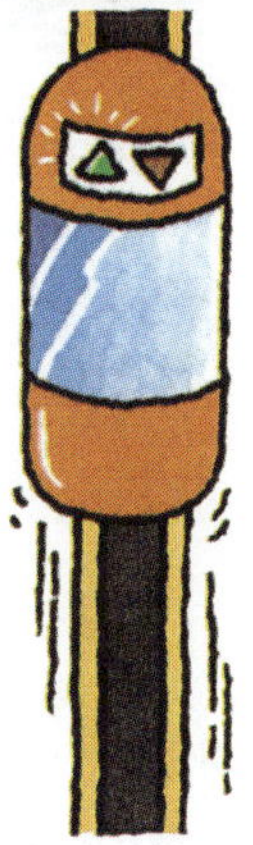

up [ʌp]
升 [shēng]

At the bird park
在飞禽公园里

- Where is Uncle Jim?
- What does Aunt Julie want?
- Who has found a pelican?
- What has David found?
- What are Susan and Penny doing?
- What do you think the kingfisher has caught?
- Which bird would you go to see? Why?

aviary [ˈeɪvɪərɪ]
鸟笼 [niǎo lóng]

entrance [ˈentrəns]
入口 [rù kǒu]

parrot [ˈpærət]
鹦鹉 [yīng wǔ]

feather [ˈfeðə]
羽毛 [yǔ máo]

chick [tʃɪk]
小鸡 [xiǎo jī]

hen [hen]
母鸡 [mǔ jī]

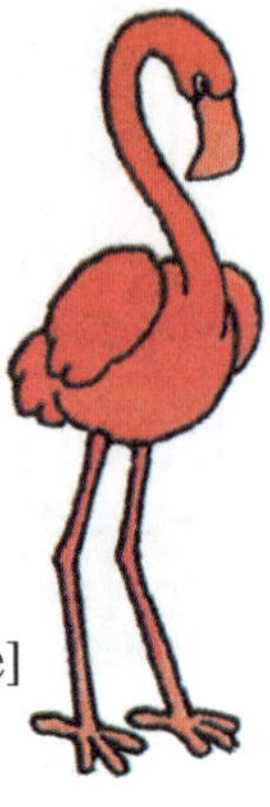

flamingo
[fləˈmɪŋgəʊ]
红鹤 [hóng hè]

pigeon [ˈpɪdʒɪn]
鸽子 [gē zi]

pelican [ˈpelɪkən]
塘鹅 [táng é]

bridge [brɪdʒ]
桥 [qiáo]

kingfisher [ˈkɪŋfɪʃə]
鱼狗 [yú gǒu]

beak [biːk]
鸟嘴 [niǎo zuǐ]

post [pəʊst]
柱子 [zhù zi]

waterfall [ˈwɔːtəfɔːl]
瀑布 [pù bù]

peacock [ˈpiːkɒk]
孔雀 [kǒng què]

goose [guːs]
鹅 [é]

peahen [ˈpiːhen]
雌孔雀 [cí kǒng què]

geese [giːs]
鹅 [é]

wing [wɪŋ]
翅膀 [chì bǎng]

fly [flaɪ]
飞 [fēi]

At the zoo 在动物园里

- What are David and Eric doing?
- Which animal is sitting with Mother and Susan?
- Who is carrying a cub?
- What is Penny doing?
- Do you think Father likes the snake?
- What would you like to do at this zoo?

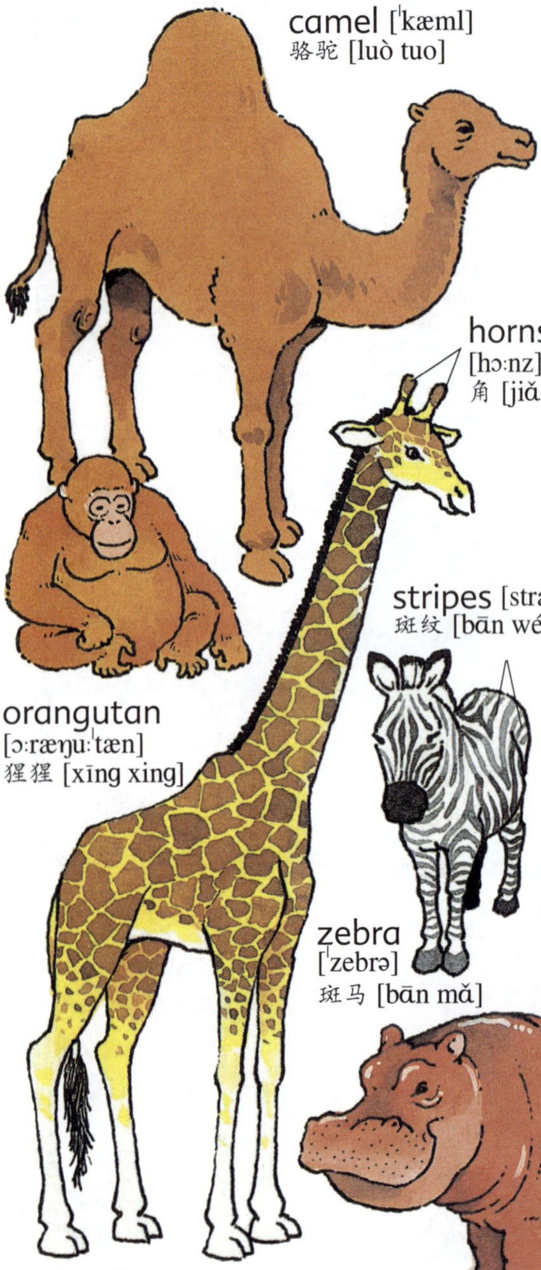

camel [ˈkæml]
骆驼 [luò tuo]

horns [hɔːnz]
角 [jiǎo]

stripes [straɪps]
斑纹 [bān wén]

orangutan [ɔːræŋuːˈtæn]
猩猩 [xīng xing]

zebra [ˈzebrə]
斑马 [bān mǎ]

monkey [ˈmʌŋkɪ]
猴子 [hóu zi]

giraffe [dʒɪˈrɑːf]
长颈鹿 [cháng jǐng lù]

hippopotamus [ˌhɪpəˈpɒtəməs]
河马 [hé mǎ]

crocodile [ˈkrɒkədaɪl]
鳄鱼 [è yú]

zookeeper [ˈzuːkiːpə]
管理员
[guǎn lǐ yuǎn]

Mother and Susan are sitting with the orangutan.
The zookeeper is carrying a cub.
Penny is talking to the monkey.

spots [spɒts] 斑点 [bān diǎn]
mane [meɪn]
鬃毛 [zōng máo]
snake [sneɪk]
蛇 [shé]
leopard [ˈlepəd]
豹 [bào]
tail [teɪl]
尾 [wěi]
tongue [tʌŋ]
舌头 [shé tou]
cub [kʌb]
小狮子
[xiǎo shī zi]
tiger [ˈtaɪɡə]
老虎 [lǎo hǔ]
rock [rɒk]
磐石 [pán shí]
lion [ˈlaɪən]
狮子 [shī zi]

At the beach

在海滩上

- Where is Mother?
- What is Gita looking for?
- Who can you see fishing?
- What has Susan made?
- What do you think Susan has been doing?
- Why is Aziz looking happy?

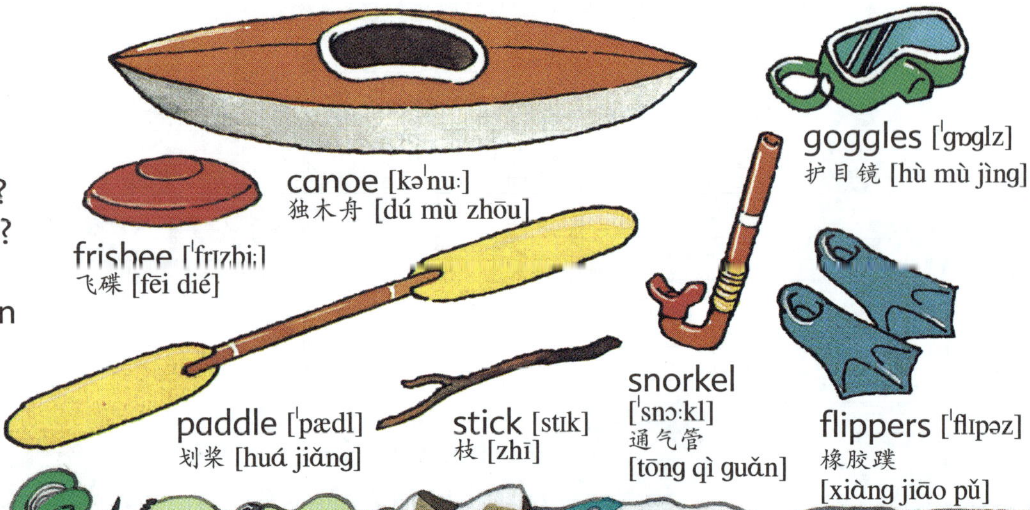

fish [fɪʃ]
鱼 [yú]

waves [weɪvz]
浪 [làng]

hermit crab [ˈhɜːmɪt kræb]
寄居蟹 [jì jū xiè]

sea [siː]
海 [hǎi]

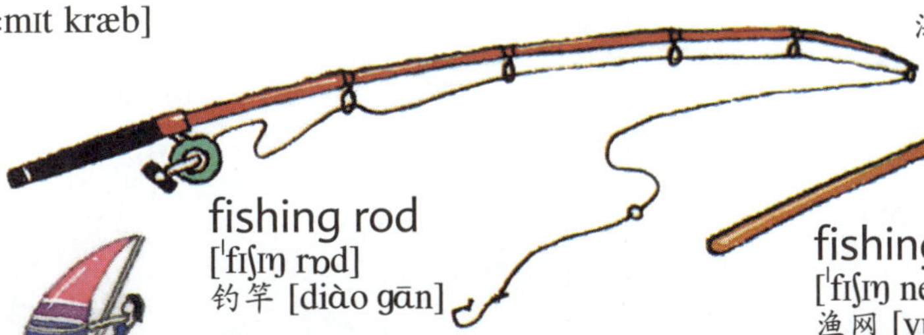

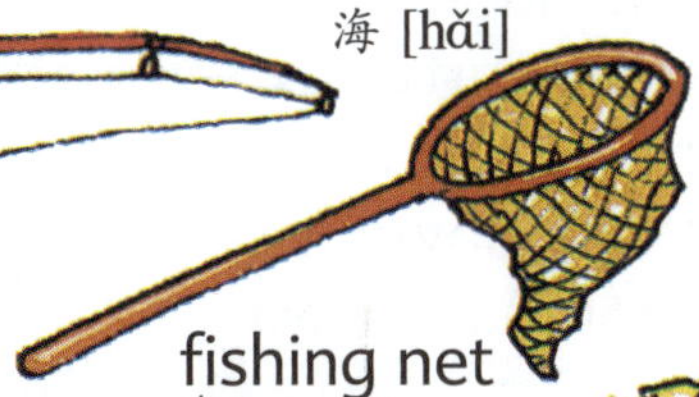

shell [ʃel]
贝壳 [bèi ké]

fishing rod
[ˈfɪʃɪŋ rɒd]
钓竿 [diào gān]

fishing net
[ˈfɪʃɪŋ net]
渔网 [yú wǎng]

sandcastle
[sændkɑːsl]
沙堡 [shā bǎo]

pebbles [ˈpebl]
卵石 [luǎn shí]

starfish [ˈstɑːfɪʃ]
海星 [hǎi xīng]

crab [kræb]
蟹 [xiè]

windsurfing [ˈwɪndˈsɜːfɪŋ]
帆板运动 [fān bǎn yùn dòng]

fishing
[ˈfɪʃɪŋ]
钓鱼 [diào yú]

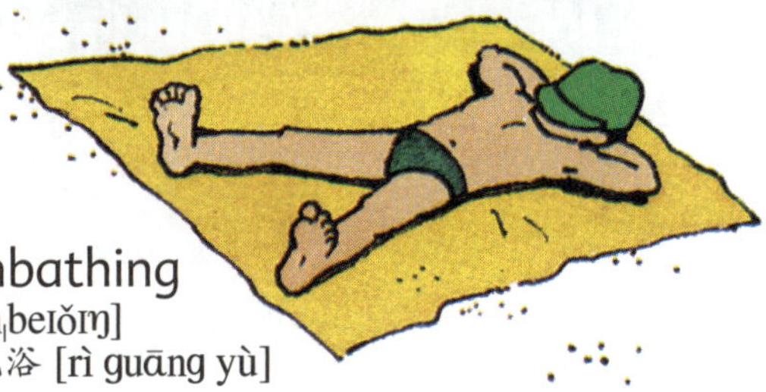

sunbathing
[ˈsʌnˌbeɪðɪŋ]
日光浴 [rì guāng yù]

At the circus 马戏团

- Can you see David and Susan?
- What is the family doing?
- Where is the circus?
- What animal are the ladies riding?
- Where are the trapeze artists?
- What is the sad clown riding?
- Why do you think the clown is sad?
- Who is in the cannon? What will happen to him?

trapeze [trəˈpiːz]
吊架 [diào jià]

trapeze artists [trəˈpiːz ˈɑːtɪsts]
空中飞人 [kōng zhōng fēi rén]

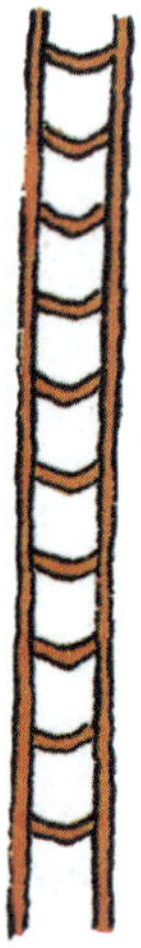

rope ladder
[rəʊp ˈlædə]
绳梯 [shéng tī]

whip [wɪp]
鞭子 [biān zi]

ringmaster
[ˈrɪŋmɑːstə]
马戏团领班
[mǎ xì tuán lǐng bān]

clown [klaʊn]
小丑 [xiǎo chǒu]

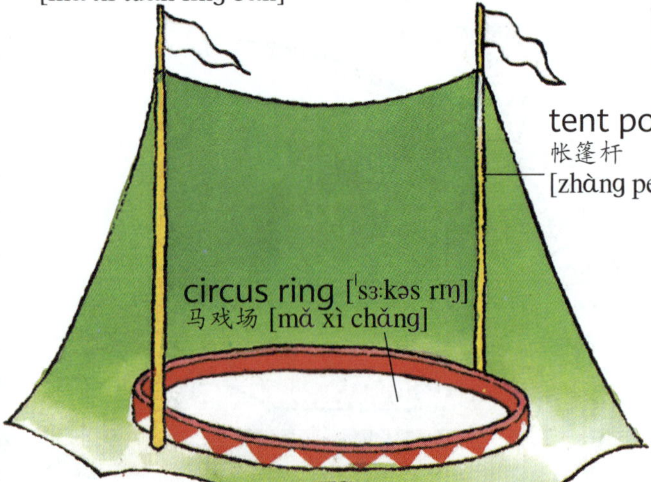

tent pole [tent pəʊl]
帐篷杆
[zhàng péng gān]

circus ring [ˈsɜːkəs rɪŋ]
马戏场 [mǎ xì chǎng]

tent [tent]
帐篷 [zhàng péng]

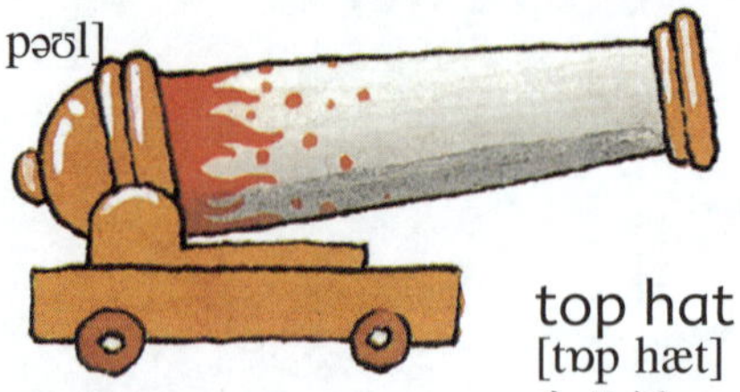

cannon [ˈkænən]
大炮 [dà pào]

top hat
[tɒp hæt]
大礼帽
[dà lǐ mào]

unicycle [ˈjuːnɪsaɪkl]
单轮自行车
[dān lún zì xíng chē]

spectators [spekˈteɪtəz]
观众 [guān zhòng]

elephant [ˈelɪfənt]
大象 [dà xiàng]

bareback rider [ˈbeəbæk ˈraɪdə]
无马鞍杂技人 [wú mǎ ān zá jì rén]

horse [hɔːs]
马 [mǎ]

sad [sæd]
悲伤的 [bēi shāng de]

happy [ˈhæpɪ]
快乐的 [kuài lè de]

popcorn [ˈpɒpkɔːn]
玉米花 [yù mǐ huā]

candyfloss
[ˈkændiflɒs]
棉花糖 [mián hua táng]

In the playground
游乐场

- Who is on the seesaw with Gita?
- Who is David playing with?
- Where is Grandmother? What is she doing?
- What is Penny trying to do?
- What is Jack going to do?
- What do you think Susan wants to play next?
- Where are Mother and Father?

swing [swɪŋ]
秋千 [qiū qiān]

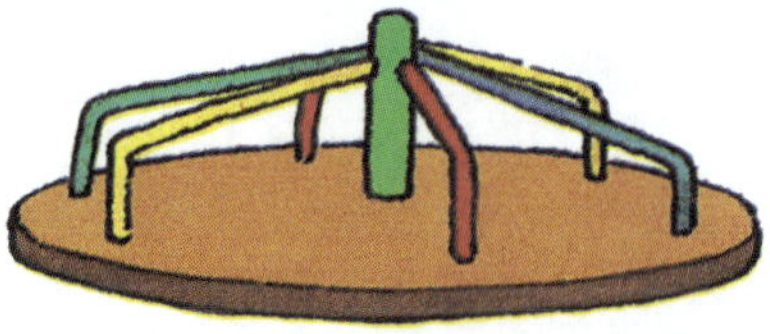

merry-go-round [ˈmerɪ-gəʊ-raʊnd]
旋转盘 [xuán zhuǎn pán]

seesaw [siːsɔː]
跷跷板 [qiāo qiāo bǎn]

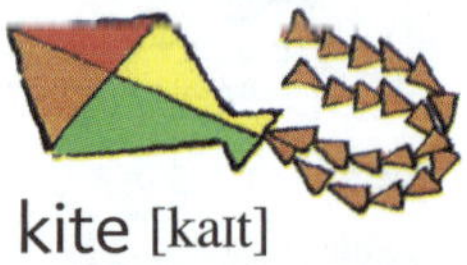

kite [kaɪt]
风筝 [fēng zheng]

bat [bæt]
球棒 [qiú bàng]

climbing frame [ˈklaɪmɪŋ freɪm]
攀玩架 [pān wán jià]

skateboard
[ˈskeɪtbɔːd]
滑板 [huá bǎn]

slide [slaɪd]
滑梯 [huá tī]

roller skates [ˈrəʊlə skeɪts]
滚轴溜冰鞋
[gǔn zhóu liū bīng xié]

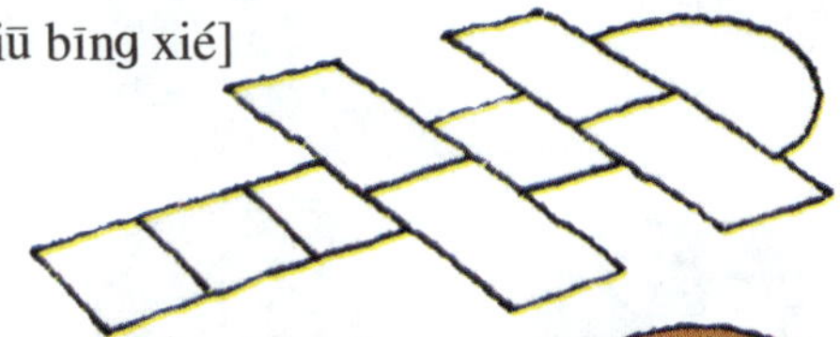

hopscotch [ˈhɒpskɒtʃ]
跳方游戏 [tiào fāng yóu xì]

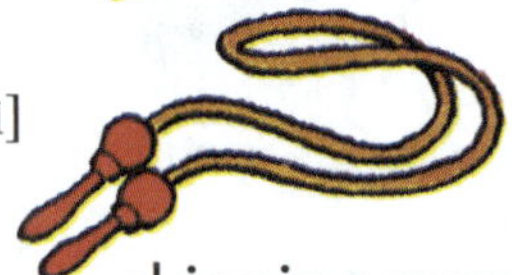

skipping rope
[skɪpɪŋ rəʊp]
绳 [shéng]

bench [bentʃ]
长椅 [cháng yǐ]

marbles
[ˈmaːblz]
弹珠 [dàn zhū]

over [ˈəʊvə]
在…上面
[zài ... shàng mian]

under [ˈʌndə]
在…下面
[zài ... xià mian]

chase [tʃeɪs]
追 [zhuī]

pull [pʊl]
拉 [lā]

through [θruː]
通过 [tōng guò]

talk [tɔːk]
说话 [shuō huà]

skip [skɪp]
跳绳 [tiào shéng]

hop [hɒp]
单足跳
[dān zú tiào]

At the park 在公园里

- What are Father and Susan doing?
- What can David see?
- What has Carol found?
- Who is jogging?
- What does Baby want to see?
- What do you think the ducks want?

nest [nest]
鸟巢 [niǎo cháo]

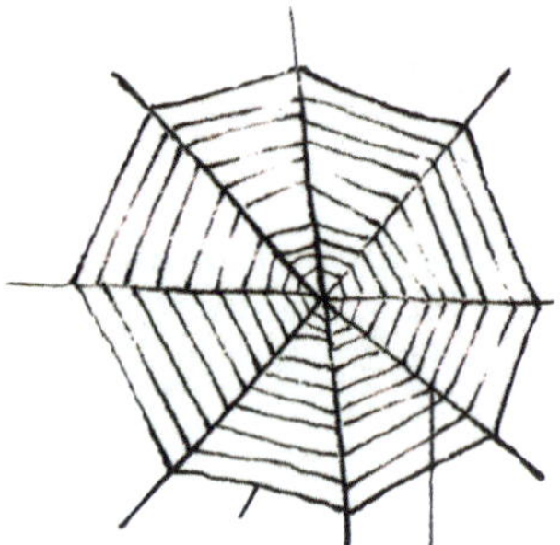

web [web]
蜘蛛网
[zhī zhū wǎng]

spider [ˈspaɪdə]
蜘蛛 [zhī zhū]

duck [dʌk]
鸭 [yā]

duckling [ˈdʌklɪŋ]
小鸭 [xiǎo yā]

frog [frɒg]
青蛙 [qīng wā]

dragonfly
[ˈdrægənflaɪ]
蜻蜓 [qīng tíng]

swan [swɒn]
天鹅 [tiān é]

butterfly
[ˈbʌtəflaɪ]
蝴蝶 [hú dié]

ant [ænt]
蚂蚁 [mǎ yǐ]

bee [biː]
蜜蜂 [mì fēng]

grasshopper
[ˈgrɑːshɒpə]
蚱蜢 [zhà měng]

caterpillar [ˈkætəpɪlə]
毛虫 [máo chóng]

flower [ˈflaʊə]
花朵 [huā duǒ]

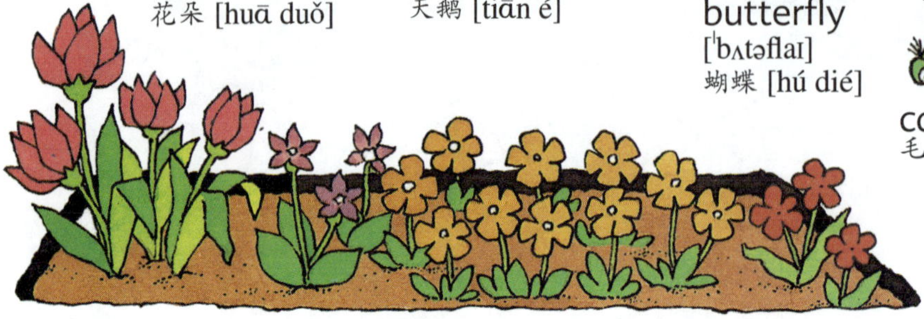

flowerbed [ˈflaʊəbed]
花坛 [huā tán]

snail [sneɪl]
蜗牛 [wō niú]

tadpoles [ˈtædpəʊlz]
蝌蚪 [kē dǒu]

Father and Susan are feeding the swan.

Mr. Nathan is jogging.

David can see tadpoles.

grass [grɑːs]
草 [cǎo]

sundial [ˈsʌndaɪəl]
日规 [rì guī]

water lily [ˈwɔːtə ˈlɪlɪ]
睡莲 [shuì lián]

fountain [ˈfaʊntɪn]
喷水池 [pēn shuǐ chí]

On the farm 农场里

- Which animal does Susan want to feed?
- What is the brown cow doing?
- What is the farmer doing?
- Where are David and Eric?
- Where do you think the farmer is going?
- What sounds would you hear on this farm?

hill [hɪl]
小山 [xiǎo shān]

fruit tree [fruːt triː]
果树 [guǒ shù]

field [fiːld]
田地 [tián dì]

farmer [ˈfɑːmə]
农夫 [nóng fū]

pigsty [ˈpɪgstaɪ]
猪圈 [zhū juàn]

hay [heɪ]
干草 [gān cǎo]

beehive [ˈbiːhaɪv]
蜂箱 [fēng xiāng]

pond [pɒnd]
池塘 [chí táng]

hen house [hen haʊs]
鸡舍 [jī shè]

turkey [ˈtɜːkɪ]
火鸡 [huǒ jī]

pig [pɪg]
猪 [zhū]

sheep [ʃiːp]
羊 [yáng]

lamb [læm]
小羊 [xiǎo yáng]

well [wel]
水井 [shuǐ jǐng]

farmhouse [ˈfɑːmhaʊs]
农舍 [nóng shè]

barn [bɑːn]
谷仓 [gǔ cāng]

trailer [ˈtreɪlə]
拖车 [tuō chē]

tractor [ˈtræktə]
拖拉机 [tuō lā jī]

Susan wants to feed the donkey.

donkey [ˈdɒŋkɪ]
驴子 [lǘ zi]

rooster [ˈruːstə]
公鸡 [gōng jī]

goat [gəʊt]
山羊 [shān yáng]

cow [kaʊ]
母牛 [mǔ niú]

calf [kɑːf]
小牛 [xiǎo niú]

bull [bʊl]
公牛 [gōng niú]

At the swimming pool 游泳池

- Where is Father?
- What are Susan and Gita doing?
- Who is diving?
- Which of the boys are having a swimming lesson?
- Who is racing with Ben?
- What do you think the coach is doing?
- Do you think Sam can swim?

goggles [ˈgɒglz]
护目镜 [hù mù jìng]

lifesaver [laɪfseɪvə]
救生圈 [jiù shēng quān]

armbands [ˈɑːmbændz]
臂圈 [bì quān]

diving board
[ˈdaɪvɪŋ bɔːd]
跳板
[tiào bǎn]

dive [ˈdaɪv]
跳水 [tiào shuǐ]

sunglasses [ˈsʌnˌglɑːsɪz]
太阳镜 [tài yáng jìng]

swimming cap
[ˈswɪmɪŋ kæp]
游泳帽 [yóu yǒng mào]

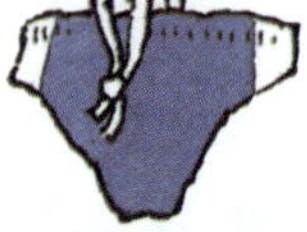

swimming trunks
[ˈswɪmɪŋ trʌŋks]
游泳裤 [yóu yǒng kù]

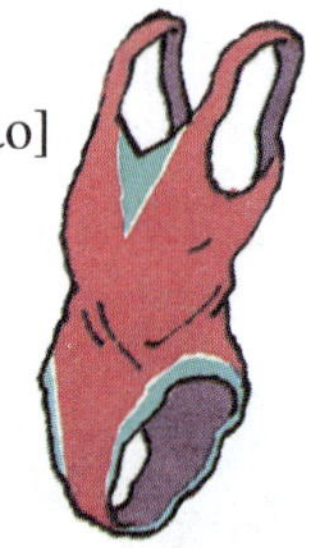

swimsuit
[ˈswɪmsuːt]
游泳衣
[yóu yǒng yī]

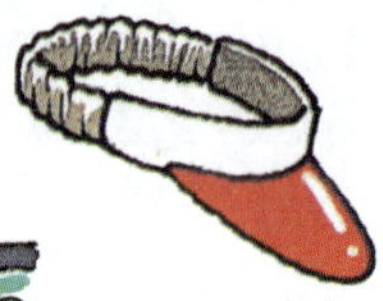

sun visor [sʌn ˈvaɪzə]
太阳帽 [tài yáng mào]

splash [splæʃ]
泼水 [pō shuǐ]

stopwatch
[ˈstɒpwɒtʃ]
秒表 [miǎo biǎo]

race [reɪs]
竞赛 [jìng sài]

sunshade [ˈsʌnʃeɪd]
太阳伞 [tài yáng sǎn]

suntan lotion
[ˈsʌntæn ˈləʊʃn]
防晒露
[fáng shài lù]

coach [ˈkəʊtʃ]
教练 [jiào liàn]

queue [kjuː]
排队 [pái duì]

stamp [stæmp]
盖章 [gài zhāng]

copy [ˈkɒpɪ]
抄写 [chāo xiě]

upside down
[ˌʌpsaɪd daʊn]
上下翻转
[shàng xià fān zhuǎn]

At the library 图书馆

- What is Mother doing?
- Who is looking at a book about frogs?
- Who is returning her books?
- Why is Jack waiting?
- Can you see the librarian?
- What is he doing?
- Why is Baby looking at his book upside down?

librarian [laɪˈbreərɪˈən]
图书馆管理员
[tú shū guǎn guǎn lǐ yuán]

pile of books
[paɪl əv bʊks]
一堆书籍
[yī duī shū jí]

cover [ˈkʌvə]
封面 [fēng miàn]

page [peɪdʒ]
页 [yè]

pop-up book
[pɒp ʌp bʊk]
立体书 [lì tǐ shū]

big book [bɪg bʊk]
大书 [dà shū]

rocket [ˈrɒkɪt]
火箭 [huǒ jiàn]

poster [ˈpəʊstə]
海报 [hǎi bào]

computer [kəmˈpjuːtə]
电脑 [diàn nǎo]

step stool
[step stuːl]
梯凳 [tī dèng]

This postman is riding a scooter.
The postman has a letter for Gita.
Grandfather is going to mail a parcel.
The postman is clearing the mailbox.

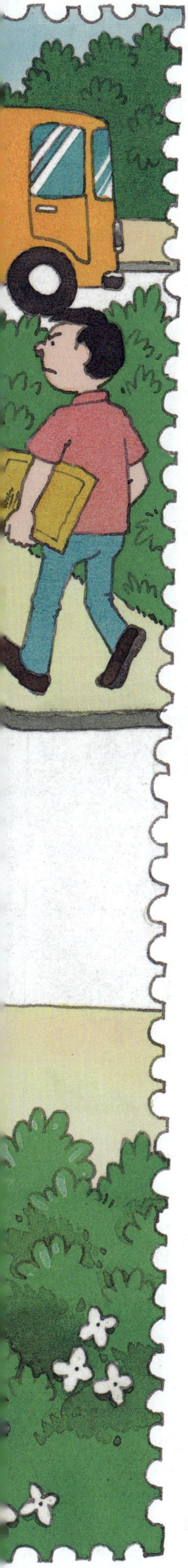

The postman 邮差

- David and Susan are watching a postman. What is he doing?
- Why is Gita happy?
- Who is riding a scooter?
- What is Grandfather going to do?
- Who else is going to the post office?

post office [pəʊst ˈɒfɪs]
邮局 [yóu jú]

postbox [ˈpəʊstbɒks]
邮箱 [yóu xiāng]

scooter [ˈsku:tə]
小型摩托车 [xiǎo xíng mó tuō chē]

postbag [ˈpəʊstbæg]
邮袋 [yóu dài]

postal van [ˈpəʊstl væn]
邮车 [yóu chē]

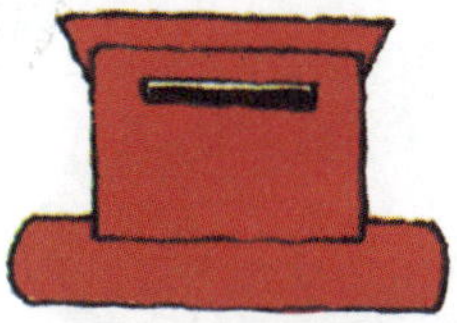

letterbox [ˈletəbɒks]
信箱 [xìn xiāng]

parcel [ˈpɑ:sl]
包裹 [bāo guǒ]

packet [ˈpækɪt]
邮包 [yóu bāo]

envelope [ˈenvələʊp]
信封 [xìn fēng]

letter [ˈletə]
信 [xìn]

deliver [dɪˈlɪvə]
送信 [sòng xìn]

postman [ˈpəʊstmən]
邮差 [yóu chāi]

post [pəʊst]
寄信 [jì xìn]

bunch of keys
[bʌntʃ əv ki:z]
一串钥匙
[yī chuàn yào shi]

stamp [stæmp]
邮票 [yóu piào]

The garbage man
清道夫

- What are the garbage men doing?
- Where are they putting the garbage?
- Who is picking up some litter?
- What is David doing?
- Why is David's dog barking?
- Why do you think the red car is passing the truck?

verge [vɜːdʒ]
路边 [lù biān]

rubbish [ˈrʌbɪʃ]
废物 [fèi wù]

litter [ˈlɪtə]
垃圾 [lā jī]

dustbin [ˈdʌstbɪn]
垃圾桶 [lā jī tǒng]

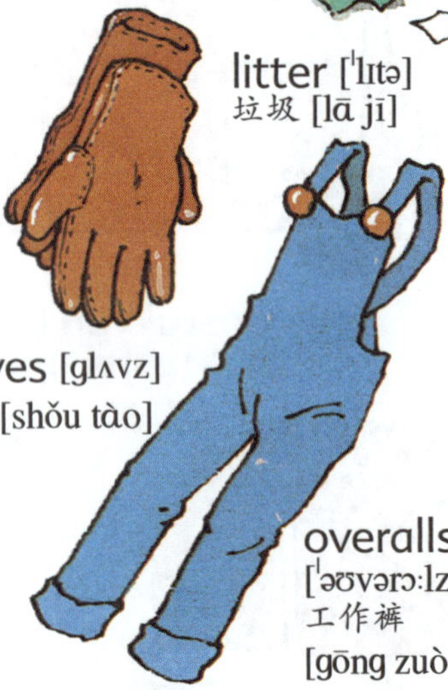

gloves [glʌvz]
手套 [shǒu tào]

overalls [ˈəʊvərɔːlz]
工作裤
[gōng zuò kù]

boots [buːts]
长靴 [cháng xuē]

dustman [ˈdʌstmən]
清洁工人
[qīng jié gōng rén]

dustmen [ˈdʌstmən]
清洁工人
[qīng jié gōng rén]

refuse truck [ˈrɪfjuːz trʌk]
垃圾车 [lā jī chē]

heavy
[ˈhevɪ]
重的
[zhòng de]

shout [ʃaʊt]
呼喊 [hū hǎn]

bark
[bɑːk]
吠 [fèi]

overtake [ˌəʊvəˈteɪk]
超越 [chāo yuè]

light [laɪt]
轻的 [qīng de]

bundle of sticks
[ˈbʌndl əv stɪks]
一束树枝 [yī shù shù zhī]

pick up [pɪk ʌp]
拾起 [shí qǐ]

throw [θrəʊ]
扔掉 [rēng diào]

The police officer 警察

- What is the police officer showing Aziz and David?
- Who is Father talking to?
- What is the police officer in the mittens doing?
- Who is at the desk in the police station?
- Why do you think the man in the police station is handcuffed?

police station [pəˈliːs ˈsteɪʃn]
警察局 [jǐng chá jú]

policewoman
[pəˈliːswʊmən]
女警察 [nǚ jǐng chá]

police officer
[pəˈliːs ɒfɪsə]
警察 [jǐng chá]

traffic police officer
[ˈtræfɪk pəˈliːs ɒfɪsə]
交通警察 [jiāo tōng jǐng chá]

lamp post [læmp pəʊst]
路灯柱 [lù dēng zhù]

police car [pəˈliːs kɑː]
警车 [jǐng chē]

police officers [pəˈliːs ɒfɪsəz]
警察 [jǐng chá]

The police officer is showing Aziz and David his whistle.

This police officer is directing the traffic.

mittens [ˈmɪtnz]
连指手套
[lián zhǐ shǒu tào]

report book
[rɪˈpɔːt bʊk]
记事簿 [jì shì bù]

cap [kæp]
警帽 [jǐng mào]

name tag [neɪm tæɡ]
名牌 [míng pái]

walkie-talkie
[ˈwɔːkɪtɔːkɪ]
对讲机 [duì jiǎng jī]

handcuffs
[ˈhændkʌfs]
手铐 [shǒu kào]

whistle [ˈwɪsl]
哨子 [shào zi]

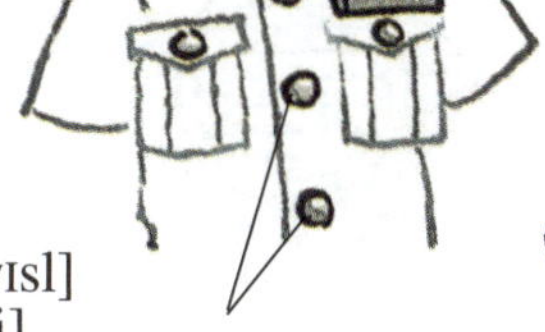

buttons [ˈbʌtnz]
钮扣 [niǔ kòu]

truck [trʌk]
货车 [huò chē]

The fire officer

消防队员

- Who are David and his friends watching?
- How many fire engines are there?
- Where is the fire?
- Can you see the fire officer with the megaphone? What is he telling the people?
- Why do you think the fire officer is pleased with Jack?

fire extinguisher [ˈfaɪə ɪkˈstɪŋgwɪʃə]
灭火器 [miè huǒ qì]

nozzle [ˈnɒzl]
喷嘴 [pēn zuǐ]

hydrant [ˈhaɪdrənt]
消防栓 [xiāo fáng shuān]

horn [hɔːn]
警报器 [jǐng bào qì]

spotlight [ˈspɒtlaɪt]
聚光灯 [jù guāng dēng]

fire engine [ˈfaɪə endʒɪn]
消防车 [xiāo fáng chē]

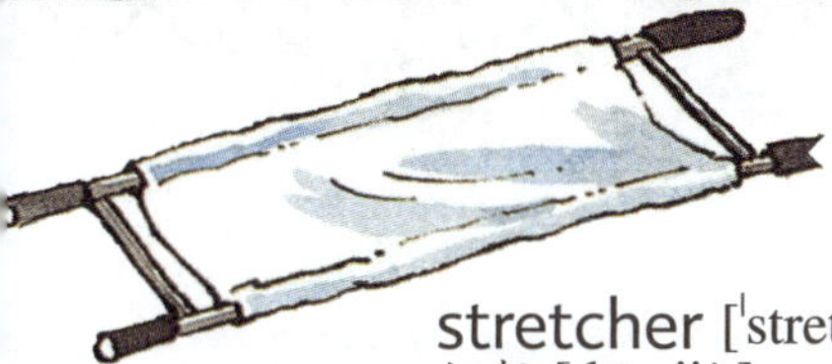

stretcher [ˈstretʃə]
担架 [dān jià]

megaphone [ˈmegəfəʊn]
扩音器 [kuò yīn qì]

oxygen tank [ˈɒksɪdʒən tæŋk]
氧气筒 [yǎng qì tǒng]

mask [mɑːsk]
防毒面具 [fáng dú miàn jù]

flames [fleɪmz]
火焰 [huǒ yàn]

first-aid kit [ˈfɜːst eɪd kɪt]
急救药箱 [jí jiù yào xiāng]

fireman's helmet [ˈfaɪəməns ˈhelmɪt]
消防头盔 [xiāo fáng tóu kuī]

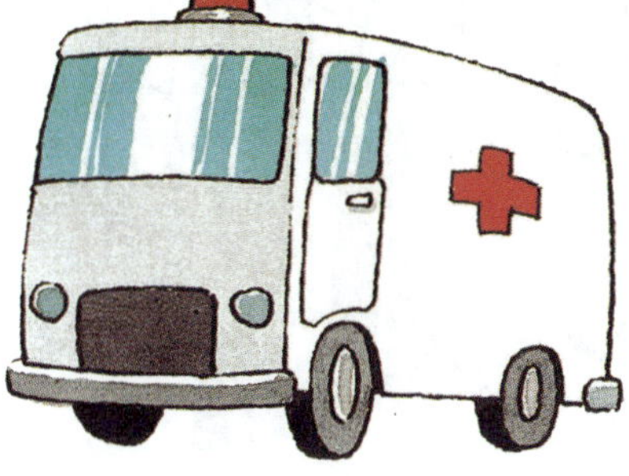

ambulance [ˈæmbjʊləns]
救护车 [jiù hù chē]

axe [æks]
斧头 [fǔ tóu]

fire officer's jacket [ˈfaɪə ɒfɪsəs ˈdʒækɪt]
消防衣 [xiāo fáng yī]

fire officer [ˈfaɪə ɒfɪsə]
消防队员 [xiāo fáng duì yuán]

fire officers [ˈfaɪə ɒfɪsəz]
消防队员 [xiāo fáng duì yuán]

The builder 建筑工人

- Where are the workmen?
- Who is looking at the plans?
- What is the dump truck doing?
- Who does Grandfather know?
- Why are all the workmen wearing safety helmets?
- Do you think David and his friends like to visit the building site? Why can't they go inside?

crane [kreɪn]
起重机 [qǐ zhòng jī]

scaffolding
[ˈskæfəldɪŋ]
棚架 [péng jià]

dump truck
[ˈdʌmp trʌk]
卸货卡车
[xiè huò kǎ chē]

cement mixer [sɪˈment mɪksə]
混凝土车 [hùn níng tǔ chē]

bag of cement
[bæg əv sɪˈment]
一袋水泥 [yī dài shuǐ ní]

excavator [ˈekskəveɪtə]
挖土机 [wā tǔ jī]

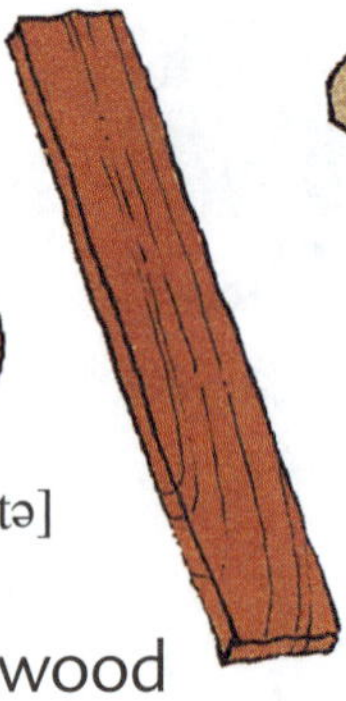

plank of wood
[plæŋk əv wʊd]
一块木板 [yī kuài mù bǎn]

workman
[ˈwɜːkmən]
工人 [gōng rén]

workmen [ˈwɜːkmən]
工人 [gōng rén]

bricks [brɪks]
砖 [zhuān]

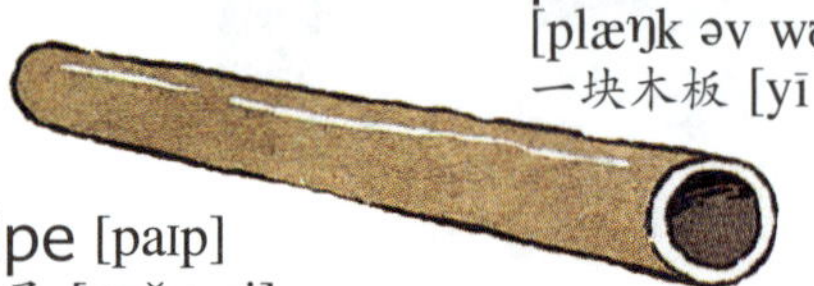

pipe [paɪp]
管子 [guǎn zi]

The workmen are at work on the building site.

Grandfather knows one of the workmen.

This builder is looking at the plans.

ladder [ˈlædə]
梯子 [tī zi]

rubble [ˈrʌbl]
瓦砾 [wǎ lì]

hook [hʊk]
吊钩
[diào gōu]

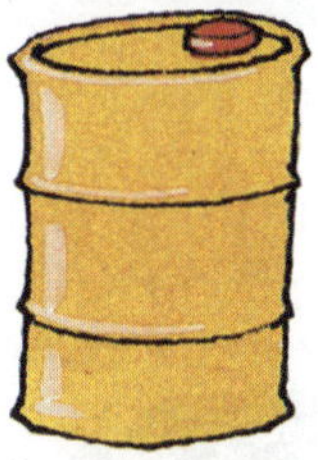

drum [drʌm]
鼓状桶
[gǔ zhuàng tǒng]

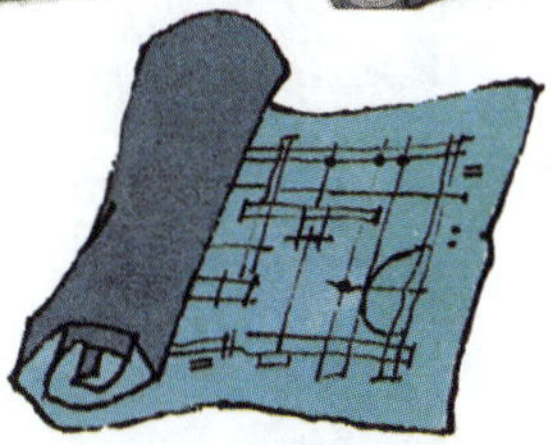

plan [plæn]
设计图 [shè jì tú]

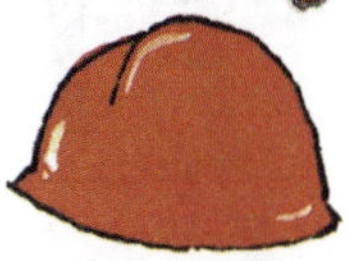

safety helmet
[ˈseɪftɪ ˌhelmɪt]
安全帽
[ān quán mào]

shovel [ˈʃʌvl]
铲 [chǎn]

metal bar [ˈmetl bɑː]
工字铁 [gōng zì tiě]

shake hands [ʃeɪk hændz]
握手 [wò shǒu]

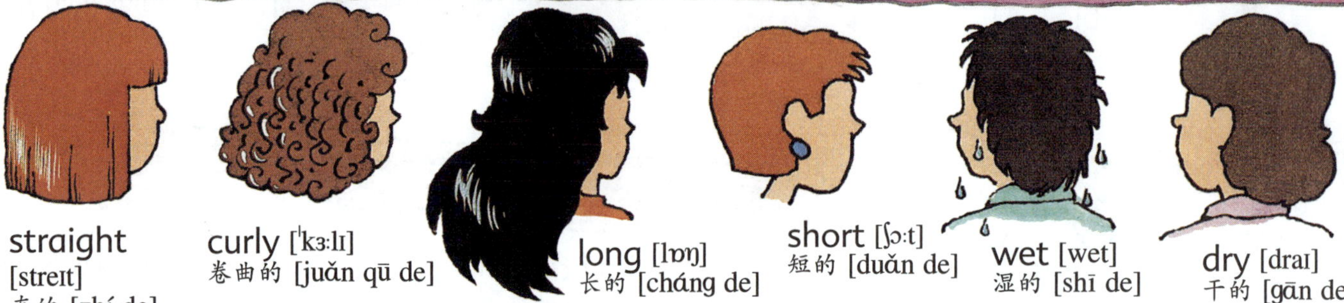

straight [streɪt] 直的 [zhí de]

curly [ˈkɜːlɪ] 卷曲的 [juǎn qū de]

long [lɒŋ] 长的 [cháng de]

short [ʃɔːt] 短的 [duǎn de]

wet [wet] 湿的 [shī de]

dry [draɪ] 干的 [gān de]

The hairdresser 理发师

- Who is having a shampoo?
- Who is having her hair cut?
- Who is blow-drying Susan's hair?
- What is the hairdresser doing?
- Why do you think Susan and David are having their hair cut? Who will be finished first?

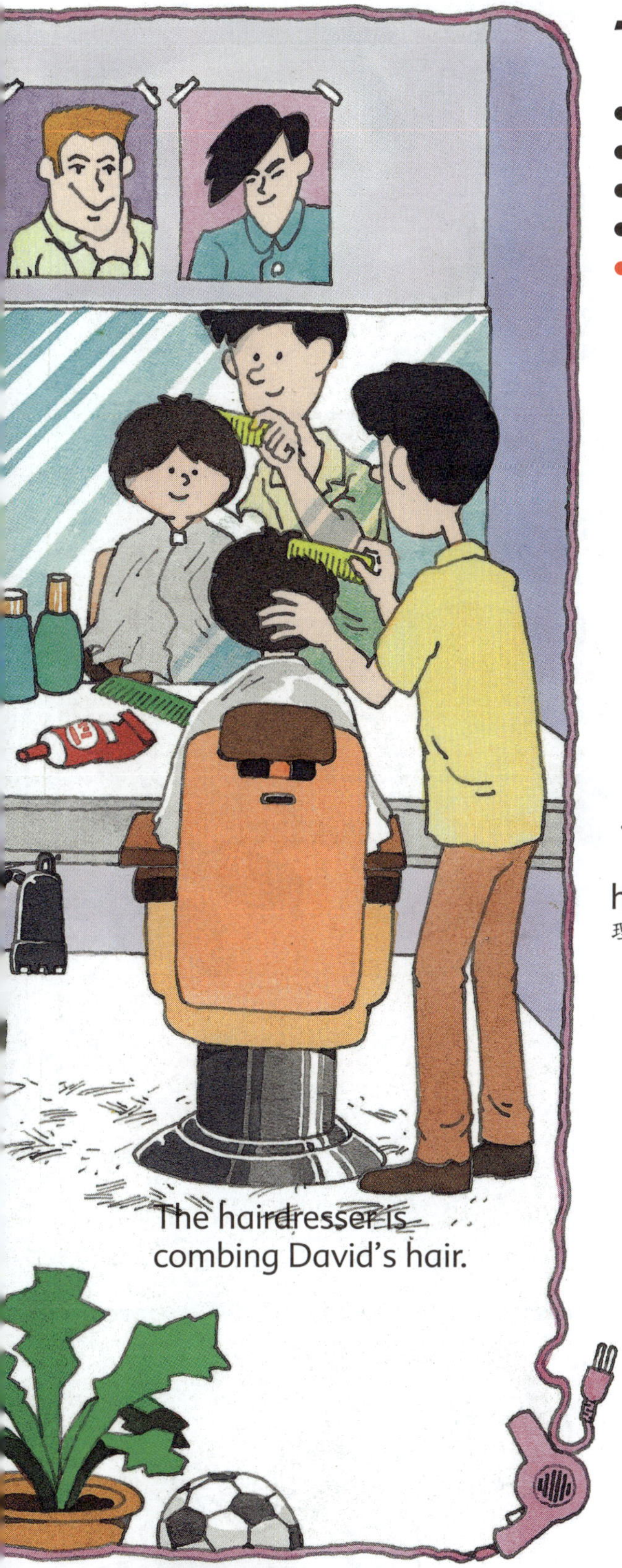

The hairdresser is combing David's hair.

perm [pɜːm]
烫发 [tàng fà]

hairdresser [ˈheədresə]
理发师 [lǐ fà shī]

hood [hʊd]
头罩 [tóu zhào]

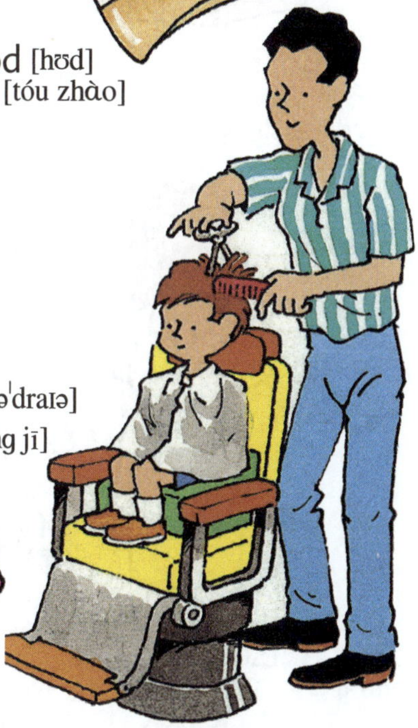

hairdresser [ˈheədresə]
理发师 [lǐ fà shī]

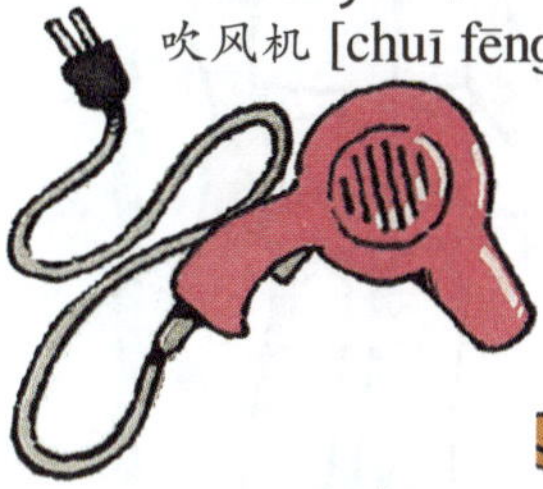

hairdryer [heəˈdraɪə]
吹风机 [chuī fēng jī]

shampoo [ʃæmˈpuː]
洗发露 [xǐ fà lù]

hair cream [heə kriːm]
发乳 [fà rǔ]

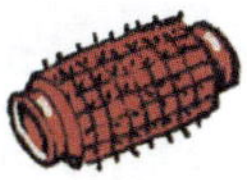

curler [kɜːlə]
卷发夹 [juǎn fà jiā]

fringe [frɪndʒ]
刘海 [liú hǎi]

hair [heə]
头发 [tóu fà]

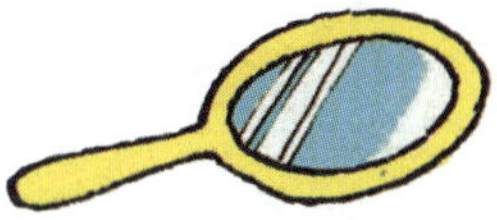

hand mirror [hænd ˈmɪrə]
镜子 [jìng zi]

hair net [heə net]
发网 [fà wǎng]

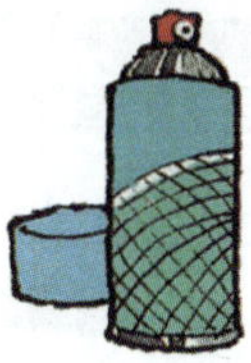

hair spray [heə spreɪ]
发胶 [fà jiāo]

cape [keɪp]
短斗篷 [duǎn dǒu péng]

The dentist 牙医

- What is the dentist going to do?
- Who is looking at an X-ray?
- Where is Susan?
- What is the matter with the man in the waiting room?
- Do you think David likes going to the dentist? Can you tell why?

X-ray machine
[ˈeks reɪ məˈʃiːn]
X射线机 [X shè xiàn jī]

X-ray [ˈeks reɪ]
X射线照片
[X shè xiàn zhào piàn]

dental nurse
[ˈdentl nɜːs]
牙科护士
[yá kē hù shi]

dentist
[ˈdentɪst]
牙医 [yá yī]

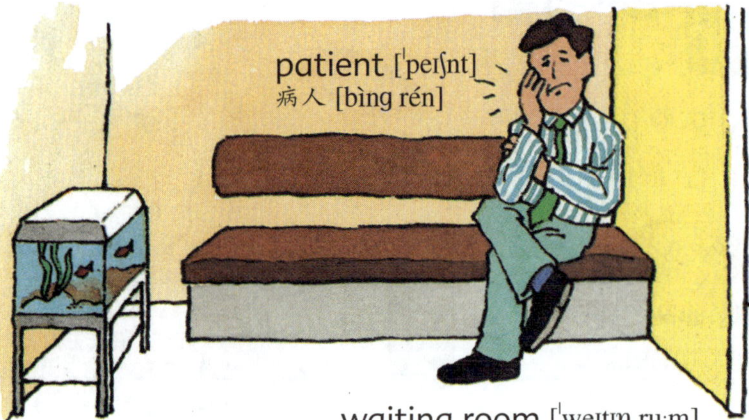

fish tank [fɪʃ tæŋk]
鱼缸 [yú gāng]

waiting room [ˈweɪtɪŋ ruːm]
候诊室 [hòu zhěn shì]

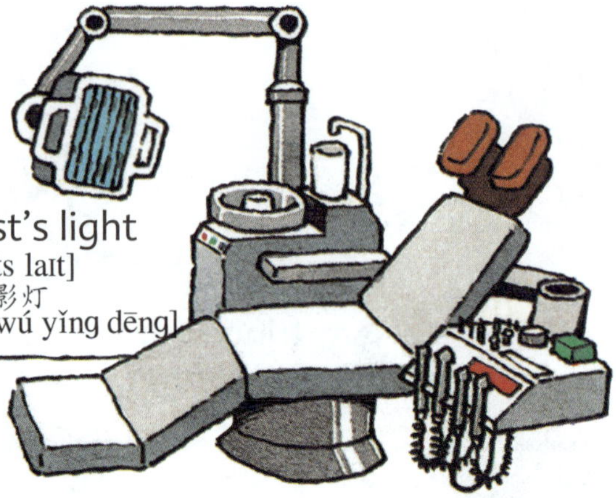

dentist's light
[ˈdentɪsts laɪt]
牙科无影灯
[yá kē wú yǐng dēng]

dentist's chair [ˈdentɪsts tʃeə]
牙科椅 [yá kē yǐ]

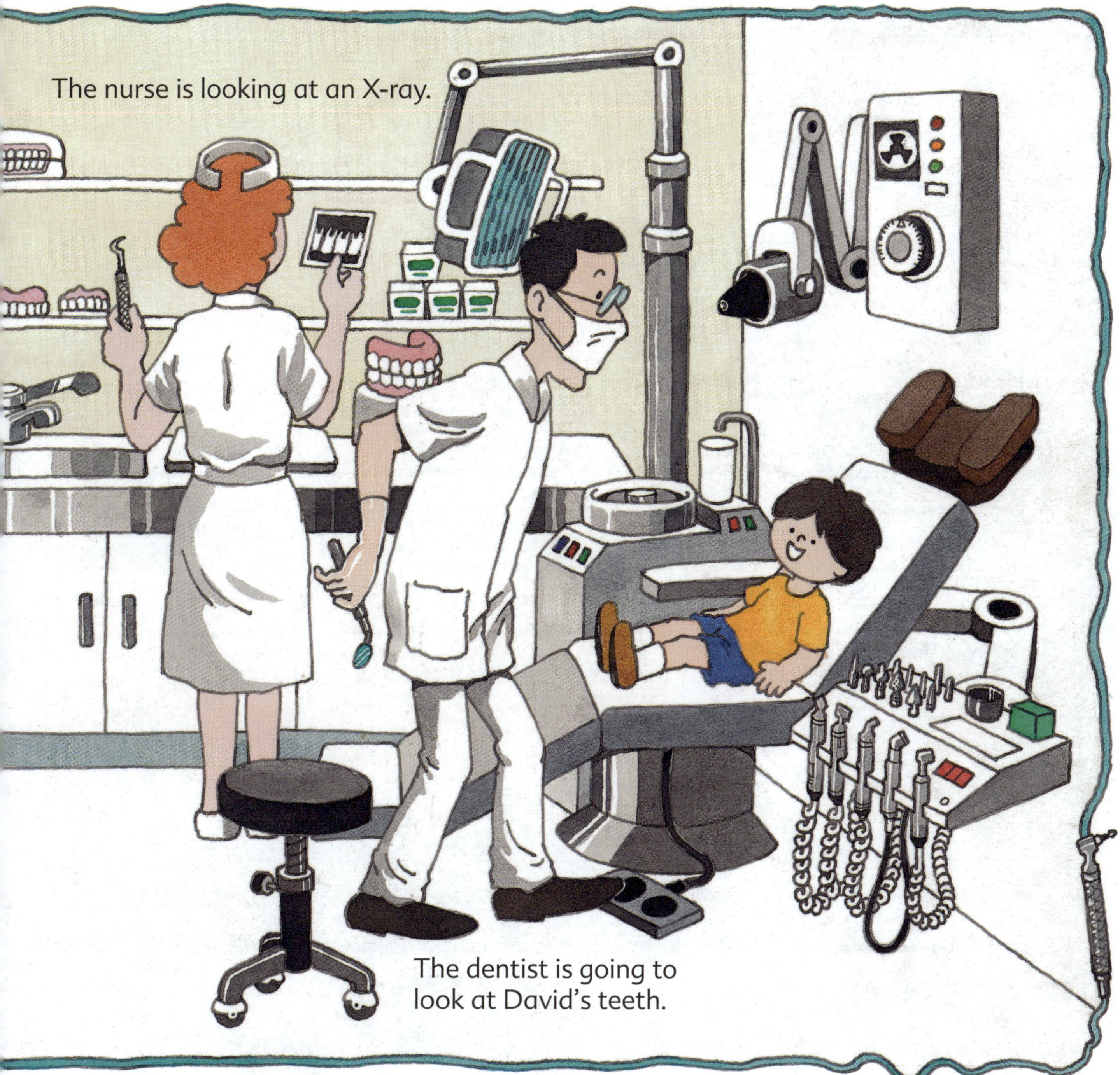

mouth mirror [maʊθ ˈmɪrə]
口镜 [kǒu jìng]

probe [prəʊb]
牙探针
[yá tàn zhēn]

drill [drɪl]
牙钻 [yá zuàn]

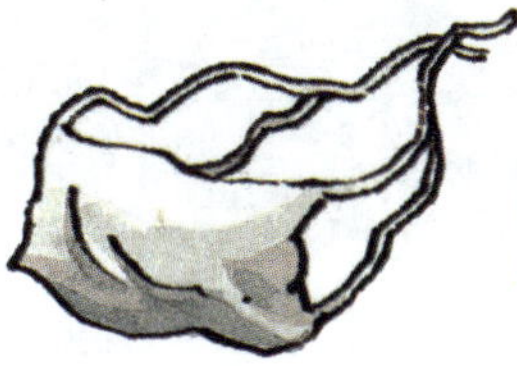

mask [mɑːsk]
卫生口罩
[wèi shēng kǒu zhào]

air and water jet
[eə ənd ˈwɔːtə dʒet]
水/气喷嘴 [shuǐ / qì pēn zuǐ]

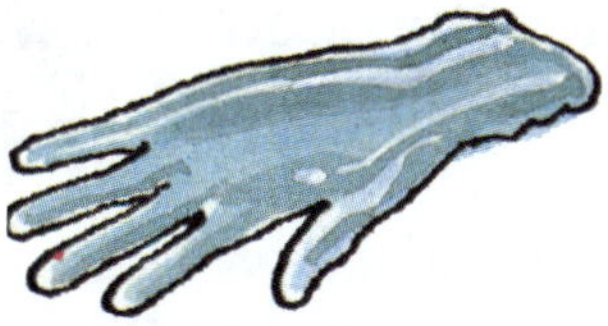

rubber glove [ˈrʌbə glʌv]
橡胶手套 [xiàng jiāo shǒu tào]

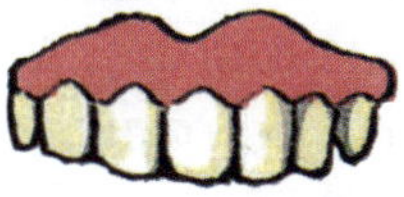

dentures [ˈdentʃəs]
假牙 [jiǎ yá]

tooth [tuːθ]
牙齿 [yá chǐ]

teeth [tiːθ]
牙齿 [yá chǐ]

toothache [ˈtuːθeɪk]
牙痛 [yá tòng]

The doctor 医生

- What is the matter with Susan?
- What is the doctor doing?
- Who has just been to see the doctor?
- What is the matter with the lady in the waiting room?
- How do you think Susan feels?
- What do you think has happened to Ben?

doctor's bag [ˈdɒktəs bæg]
医生工具箱
[yī shēng gōng jù xiāng]

plaster
[ˈplɑ:stə]
胶布 [jiāo bù]

thermometer
[θəˈmɒmɪtə]
探热计 [tàn rè jì]

needle [ni:dl]
针 [zhēn]

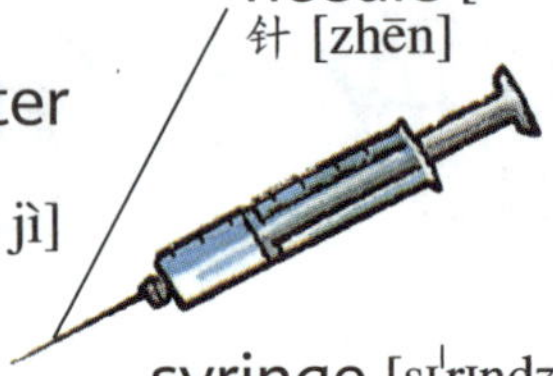

syringe [sɪˈrɪndʒ]
注射器 [zhù shè qì]

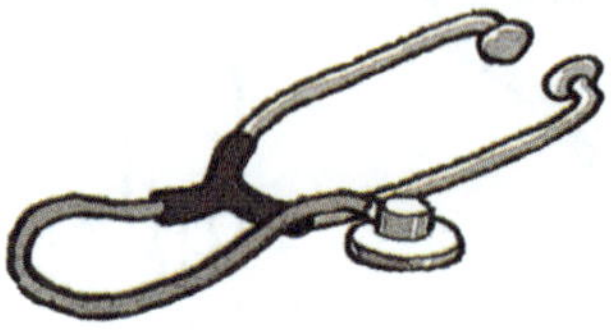

stethoscope [ˈsteθəskəʊp]
听诊器 [tīng zhěn qì]

nurse [nɜ:s]
护士 [hù shì]

doctor [ˈdɒktə]
医生 [yī shēng]

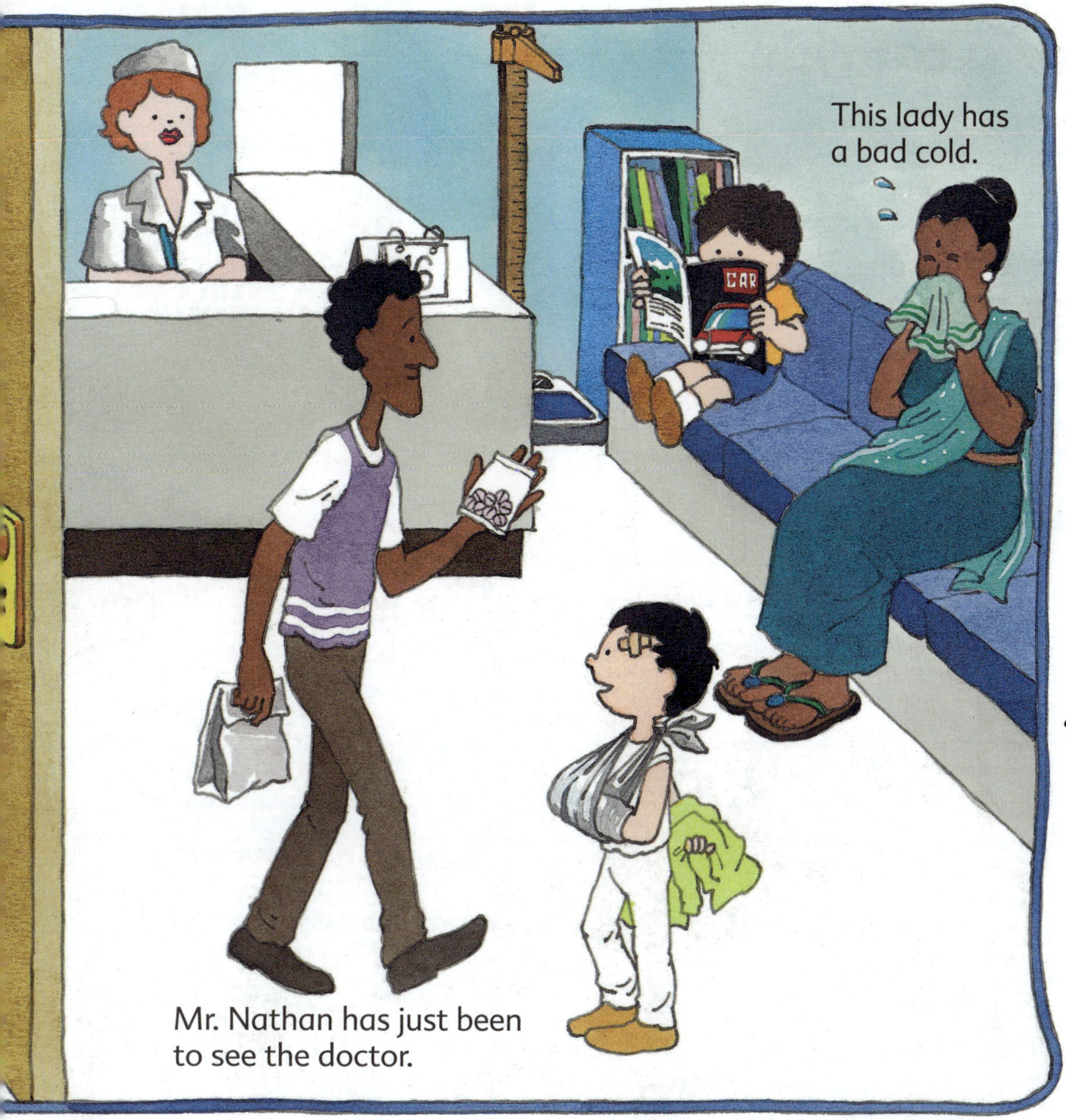

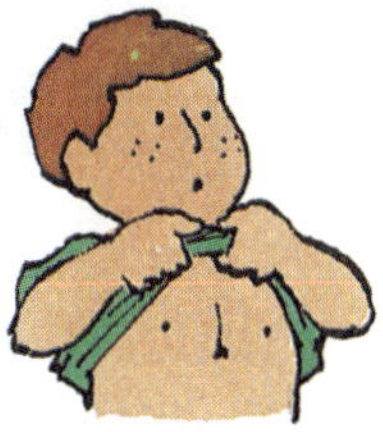

chest [tʃest]
胸部 [xiōng bù]

tablet [ˈtæblɪt]
药片 [yào piàn]

medicine [ˈmedsn]
药 [yào]

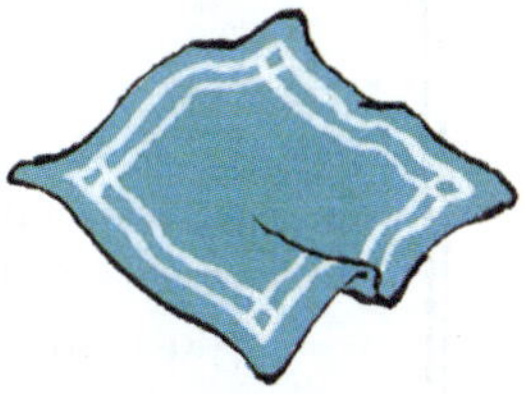

handkerchief
[ˈhæŋkətʃɪf]
手帕 [shǒu pà]

scale
[skeɪl]
体重计
[tǐ zhòng jì]

torch [tɔ:tʃ]
手电筒
[shǒu diàn tǒng]

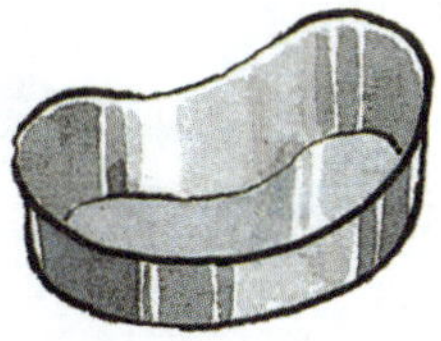

kidney dish
[ˈkɪdnɪ dɪʃ]
肾形盘 [shèn xíng pán]

cotton wool
[kɒtn wʊl]
药棉 [yào mián]

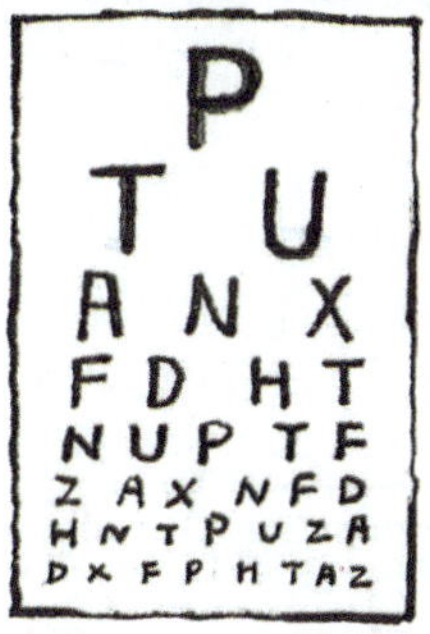

eye chart [aɪ tʃa:t]
视力检验表
[shì lì jiǎn yàn biǎo]

couch [kaʊtʃ]
长沙发椅 [cháng shā fā yǐ]

bandage [ˈbændɪdʒ]
绷带 [bēng dài]

sling [slɪŋ]
吊带 [diào dài]

sneeze [sni:z]
打喷嚏 [dǎ pēn tì]

Let's go for a car ride 我们去兜风

- Who is going for a ride with Father?
- What is Ben doing?
- Who is Grandfather talking to?
- What has Uncle Fred bought?
- Why do you think Mr. Nathan is running?

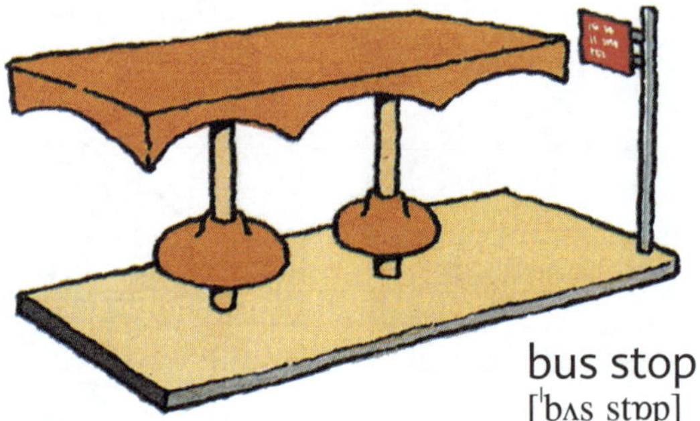

bus stop
[ˈbʌs stɒp]
公共汽车车站
[gōng gòng qì chē chē zhàn]

road sign
[rəʊd saɪn]
路标 [lù biāo]

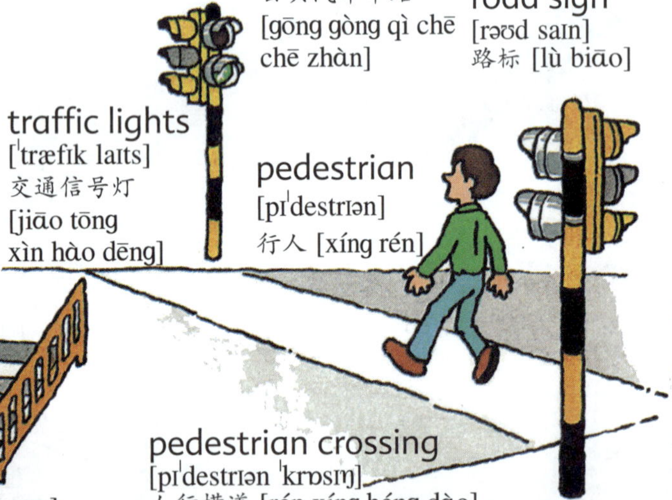

traffic lights
[ˈtræfɪk laɪts]
交通信号灯
[jiāo tōng xìn hào dēng]

pedestrian
[pɪˈdestrɪən]
行人 [xíng rén]

pedestrian crossing
[pɪˈdestrɪən ˈkrɒsɪŋ]
人行横道 [rén xíng héng dào]

subway [ˈsʌbweɪ]
行人隧道 [xíng rén suì dào]

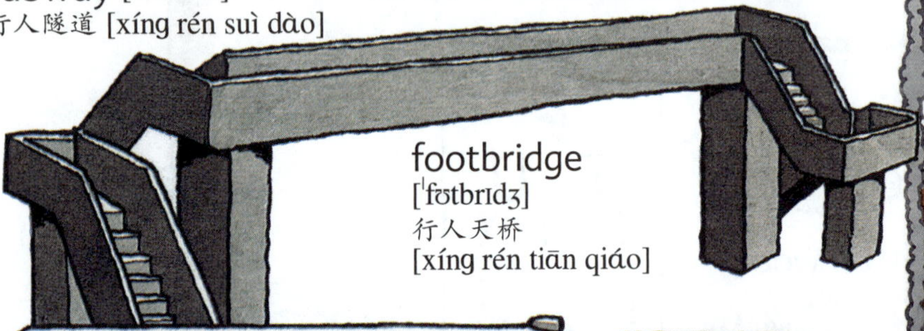

footbridge
[ˈfʊtbrɪdʒ]
行人天桥
[xíng rén tiān qiáo]

double-decker bus [ˈdʌblˈdekə bʌs]
双层公共汽车 [shuāng céng gōng gòng qì chē]

newsstand
[ˈnjuːzstænd]
书报摊
[shū bào tān]

drill [drɪl]
钻孔 [zuān kǒng]

trash can [træʃ kæn]
废物箱 [fèi wù xiāng]

cyclist [ˈsaɪklɪst]
骑自行车的人
[qí zì xíng chē de rén]

taxi [ˈtæksɪ]
计程车 [jì chéng chē]

sports car
[ˈspɔːts kɑː]
跑车 [pǎo chē]

container lorry [kənˈteɪnə ˈlɒrɪ]
货柜车 [huò guì chē]

At the garage 修车厂

- What is Father doing?
- Who else needs gasoline?
- What is Mother going to do?
- Who is putting air in the tyres?
- Can you see Ben? What do you think he wants?
- Who do you think David is waving to?

petrol cap [ˈpetrəl kæp] 油箱盖 [yóu xiāng gài]

trunk [trʌŋk] 车尾箱 [chē wěi xiāng]

mechanic [mɪˈkænɪk] 技工 [jì gōng]

steering wheel [ˈstɪərɪŋ wiːl] 驾驶盘 [jià shǐ pán]

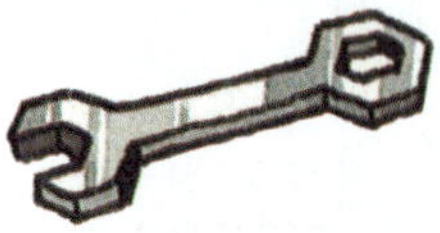

spanner [ˈspænə] 扳钳 [bān qián]

screwdriver [ˈskruːdraɪvə] 螺丝起子 [luó sī qǐ zi]

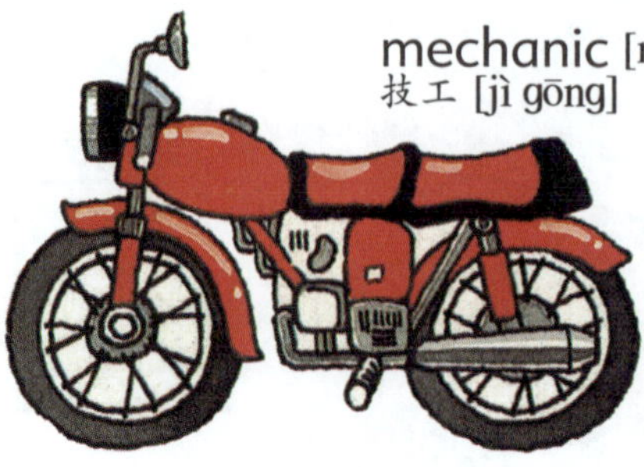

motorcycle [ˈməʊtəsaɪkl] 摩托车 [mó tuō chē]

can of oil [kæn əv ɔɪl] 一罐油 [yī guàn yóu]

petrol pump [ˈpetrəl pʌmp] 加油器 [jiā yóu qì]

Grandfather is putting air in the tyres.

Father is filling the car up with gasoline.

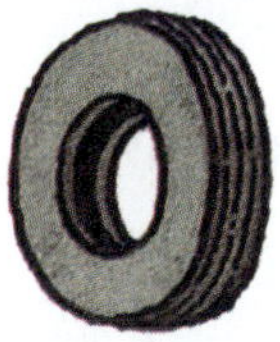

tyre [ˈtaɪə]
轮胎 [lún tāi]

wheel [wiːl]
车轮 [chē lún]

crash helmet
[kræʃ ˈhelmɪt]
安全帽 [ān quán mào]

tow truck [təʊ trʌk]
拖吊车 [tuō diào chē]

pedal [ˈpedl]
踏板 [tà bǎn]

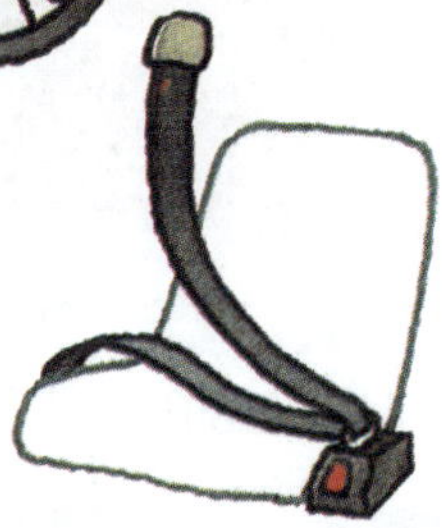

safety belt [ˈseɪftɪ belt]
安全带 [ān quán dài]

car wash [kɑː wɒʃ]
自动洗车机 [zì dòng xǐ chē jī]

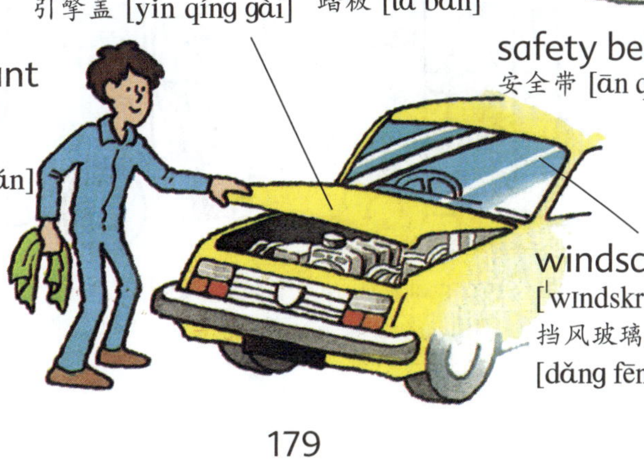

attendant
[əˈtendənt]
服务员
[fú wù yuán]

bonnet [ˈbɒnɪt]
引擎盖 [yǐn qíng gài]

windscreen
[ˈwɪndskriːn]
挡风玻璃
[dǎng fēng bō lí]

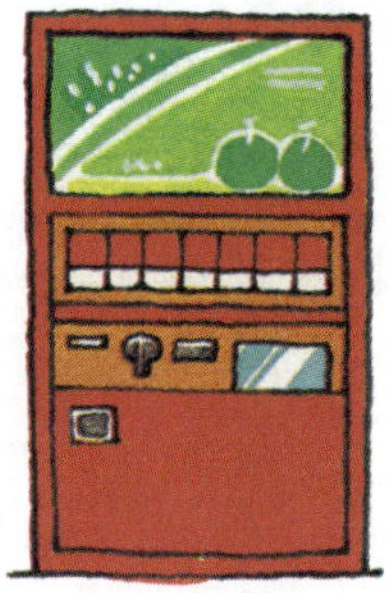

drink machine
[drɪŋk məˈʃiːn]
饮料贩卖机
[yǐn liào fàn mài jī]

sit down [sɪt daʊn]
坐下 [zuò xià]

stand up [stænd ʌp]
站立 [zhàn lì]

get on [get ɒn]
上车 [shàng chē]

get off [get ɒf]
下车 [xià chē]

used ticket box
[ju:zd ˈtɪkɪt bɒks]
废票箱 [fèi piào xiāng]

coins [kɔɪnz]
硬币 [yìng bì]

Let's ride in a bus
我们乘公共汽车

- Who is getting on the bus?
- Where is Susan sitting?
- Why are some people standing up?
- What is David doing?
- Where do you think David will sit?
- Who do you think has left the umbrella behind?

bus driver [bʌs ˈdraɪvə]
公共汽车司机
[gōng gòng qì chē sī jī]

ticket machine [ˈtɪkɪt məˈʃiːn]
售票机
[shòu piào jī]

ticket [ˈtɪkɪt]
车票 [chē piào]

coin box [kɔɪn bɒks]
钱箱 [qián xiāng]

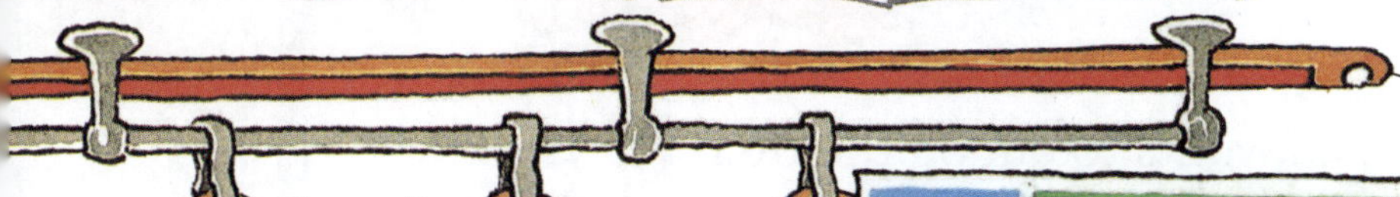

bell strip [bel strɪp]
拉铃 [lā líng]

handle
[ˈhændl]
扶手 [fú shǒu]

advertisement [ədˈvɜːtɪsmənt]
广告 [guǎng gào]

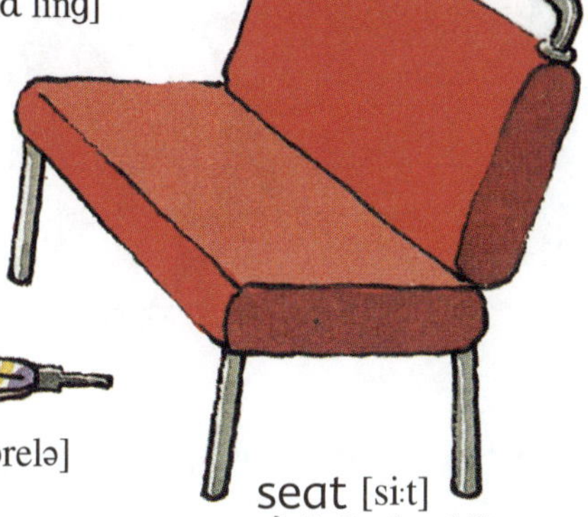

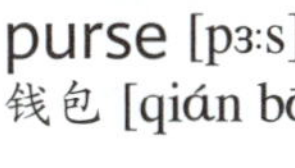

purse [pɜːs]
钱包 [qián bāo]

handbag [ˈhændbæg]
手提包 [shǒu tí bāo]

umbrella [ʌmˈbrelə]
雨伞 [yǔ sǎn]

seat [siːt]
座位 [zuò wèi]

Let's ride on the subway

我们乘地铁

- Which train is coming into the station?
- What is Father doing?
- What does David want to do?
- Where are Mother and Susan?
- Why is Mother holding Susan's hand?
- Which train will leave the station first?

tunnel [ˈtʌnl]
隧道 [suì dào]

train [treɪn]
火车 [huǒ chē]

headlight [ˈhedlaɪt]
车头灯 [chē tóu dēng]

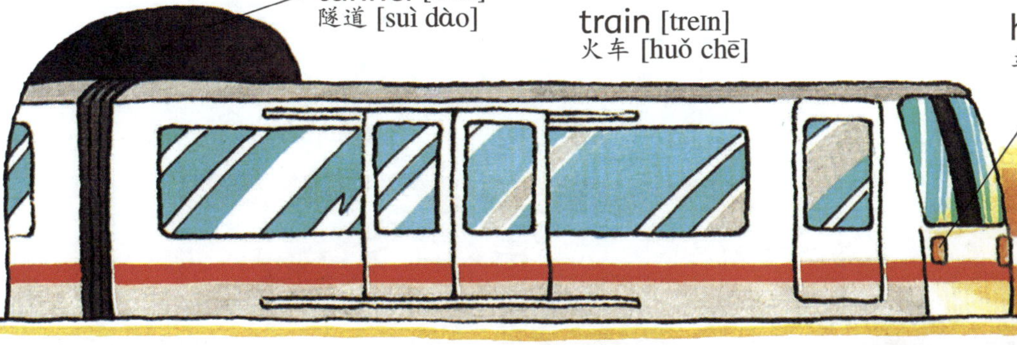

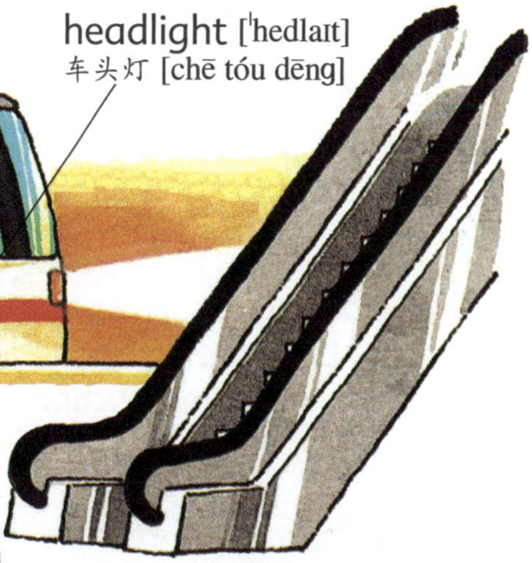

platform [ˈplætfɔːm]
月台 [yuè tái]

escalator [ˈeskəleɪtə]
电动楼梯 [diàn dòng lóu tī]

tourist [ˈtʊərɪst]
游客 [yóu kè]

sign [saɪn]
标志 [biāo zhì]

briefcase [ˈbriːfkeɪs]
公事包 [gōng shì bāo]

map [mæp]
地图 [dì tú]

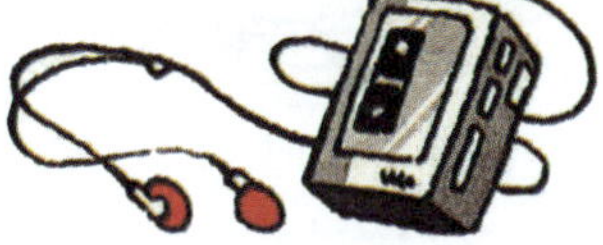

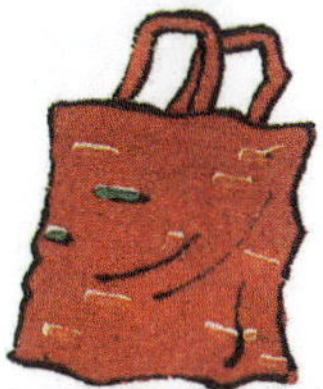

Walkman® [ˈwɔːkmən]
随身听 [suí shēn tīng]

shopping bag
[ˈʃɒpɪŋ bæg]
购物袋 [gòu wù dài]

open [ˈəʊpən]
开的 [kāi de]

close [kləʊs]
关闭的 [guān bì de]

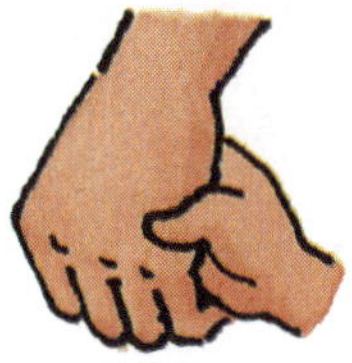

listen [ˈlɪsn]
听 [tīng]

hold [həʊld]
握住 [wò zhù]

Let's go for a boat ride

我们乘游艇兜风

- Where is the ferry going?
- Who is steering the ferry?
- Where are Mother and Baby?
- What is the sailor doing?
- What do you think Father is showing David?
- What do you think Susan is asking Grandfather?

container ship [kənˈteɪnə ʃɪp]
货柜船 [huò guì chuán]

funnel [ˈfʌnl]
烟囱 [yān cōng]

ship [ʃɪp]
船 [chuán]

buoy
[bɔɪ]
浮标
[fú biāo]

oar [ɔː]
划桨 [huá jiǎng]

boat [ˈbəʊt]
艇 [tǐng]

sail
[seɪl]
帆 [fān]

sailboat [ˈseɪlbəʊt]
帆船 [fān chuán]

deck [dek]
甲板 [jiǎ bǎn]

cabin [ˈkæbɪn]
船舱 [chuán cāng]

tugboat [ˈtʌgbəʊt]
拖船 [tuō chuán]

lifeboat
[ˈlaɪfbəʊt]
救生艇
[jiù shēng tǐng]

ferry [ˈferɪ]
渡轮 [dù lún]

steering wheel
[ˈstɪərɪŋ wiːl]
舵轮 [duò lún]

lighthouse
[ˈlaɪthaʊs]
灯塔 [dēng tǎ]

anchor [ˈæŋkə]
锚 [máo]

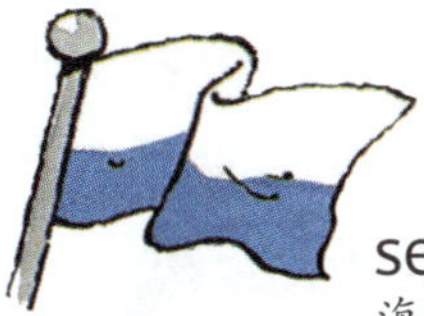

flag [flæɡ]
旗帜 [qí zhì]

seagull [ˈsiːɡʌl]
海鸥 [hǎi ōu]

rope [rəʊp]
绳索 [shéng suǒ]

point [ˈpɔɪnt]
指向 [zhǐ xiàng]

island [ˈaɪlənd]
岛屿 [dǎo yǔ]

pier [pɪə]
码头 [mǎ tou]

pilot [ˈpaɪlət]
舵手 [duò shǒu]

sailor [ˈseɪlə]
水手 [shuǐ shǒu]

row [rəʊ]
划船 [huá chuán]

At the train station

在火车站

- What is Grandfather doing?
- What can Ben and David see?
- Which train is leaving?
- What is Father doing?
- Can you see Grandmother, Mother, Susan and Baby? What are they doing?

This train is leaving.

platform number
[ˈplætfɔ:m nʌmbə]
月台号码 [yuè tái hào mǎ]

barrier [ˈbærɪə]
隔板 [gé bǎn]

ticket collector
[ˈtɪkɪt kəˈlektə]
收票员 [shōu piào yuán]

porter [ˈpɔ:tə]
行李搬运员
[xíng lǐ bān yùn yuán]

suitcase [ˈsu:tkeɪs]
手提箱
[shǒu tí xiāng]

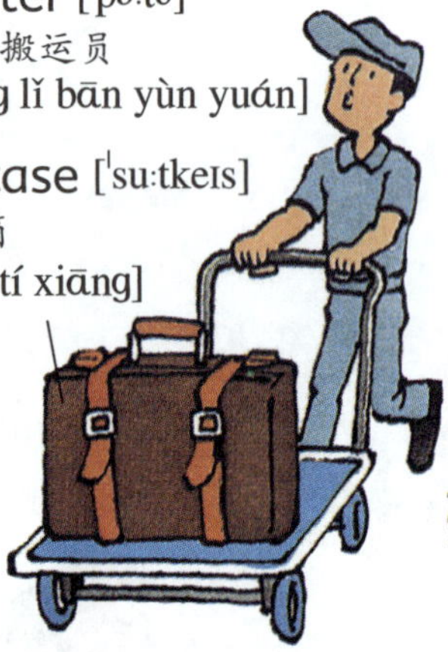

guard [gɑ:d]
列车员 [liè chē yuán]

engineer [endʒɪˈnɪə]
火车司机 [huǒ chē sī jī]

luggage [ˈlʌgɪdʒ]
行李 [xíng lǐ]

luggage rack [ˈlʌgɪdʒ ræk]
行李架 [xíng lǐ jià]

diesel engine
[ˈdi:zl endʒɪn]
火车头[huǒ chē tóu]

sleeper [ˈsli:pə]
枕木 [zhěn mù]

railway [ˈreɪlweɪ]
铁路路轨 [tiě lù lù guǐ]

buffer [ˈbʌfə]
缓冲器 [huǎn chōng qì]

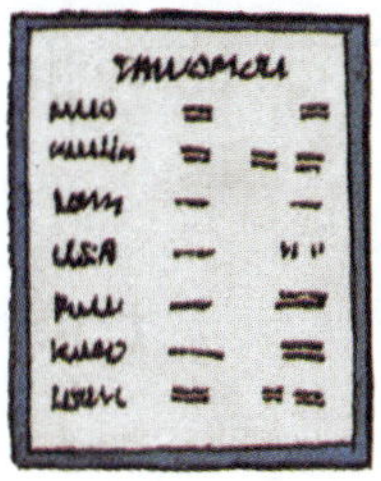

train schedule
[treɪn ˈʃedjuːl]
火车时间表
[huǒ chē shí jiān biǎo]

ticket control
[tɪkɪt kənˈtrəʊl]
售票处 [shòu piào chù]

waiting room
[ˈweɪtɪŋ ruːm]
候车室 [hóu chē shì]

arrive [əˈraɪv]
到达 [dào dá]

leave [liːv]
离开 [lí kāi]

At the airport 在飞机场

- Who can David see?
- What is the stewardess doing?
- Which aeroplane is landing?
- What is the blue aeroplane doing?
- Why are the bus and baggage train empty? Where are they going?

hangar [ˈhæŋə]
飞机棚 [fēi jī péng]

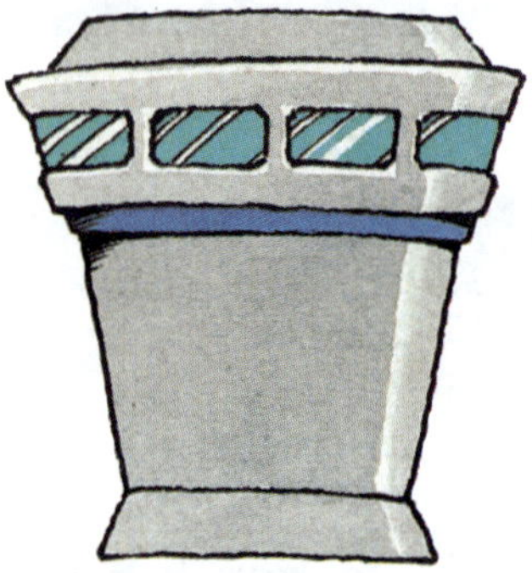

control tower [kənˌtrəʊl ˈtaʊə]
机场指挥塔 [jī chǎng zhǐ huī tǎ]

baggage train [ˈbægɪdʒ treɪn]
行李列车 [xíng lǐ liè chē]

propeller [prəˈpelə]
螺旋桨 [luó xuán jiǎng]

airport bus [ˈeəpɔːt bʌs]
机场汽车 [jī chǎng qì chē]

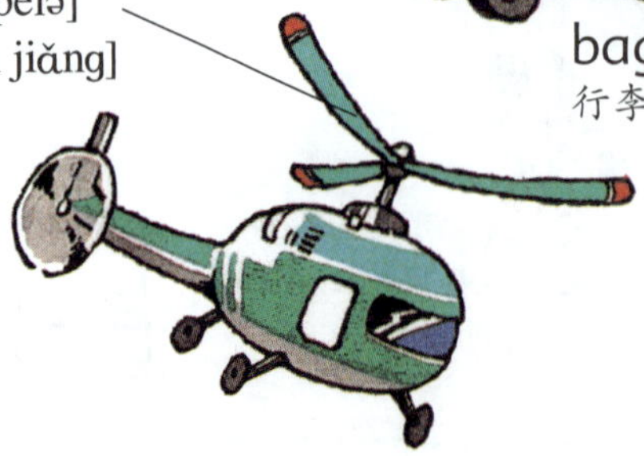

helicopter [ˈhelɪkɒptə]
直升机 [zhí shēng jī]

wing [wɪŋ]
机翼 [jī yì]

tail [teɪl]
机尾 [jī wěi]

jet engine [dʒet ˈendʒɪn]
喷射发动器 [pēn shì fā dòng qì]

aeroplane [ˈeərəpleɪn]
飞机 [fēi jī]

controller [kənˈtrəʊlə]
信号员 [xìn hào yuán]

earmuffs [ˈɪəmʌfs]
耳罩 [ěr zhào]

food truck [fuːd trʌk]
食物货车 [shí wù huò chē]

pilot [ˈpaɪlət]
飞行驾驶员 [fēi xíng jià shǐ yuán]

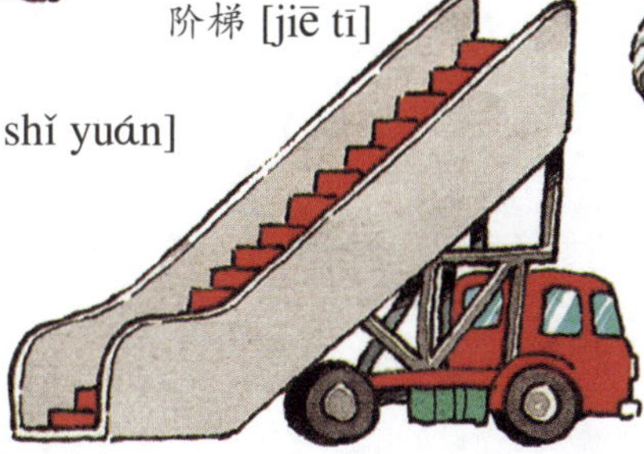

stairs [steəz]
阶梯 [jiē tī]

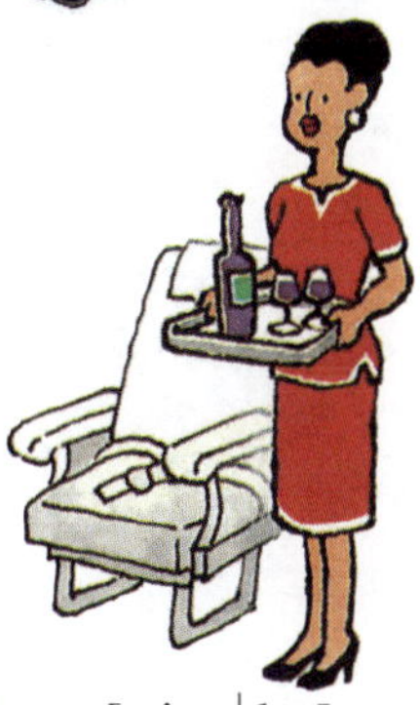

stewardess [stjuːəˈdes]
空中小姐 [kōng zhōng xiǎo jiě]

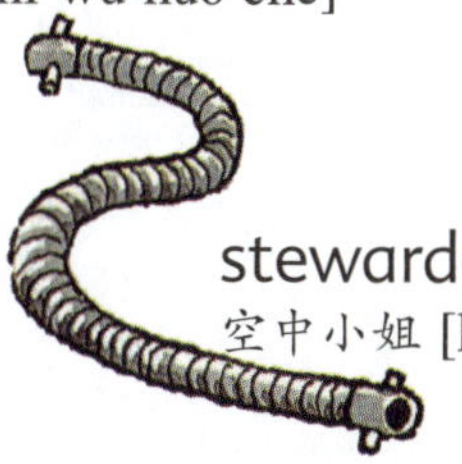

fuel hose [fjʊəl həʊz]
输油软管 [shū yóu ruǎn guǎn]

take off [teɪk ɒf]
起飞 [qǐ fēi]

runway [ˈrʌnweɪ]
飞机跑道 [fēi jī pǎo dào]

land [lænd]
降落 [jiàng luò]

TIMES 1000 WORD DICTIONARY

Myra Ellis

Illustrated by May Kong

A Note to Parents

This section of the book consists of a 1000-WORD DICTIONARY which has been compiled with the aim of making learning both stimulating and fun for students. The meaning of all the entries in the dictionary are shown in ordinary sentence form, with illustration in full colour for further clarification. Where there are different meanings for one word, these are shown in separate sentences.

Additional useful information is given alongside certain types of entries:

- the present participle and past simple tense of all verb entries
- the plural of noun entries with irregular forms
- the other pronoun forms of the subject pronoun entries

To enable students to learn a word in the context of a group it is associated with, certain words have been grouped together under one entry (e.g. building, machine, shape). Similarly, there are five supplements at the end of the dictionary covering the calendar, the family tree, festivals, numbers and times.

The artist has chosen a group of names and given each a special character. These characters are featured in the illustrations according to the characteristics that suit the mood of a particular sentence. This along with the warmth and humour of the illustrations add a unique quality to this part.

给家长的话

本部分有一千个词，不但要达到激发学生们学习的目的，也希望他们能在学习中得到无穷的乐趣。字典中每个词的意思，除了透过简单的造句加以说明外，还配上了色彩鲜艳的图画以加强说明。当词有超过一个以上的意思时，都会透过不同的句子加以说明。

额外有用的资料会附加在词的旁边:

- 动词的过去时态及过去分词
- 名词的不规律复数形式
- 主词代词的其他代词形式

为了让学生在一组事物中学习个别的词汇，我们也把相关的一组词归类于某个特定的词类中，例如：**building**、**machine** 和 **shape**。字典末亦设有五个附录：月历、家族表、节日、数目和时间。

插图者也在本部分安排了一组 格各异的人物。他们将按照不同句子的要求，以他们独特的性格和学生们见面。亲切活泼，充满趣味的图画，也是本部分一大特色。

a [eɪ] **an**
一个 [yī gè]

Sandra has **an** apple and **a** pear.

accident [ˈæksɪdənt]
意外 [yì wài]

Polly had an **accident**.

across [əˈkrɒs] 横过 [héng guò]

The elephant is walking **across** the road.

act [ækt] **acting, acted**
演出 [yǎn chū]

Patrick likes to **act**.

add [æd] **adding, added**
添、加 [tiān, jiā]

The builder **adds** one brick to the wall.

aeroplane [ˈeərəpleɪn]
飞机 [fēi jī]

An **aeroplane** flies in the sky.

afraid [əˈfreɪd] 害怕 [hài pà]

Sally is **afraid** of monsters.

after [ˈɑːftə] 之后 [zhī hòu]

B comes **after** A.

afternoon [ˌɑːftəˈnuːn]
下午 [xià wǔ]

It is after twelve o'clock. It is the **afternoon**.

again [əˈgen] 又 [yòu]

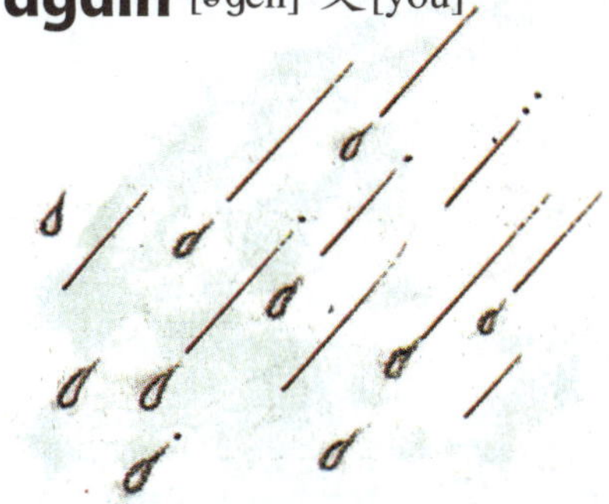

It rained this morning. It is raining **again** now.

against [əˈgenst] 倚 [yǐ]

The elephant is leaning **against** the wall.

age [eɪdʒ] 年龄 [nián líng]

Sandra is four years old.
That is her **age**.

agree [əˈɡriː] **agreeing, agreed**
同意 [tóng yì]

'Yes, let's race.'
We **agree** to run a race.

alike [əˈlaɪk]
一样的 [yī yàng de]

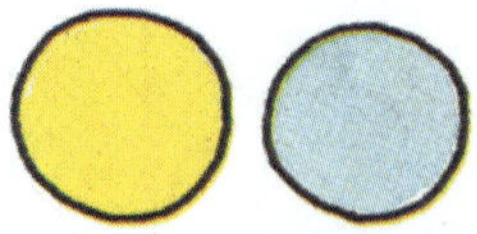

These two shapes are **alike**.

These two shapes are not **alike**.

alive [əˈlaɪv] 活的 [huó de]

My dog is playing dead, but he is **alive**.

all [ɔːl] 所有 [suǒ yǒu]

All these men are digging.

allow [əˈlaʊ] **allowing, allowed**
允许 [yǔn xǔ]

My father **allows** me to wear his shirt.

alone [əˈləʊn] 一个人 [yī gè rén]

Everyone has left. Mrs. Lee is **alone**.

along [əˈlɒŋ] 沿着 [yán zhe]

The cat is walking **along** the wall.

also [ˈɔːlsəʊ] 也 [yě]

Harry wants the book. Sandra **also** wants the book.

always [ˈɔːlweɪz]
总是 [zǒng shì]

Patrick **always** brushes his teeth in the morning.

am [eɪˈem] **was** 是 [shì]

I **am** ten years old. Last year I **was** nine.

ambulance [ˈæmbjʊləns]
救护车 [jiù hù chē]

An **ambulance** takes people to the hospital.

among [ˈəmʌŋ]
当中 [dāng zhōng]

Toby is hiding **among** the boxes. Can you see him?

anchor [ˈæŋkə] 锚 [máo]

An **anchor** stops a boat from moving. It is very heavy.

and [ənd] 和 [hé]

Omar has a bat. He also has a ball. Omar has a bat **and** a ball.

angry [ˈæŋgrɪ] 生气的 [shēng qì de]

Uncle Bob is **angry** with Dick. Dick broke his window.

animals [ˈænɪml]
动物 [dòng wù]
Here are some **animals**.

bat [bæt]
蝙蝠 [biān fú]

hippopotamus [ˌhɪpəˈpɒtəməs]
河马 [hé mǎ]

guinea pig [ˈgɪnɪ pɪg]
豚鼠 [tún shǔ]

deer [dɪr]
鹿 [lù]

ankle [ˈæŋkl] 踝 [huái]

Ali is holding his **ankle**.

answer [ˈɑ:nsə]
答案 [dá àn]

Betty knows the **answer**.

ant [ænt] 蚂蚁 [mǎ yǐ]

An **ant** is a small insect. It has six legs.

any [ˈenɪ] 任何 [rèn hé]

Mrs. Lee does not have **any** food. Her plate is empty.

anyone [ˈenɪwʌn]
任何人 [rèn hé rén]

Is **anyone** at home?

anything [ˈenɪθɪŋ]
任何东西 [rèn hé dōng xi]

Norman does not want to eat **anything**. He is full.

apple [ˈæpl] 苹果 [píng guǒ]

An **apple** is a fruit. **Apples** can be red, green or yellow.

aquarium [əˈkweərɪəm] 鱼缸 [yú gāng]

We keep fish in an **aquarium**. It has glass sides.

are [ɑ:] **were** 是 [shì]

There **are** two buns on the table. There **were** six buns a minute ago.

argue [ɑ:gju:] **arguing, argued** 争吵 [zhēng chǎo]

Sandra and Polly want the bicycle. They **argue** over it.

arm [ɑ:m] 手臂 [shǒu bì]

Your hand is at the end of your **arm**. You have two **arms**.

army [ˈɑ:mɪ] **armies** 军队 [jūn duì]

An **army** is a large group of soldiers.

around [əˈraʊnd] 绕着 [rào zhe]

Grandfather is chasing the monkey **around** the tree.

arrange [əˈreɪndʒ] **arranging, arranged** 整理 [zhěng lǐ]

Mother is **arranging** the flowers in a vase.

arrive [əˈraɪv] **arriving, arrived** 抵达 [dǐ dá]

The train will **arrive** soon.

arrow [ˈærəʊ] 箭 [jiàn]

Omar shoots his sharp **arrow**.

artist [ˈɑ:tɪst] 画家 [huà jiā]

An **artist** draws or paints.

ask [ɑ:sk] **asking, asked** 请求 [qǐng qiú]

Harry will **ask** his mother for some dessert.

asleep [əˈsliːp]
睡着了 [shuì zháo le]

The baby's eyes are closed. He is **asleep**.

assembly [əˈsemblɪ] **assemblies**
聚会 [jù huì]

The schoolchildren are in **assembly**.

astronaut [ˈæstrənɔːt]
太空人 [tài kōng rén]

An **astronaut** travels in a spaceship. He can go to the moon.

at [ət] 在 [zài]

Ali is waiting **at** the station. He is looking **at** the train.

attention [əˈtenʃn]
注意力 [zhù yì lì]

Rita is not paying **attention** to the teacher.

aunt [ɑːnt]
姑母、姨母 [gū mǔ, yí mǔ]

Your **aunt** is the sister of your father or mother.

awake [əˈweɪk] 醒来 [xǐng lái]

The baby's eyes are open. He is **awake**.

away [əˈweɪ] 离开 [lí kāi]

My friends are leaving. They are going **away** from my house.

baby [ˈbeɪbɪ] **babies**
婴儿 [yīng ér]

The **baby** is drinking some milk.

back [bæk] 背 [bèi]

Mrs. Lee is carrying a sack on her **back**.

bad [bæd] 坏的 [huài de]

Norman cannot eat his apple. It is **bad**.

badge [bædʒ] 徽章 [huī zhāng]

Harry has a **badge** on his cap.

bag [bæg] 袋、包 [dài, bāo]

You carry your school books in a **bag**.

bake [beɪk] **baking, baked**
烘烤 [hōng kǎo]

Grandmother **bakes** food in an oven.

balcony [ˈbælkənɪ] **balconies**
阳台 [yáng tái]

This house has a **balcony**.

ball [bɔ:l] 球 [qiú]

Dick is kicking a **ball**. Balls are round.

balloon [bəˈlu:n] 气球 [qì qiú]

Uncle Bill is blowing up a blue **balloon**.

banana [bəˈnɑ:nə]
香蕉 [xiāng jiāo]

A **banana** is a fruit with a yellow or green skin.

bang [bæŋ] **banging, banged**
砰 [pēng]

A **bang** is a sudden loud noise. The balloon burst with a big **bang**.

bank [bæŋk] 银行 [yín háng]

A **bank** is a safe place to keep money.

barbecue [ˈbɑ:bɪkju:]
烧烤 [shāo kǎo]

We are having a **barbecue** with chicken and beef.

bark [bɑ:k] **barking, barked**
吠 [fèi]

A **bark** is the noise a dog makes.

basket [ˈbɑ:skɪt] 篮子 [lán zi]

Mother carries her shopping in a **basket**.

bat [bæt] 球棒 [qiú bàng]

We use a **bat** to hit a ball.

beach [bi:tʃ] **beaches**
海滩 [hǎi tān]

A **beach** is found beside a sea.

bear [beə] 熊 [xióng]

A **bear** is an animal with brown or black fur.

bath [bɑ:θ]洗澡 [xǐ zǎo]

Patrick is having a **bath**.

beak [bi:k] 喙 [huì]

This bird has an orange **beak**.

beard [bɪəd] 胡子 [hú zi]

This king has a long black **beard**.

bathe [beɪð] **bathing, bathed**
戏水 [xì shuǐ]

We are **bathing** in the sea.

bean [bi:n] 豆 [dòu]

A **bean** is a vegetable.

beat [bi:t] **beating, beat** 打 [dǎ]

The drummer is **beating** his drum.

bathroom [bɑ:θru:m]
浴室 [yù shì]

Toby will take a bath in the **bathroom**.

bean sprout [bi:n spraʊt]
豆芽 [dòu yá]

Sally likes to eat **bean sprouts**. **Bean sprouts** are a vegetable.

beautiful [ˈbju:tɪfl]
美丽的 [měi lì de]

These flowers are **beautiful**. They are lovely to look at.

bed [bed] 床 [chuáng]

A **bed** is a place to sleep or rest.

bedroom [bedru:m]
睡房 [shuì fáng]

You sleep in your **bedroom**.

bee [bi:] 蜜蜂 [mì fēng]

A **bee** is an insect. It makes honey.

beef [bi:f] 牛肉 [niú ròu]

Beef is the meat from a cow.

beetle [ˈbi:tl]
甲虫 [jiǎ chóng]

A **beetle** is an insect.

before [bɪˈfɔ:]
之前 [zhī qián]

You take off your shoes **before** you enter a bathtub.

begin [bɪˈgɪn] **beginning, began**
开始 [kāi shǐ]

The play will **begin** soon. We are waiting for it to start.

behind [bɪˈhaɪnd]
后面 [hòu mian]

Harry is walking **behind** his dog.

bell [bel] 铃 [líng]

The woman rings the **bell**.

belong [bɪˈlɒŋ] **belonging, belonged**
属于 [shǔ yú]

The dog has a bone. It **belongs** to him.

below [bɪˈləʊ] 下面 [xià mian]

I can see people **below** me.

belt [belt]
腰带、皮带 [yāo dài, pí dài]

Norman wears a black **belt**.

bench [bentʃ] **benches**
长椅 [cháng yǐ]

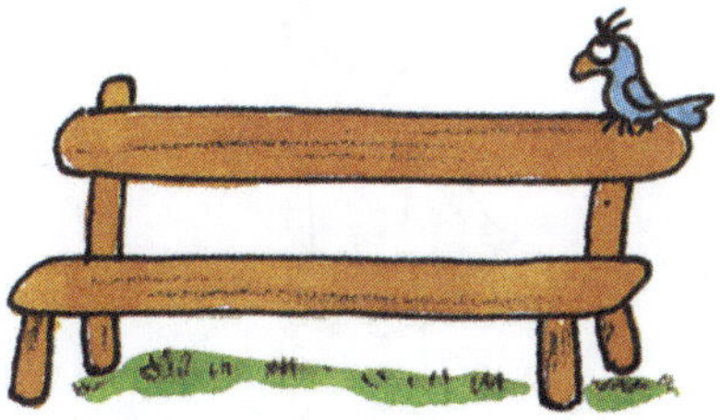

A **bench** is a long seat.

beside [bɪˈsaɪd]
旁边 [páng biān]

The chair is **beside** the door.

between [bɪˈtwiːn] 中间
[zhōng jiān]

Harry is sitting **between** his father and his mother.

bicycle [ˈbaɪsɪkl]
自行车 [zì xíng chē]

A **bicycle** has two wheels.

big [bɪg] 大的 [dà de]

An elephant is **big**.
A mouse is not **big**.

bird [bɜːd] 鸟 [niǎo]

pigeon [ˈpɪdʒɪn]
鸽子[gē zi]

woodpecker
[wʊdˈpekə]
啄木鸟
[zhuó mù niǎo]

sparrow
[ˈspærəʊ]
麻雀 [má què]

crow [krəʊ]
乌鸦 [wū yā]

A **bird** has feathers. Most **birds** fly.

birthday [ˈbɜːθdeɪ]
生日 [shēng rì]

It is my **birthday** today. My brother says, "Happy **Birthday**!"

biscuit [ˈbɪskɪt]
饼干 [bǐng gān]

Many children love to eat **biscuits**.

black [blæk]
黑色的 [hēi sè de]

This **black** dog is chasing the **black** cat.

blackboard [blækbɔːd]
黑板 [hēi bǎn]

Omar writes his name on the **blackboard**.

blank [blæŋk]
空白的 [kōng bái de]

This paper is **blank**. There is no writing on it.

blanket [blæŋkɪt] 毛毯 [máo tǎn]

A **blanket** is a warm cover. We put a **blanket** on a bed.

blind [blaɪnd] 瞎的 [xiā de]

This woman is **blind**. She cannot see.

blocks [blɒkes] 积木 [jī mù]

Rita is building a tower with **blocks**.

blouse [blaʊz]
女装衬衫 [nǚ zhuāng chèn shān]

Sandra does not like her sister's **blouse**.

blow [bləʊ] **blowing, blew**
吹 [chuī]

The wind **blows** the trees.

blue [bluː] 蓝色的 [lán sè de]

Uncle Bob drives a **blue** car.

boat [bəʊt] 船 [chuán]

A **boat** floats on the water.

body [ˈbɒdɪ] **bodies**
身体 [shēn tǐ]

You should take care of your **body**.

bone [bəʊn] 骨头 [gǔ tou]

A dog likes to have a **bone**. A **bone** is hard.

book [bʊk] 书 [shū]

Mother reads a **book** to me.

borrow [ˈbɒrəʊ] **borrowing, borrowed** 借 [jiè]

I **borrow** a pen from my sister. I will return it later.

both [bəʊθ] 两者 [liǎng zhě]

Father will buy bananas and biscuits.
He will buy them **both**.

bottle [ˈbɒtl]瓶子 [píng zi]

Toby pours a drink from the **bottle**.

bottom [ˈbɒtəm] 底 [dǐ]

Patrick is at the top of the ladder.
The dog is at the **bottom**.

bow [bəʊ] 蝴蝶结 [hú dié jié]

Mrs. Lee has a **bow** in her hair.

bow [baʊ] **bowing, bowed**
鞠躬 [jū gōng]

The man **bows** to the lady.

bowl [bəʊl] 碗 [wǎn]

Ali has some soup in his **bowl**.

box [bɒks] **boxes** 盒子 [hé zi]

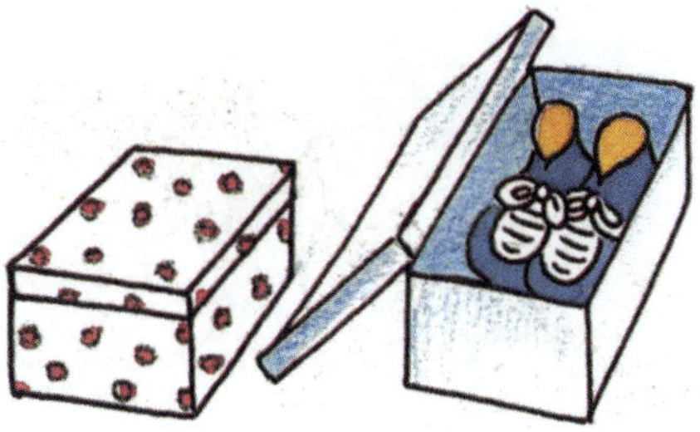

These new shoes are in a **box**.

boy [bɔɪ] 男孩 [nán hái]

These **boys** are playing soccer.

branch [brɑ:ntʃ] **branches**
树枝 [shù zhī]

A **branch** is part of a tree.
Branches grow from the trunk.

bread [bred] 面包 [miàn bāo]

This shop sells lots of **bread**.
Bread is made from flour.

break [breɪk] **breaking, broke**
打破 [dǎ pò]

Glass will **break** if you drop it.

breakfast [ˈbrekfəst]
早餐 [zǎo cān]

We eat **breakfast** in the morning.

breath [breθ] 呼吸 [hū xī]

Norman takes a deep **breath**.

brick [brɪk] 砖 [zhuān]

This man is building a wall with **bricks**.

bridge [brɪdʒ] 桥 [qiáo]

Uncle Tom is crossing the **bridge**.

bring [brɪŋ] **bringing, brought**
拿 [ná]

Grandmother will **bring** the food to the table.

broom [bru:m] 扫帚 [sào zhǒu]

We sweep the floor with a **broom**.

brown [braʊn]
褐色的 [hè sè de]

Omar is wearing a **brown** shirt and **brown** trousers.

brush [brʌʃ] 刷子 [shuā zi]

Mother scrubs the floor with a **brush**.

bubble [ˈbʌbl] 泡泡 [pào pao]

A **bubble** is round and filled with air. It is fun to blow **bubbles**.

bucket [ˈbʌkɪt] 桶子 [tǒng zi]

The worker carries sand in a **bucket**.

buffalo [ˈbʌfələʊ] **buffaloes**
水牛 [shuǐ niú]

A **buffalo** is a big, strong animal. **Buffaloes** have long curved horns.

build [bɪld] **building, built**
筑盖 [zhù gài]

We **built** a house with our blocks.

building [bɪldɪŋ] 建筑物 [jiàn zhù wù]

Here are some **buildings**.

school [skuːl]
学校 [xué xiào]

fire station [ˈfaɪə ˈsteɪʃn]
消防局 [xiāo fáng jú]

house [haʊs]
房屋 [fáng wū]

cinema [ˈsɪnəmaː]
影院 [yǐng yuàn]

shop [ʃɒp]
商店 [shāng diàn]

factory [ˈfæktərɪ]
工厂 [gōng chǎng]

bun [bʌn]
小圆面包 [xiǎo yuán miàn bāo]

Sandra is eating a **bun**.

burn [bɜːn] **burning, burned**
烧 [shāo]

The wood is **burning**.

bus [bʌs] **buses**
公共汽车 [gōng gòng qì chē]

The boy wants to catch the **bus**.
A **bus** can carry many people.

bus stop [bʌn stɒp]
公共汽车车站
[gōng gòng qì chē chē zhàn]

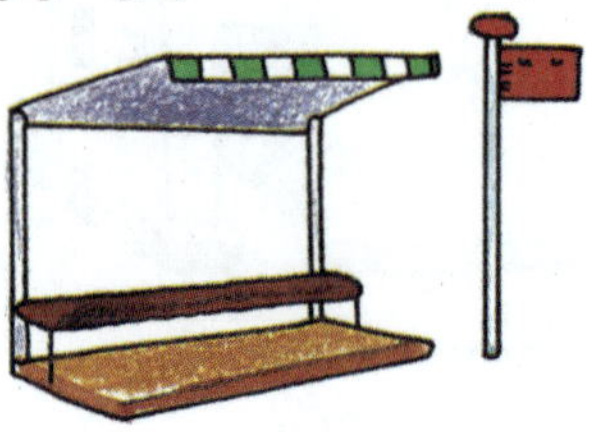

People get on and off at the **bus stop**.

busy [ˈbɪzɪ]
忙碌的 [máng lù de]

Mrs. Lee has a lot of work to do.
She is **busy**.

but [bʌt]
但是 [dàn shì]

A giraffe is tall **but** a duck is short.

butcher [ˈbʊtʃə]
肉贩 [ròu fàn]

Mother goes to the **butcher** to buy meat.

butter [ˈbʌtə]
牛油 [niú yóu]

We spread **butter** on bread.

butterfly [ˈbʌtəflaɪ] **butterflies**
蝴蝶 [hú dié]

A **butterfly** is an insect.
It has pretty wings.

button [ˈbʌtn] **buttoning, buttoned** 钮扣 [niǔ kòu]

My shirt has five **buttons**.
I can **button** it myself.

buy [baɪ] **buying, bought**
买 [mǎi]

We **buy** things with money.

by [baɪ] 旁边 [páng biān]

Patrick is standing **by** the bus stop. He will go to school **by** bus.

calf [kɑ:f] **calves**
[xiǎo niú] 小牛

A **calf** is a young cow.

can [kæn] **could**
会、能 [huì, néng]

I know how to swim. I **can** swim now, but I **could** not swim last month.

cage [keɪdʒ] 笼子 [lǒng zi]

These monkeys are in their **cage**.

call [kɔ:l] **calling, called**
叫 [jiào]

Sandra is **calling** to her dog.

canary [kəˈneərɪ] **canaries**
金丝雀 [jīn sī què]

A **canary** is a small yellow bird. It sings sweetly.

cake [keɪk] 蛋糕 [dàn gāo]

A **cake** is sweet. It is made from flour, eggs, butter and sugar.

camera [ˈkæmərə]
照相机 [zhào xiàng jī]

We take photographs with a **camera**.

candle [ˈkændl]
蜡烛 [là zhú]

There is only one **candle** on the cake.

calendar [ˈkælɪndə] 日历 [rì lì]

We look at a **calendar** to find the date.

camp [kæmp] 露营 [lù yíng]

There are two tents in this **camp**.

canteen [kænˈti:n]
食堂 [shí táng]

We buy food and drink at the school **canteen.**

cap [kæp] 便帽 [biàn mào]

Do you like my new red **cap**?

car [kɑ:] 汽车 [qì chē]

Father wants to buy the big **car**.

card [kɑ:d] 卡 [kǎ]

Sally gave me a **card.** We are playing games with **cards** on my birthday.

careful [ˈkeəfl]
小心的 [xiǎo xīn de]

I am **careful**. I will not drop the tray.

careless [ˈkeəlɪs]
大意的 [dà yì de]

Dick is **careless**. He has dropped the plates.

carpenter [ˈkɑ:pəntə]
木匠 [mù jiang]

A **carpenter** makes things out of wood.

carpet [ˈkɑ:pɪt] 地毯 [dì tǎn]

A **carpet** is used to cover the floor.

carrot [ˈkærət]
红萝卜 [hóng luó bo]

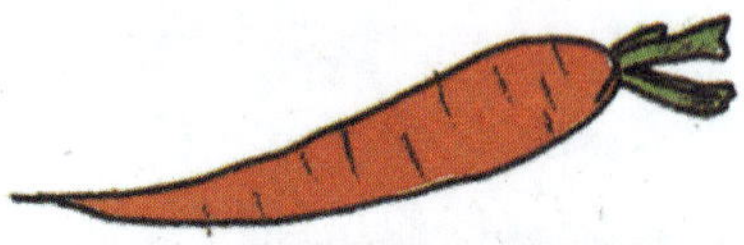

A **carrot** is a vegetable. It grows underground.

carry [ˈkærɪ] **carrying, carried**
抱 [bào]

Sandra can **carry** the puppy home.

cart [kɑ:t] 大车 [dà chē]

The ox is pulling the **cart** along the road.

cartoon [kɑ:ˈtu:n]
卡通 [kǎ tōng]

Harry likes to watch **cartoons** on television.

cat [kæt] 猫 [māo]

This **cat** is eating.

catch [kætʃ] **catching, caught**
接 [jiē]

Toby tried to **catch** the ball. Rita **caught** it.

caterpillar [ˈkætəpɪlə]
毛虫 [máo chóng]

A **caterpillar** has many legs. It will turn into a butterfly.

cave [keɪv] 山洞 [shān dòng]

A **cave** is a hole in the mountain/hill/cliff.
Bears live in this **cave**.

ceiling [ˈsiːlɪŋ]
天花板 [tiān huā bǎn]

Father is painting the **ceiling** of the room.

cent [sent] 分 [fēn]

A **cent** is a coin. There are one hundred **cents** in a dollar.

centre [ˈsentə]
中心 [zhōng xīn]

Betty is in the **centre** of the circle.

chair [tʃeə] 椅子 [yǐ zi]

Is the **chair** too big for Dick?

chalk [tʃɔːk] 粉笔 [fěn bǐ]

Ali likes to draw with **chalk**.

change [tʃeɪndʒ] **changing, changed** 换 [huàn]

The children **changed** their clothes after school.

chase [tʃeɪs] **chasing, chased**
追捕 [zhuī bǔ]

The policeman **chases** after the thief.

cheek [tʃiːk] 面颊 [miàn jiá]

Rita is pointing at her **cheeks**.

cheese [tʃi:z] 干酪 [gān lào]

Cheese is a food made from milk.

chest [tʃest] 胸部 [xiōng bù]

Dick is beating his **chest**.

chick [tʃɪk] 小鸡 [xiǎo jī]

A **chick** is a baby hen. **Chicks** are yellow.

child [tʃaɪld] **children**
儿童 [ér tóng]

A **child** is a boy or a girl who is not yet grown up. These **children** are playing.

chilli [ˈtʃɪlɪ] **chillies** 辣椒 [là jiāo]

A **chilli** can be red or green. **Chillies** make food taste hot.

chocolate [ˈtʃɒklət]
巧克力 [qiǎo kè lì]

Chocolate is brown and sweet. Mmm, that **chocolate** looks good.

choose [tʃu:z] **choosing, chose**
选择 [xuǎn zé]

Sally is trying to **choose** a dress.

chop [tʃɒp] **chopping, chopped**
砍、劈 [kǎn, pī]

Mr. Smiley **chops** the wood.

chopsticks [ˈtʃɒpstɪk]
筷子 [kuài zi]

The Chinese usually eat with **chopsticks**.

church [ˈtʃɜ:t] **churches**
教堂 [jiào táng]

Many people go to **church** every Sunday.

circle [ˈsɜ:kl] 圈 [quān]

Patrick has drawn a **circle** around the answer.

circus [ˈsɜːkəs]
马戏团 [mǎ xì tuán]

A **circus** is a big show. Polly loves going to the **circus**.

claw [klɔː] 爪 [zhǎo]

Some birds and animals have **claws** on their feet.

climb [klaɪm] **climbing, climbed**
爬 [pá]

Do you like to **climb** trees?

city [ˈsɪtɪ] **cities**
城市 [chéng shì]

A **city** is a very large town.

clean [kliːn]
干净的 [gān jìng de]

Toby has **clean** hands. His feet are not **clean**.

clinic [ˈklɪnɪk]
诊所 [zhěn suǒ]

Norman is ill. He goes to the **clinic** to see the doctor.

clap [klæp] **clapping, clapped**
鼓掌 [gǔ zhǎng]

They **clap** their hands when the play ends.

clear [klɪə] 清澈 [qīng chè]

The water is **clear**. I can see my feet through it.

clock [klɒk] 时钟 [shí zhōng]

A **clock** tells us what time it is.

class [klɑ:s] **classes**
班 [bān]

There are only six pupils in this **class**.

clever [ˈklevə]
聪明的 [cōng míng de]

Betty is **clever**. Her answers are all correct.

close [kləʊs] **closing, closed**
关 [guān]

Mother asked me to **close** the door.

clothes [kləʊð] 衣物 [yī wù]

Clothes are things we wear.

shorts [ʃɔ:ts]
短裤 [duǎn kù]

shoes [ʃu:z]
鞋 [xié]

shirt [ʃɜ:t]
衬衫 [chèn shān]

T-shirt [ti:ʃɜ:t]
汗衫 [hán shān]

socks [sɒkz]
短袜 [duǎn wà]

tie [tai]
领带 [lǐng dài]

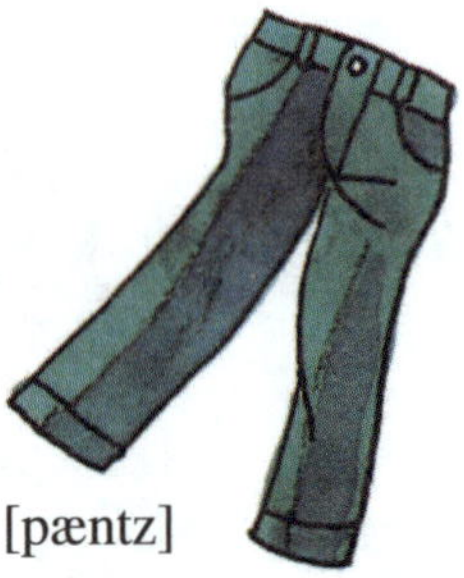

pants [pæntz]
长裤 [cháng kù]

pyjamas [pɪˈʒa:məz]
睡衣 [shuì yī]

cap [kæp]
帽 [mào]

dress [dres]
裙 [qún]

raincoat [ˈreɪnkəʊt]
雨衣 [yǔ yī]

skirt [skɜ:t]
短裙 [duǎn qún]

blouse [blaʊz]
女装衬衫
[nǚ zhuāng
chèn shān]

panties
[ˈpæntɪz]
内裤 [nèi kù]

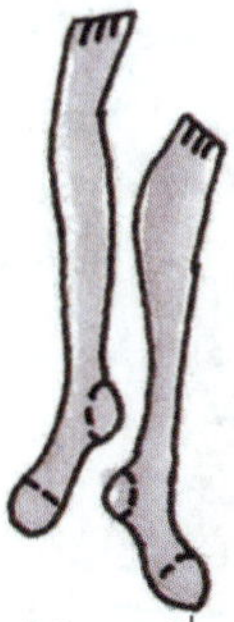

stockings [ˈstɒkɪŋz]
长袜 [cháng wà]

sandals
[sændlz]
凉鞋 [liáng xié]

hat [hæt]
帽子 [mào zi]

nightdress [ˈnaɪtdres]
女装睡衣 [nǚ zhuāng shuì yī]

cloud [klaʊd] 云 [yún]

I see a **cloud** in the sky. **Clouds** bring rain.

clown [klaʊn] 小丑 [xiǎo chǒu]

A **clown** tries to make us laugh. He wears funny clothes.

coast [kəʊst] 海岸 [hǎi àn]

The **coast** is the land by the sea.

cobra [ˈkəʊbrə]
眼镜蛇 [yǎn jìng shé]

A **cobra** is a dangerous snake.

cobweb [ˈkɒbweb]
蜘蛛网 [zhī zhū wǎng]

A spider makes a **cobweb** to catch insects.

cock [kɒk] 公鸡 [gōng jī]

A **cock** is a bird. It makes a lot of noise when the sun rises.

cockroach [ˈkɒkrəʊtʃ]
cockroaches 蟑螂 [zhāng láng]

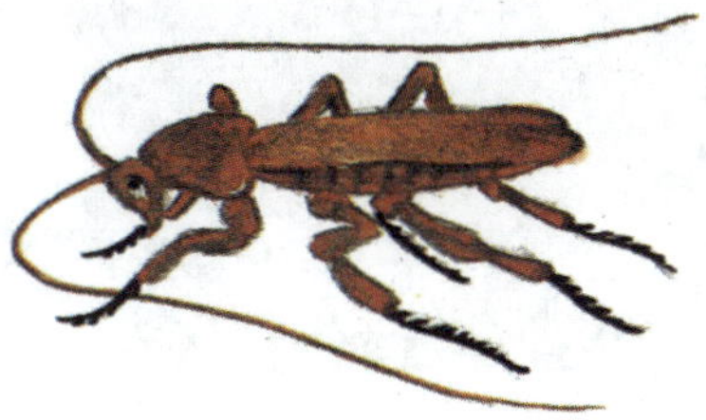

A **cockroach** is a dark brown insect.

coconut [ˈkəʊkənʌt]
椰子 [yē zi]

Coconuts grow on trees. A **coconut** has a hard brown shell.

coffee [ˈkɒfɪ] 咖啡 [kā fēi]

Mrs. Lee drinks **coffee** at breakfast time.

coin [kɔɪn] 硬币 [yìng bì]

A **coin** is a piece of money. Patrick collects **coins**.

cold [kəʊld] 冷的 [lěng de]

The water is too **cold** for Sandra.

collect [kəˈlekt] **collecting, collected** 拾 [shí]

Sally **collects** many seashells. Mother **collects** me from school every day.

colour [ˈkʌlə] 颜色 [yán sè]

A rainbow has seven **colours**.

comb [kəʊm] 梳子 [shū zi]

Sandra's **comb** is red.

come [kʌm] **coming, came**
来 [lái]

Sandra's mother is telling her to **come** home.

cook [kʊk] 厨子 [chú zi]

Sally wants to be a good **cook**.

count [kaʊnt] **counting, counted**
数一数 [shǔ yī shǔ]

How many flowers are there? **Count** them.

compare [kəmˈpeə] **comparing, compared** 比较 [bǐ jiào]

They **compare** shoes. His are large, but hers are small.

corner [ˈkɔːnə]
角落 [jiǎo luò]

There is a tree in the **corner** of the garden. This table has sharp **corners**.

country [ˈkʌntrɪ] **countries**
国家 [guó jiā]

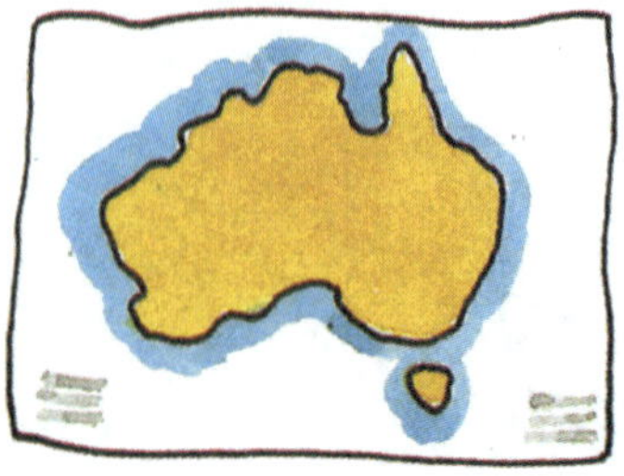

This map shows the **country** of Australia.

cone [kəʊn] 圆锥 [yuán zhuī]

A **cone** is a shape.
This hat is **cone**-shaped.

correct [kəˈrekt]
正确的 [zhèng què de]

Betty has given the **correct** answers.

cover [ˈkʌvə] **covering, covered**
盖 [gài]

Mother **covers** Sandra with a blanket.

continue [kənˈtɪnjuː] **continuing, continued** 继续 [jì xù]

Omar has stopped playing.
Ali will **continue** for a while.

cot [kɒt] 婴儿床 [yīng ér chuáng]

A baby sleeps in a **cot**.

cow [kaʊ] 牛 [niú]

A **cow** is an animal.
Cows give us milk.

cowboy [ˈkaʊbɔɪ]
牧童 [mù tóng]

A **cowboy** rides a horse and looks after cows and bulls.

crab [kræb] 蟹 [xiè]

A **crab** is an animal with a hard shell. It has two claws and eight legs.

crane [kreɪn]
起重机 [qǐ zhòng jī]

A **crane** is a machine which lifts things.

crash [kræʃ]
哗啦一声 [huā lā yī shēng]

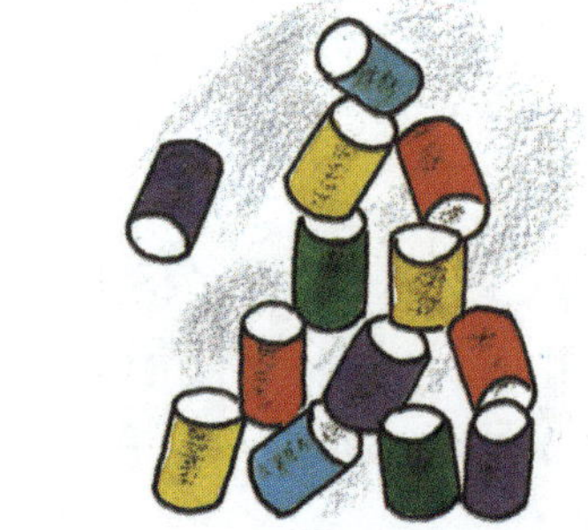

Crash! The cans fell to the floor.

crawl [krɔːl] **crawling, crawled**
爬行 [pá xíng]

A baby **crawls** on his hands and knees.

crayon [ˈkreɪən] 蜡笔 [là bǐ]

Rita is drawing with a blue **crayon**.

croak [krəʊk]
呱呱叫 [guā guā jiào]

A **croak** is the noise a frog makes.

crocodile [ˈkrɒkədaɪl]
鳄鱼 [è yú]

A **crocodile** is a large animal that lives in the water.

crooked [ˈkrʊkɪd]
弯曲的 [wān qū de]

This line is **crooked**. It is not straight.

cross [krɒs] **crossing, crossed**
过 [guò]

The children can **cross** the road now.

crow [krəʊ] 乌鸦 [wū yā]

A **crow** is a black bird. **Crows** are noisy.

crowd [kraʊd] 人群 [rén qún]

A **crowd** is a lot of people all together in one place.

cry [kraɪ] **crying, cried**
哭 [kū]

The baby is **crying** because he is hungry.

cucumber [ˈkju:kʌmbə]
黄瓜 [huáng gua]

A **cucumber** is a vegetable. **Cucumbers** are green.

cup [kʌp] 杯 [bēi]

Mother pours orange juice into her **cup**.

cupboard [ˈkʌbəd]
碗柜 [wǎn guì]

Father will mend the **cupboard**.

curry [ˈkʌrɪ] 咖喱 [gā lí]

Your mouth feels hot when you eat **curry**.

cut [kʌt] **cutting, cut**
剪 [jiǎn]

Sally will **cut** the paper with her scissors.

cycle [ˈsaɪkl] **cycling, cycled**
骑自行车 [qí zì xíng chē]

Brian is **cycling** in the park.

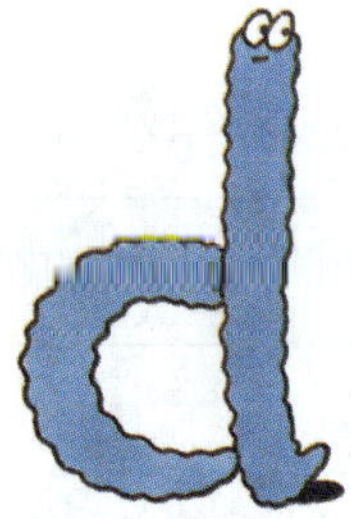

dance [dɑ:ns] **dancing, danced**
跳舞 [tiào wǔ]

Rita and Ali are **dancing** to the music.

danger [ˈdeɪndʒə]
危险 [wēi xiǎn]

This sign warns you of **danger**. You must not go in.

dark [dɑ:k] 深的 [shēn de]

It is **dark** at night.

date [deɪt] 日期 [rì qī]

What is the **date** today? It is the 5th of May.

day [deɪ] 白天 [bái tiān]

It is **day** when it is light outside. Do you know the **days** of the week?

dead [ded] 已死的 [yǐ sǐ de]

The bird is **dead**. It is not breathing.

deaf [def] 聋的 [lóng de]

Grandfather is **deaf**. He cannot hear.

deep [diːp] 深的 [shēn de]

The water is **deep**. It is a long way to the bottom of the pool.

deer [dɪə] **deer**
鹿 [lù]

A **deer** is an animal. **Deer** eat grass and vegetables.

dentist [ˈdentɪst]
牙医 [yá yī]

A **dentist** looks after your teeth.

desk [desk]
桌子 [zhuō zi]

We sit at our **desks** to write.

different [ˈdɪfrənt]
不同的 [bù tóng de]

A leopard is **different** from a tiger. It is not like a tiger.

dig [dɪɡ] **digging, dug**
挖 [wā]

Uncle Bill is **digging** a hole.

dining room [dɪnɪŋ rʊm]
饭厅 [fàn tīng]

A **dining room** is the place in which you eat your meals.

dinner
[ˈdɪnə] 晚餐 [wǎn cān]

We eat **dinner** in the evening.

dirty
[ˈdɜːtɪ]
肮脏的 [āng zāng de]

Dick is **dirty**. He is not clean.

dive
[daɪv] **diving, dived**
跳水 [tiào shuǐ]

Patrick can **dive** into the swimming pool.

divide
[dɪˈvaɪd] **dividing, divided**
分 [fēn]

Mrs. Lee **divides** the cake into four pieces.

do
[duː] **doing, did**
做 [zuò]

I **do** my homework when I come home from school. Mother **does** the cooking. She **did** the washing this morning.

doctor
[ˈdɒktə] 医生 [yī shēng]

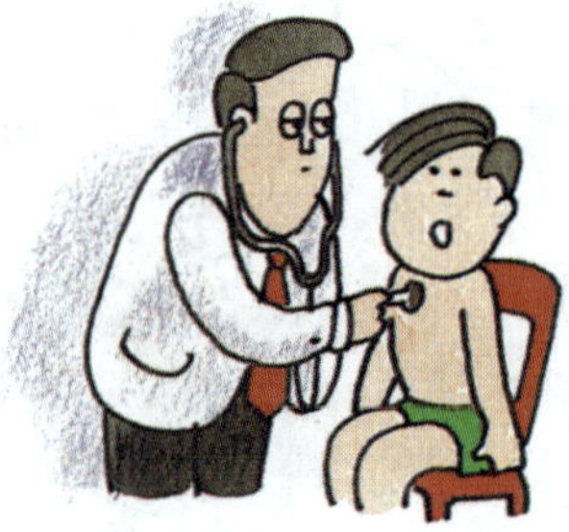

A **doctor** looks after sick people.

dog
[dɒg] 狗 [gǒu]

The **dog** is an animal with four legs.
Dogs bark.

doll
[dɒl]
洋娃娃 [yáng wá wa]

Sandra is playing with her **doll**.

dollar
[ˈdɒlə] 元 [yuán]

Each week Harry saves one **dollar**. He now has five **dollars**.

donkey
[ˈdɒŋkɪ] 驴 [lǘ]

A **donkey** is an animal with long ears.

door [dɔː] 门 [mén]

We go in and out of a house through **doors**. This **door** is open.

dot [dɒt] 点 [diǎn]

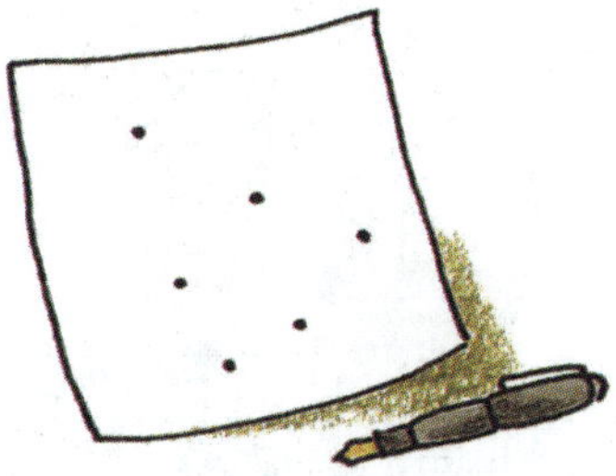

A **dot** is a small mark. There are six **dots** on the paper.

down [daʊn] 下去 [xià qu]

Dick goes **down** the slide.

downstairs [ˈdaʊnˈsteəz] 下楼 [xià lóu]

Sally is coming **downstairs**.

dragonfly [ˈdræɡənflaɪ] **dragonflies** 蜻蜓 [qīng tíng]

A **dragonfly** is an insect. Many **dragonflies** have bright colours on their bodies.

drain [dreɪn] 沟渠 [gōu qú]

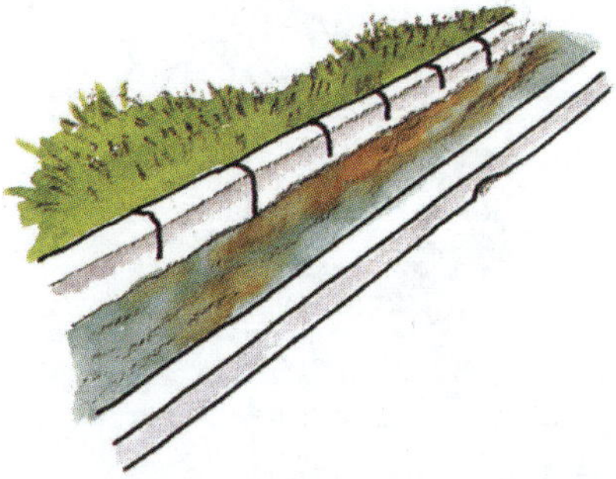

A **drain** carries water away.

draw [drɔː] **drawing, drew** 画 [huà]

I will **draw** my father.

drawer [ˈdrɔː] 抽屉 [chōu ti]

Toby keeps his pen in the **drawer**.

dream [driːm] 做梦 [zuò mèng]

Sally is asleep. She is having a **dream**.

dress [dres] **dresses** 裙子 [qún zi]

Rita wants to wear her red **dress**.

drink [drɪŋk] 饮品 [yǐn pǐn]

Which **drink** would you like?

drive [draɪv] **driving, drove**
驾驶 [jià shǐ]

This man **drives** a bus.

driver [ˈdraɪvə] 司机 [sī jī]

My uncle is a taxi **driver**. He drives a taxi.

drop [drɒp] **dropping, dropped**
掉 [diào]

Mrs. Lee **drops** the vase.

drum [drʌm] 鼓 [gǔ]

Toby likes to beat his **drum**.

dry [draɪ] 干的 [gān de]

The clothes are **dry**. Mother is collecting them.

duck [dʌk] 鸭 [yā]

A **duck** is a bird. **Ducks** can swim and fly.

duckling [ˈdʌklɪŋ]
小鸭 [xiǎo yā]

A **duckling** is a young duck.

during [ˈdjʊərɪŋ]
在……期间 [zài…qī jiān]

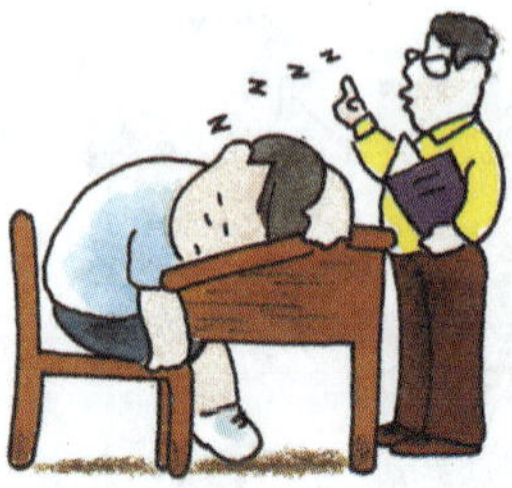

Norman fell asleep **during** a lesson.

dust [dʌst] 灰尘 [huī chén]

There is a lot of **dust** in the flat.

dustbin [ˈdʌstbɪn]
垃圾桶 [lā jī tǒng]

You should throw litter into the **dustbin**.

duster [ˈdʌstə]
粉笔刷 [fěn bǐ shuā]

The teacher is wiping the blackboard with a **duster**.

dwarf [dwɔːf] 矮子 [ǎi zi]

A **dwarf** is a very small person. There are **dwarfs** in some fairy tales.

early [ˈɜːlɪ] 早的 [zǎo de]

Uncle Bob is **early**. The shop is not open yet.

egg [eg] 鸡蛋 [jī dàn]

Birds lay **eggs**. Baby birds hatch from the **eggs**.

each [iːtʃ] 每个 [měi gè]

Each child wears a different hat.

earth [ɜːθ] 地球 [dì qiú]

The **earth** is big and round. Dogs like to dig in the **earth**.

elbow [ˈelbəʊ] 肘 [zhǒu]

Your **elbow** is where your arm bends.

eagle [ˈiːgl] 鹰 [yīng]

An **eagle** is a large bird. It eats small animals and birds.

earthquake [ˈɜːθkweɪk] 地震 [dì zhèn]

During an **earthquake** the earth moves and cracks.

electricity [ɪˈlekˈtrɪsətɪ] 电力 [diàn lì]

electric lamp
[ɪˈlektrɪk læmp]
电灯 [diàn dēng]

electric iron
[ɪˈlektrɪk ˈaɪən]
熨斗 [yùn dǒu]

television
[ˈtelɪvɪʒn]
电视机 [diàn shì jī]

electric fan
[ɪˈlektrɪk fæn]
风扇 [fēng shàn]

Electricity makes many things work.

ear [ɪə] 耳朵 [ěr duo]

You hear with your **ears**.

eat [iːt] eating, ate 吃 [chī]

Norman **eats** breakfast at seven o'clock.

elephant [ˈelɪfənt] 象 [xiàng]

An **elephant** is a large animal with a long trunk.

elf [elf] **elves**
小精灵 [xiǎo jīng líng]

An **elf** is a creature found in fantasy stories. **Elves** play tricks on people.

empty [ˈemptɪ]
空的 [kōng de]

Norman's bowl is **empty**. There is nothing in it.

engine [ˈendʒɪn]
引擎 [yǐn qíng]

The car will not go. Father must repair the **engine**.

enjoy [ɪnˈdʒɔɪ] **enjoying, enjoyed**
喜欢 [xǐ huan]

We **enjoy** swimming. We like it very much.

enough [ɪˈnʌf] 够 [gòu]

Tim is tall **enough** to reach the book.

enter [ˈentə] **entering, entered**
[jìn] 进

Our teacher **enters** our classroom.

entrance [ˈentrəns]
入口 [rù kǒu]

An **entrance** is the way into a place or a building.

envelope [ˈenvələʊp]
信封 [xìn fēng]

You put a letter in an **envelope**.

equal [ˈiːkwəl]
相同的 [xiāng tóng de]

Brian and Harry have an **equal** number of marbles.

eraser [ɪˈreɪzə]
橡皮 [xiàng pí]

Rita uses an **eraser** to rub out the word.

escalator [ˈeskəleɪtə]
自动扶梯 [zì dòng fú tī]

An **escalator** is a moving staircase.

estate [ɪˈsteɪt]
住宅区 [zhù zhái qū]

I live on an **estate**. There are many flats on my **estate**.

evening [ˈiːvnɪŋ]
傍晚 [bàng wǎn]

Evening is the time between day and night.

every [ˈevrɪ]
每一个 [měi yī gè]

There are flowers on **every** table.

exercise [ˈeksəsaɪz]
运动 [yùn dòng]

They are doing some **exercise**.

exit [ˈeksɪt] 出口 [chū kǒu]

An **exit** is the way out of a building.

eye [aɪ] 眼睛 [yǎn jing]

You see with your **eyes**. Everyone has two **eyes**.

face [feɪs] 脸 [liǎn]

Rita can see her **face** in the mirror.

factory [ˈfæktərɪ] **factories**
工厂 [gōng chǎng]

A **factory** is a building where things are made.

fairy [ˈfeərɪ] **fairies**
仙女 [xiān nǚ]

I like to read **fairy** tales. **Fairies** can do magic things.

fall [fɔːl] **falling, fell** 跌 [diē]

Toby is **falling** off his chair.

family [ˈfæməlɪ] **families**
家庭 [jiā tíng]

This is a photograph of Sandra's **family**.

fan [fæn]
风扇 [fēng shàn]

A **fan** makes us feel cool.

farm [fɑːm] 农场 [nóng chǎng]

A **farm** is a place for growing food and keeping animals.

farmer [fɑːmə] 农夫 [nóng fū]

A **farmer** looks after the plants and animals on his farm.

fast [fɑːst] 快的 [kuài de]

This car is going very **fast**.

fat [fæt] 胖的 [pàng de]

Norman is **fat**. He eats too much.

feather [ˈfeðə] 羽毛 [yǔ máo]

A **feather** is light and soft. Birds have **feathers**.

feed [fiːd] **feeding, fed** 喂 [wèi]

Sally **feeds** the cat every day. She gives it milk and fish to eat.

feel [fiːl] **feeling, felt**
感到 [gǎn dào]

I **feel** happy when I play with my dog. My dog's fur **feels** soft.

fence [fens] 围墙 [wéi qiáng]

Mr. Smiley is putting a **fence** around his garden.

field [fi:ld] 田野 [tián yě]

A **field** is a large piece of open ground. There are cows in this **field**.

film [fɪlm]
电影 [diàn yǐng]

Do you like to watch **films**? This **film** is about cowboys.

fern [fɜ:n]
羊齿植物 [yáng chǐ zhí wù]

A **fern** is a plant.

fierce [fɪəs]
凶恶的 [xiōng è de]

This lion looks very **fierce**. I will not go near it.

find [faɪnd] **finding, found**
找 [zhǎo]

Rita cannot **find** her pen. She is looking for it.

ferry [ˈferɪ] **ferries**
渡轮 [dù lún]

A **ferry** is a boat. This **ferry** is carrying people to the island.

fight [faɪt] 打架 [dǎ jià]

The dogs are having a **fight**.

fill [fɪl] **filling, filled**
装满 [zhuāng mǎn]

Harry will **fill** the tank with water.

finger [ˈfɪŋgə] 手指 [shǒu zhǐ]

Mrs. Lee has cut her **finger**.

fingernail [ˈfɪŋgəneɪl]
指甲 [zhǐ jia]

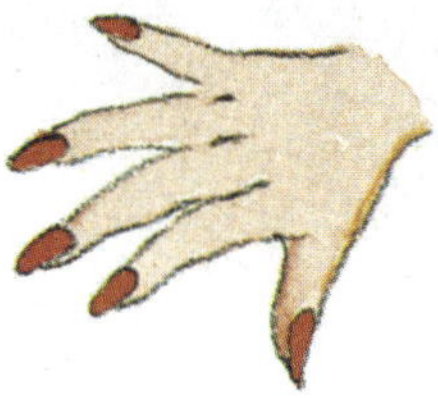

Mother paints her **fingernails** red.

finish [ˈfɪnɪʃ] **finishing, finished**
完成 [wán chéng]

Tim cannot **finish** the cakes.

fire [ˈfaɪə] 火 [huǒ]

A **fire** is very hot. We can cook food over a **fire**.

fire engine [ˈfaɪə ˈendʒɪn]
消防车 [xiāo fáng chē]

A **fire engine** is used to put out big fires.

fireman [ˈfaɪəmən] **firemen**
消防队员 [xiāo fáng duì yuán]

A **fire officer** puts out fires.

fish [fɪʃ] 鱼 [yú]

Fish live in water.

fisherman [ˈfɪʃəmən]
fishermen 渔夫 [yú fū]

A **fisherman** catches fish.

flag [flæg] 旗子 [ˈqí zi]

A **flag** is made of cloth and it hangs on a pole.

flat [flæt] 平的 [píng de]
公寓 [gōng yù]

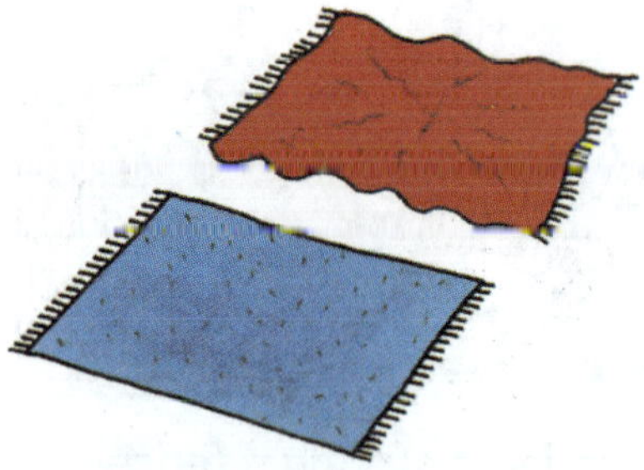

The blue carpet lies **flat** on the floor. The red one is not **flat**.

We live in this block of **flats.** Our **flat** is on the sixth floor.

float [fləʊt] **floating, floated**
飘、浮 [piāo, fú]

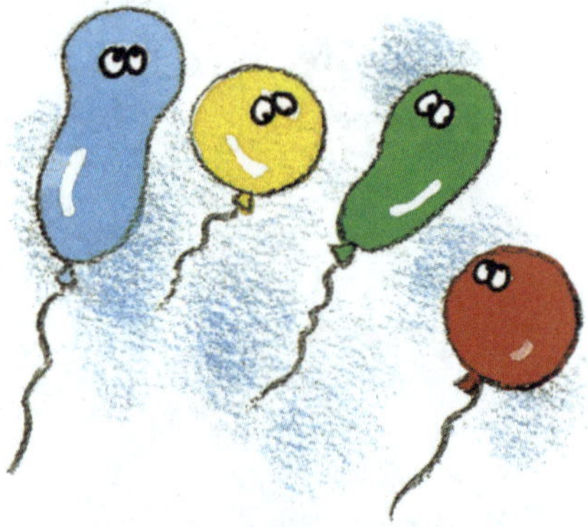

These balloons are **floating** in the air. Sandra can **float** on top of the water.

flood [flʌd] 水灾 [shuǐ zāi]

In a **flood** water covers the ground.

floor [flɔ:] 地上 [dì shang]

The boys are lying on the **floor**.

flour [ˈflaʊə] 面粉 [miàn fěn]

Mother uses **flour** to make cakes and bread.

flower [ˈflaʊə] 花 [huā]

tulip [ˈtju:lɪp]
郁金香
[yù jīn xiāng]

daisy [ˈdeɪzɪ]
雏菊 [chú jú]

Harry gave his mother some **flowers**. Many plants have **flowers**.

fly [flaɪ] **flies**
苍蝇、飞 [cāng ying, fēi]

A **fly** is a small insect. **Flies** have wings.

Birds can **fly**. They use their wings to move through the air.

foot [fʊt] **feet**
脚 [jiǎo]

Your **foot** is at the end of your leg. You have two **feet**.

football [fʊtbɔ:l]
足球 [zú qiú]

They are kicking the **football**. **Football** is a good game.

for [fə] 替 [tì]

My sister cannot open the door. I do it **for** her.

forehead [ˈfɒrɪd] 前额 [qián é]

She has a mark in the middle of her **forehead**.

forest [ˈfɒrɪst] 森林 [sēn lín]

There are many trees in a **forest**.

forget [fəˈget] **forgetting, forgot**
忘记[wàng jì]

I often **forget** to bring my lunch. Then I go hungry.

fork [fɔːk] 叉 [chā]

Norman eats his food with a **fork**.

form [fɔːm] **forming, formed**
形成、制作 [xíng chéng, zhì zuò]

Patrick **forms** a square with the bricks.

fox [fɒks] **foxes** 狐狸 [hú li]

A **fox** is an animal. It has a long bushy tail.

friend [frend] 朋友 [péng you]

A **friend** is somebody you like very much.

frog [frɒg] 青蛙 [qīng wā]

A **frog** is a small animal. **Frogs** live in or near the water.

front [frʌnt] 前面 [qián mian]

There is a zipper down the **front** of Dick's shirt. Polly is standing in **front** of Dick.

fruit [fruːt] 水果 [shuǐ guǒ]

pear [peə]
梨 [lí]

tomato [təˈmɑːtəʊ]
蕃茄 [fān qié]

durian [ˈdjʊərɪən]
榴槤 [liú lián]

star fruit [stɑː fruːt]
杨桃 [yáng táo]

pomelo [ˈpʌmələʊ]
柚子 [yòu zi]

cherry [ˈtʃerɪ]
樱桃 [yīng táo]

mangosteen [ˈmæŋgəʊstiːn]
山竹 [shān zhú]

grapes [greɪpz]
葡萄 [pú táo]

Which **fruit** do you like best?

fry [fraɪ] **frying, fried**
煎 [jiān]

Mother is **frying** some chicken. She is cooking it in hot oil.

full [fʊl] 满的 [mǎn de]

The tank is **full**. You cannot put any more water in it.

fun [fʌn] 乐趣 [lè qù]

We have great **fun** playing in the water.

funny [ˈfʌnɪ] 滑稽 [huá jī]

He looks so **funny** that he makes me laugh.

fur [fɜː] 软毛 [ruǎn máo]

Many animals are covered with soft **fur**.

furniture [ˈfɜːnɪtʃə] 家具 [jiā jù]

Here are some pieces of **furniture** we use in the house.

g

game [geɪm] 游戏、运动 [yóu xì, yùn dòng]

The children are playing a **game**. What **games** do you like?

basketball
[bɑ:skɪtbɔ:l]
篮球 [lán qiú]

sack race [sæk reɪs]
套袋赛跑 [tào dài sài pǎo]

hopscotch [ˈhɒpskɒtʃ]
跳方格游戏 [tiào fāng gé yóu xì]

blind man's buff
[blaɪnd mænz bʌf]
捉迷藏 [zhuō mí cáng]

card game [kɑ:d geɪm]
纸牌游戏 [zhǐ pái yóu xì]

skipping [skɪpɪŋ]
跳绳 [tiào shéng]

football [ˈfʊtbɔ:l]
足球 [zú qiú]

garage [ˈgærɑ:ʒ]
车房 [chē fáng]

We keep our car in the **garage**.

garden [ˈgɑ:dn]
花园 [huā yuán]

A **garden** is a place where flowers or vegetables grow.

gardener [ˈgɑ:dnə]
园丁 [yuán dīng]

A **gardener** grows and looks after the plants in a garden.

gas [gæs] 煤气 [méi qì]

My mother has a **gas** cooker.

gate [geɪt] 大门 [dà mén]

The **gate** is shut. Ali cannot get out.

ghost [gəʊst] 鬼 [guǐ]

He thought he saw a **ghost**. **Ghost** stories make you feel afraid.

giant [ˈdʒaɪənt] 巨人 [jù rén]

A **giant** is a very big and tall man. There are **giants** in some fairy tales.

giraffe [dʒɪˈrɑ:f]
长颈鹿 [cháng jǐng lù]

A **giraffe** is a tall animal with a long neck.

girl [gɜ:l] 女孩 [nǚ hái]

This **girl** looks beautiful.

give [gɪv] **giving, gave**
给 [gěi]

Please, will you **give** me a sweet?

glass [glɑ:s] 玻璃 [bō li]

Glass is hard and smooth. **Glass** will break if you drop it.

glide [glaɪd] **gliding, glided**
滑行 [huá xíng]

Norman **glides** over the ice. Dick is **gliding** behind him.

glove [glʌv]
手套 [shǒu tào]

Brian is trying on the **glove**.

glue [glu:] 胶水 [jiāo shuǐ]

We use **glue** to stick things together.

go [gəʊ] **going, went**
去 [qù]

I **go** to school by bus.

goat [gəʊt] 山羊 [shān yáng]

A **goat** is an animal. **Goats** can climb well.

gold [gəʊld] 黄金 [huáng jīn]

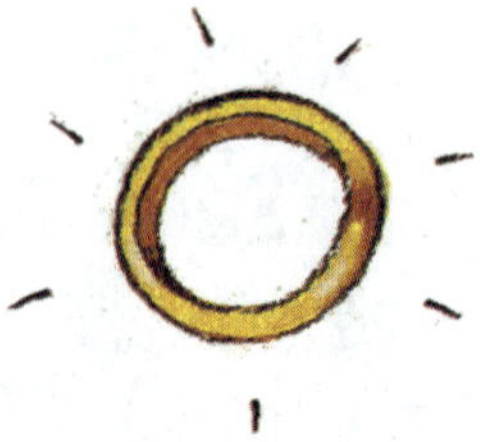

Mother would like that **gold** ring. **Gold** costs a lot of money.

goldfish [ˈgəʊldfɪʃ]
金鱼 [jīn yú]

I like to watch my **goldfish** swim.

good [gʊd] 好的 [hǎo de]

This is a **good** book. I like to read it.

goodbye [ˈgʊdˈbaɪ]
再见 [zài jiàn]

Sally waves **goodbye** to her friend.

goose [gu:s] **geese**
鹅 [é]

A **goose** is a large bird with a long neck.

grape [greɪp] 葡萄 [pú táo]

A **grape** is a small, round fruit. **Grapes** are green, black or red.

grass [grɑ:s] 草 [cǎo]

Father cuts the **grass**.

grasshopper [ˈgrɑ:shɒpə]
蚱蜢 [zhà měng]

A **grasshopper** is a green insect. **Grasshoppers** eat plants.

great [greɪt] 大的 [dà de]

He has climbed up the **great** building. "**Great**! Now I can see so far," he said.

greedy [ˈgri:dɪ]
贪心的 [tān xīn de]

Norman is **greedy**. He eats too much.

green [gri:n] 绿色 [lǜ sè]

Green is a color. Grass is **green**.

grey [greɪ] 灰色 [huī sè]

These clouds are **grey**.

grocer [ˈgrəʊsə]
杂货商 [zá huò shāng]

A **grocer** sells many things we use in the house every day.

ground [graʊnd]
地上 [dì shang]

Dick dropped his books on the **ground**. Plants grow in the **ground**.

group [gru:p] 一群 [yī qún]

There is a **group** of people waiting at the bus stop.

group [gru:p] 分组 [fēn zǔ]

I will **group** these bricks. I put the red ones on my left and the blue ones on my right.

grow [grəʊ] **growing, grew**
生长 [shēng zhǎng]

Harry **grows** taller each year.

guinea pig [ˈgɪnɪ pɪg]
豚鼠 [tún shǔ]

A **guinea pig** is a small animal. It eats grass.

guitar [gɪˈtɑː] 吉他 [jí tā]

Toby loves to play the **guitar**.

gun [gʌn] 枪 [qiāng]

The teacher shoots the **gun** to start the race.

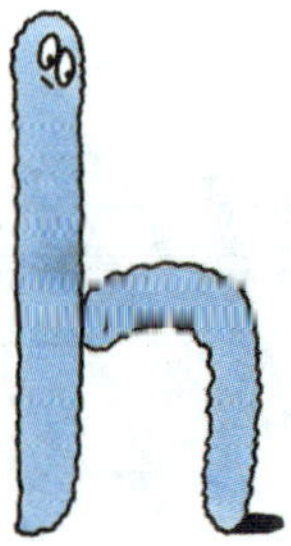

hair [heə] 头发 [tóu fà]

Hair grows on your head.

half [hɑːf] **halves**
半 [bàn]

Omar cuts his apple in **half**. The two **halves** are of the same size.

hammer [ˈhæmə]
锤子 [chuí zi]

Uncle Bill is hitting the nail with his **hammer**.

hand [hænd] 手 [shǒu]

Your **hand** is at the end of your arm. You hold things with your **hands**.

handkerchief [ˈhæŋkətʃɪf]
手帕 [shǒu pà]

Sandra wipes her eyes with a **handkerchief**.

handsome [ˈhænsəm]
英俊 [yīng jùn]

Ali is a **handsome** boy. People like to look at him.

hang [hæŋ] **hanging, hung**
挂 [guà]

Rita **hangs** out the clothes to dry.

happy [ˈhæpɪ]
高兴的 [gāo xìng de]

They are **happy** to see their father.

harbour [ˈhɑːbə]
港口 [gǎng kǒu]

There are many ships in the **harbour**.

hard [hɑːd] 硬的 [yìng de]

Stone is **hard**. It is **hard** to break it.

hardworking [hɑːdwɜːkɪŋ]
勤劳的 [qín láo de]

Patrick always does his work. He is **hardworking**.

has [həz] **have**
有 [yǒu]

Norman **has** a motorcycle. I **have** a bicycle.

hat [hæt] 帽子 [mào zi]

This **hat** is too big for my head.

hatch [hætʃ] **hatching, hatched**
孵出 [fū chū]

The chickens **hatch** out of the eggs. They break open their shells.

hawk [hɔːk] 鹰 [yīng]

A **hawk** is a bird. It kills other birds and small animals for food.

he [hiː] **him, his**
他 [tā]

Omar is a boy. **He** has a ball. Rita gave it to **him**. It is **his** ball.

head [hed] 头 [tóu]

This is a picture of my **head**.

headmaster [hedˈmɑːstə]
校长 [xiào zhǎng]

A **headmaster** is the man who looks after a school.

headmistress [ˈhedˈmɪstrəs]
女校长 [nǚ xiào zhǎng]

A **headmistress** is the woman who looks after a school.

hear [hɪə] **hearing, heard** 听 [tīng]

Can you **hear** the music? You **hear** with your ears.

height [haɪt] 高度 [gāo dù]

Father measures my **height**. I am one metre tall.

help [help] **helping, helped**

帮助 [bāng zhù]

Sally **helps** the old lady cross the road.

heart [hɑ:t] 心 [xīn]

Put your hand on your chest and you can feel your **heart** beating.

helicopter [ˈhelɪkɒptə]

直升机 [zhí shēng jī]

Uncle Bill flies a **helicopter**.

hen [hen] 母鸡 [mǔ jī]

A **hen** lays eggs.

heavy [ˈhevɪ]

重的 [zhòng de]

This stone is very **heavy**. Tim cannot move it.

hello [həˈləʊ] 你好 [nǐ hǎo]

Brian said **hello** when he saw his friend.

here [hɪə] 这里 [zhè lǐ]

Please put the flowers **here**.

heel [hi:l] 踝 [huái]

Your **heel** is the back part of your foot.

helmet [ˈhelmɪt]

头盔 [tóu kuī]

Mr. Smiley wears a **helmet** on his head. The **helmet** keeps his head from getting hurt.

hide [haɪd] **hiding, hid**

躲 [duǒ]

The dogs **hide** under the table. Harry cannot see them.

high [haɪ] 高的 [gāo de]

This building is very **high**.

hill [hɪl] 小山 [xiǎo shān]

A **hill** is high ground with sloping sides.

hit [hɪt] **hitting, hit**
撞、碰 [zhuàng, pèng]

Oh dear! Toby **hit** his head.

hold [həʊld] **holding, held**
抱 [bào]

I like to **hold** my doll. I **hold** it in my arms.

hole [həʊl] 洞 [dòng]

Uncle Bob does not see the **hole** in the road.

holiday [ˈhɒlɪdeɪ] 假期 [jià qī]

We are going on **holiday** for one week.

home [həʊm] 家 [jiā]

Your **home** is where you live.

honey [ˈhʌnɪ] 蜂蜜 [fēng mì]

Bees make **honey**. **Honey** is sweet and good to eat.

hoof [huːf] **hooves** 蹄 [tí]

A **hoof** is the hard part of an animal's foot. Cows and goats have **hooves**.

hook [hʊk] 钩子 [gōu zi]

Polly hangs her bag on a **hook**.

hoop [huːp] 环、圈 [huán, quān]

A **hoop** is a big ring. The dog jumps through the **hoop**.

hop [hɒp] **hopping, hopped**
跳 [tiào]

Sally can **hop** like a kangaroo.

hot [hɒt] 热的 [rè de]

The sun is shining brightly. Everyone feels **hot**.

how [haʊ] 怎样 [zěn yàng]

I must cross the river. **How** can I do it?

horn [hɔ:n] 角 [jiǎo]

Some animals have **horns**.

hotel [həʊˈtel] 酒店 [jiǔ diàn]

A **hotel** is a building where people away from home can sleep.

hungry [ˈhʌŋgrɪ] 饿 [è]

The children are **hungry**. They want something to eat.

horse [hɔ:s] 马 [mǎ]

Rita rides her **horse** every day. Some **horses** work for us.

hour [ˈaʊə] 小时 [xiǎo shí]

There are sixty minutes in one **hour**. A day has 24 **hours**.

hurt [hɜ:t] **hurting, hurt**
伤 [shāng]

Rita has **hurt** her arm. It is sore.

hospital [ˈhɒspɪtl]
医院 [yī yuàn]

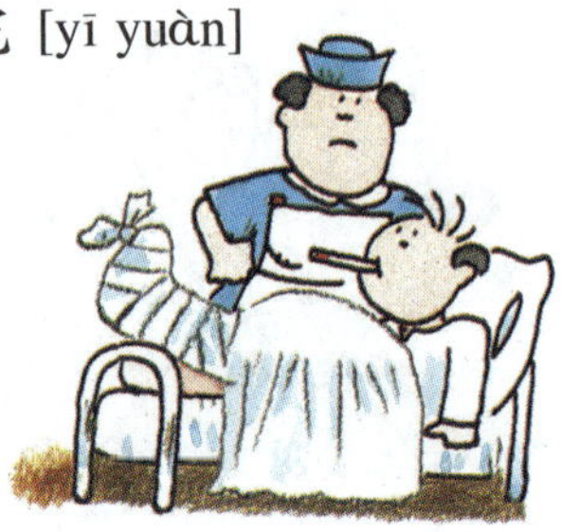

You go to the **hospital** when you are very ill.

house [haʊs] 房子 [fáng zi]

This is our new **house**. We are going to live here.

I [aɪ] **me, my** 我 [wǒ]

I am Sandra. That is **my** book. Please give it to **me**.

ice [aɪs] 冰 [bīng]

Ice is very cold. **Ice** is frozen water.

ice cream [aɪs kriːm] 冰激凌 [bīng ji líng]

Norman loves to eat **ice cream**.

ice cube [aɪs kjuːb] 冰块 [bīng kuài]

Jimmy puts an **ice cube** into his drink. The **ice cube** makes his drink cold.

idea [aɪˈdɪə] 主意 [zhǔ yì]

Sally thinks of an **idea** for her story. She knows what to write.

ill [ɪl] 生病的 [shēng bìng de]

Norman is **ill**. He is in bed.

in [ɪn] 里 [lǐ]

The apple is **in** the basket.

insect [ˈɪnsekt] 昆虫 [kūn chóng]

Insects are small animals with six legs.

beetle [ˈbiːtl] 甲虫 [jiǎ chóng]

dragonfly [ˈdrægənflaɪ] 蜻蜓 [qīng tíng]

bee [biː] 蜜蜂 [mì fēng]

flea [flɪː] 跳蚤 [tiào zao]

grasshopper [ˈgrɑːshɒpə] 蚱蜢 [zhà měng]

ladybird [ˈleɪdɪbəːd] 瓢虫 [piáo chóng]

mosquito [məˈskiːtəʊ] 蚊子 [wén zi]

inside [ɪnˈsaɪd] 里面 [lǐ miàn]

The lion is **inside** its cage.

into [ˈɪntə] 进入 [jìn rù]

Mrs. Lee is coming **into** the room.

invite [ɪnˈvaɪt] **inviting, invited**
邀请 [yāo qǐng]

I **invite** my friend to my party.
I ask her to come to my party.

iron [ˈaɪən] 熨斗 [yùn dǒu]

Mother is using her new **iron**.

is [ɪz] **was**
是 [shì]

This **is** my dog. I bought him when he **was** a puppy.

island [ˈaɪlənd] 岛 [dǎo]

An **island** is land with water all around it.

it [ɪt] 它 [tā]

Grandfather has a bag. He is holding **it**.

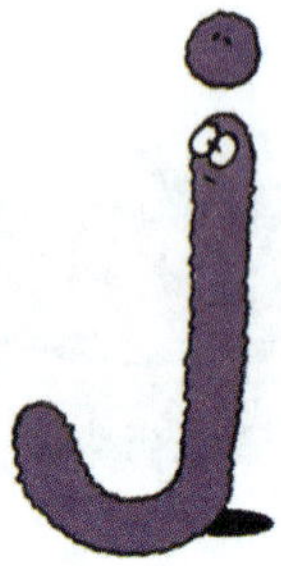

jam [dʒæm] 果酱 [guǒ jiàng]

Norman puts **jam** on his bread. **Jam** is made from fruit and sugar.

jar [dʒɑ:] 罐 [guàn]

What a big **jar** of cookies!

jaw [dʒɔ:] 下颚 [xià è]

Your **jaw** is part of your mouth. It moves up and down when you are talking or eating.

jeans [dʒi:nz]
牛仔裤 [niú zǎi kù]

Brian is wearing a pair of blue **jeans**.

jeep [dʒi:p] 吉普车 [jì pǔ chē]

A **jeep** can travel over rough ground.

jelly [ˈdʒelɪ] 果冻 [guǒ dòng]

Mother makes a good **jelly** from fruit juice and sugar.

jellyfish [ˈdʒelɪfɪʃ]
水母 [shuǐ mǔ]

A **jellyfish** lives in the sea.

jetty [ˈdʒetɪ] 码头 [mǎ tou]

A **jetty** is made of wood or stone.

jigsaw [ˈdʒɪgsɔː]
拼图游戏 [pīn tú yóu xì]

Do you enjoy doing **jigsaw** puzzles?

jog [dʒɒg] 慢跑 [màn pǎo]

We go for a **jog** round the field.

join [dʒɔɪn] **joining, joined**
连接 [lián jiē]

Patrick **joins** the strings together

joke [dʒəʊk] 笑话 [xiào hua]

A **joke** is something funny to make you laugh.

jug [dʒʌg] 壶 [hú]

There is a **jug** of water on the table.

juice [dʒuːs] 汁 [zhī]

Omar is squeezing the **juice** of the lemon.

jump [dʒʌmp] 跳 [tiào]

The cat **jumps** over the branch.

jungle [ˈdʒʌŋgl] 丛林 [cóng lín]

There are many trees and animals in the **jungle**.

key [kiː] 钥匙[yào shi]

Toby will open the door with the **key**.

king [kɪŋ] 国王 [guó wáng]

A **king** is the ruler of a country. He lives in a palace.

kangaroo [ˌkæŋgəˈruː] 袋鼠 [dài shǔ]

A **kangaroo** is a big animal that hops.

kick [kɪk] **kicking, kicked** 踢 [tī]

Dick is going to **kick** the ball.

kiss [kɪs] 吻 [wěn]

Sandra gives her mother a **kiss**.

keep [kiːp] **keeping, kept** 保留 [bǎo liú]

Harry wants to **keep** the train. He does not want to give it to his brother.

kid [kɪd] 小山羊 [xiǎo shān yáng]

A **kid** is a young goat.

kitchen [ˈkɪtʃɪn] 厨房 [chú fáng]

We cook food in the **kitchen**.

kettle [ˈketl] 水壶 [shuǐ hú]

You boil water in a **kettle**.

kind [kaɪnd] 善良的 [shàn liáng de]

Sally is a **kind** girl. She gave the hungry boy some food.

kite [kaɪt] 风筝 [fēng zheng]

My **kite** flies high in the sky.

kitten [ˈkɪtn] 小猫 [xiǎo māo]

A **kitten** is a baby cat.

knee [niː] 膝 [xī]

Sandra puts her hands on her **knees**.

knife [naɪf] **knives**
刀子 [dāo zi]

A **knife** is for cutting things. I cut up my food with my **knife**.

knock [nɒk] **knocking, knocked**
敲 [qiāo]

The mailman is **knocking** on the door.

knot [nɒt] 结 [jié]

Patrick tied a **knot** in the string.

know [nəʊ] **knowing, knew**
知道、懂得 [zhī dào, dǒng de]

Betty **knows** the numbers 1 to 10. She is saying them.

labourer [ˈleɪbərə]
工人 [gōng rén]

These **labourers** are helping to build a road.

ladder [ˈlædə] 梯子 [tī zi]

Mr. Smiley is climbing up the **ladder**.

ladle [ˈleɪdl]
长柄勺子 [cháng bǐng sháo zi]

Polly uses a **ladle** to put soup into her bowl.

lamb [læm] 羔羊 [gāo yáng]

A **lamb** is a young sheep.

lamp [læmp] 灯 [dēng]

A **lamp** gives us light.

land [lænd] 陆地 [lù dì]

We stepped off the boat onto dry **land**.

lantern [ˈlæntən]
灯笼 [dēng long]

Toby carries a **lantern** to help him see his way.

lap [læp] 腿上 [tuǐ shàng]

The baby is sitting on his mother's **lap**.

large [lɑ:dʒ] 大的 [dà de]

Large means big. The mouse thinks the elephant is **large**.

last [lɑ:st] 最后 [zuì hòu]

Who will have the **last** banana?

late [leɪt] 迟到 [chí dào]

I am **late** for dinner. Everyone is waiting for me.

laugh [lɑ:f] **laughing, laughed**
[xiào] 笑

The clown looks funny. We **laugh** at him.

lay [leɪ] **laying, laid**
生 [shēng]

These hens **lay** eggs every day.

lazy [ˈleɪzɪ] 懒惰的 [lǎn duò de]

Norman is **lazy**. He does not like to work.

lead [li:d] **leading, led**
带领 [dài lǐng]

Mother Duck will **lead** her ducklings to the pond.

leaf [li:f] **leaves** 叶 [yè]

A **leaf** grows on a plant. Most **leaves** are green.

learn [lɜ:n] **learning, learned**
学 [xué]

Mrs. Lee is **learning** to ride her bicycle.

leave [liːv] **leaving, left**
离开 [lí kāi]

I will **leave** the house now. I must go to school.

left [left] 左 [zuǒ]

Patrick is holding up his **left** hand.

leg [leg] 脚 [jiǎo]

ant [ænt]
蚂蚁 [mǎ yǐ]

bird [bɜːd]
鸟 [niǎo]

rabbit [ˈræbɪt]
兔子 [tù zi]

caterpillar [ˈkætəpɪlə]
毛虫 [máo chóng]

You use your **legs** to walk. How many **legs** do these animals have?

lemon [ˈlemən] 柠檬 [níng méng]

A **lemon** is a yellow fruit. **Lemons** taste sour.

length [leŋθ] 长度 [cháng dù]

Rita measures the **length** of the table. She wants to know how long it is.

leopard [ˈlepəd] 豹 [bào]

A **leopard** is a big animal. A **leopard** has black spots on its body.

less [les] 少 [shǎo]

Sally has **less** cake than Polly.

lesson [ˈlesn] 课 [kè]

We are taking an English **lesson**.

letter [ˈletə] 信 [xìn]

I am writing a **letter** to my grandmother.

library [ˈlaɪbrərɪ] **libraries**
图书馆 [tú shū guǎn]

You can borrow books from the **library**.

lick [lɪk] **licking, licked**
舔 [tiǎn]

Norman is **licking** his ice cream.

lift [lɪft] **lifting, lifted**
升降机、提起
[shēng jiàng jī], [tí qǐ]

We go up a tall building in a **lift**.

Patrick is trying to **lift** the basket.

light [laɪt]
灯、轻的 [dēng], [qīng de]

At night we must turn on the **light**. This feather is **light**. It is not heavy.

lightning [ˈlaɪtnɪŋ]
闪电 [shǎn diàn]

Do not play outside when there is **lightning** in the sky.

like [laɪk] **liking, liked**
喜欢 [xǐ huan]

I **like** to paint. Ali **likes** to draw.

lily [ˈlɪlɪ] **lilies** 百合 [bǎi hé]

A **lily** is a flower. **Lilies** can be orange, white or pink.

line [laɪn] 线 [xiàn]

I have drawn a **line** down my page.

lion [ˈlaɪən] 狮子 [shī zi]

A **lion** likes to eat meat. **Lions** roar.

lips [lɪpz] 唇 [chún]

Mother has red **lips**.

listen [ˈlɪsn] **listening, listened**
听 [tīng]

We are **listening** to the story. We want to hear it.

litter [ˈlɪtə] 垃圾 [lā jī]

Put your **litter** into the can.

little [ˈlɪtl] 小的 [xiǎo de]

Little means small. This is a **little** baby.

live [lɪv] **living, lived**
住 [zhù]

Sally **lives** near a school.

lobster [ˈlɒbstə] 龙虾 [lóng xiā]

A **lobster** lives in the sea. **Lobsters** have hard shells.

lock [lɒk] 锁 [suǒ]

Toby turns the key in the **lock**.

long [lɒŋ] 长 [cháng]

Polly has very **long** hair. Dick has short hair.

long bean [lɒŋ biːn]
长豆 [cháng dòu]

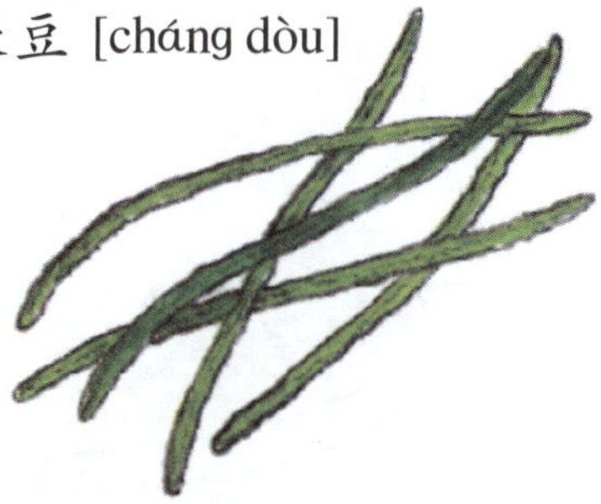

A **long bean** is a green vegetable. **Long beans** are thin and long.

look [lʊk] **looking, looked**
看 [kàn]

Look at the monkey. See how he swings!

lorry [ˈlɒrɪ] **lorries**
货车 [huò chē]

Father drives a big **lorry**.

lose [luːz] **losing, lost**
丢失 [diū shī]

I often **lose** my pencils. I cannot find them, and I have to buy new ones.

loud [laʊd]
大声的 [dà shēng de]

The aeroplane is going to fly. It makes a **loud** noise.

love [lʌv] 爱 [ài]

My parents give me lot of **love**.

low [ləʊ] 低 [dī]

My chair is too **low**. I need a higher one.

lunch [lʌntʃ] 午餐 [wǔ cān]

You eat **lunch** in the middle of the day.

machine [məˈʃiːn] 机器 [jī qì]

A **machine** does work for us.
Here are some **machines**.

iron [ˈaɪən]
熨斗 [yùn dǒu]

bulldozer [bʊldəʊzə]
推土机 [tuī tǔ jī]

vacuum cleaner
[ˈvækjʊəm kliːnə]
吸尘机 [xī chén jī]

typewriter [ˈtaɪpraɪtə]
打字机 [dǎ zì jī]

sewing machine
[ˈsəʊɪŋ məˈʃiːn]
缝纫机 [féng rèn jī]

toaster [ˈtəʊstə]
烤面包机 [kǎo miàn bāo jī]

computer [kəmˈpjuːtə]
电脑 [diàn nǎo]

magic [ˈmædʒɪk] 魔术 [mó shù]

In my dream I flew on a **magic** carpet.

magician [məˈdʒɪʃn]
魔术师 [mó shù shī]

A **magician** can do tricks that look like magic.

make [meɪk] **making, made**
做 [zuò]

Mrs. Lee likes to **make** cakes.

man [mæn] **men**
男人 [nán rén]

When Harry grows up, he will be a **man**. Harry's father is a **man**.

mandarin [ˈmændərɪn]
柑 [gān]

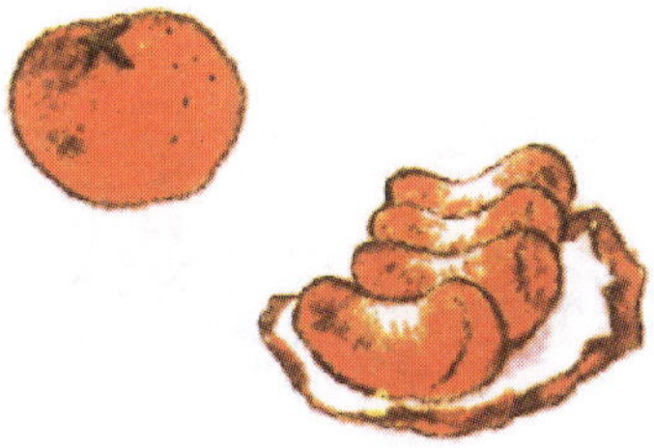

A **mandarin** is a small, orange fruit.

mango [ˈmæŋgəʊ]
芒果 [máng guǒ]

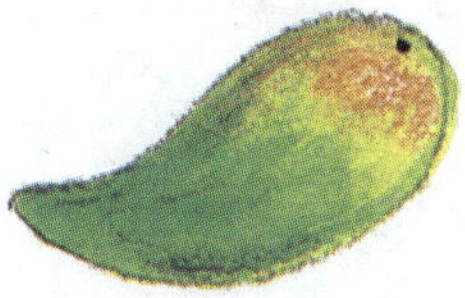

A **mango** is a fruit. It has one seed.

mangosteen [ˈmæŋgəʊstiːn]
山竹 [shān zhú]

A **mangosteen** is a fruit. It has a thick skin, and the fruit inside is white.

many [ˈmenɪ] 很多 [hěn duō]

There are **many** apples on the tree.

map [mæp] 地图 [dì tú]

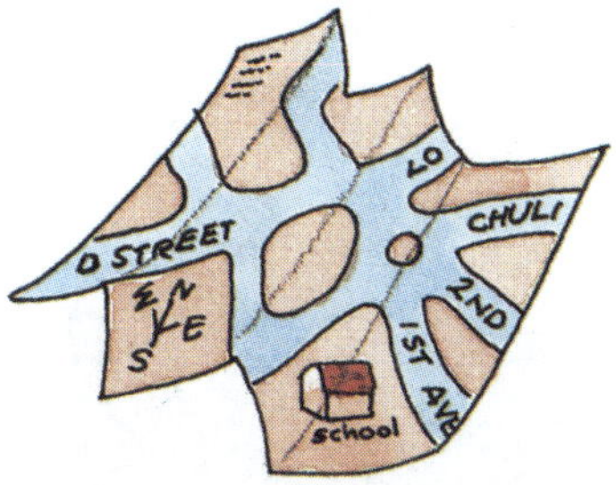

A **map** shows you how to find places.

marble [ˈmɑːbl] 弹珠 [dàn zhū]

We are playing with **marbles**.

march [mɑːtʃ] **marching, marched** 步操走 [bù cāo zǒu]

The soldiers **march** along the road.

margarine [ˈmɑːdʒəˈriːn]
人造牛油 [rén zào niú yóu]

We spread **margarine** on bread.

market [ˈmɑːkɪt]
市场、街市 [shì chǎng, jiē shì]

You can buy many things at a **market**.

mask [mɑːsk] 面具 [miàn jù]

Patrick has a **mask** on his face.

mat [mæt] 地席 [dì xí]

You wipe your shoes on the **mat**.

match [mætʃ] **matches**
火柴、比赛 [huǒ chái], [bǐ sài]

Grandfather uses a **match** to light the fire. I love to watch a soccer **match**.

match [mætʃ] **matching, matched** 相配 [xiāng pèi]

Sally's socks **match** but Toby's do not **match**.

mattress [ˈmætrɪs] **mattresses**
床垫 [chuáng diàn]

I have a new **mattress** on my bed.

may [meɪ] 可以 [kě yǐ]

"**May** I have an ice cream?" asks Sandra. "You **may**," says her mother. She allows Sandra to have one.

meal [miːl] 餐 [cān]

You eat food at a **meal**.

measure [ˈmeʒə]
measuring, measured 量度 [liàng dù]

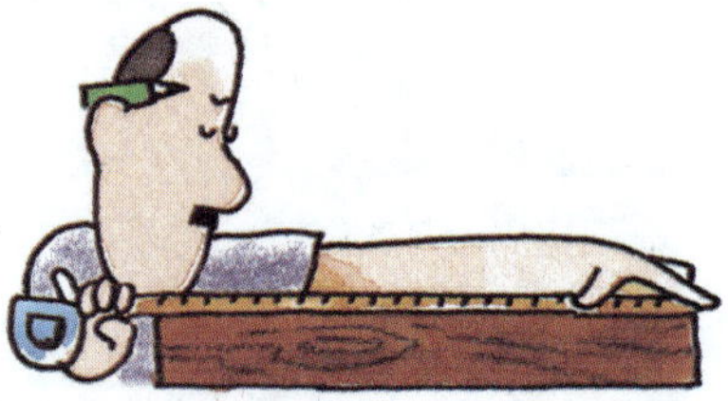

Uncle Bill will **measure** the piece of wood. He wants to know its size.

meat [miːt] 肉 [ròu]

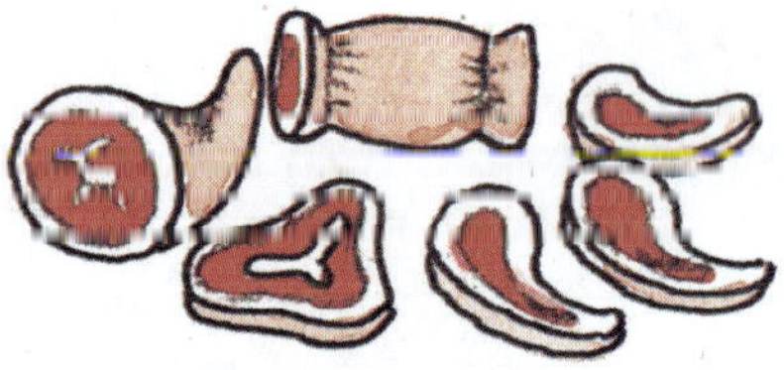

Meat is the flesh of an animal.

medicine [ˈmedsn] 药 [yào]

The doctor gives Norman some **medicine**. It will make him feel better.

meet [miːt] **meeting, met**
遇见 [yù jiàn]

Mother **met** Mr. Smiley at the supermarket.

mend [mend] **mending, mended**
修好 [xiū hǎo]

I must **mend** my toy. It is broken.

merry-go-round
[ˈmerɪ gəʊ raʊnd]
旋转木马 [xuán zhuǎn mù mǎ]

We love to sit on the **merry-go-round.** It goes up and down and round and round.

metre [ˈmiːtə] 公尺 [gōng chǐ]

Mrs. Lee wants one **metre** of cloth.

middle [ˈmɪdl] 中间 [zhōng jiān]

The baby is sitting in the **middle** of the rug. The **middle** flower is red.

milk [mɪlk] 牛奶 [niú nǎi]

Milk comes from cows. It is good for your body.

mine [maɪn]
矿场、我的 [kuàng chǎng], [wǒ de]

These men are working in a **mine**. This cat is **mine**. It belongs to me.

minute [ˈmɪnɪt]
分钟 [fēn zhōng]

There are sixty **minutes** in one hour. One **minute** is sixty seconds long.

mirror [ˈmɪrə] 镜 [jìng]

I can see myself in the **mirror**.

miss [mɪs] missing, missed
赶不上、想念
[gǎn bu shàng], [xiǎng liàn]

Polly **missed** the bus. It left without her. I will **miss** my grandmother.

mix [mɪks] mixing, mixed
混合 [hùn hé]

I **mix** yellow and blue to make green.

money [ˈmʌnɪ] 钱 [qián]

We use **money** to buy things.

monkey [ˈmʌŋkɪ]
猴子 [hóu zi]

A **monkey** has a long tail.
Monkeys like to swing in trees.

monster [ˈmɒnstə]
妖怪 [yāo guài]

Jimmy is reading a story about an ugly **monster**.

month [mʌnθ] 月份 [yuè fèn]

This **month** is February. Next **month** will be March.

moon [muːn] 月亮 [yuè liàng]

At night you can see the **moon** in the sky.

mop [mɒp] 拖把 [tuō bǎ]

Grandmother uses a **mop** to clean the floor.

more [mɔː] 多 [duō]

Norman has already eaten his ice cream. He would like some **more**.

morning [ˈmɔːnɪŋ]
早上 [zǎo shang]

It is **morning** when the sun rises. We have breakfast in the **morning**.

mosque [mɒsk]
清真寺 [qīng zhēn sì]

Ali prays in the **mosque** on Fridays.

mosquito [məˈskiːtəʊ]
mosquitoes 蚊子 [wén zi]

A **mosquito** is a small insect.
Mosquitoes bite people.

most [məʊst] 最多 [zuì duō]

Patrick has some sweets. Sally has more sweets than Patrick.
Norman has the **most** sweets.

motorcycle [ˈməʊtəsaɪkl]
摩托车 [mó tuō chē]

Mr. Smiley goes fast on his black **motorcycle**.

mountain [ˈmaʊntɪn]
高山 [gāo shān]

A **mountain** is bigger and higher than a hill.

mouse [maʊs] **mice**
老鼠 [lǎo shǔ]

A **mouse** has a long tail. **Mice** like cheese.

mouth [maʊθ] 口 [kǒu]

You use your **mouth** to talk and eat.

move [muːv] **moving, moved**
移 [yí]

We will **move** the table. We will put it by the window.

much [mʌtʃ] 多少 [duō shǎo]

How **much** do the cakes cost? Does your thumb hurt **much**?

mud [mʌd] 泥浆 [ní jiāng]

Norman has fallen into the **mud**. **Mud** is soft, wet earth.

mug [mʌg] 大杯 [dà bēi]

Grandfather is holding a **mug** of tea.

muscle [ˈmʌsl] 肌肉 [jī ròu]

Every **muscle** in your body helps you to move.

museum [mjuːˈzɪəm]
博物馆 [bó wù guǎn]

We are visiting the **museum**. We look at many old things.

music [ˈmjuːzɪk] 音乐 [yīn yuè]

They are making **music**. **Music** is made up of sounds we like to hear.

must [məst] 必须 [bì xū]

I **must** run or I will get wet.

mutton [ˈmʌtn] 羊肉 [yáng ròu]

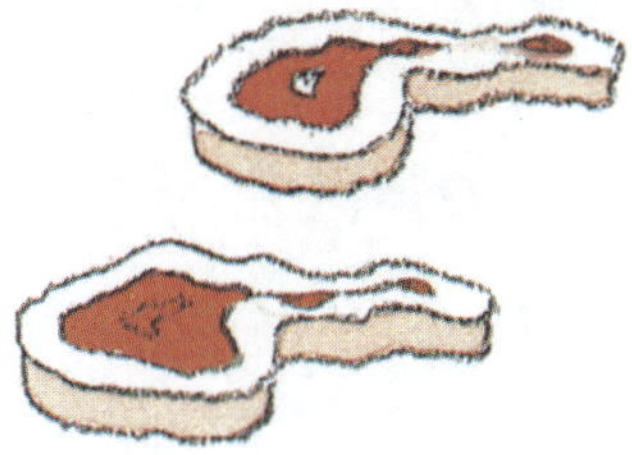

Mutton is the meat from a sheep.

my [maɪ] 我的 [wǒ de]

This is **my** pencil. I bought it.

nail [neɪl] 钉 [dīng]

Uncle Bill is hammering a **nail** into the wood.

name [neɪm] 名字 [míng zì]

Betty has written her **name** on her book.

narrow [ˈnærəʊ]
狭窄的 [xiá zhǎi de]

The doorway is too **narrow** for Norman to go through.

naughty [ˈnɔːtɪ]
顽皮的 [wán pí de]

Dick is very **naughty**. He is drawing on the wall.

near [nɪə] 接近 [jiē jìn]

Omar is swimming **near** the edge of the pool. The edge is not far from him.

neck [nek] 颈 [jǐng]

Your **neck** joins your head to your body.

necktie [ˈnektaɪ] 领带 [lǐng dài]

Uncle Bob is wearing a green **necktie**.

need [niːd] **needing, needed**
需要 [xū yào]

Toby **needs** new shoes. One shoe has a hole in it.

needle [niːdl] 针 [zhēn]

Mother is pulling the thread through the **needle**.

neighbour [neɪbə]
邻居 [lín jū]

Your **neighbour** lives in the house next to yours.

nest [nest] 巢 [cháo]

Birds live in a **nest**. **Nests** are made of sticks and leaves.

never [ˈnevə] 决不 [jué bù]

Never play with matches. Don't play with them at any time.

new [nju:] 新的 [xīn de]

I have a **new** bicycle. I am riding it for the first time.

news [nju:z] 新闻 [xīn wén]

News is something that has happened. We watch the **news** on television.

newspaper [ˈnju:speɪpə] 报纸 [bào zhǐ]

People read the **newspaper** to find out the news.

next [nekst] 在 ...... 旁边 [zài ...... páng biān]

Rita is standing **next** to Polly.

night [naɪt] 晚上 [wǎn shang]

It is dark during the **night**.

nobody [ˈnəʊbədɪ] 没有人 [méi yǒu rén]

There is **nobody** in the park.

noise [nɔɪz] 声音 [shēng yīn]

The children are making a lot of **noise**.

none [nʌn] 一点也没有 [yī diǎn yě méi yǒu]

The cat wants some milk. There is **none** left.

noodle [ˈnu:dl] 面 [miàn]

We are eating **noodles** for lunch.

nose [nəʊz] 鼻子 [bí zi]

You breathe and smell things with your **nose**.

nothing [ˈnʌθɪŋ]
没有东西
[méi yǒu dōng xi]

There is **nothing** in this box.
It is empty.

number [ˈnʌmbə]
号码 [hào mǎ]

Each player has a **number** on his T-shirt.

nurse [nɜːs] 护士 [hù shi]

A **nurse** looks after sick people.

nut [nʌt] 果仁 [guǒ rén]

hazelnut
[ˈheɪzlnʌt]
榛子
[zhēn zi]

peanut [ˈpiːnʌt]
花生 [huā shēng]

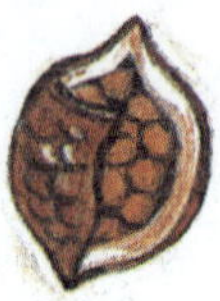

walnut
[ˈwɔːlnʌt]
胡桃
[hú táo]

I like eating **nuts. Nuts** have shells.

oar [ɔː] 桨 [jiǎng]

You use an **oar** to row a boat.

ocean [ˈəʊʃn] 海洋 [hǎi yáng]

The **ocean** is a very big sea.

octopus [ˈɒktəpəs]
章鱼 [zhāng yú]

An **octopus** lives in the sea.
It has eight arms.

of [ev] 的 [de]

All **of** us have a cup of milk. The cups are made **of** plastic.

of course [ev kɔːs]
当然 [dāng rán]

"May I have some lunch?" asks Harry. "**Of course**," replies his mother.

office [ˈɒfɪs]
办公室 [bàn gōng shì]

These people work in an **office**.

office boy [ˈɒfɪs bɔɪ]
杂工 [zá gōng]

Oliver is an **office boy**. He helps to keep the office tidy and posts the letters.

officer [ˈɒfɪsə] 军官 [jūn guān]

Uncle Bob is an **officer** in the army. He tells the soldiers what to do.

often [ˈɒfn] 经常 [jīng cháng]

Grandmother **often** comes to visit us. She comes to see us many times.

oil [ɔɪl] 油 [yóu]

Uncle Bill puts **oil** in the engine.

old [əʊld] 旧的 [jiù de]

My trousers are **old**. I have had them a long time.

on [ɒn] 上面 [shàng mian]

The food is **on** the table.

only [ˈəʊnlɪ] 唯一的 [wéi yī de]

Brian is the **only** boy in the group. The others are all girls.

open [ˈəʊpən] 开着的 [kāi zhe de]

The door is **open**.

opposite [ˈɒpəzɪt] 对面 [duì miàn]

I will sit **opposite** to Sally. Down is the **opposite** of up.

or [ɔː] 或 [huò]

I can have some chocolates **or** some sweets. I cannot have both.

orangutan [ɔːræŋuːˈtæŋ] 大猩猩 [dà xīng xing]

An **orangutan** has brown hair and long arms. It lives in the jungle.

orange [ˈɒrɪndʒ] 橙、橙色 [chéng, chéng sè]

An **orange** is a round fruit. **Orange** is a colour.

orchard [ˈɔːtʃəd] 果园 [guǒ yuán]

An **orchard** is a field of fruit trees. This is an apple **orchard**.

orchestra [ˈɔ:kɪstrə]
交响乐队 [jiāo xiǎng yuè duì]

An **orchestra** is a group of people who make music together.

orchid [ˈɔ:kɪd] 兰花 [lán huā]

An **orchid** is a flower. There are many kinds of **orchids**.

organ [ˈɔ:gən] 风琴 [fēng qín]

Rita can play the **organ**.
An **organ** makes music.

out [aʊt] 出 [chū]

We pulled Norman **out** of the hole.

outside [ˈaʊtˈsaɪd]
外面 [wài mian]

Uncle Bill is working **outside** his house.

oven [ˈʌvn] 烤炉 [kǎo lú]

Mother puts cakes in the **oven** to cook.

over [ˈəʊvə] 过 [guò]

Omar jumps **over** the box.

owl [aʊl] 猫头鹰 [māo tóu yīng]

An **owl** is a bird with big eyes.
You can see **owls** at night.

own [əʊn] 自己的 [zì jǐ de]

Sandra has her **own** puppy.
It belongs to her.

pack [pæk] **packing, packed**
[shōu shí] 收拾

We are **packing** our bags.

page [peɪdʒ] 页 [yè]

Patrick turns the **page** of his book.

pain [peɪn] 痛 [tòng]

Norman has a **pain** in his stomach. It hurts him.

paint [peɪnt] 油漆 [yóu qī]

The men are using yellow **paint**.

pair [peə] 双 [shuāng]

Toby has a new **pair** of shoes. A **pair** means two things that belong together.

palm [pɑ:m] 手掌 [shǒu zhǎng]

Rita looked at the **palm** of my hand.

papaya [pəˈpaɪə] 木瓜 [mù guā]

A **papaya** is a large fruit. Its flesh is red or orange.

paper [ˈpeɪpə] 纸张 [zhǐ zhāng]

We write and draw on **paper**. Mother wraps the present in colored **paper**.

parachute [ˈpærəʃu:t] 降落伞 [jiàng luò sǎn]

A **parachute** helps you fall safely to the ground.

parcel [ˈpɑ:sl] 包裹 [bāo guǒ]

The mailman brought me a **parcel**.

park [pɑ:k] **parking, parked** 停泊、公园 [tíng bó], [gōng yuán]

Uncle Bob is trying to **park** his car.

I am playing with my friends in the **park**.

parrot [ˈpærət] 鹦鹉 [yīng wǔ]

A **parrot** is a bird. You can teach a **parrot** to talk.

part [pɑːt] 部分 [bù fèn]

Harry has painted **part** of the door blue. The other **part** is yellow.

party [ˈpɑːtɪ] 派对 [pài duì]

We are all enjoying the **party**.

pat [pæt] **patting, patted**
轻拍 [qīng pāi]

Mother gives the baby a **pat** on the leg.

pattern [ˈpætn]
图案、纸样 [tú àn, zhǐ yàng]

Mother uses a **pattern** to make her dress.

pavement [ˈpeɪvmənt]
人行道 [rén xíng dào]

People walk on the **pavement** by the side of a road.

paw [pɔː] 爪 [zhǎo]

My dog has one white **paw** and three black **paws**.

pay [peɪ] **paying, paid**
付 [fù]

Polly handed over some money to **pay** for the bread.

pea [piː] 豆 [dòu]

A **pea** is a small round vegetable. **Peas** are green.

peacock [ˈpiːkɒk]
孔雀 [kǒng què]

A **peacock** is a bird. **Peacocks** have beautiful tail feathers.

pear [peə] 梨 [lí]

We are picking **pears** from the trees. **Pears** are good to eat.

pedestrian [pɪˈdestrɪən]
行人 [xíng rén]

A **pedestrian** is a person who is walking along the road.

pedestrian crossing
[pɪˈdestrɪən ˈkrɒsɪŋ]
人行横道 [rén xíng héng dào]

You cross the road at a **pedestrian crossing**.

peel [piːl] **peeling, peeled**
剥 [bō]

You **peel** the skin off a banana before you eat it.

peep [piːp] **peeping, peeped**
偷看 [tōu kàn]

I am **peeping** through a hole in the wall.

peg [peg] 衣夹 [yī jiā]

Rita is using **pegs** to hang out the clothes.

pen [pen] 笔 [bǐ]

I write with my **pen**. A **pen** uses ink.

pencil [ˈpensl] 铅笔 [qiān bǐ]

A **pencil** is for writing or drawing.

penguin [ˈpeŋgwɪn] 企鹅 [qǐ é]

A **penguin** is a bird that lives in very cold places. **Penguins** cannot fly.

people [ˈpiːpl] 人 [rén]

There are a lot of **people** on the beach.

person [ˈpɜːsn] 人 [rén]

Omar is the only **person** in the classroom.

pet [pet] 宠物 [chǒng wù]

A **pet** is an animal you like and look after. These animals are kept as **pets**.

petal [ˈpetl] 花瓣 [huā bàn]

This flower has five red **petals**.

petrol [ˈpetrəl] 汽油 [qì yóu]

Father puts **petrol** in his car to make it go.

petrol station [petrəl ˈsteɪʃn]
加油站 [jiā yóu zhàn]

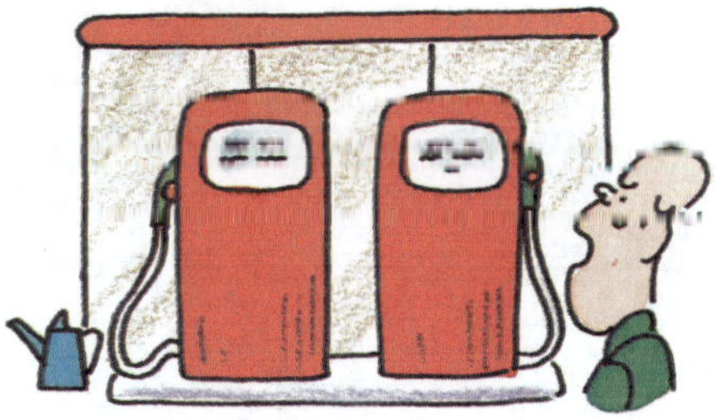

Uncle Bob goes to the **petrol station** to buy petrol.

photograph [ˈfəʊtəgrɑ:f]
照片 [zhào piàn]

This is a **photograph** of my grandfather and grandmother.

piano [pɪˈænəʊ] 钢琴 [gāng qín]

Sally plays the **piano** very well.
A **piano** makes music.

pick [pɪk] **picking, picked**
拾、摘 [shí], [zhāi]

He is **picking** up the toy. We must not **pick** the flowers in the park.

picnic [ˈpɪknɪk] 野餐 [yě cān]

We are having a **picnic** in the park.

picture [ˈpɪktʃə] 画 [huà]

I am drawing a **picture** of myself.

piece [pi:s] 块 [kuài]

Norman is eating a **piece** of cake.

pig [pɪg] 猪 [zhū]

A **pig** is a farm animal. **Pigs** are kept for their meat.

piglet [ˈpɪglɪt] 小猪 [xiǎo zhū]

A **piglet** is a young pig.

pillow [ˈpɪləʊ] 枕头 [zhěn tou]

Toby is sleeping on two **pillows**.

pilot [ˈpaɪlət]
飞行驾驶员 [fēi xíng jià shǐ yuán]

A **pilot** flies an aeroplane.

pin [pɪn] 大头针 [dà tóu zhēn]

The **pin** is holding the cloth together.

pineapple [ˈpaɪnæpl]
菠萝 [bō luó]

A **pineapple** is a large sweet fruit. It has yellow flesh.

pink [pɪŋk]
粉红色 [fěn hóng sè]

Sandra has a new **pink** dress.

pipe [paɪp] 水管 [shuǐ guǎn]

The **pipe** has a hole in it.

pirate [ˈpʌɪrət] 海盗 [hǎi dào]

A **pirate** robs ships at sea.

place [pleɪs] 地方 [dì fang]

Harry went to these **places** today.

zoo [zu:]
动物园 [dòng wù yuán]

beach [bi:tʃ]
海滩 [hǎi tān]

playground [ˈpleɪgraʊnd]
游乐场 [yóu lè chǎng]

plant [plɑ:nt] **planting, planted**
种植、植物 [zhòng zhí], [zhí wù]

Father will **plant** the flowers. He has many **plants** in the garden.

plastic [ˈplæstɪk] 塑胶 [sù jiāo]

bag [bæg]
袋 [dài]

bucket [ˈbʌkɪt]
桶 [tǒng]

lunch box [lʌntʃ bɒks]
午餐盒 [wǔ cān hé]

raincoat
[ˈreɪnkəʊt]
雨衣 [yǔ yī]

These things are made of **plastic**. Some **plastic** is soft and some is hard.

plate [pleɪt] 碟 [dié]

We put food on a **plate**.

play [pleɪ] **playing, played**
玩 [wán]

After school we **play** a game of marbles.

playground [ˈpleɪgraʊnd]
游乐场 [yóu lè chǎng]

There are swings and see-saws in this **playground**.

please [pliːz] 请 [qǐng]

When you want something, say **please**.

plenty [ˈplentɪ] 很多 [hěn duō]

Mrs. Lee has **plenty** of food. She does not need any more.

pocket [ˈpɒkɪt] 袋 [dài]

I keep my handkerchief in my **pocket**.

point [pɔɪnt] 点 [diǎn]

My pencil has a sharp **point**.

pole [pəʊl] 杆 [gān]

Toby is trying to climb the **pole**.

police station [pəˈliːs ˈsteɪʃn]
警察局 [jǐng chá jú]

Rita has lost her bag. She goes to the **police station** to ask the police to help her find it.

police officer [pəˈliːs ˈɒfɪsə]
警察 [jǐng chá]

The **police officer** is stopping the traffic.

pond [pɒnd] 池塘 [chí táng]

We can see many fish in the **pond**.

pony [ˈpəʊnɪ] 小马 [xiǎo mǎ]

A **pony** is a small horse.

pool [puːl] 水池 [shuǐ chí]

We love to splash in the **pool**.

poor [pɔː] 穷的 [qióng de]

This man is **poor**. He does not have much money.

pork [pɔːk] 猪肉 [zhū ròu]

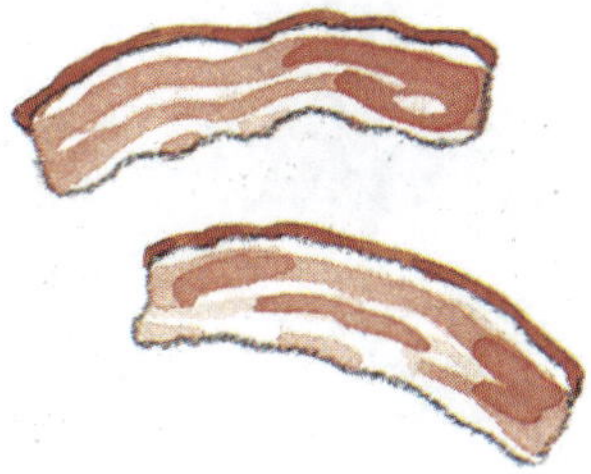

Pork is the meat from a pig.

port [pɔːt] 港口 [gǎng kǒu]

A **port** is a safe place for ships to stay.

post [pəʊst] **posting, posted**
寄、邮政 [jì], [yóu zhèng]

Patrick **posts** a letter and a parcel at the **post** office.

postman [ˈpəʊstmən] **postmen**
邮差 [yóu chāi]

The **postman** brings letters to your home.

pot [pɒt] 锅子 [guō zi]

The food is cooking in the **pot**.

potato [pəˈteɪtəʊ] **potatoes**
马铃薯 [mǎ líng shǔ]

A **potato** is a vegetable. There are many different ways to cook **potatoes**.

pour [pɔː] **pouring, poured**
倒出 [dào chū]

Harry is **pouring** water into a glass.

prawn [prɔːn] 虾 [xiā]

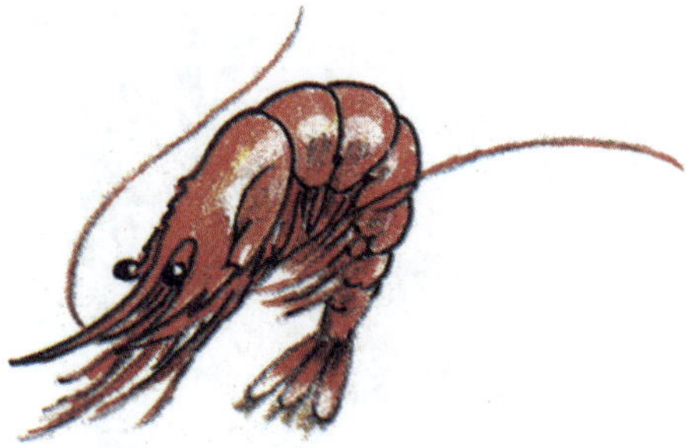

A **prawn** lives in the sea. **Prawns** are good to eat.

pray [preɪ] **praying, prayed**
祈祷 [qí dǎo]

These people are **praying**. People **pray** in different ways.

present [ˈpreznt] 礼物 [lǐ wù]

There are many **presents** for Polly on her birthday.

press [pres] **pressing, pressed**
按 [àn]

Press this button to start the machine.

pretty [ˈprɪtɪ] 美丽的 [měi lì de]

These flowers are **pretty**. They are nice to look at.

prince [prɪns] 王子 [wáng zǐ]

A **prince** is the son of a king and a queen.

princess [prɪnˈses] **princesses**
公主 [gōng zhǔ]

A **princess** is the daughter of a king and a queen.

prize [praɪz] 奖品 [jiǎng pǐn]

Toby won first **prize**. He ran well.

pull [pʊl] **pulling, pulled**
拉 [lā]

My dog tries to **pull** me along.

punch [pʌntʃ] **punching, punched**
用拳头打 [yòng quán tóu dǎ]

It is not kind to **punch** anybody.

pupil [ˈpjuːpl] 学生 [xué sheng]

The teacher is talking to his **pupils**.

puppet [ˈpʌpɪt] 木偶 [mù ǒu]

It is fun to play with **puppets**.

puppy [ˈpʌpɪ] 小狗 [xiǎo gǒu]

A **puppy** is a young dog.

purple [ˈpɜːpl] 紫色 [zǐ sè]

We are painting this wall **purple**.

purse [pɜːs] 钱包 [qián bāo]

Mrs. Lee has too much money in her **purse**.

push [pʊʃ] **pushing, pushed**
推 [tuī]

I **push** my bicycle up the hill.

put [pʊt] **putting, put**
放 [fàng]

Mother **puts** the baby into the crib.

pyjamas [pəˈdʒɑːməz]
睡衣 [shuì yī]

Ali wears **pyjamas** to go to bed.

python [ˈpaɪθn]
蟒蛇 [mǎng shé]

A **python** is a large snake.

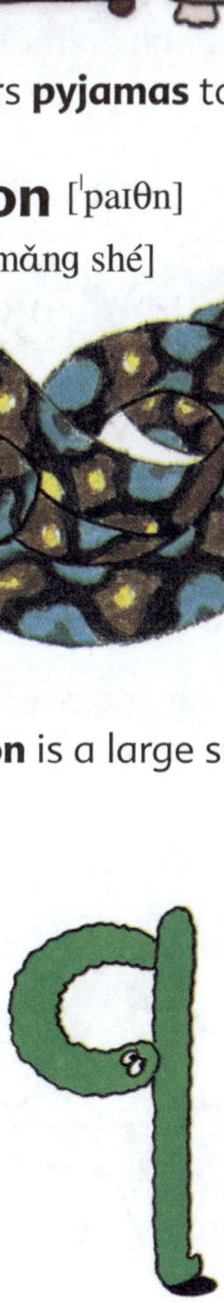

quack [kwæk] **quacking, quacked**
嘎嘎 [gā gā]

Ducks **quack**. A **quack** is the noise made by a duck.

quarter [ˈkwɔːtə]
四分之一 [sì fēn zhī yī]

I have painted in a **quarter** of the square.

quay [kiː] 码头 [mǎ tou]

Ships load and unload at a **quay**.

queen [kwiːn] 王后 [wáng hòu]

A **queen** is a king's wife. Some **queens** rule a country.

question [ˈkwestʃən]
问题 [wèn tí]

He asks her a **question**.

quick [kwɪk] 快的 [kuài de]

We must be **quick**, or we will get wet.

quiet [ˈkwaɪət]
安静的 [ān jìng de]

You must be **quiet** in the library. You must not make a noise.

quite [kwaɪt] 颇 [pō]

It is **quite** dark. It will be darker soon.

rabbit [ˈræbɪt] 白兔 [bái tù]

A **rabbit** is a small animal. It has long ears.

race [reɪs] 比赛 [bǐ sài]

Omar is running against Toby. Who will win the **race**?

radio [ˈreɪdɪəʊ]
收音机 [shōu yīn jī]

Brian is listening to the **radio**.

railway [ˈreɪlweɪ] 铁路 [tiě lù]

A train moves on the **railway**. People get on and off the trains at the **railway** station.

rain [reɪn] 雨 [yǔ]

Rain is water that falls from the sky.

rainbow [ˈreɪnbəʊ]
彩虹 [cǎi hóng]

Look at the **rainbow** in the sky. It has seven colours in it.

raincoat [ˈreɪnkəʊt]
雨衣 [yǔ yī]

A **raincoat** keeps you dry when it rains.

rash [ræʃ] 皮疹 [pí zhěn]

Norman has a **rash** all over his body.

rat [ræt] 老鼠 [lǎo shǔ]

A **rat** is an animal. **Rats** have long tails.

rattle [ˈrætl]
拨浪鼓 [bō làng gǔ]

The baby is shaking the **rattle**.

raw [rɔː] 生的 [shēng de]

All this food is **raw**. It has not been cooked.

reach [riːtʃ] **reaching, reached**
触到 [chù dào]

The dog cannot **reach** the meat. It is too short.

read [riːd] **reading, read**
读 [dú]

Mother **reads** me a story before I go to sleep.

ready [ˈredɪ]
准备好 [zhǔn bèi hǎo]

We are **ready** to go swimming. Rita is not **ready**. She still has her clothes on.

real [rɪəl] 真的 [zhēn de]

Toby has a **real** dog. Polly's dog is not **real**.

recess [rɪˈses] 休息 [xiū xi]

It is time for **recess**. We will have a short break from our lessons.

rectangle [ˈrektæŋgl]
长方形 [cháng fāng xíng]

A **rectangle** is a shape with four sides.

red [red] 红色的 [hóng sè de]

Polly has a **red** ball.

refrigerator [rɪˈfrɪdʒəreɪtə]
冰箱 [bīng xiāng]

A **refrigerator** keeps food and drinks cold.

remember [rɪˈmembə]
remembering, remembered
记得 [jì dé]

Omar cannot **remember** which way to go.

repair [rɪˈpeər] **repairing, repaired**
修理 [xiū lǐ]

Uncle Tom must **repair** his lorry. It will not start.

reply [rɪˈplaɪ] **replying, replied**
回复 [huí fù]

Patrick is writing a **reply** to Ali.

rest [rest]
其余、休息 [qǐ yú], [xiū xi]

Toby takes some of the chocolate. He gives his friend the **rest**. Grandmother takes a **rest** when she feels tired.

restaurant [ˈrestərənt]
餐厅 [cān tīng]

We like to eat in this **restaurant.**

rhinoceros [raɪˈnɒsərəs]
犀牛 [xī niú]

A **rhinoceros** is a large animal with a thick skin. It has one or two horns on its head.

ribbon [ˈrɪbən] 丝带 [sī dài]

Polly will tie a pink **ribbon** around the present.

rice [raɪs] 米 [mǐ]

Rice is food. It can be cooked in many ways.

rich [rɪtʃ] 富有的 [fù yǒu de]

The king has a lot of money. He is **rich**.

ride [raɪd] **riding, rode**
骑 [qí]

Sally is learning to **ride** a horse.

right [raɪt] 对、右 [duì], [yòu]

Betty gave the **right** answer.
The car is turning **right**.

ring [rɪŋ] **ringing, rang**
响 [xiǎng]

I will **ring** the bell.
The telephone is **ringing**.

river [ˈrɪvə] 河 [hé]

He is rowing down the **river**.

road [rəʊd] 路 [lù]

There are many cars on the **road**.

roar [rɔː] 吼 [hǒu]

A **roar** is the sound a lion makes.

rock [rɒk] **rocking, rocked**
石、摇 [shí], [yáo]

We love to climb over the **rocks**.

Grandmother is sitting in a **rocking** chair.

rocket [ˈrɒkɪt] 火箭 [huǒ jiàn]

A **rocket** travels into space.

roll [rəʊl] **rolling, rolled**
滚 [gǔn]

A ball and a wheel are **rolling** down the hill.

roof [ruːf] 屋顶 [wū dǐng]

Our house has a red **roof**.

room [ru:m] 房间 [fáng jiān]

Harry cannot get inside the **room**. There are too many people there.

root [ru:t] 根 [gēn]

Every plant has **roots** which grow under the ground. They take in water for the plant.

rope [rəʊp] 绳 [shéng]

They pulled Toby up with a **rope**.

rose [ˈrəʊz] 玫瑰 [méi gui]

A **rose** is a flower. There are **roses** of different colours.

rough [rʌf]
不平坦的 [bù píng tán de]

It is difficult to ride on a **rough** road.

round [raʊnd] 圆的 [yuán de]

These balls are **round**. The box is not **round**.

row [rəʊ] **rowing, rowed**
行、划船 [háng], [huá chuán]

Toby arranges the chairs in a **row**. They are in a straight line.

Omar is **rowing** across the lake.

rubber [ˈrʌbə]
橡胶 [xiàng jiāo]

eraser [ɪˈreɪzə]
橡皮 [xiàng pí]

boots [bu:ts]
靴 [xuē]

slippers [ˈslɪpəz]
拖鞋 [tuō xié]

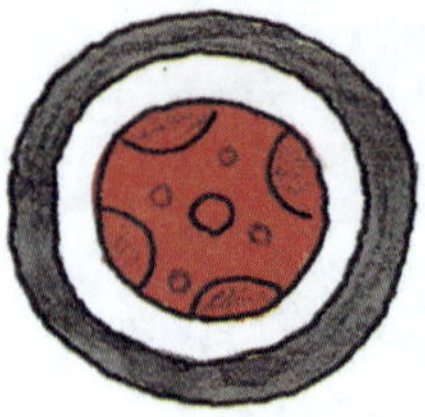

tyre [ˈtaɪə]
轮胎 [lún tāi]

ball [bɔ:l]
球 [qiú]

Rubber comes from a tree. These things are made from **rubber**.

rug [rʌg] 小地毯 [xiǎo dì tǎn]

There is a **rug** on the floor beside the bed.

ruler [ˈru:lə] 尺 [chǐ]

A **ruler** helps you draw straight lines. It helps you measure things.

run [rʌn] **running, ran** 跑 [pǎo]

Can you **run** as fast as I can?

sack [sæk] 袋 [dài]

A **sack** is a big bag. Here is a **sack** of rice.

sad [sæd] 悲伤的 [bēi shāng de]

Sally has lost her pen. She feels **sad**.

safe [seɪf] 安全的 [ān quán de]

The three kids are **safe**. The wolf cannot reach them.

sail [seɪl] 帆 [fān]

My boat has a yellow **sail**.

salt [sɔːlt] 盐 [yán]

Sally puts **salt** on her food.

same [seɪm]
一样的 [yī yàng de]

We have the **same** books.

sand [sænd] 沙 [shā]

Beaches are full of **sand**. Brian is drawing in the **sand**.

sandals [ˈsændlz]
凉鞋 [liáng xié]

Sandals are cool to wear in hot weather.

sandwich [ˈsænwɪdʒ]
sandwiches 三明治 [sān míng zhì]

A **sandwich** is two slices of bread with a filling in between.

saucepan [ˈsɔːspən]
有柄平底锅 [yǒu bǐng píng dǐ guō]

You cook food in a **saucepan**.

saucer [ˈsɔːsə]
浅碟 [qiǎn dié]

Mrs. Lee puts her cup on the **saucer**.

sausage [ˈsɒsɪdʒ]
香肠 [xiāng cháng]

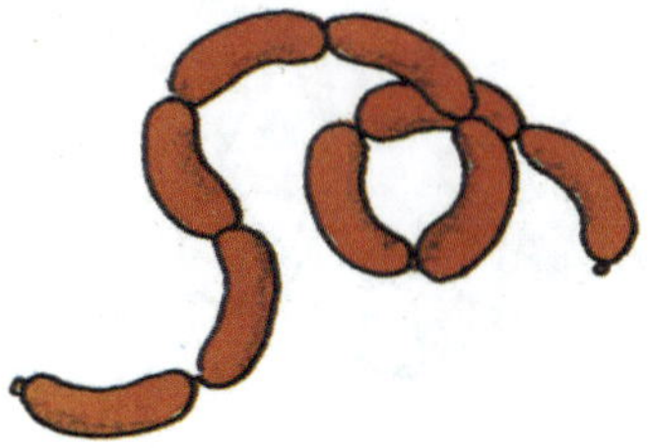

A **sausage** is made of meat.

saw [sɔː] 锯子 [jù zǐ]

Uncle Bill cuts the wood with his **saw**.

say **saying, said** [seɪ] 说 [shuō]

"Good morning, Mother," **say** the children.

scare [ˈskeə] **scaring, scared**
吓 [xià]

Harry is trying to **scare** his sister. He wants to frighten her.

scarf [skɑːf] 围巾 [wéi jīn]

Sally is wearing a **scarf** round her neck. Rita is wearing a **scarf** on her head.

school [skuːl] 学校 [xué xiào]

We go to **school** to learn and play.

scissors [ˈsɪzəz] 剪刀 [jiǎn dāo]

Polly is cutting the paper with a pair of **scissors**.

scream [skriːm] **screaming, screamed** 尖叫 [jiān jiào]

Sandra **screams** when she sees a mouse. She is scared of mice.

screw [skruː] 螺丝 [luó sī]

A **screw** holds things together.

screwdriver [ˈskruːdraɪvə]
螺丝起子 [luó sī qǐ zi]

He is using a **screwdriver** to put in the screw.

sea [siː] 海 [hǎi]

The **sea** is the salty water all around the coast. Many fish live in the **sea**.

seagull [siːgʌl] 海鸥 [hǎi ou]

A **seagull** is a bird which lives near the sea.

seat [siːt] 座位 [zuò wèi]

A **seat** is something for us to sit on.

second [ˈsekənd] 秒 [miǎo]

A **second** is a very short time. There are sixty **seconds** in one minute.

secret [ˈsiːkrɪt] 秘密 [mì mì]

Rita tells Polly a **secret**. Nobody else can hear what she is saying.

see [siː] **seeing, saw**
看见 [kān jiàn]

Sandra can **see** three snails. Can you **see** them?

seed [siːd] 种子 [zhǒng zi]

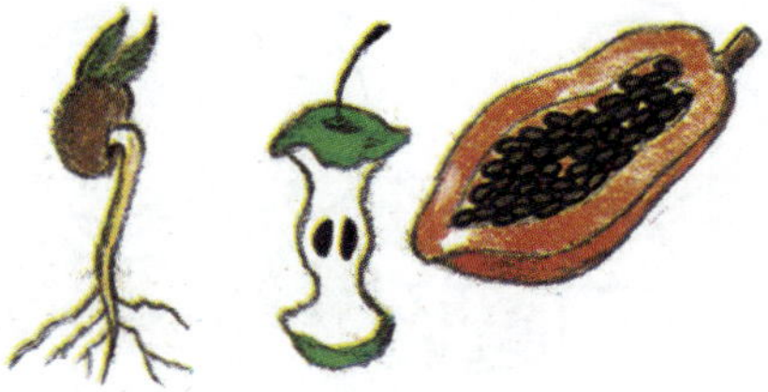

This **seed** will grow into a plant. You can find **seeds** in many fruits.

see-saw [siːsɔː]
跷跷板 [qiāo qiāo bǎn]

They are playing on the **see-saw**. It goes up and down.

sell [sel] **selling, sold**
卖 [mài]

These men **sell** drinks.

set [set]
套 [tào]

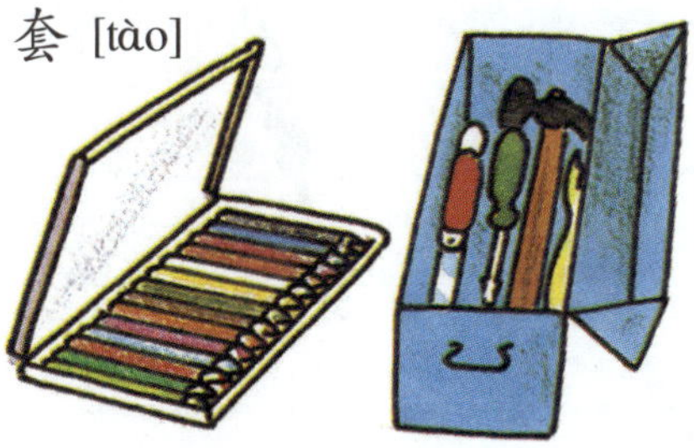

Ali bought this **set** of color pencils. Uncle Bill bought a **set** of tools.

sew [səʊ] **sewing, sewed**
缝 [féng]

Grandmother is **sewing** the button onto the shirt.

shade [ʃeɪd] 荫 [yīn]

The dog is sitting in the **shade** of the tree. It is cool in the **shade**.

shadow ['ʃædəʊ]
影子 [yǐng zi]

My **shadow** is long. The pole's **shadow** is even longer.

shake [ʃeɪk] **shaking, shook**
摇 [yáo]

Omar and Patrick are **shaking** hands.

shallow ['ʃæləʊ] 浅的 [qiǎn de]

The water is too **shallow**. I cannot swim in it.

shape [ʃeɪp]
形状 [xíng zhuàng]

circle ['sɜ:kl]
[yuán xíng]
圆形

cone [kəʊn]
[zhuī xíng]
锥形

triangle['traɪæŋgl]
三角形
[sān jiǎo xíng]

square ['skweə]
正方形
[zhèng fāng xíng]

rectangle ['rektæŋgl]
长方形
[cháng fāng xíng]

These things have different **shapes**.

share [ʃeə] **sharing, shared**
分享 [fēn xiǎng]

Sally **shares** her sweets with her friends. She gives her friends some of her sweets.

shark [ʃɑ:k] 鲨鱼 [shā yú]

A **shark** is a large fish. **Sharks** live in the sea.

sharp [ʃɑ:p]
锋利的 [fēng lì de]

This knife is very **sharp**. It cuts the meat easily.

sharpener ['ʃɑ:pənə]
铅笔削具 [qiān bǐ xiāo jù]

Jimmy is using a **sharpener** to make his pencil sharp.

she [ʃi:] **her, hers** 她 [tā]

Sandra has a doll. **She** likes it very much. Mother gave it to **her**. It is **hers**.

sheep [ʃi:p] 绵羊 [mián yáng]

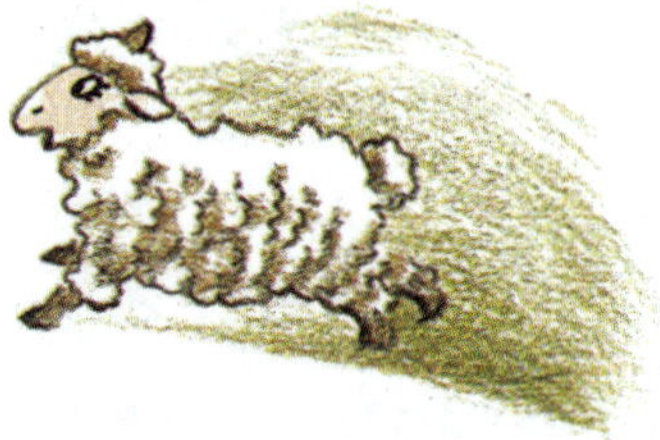

A **sheep** is a farm animal. It is covered with wool.

shell [ʃel] 壳 [ké]

I found a **shell** on the beach. Eggs and nuts have **shells**.

shoe [ʃu:] 鞋子 [xié zi]

Sandra has put on one **shoe**.

short [ʃɔ:t] 短的 [duǎn de]

Tim's trousers are too **short**.

shine [ʃaɪn] **shining, shone**
发光 [fā guāng]

The lights **shine** in the dark.

shoot [ʃu:t] **shooting, shot**
射 [shè]

He wants to **shoot** the duck with the gun.

shorts [ʃɔ:ts] 短裤 [duǎn kù]

Brian is wearing red **shorts**.

ship [ʃɪp] 轮船 [lún chuán]

A **ship** carries people and things across the sea.

shop [ʃɒp] 商店 [shāng diàn]

A **shop** sells things. This **shop** sells toys.

shovel [ˈʃʌvl] 铲 [chǎn]

Uncle Bill uses a **shovel** to dig a hole.

shirt [ʃɜ:t] 衬衫 [chèn shān]

Do you like my new **shirt**?

shopkeeper [ˈʃɒpki:pə]
店主 [diàn zhǔ]

A **shopkeeper** is a person who owns or manages a shop. This **shopkeeper** owns a shoes shop.

show [ʃəʊ] **showing, showed**
表演 [biǎo yǎn]

Harry is **showing** a frog to his sister.

shut [ʃʌt]
关闭的 [guān bì de]

The door is **shut**. It is not open.

sing [sɪŋ] **singing, sang**
唱歌 [chàng gē]

Patrick likes to **sing** in the shower.

size [saɪz] 尺码 [chǐ mǎ]

Norman needs larger **size** shoes. These are the wrong **size**.

sick [sɪk]
有病的 [yǒu bìng de]

Norman is **sick**. He does not feel well.

sink [sɪŋk] 洗涤槽 [xǐ dí cáo]

Sally washes the plates in the **sink**.

skate [skeɪt]
滚轴溜冰鞋 [gǔn zhóu liū bīng xié]

Dick has some new **skates**.

side [saɪd] 旁边 [páng biān]

Father is washing the **side** of the car.

sit [sɪt] **sitting, sat** 坐 [zuò]

Grandfather **sits** on the bench.

skin [skɪn] 皮肤 [pí fū]

Skin covers the whole of your body.

signal [ˈsɪgnəl] 讯号 [xùn hào]

The **signal** is green. The train can go.

sitting room [ˈsɪtɪŋ ruːm]
客厅 [kè tīng]

We watch television in our **sitting room**.

skip [skɪp] **skipping, skipped**
跳绳 [tiào shéng]

Polly can **skip** with her rope.

skirt [skɜːt] 裙子 [qún zi]

I am wearing a blue **skirt**.

sky [skaɪ] **skies** 天空 [tiān kōng]

I can see an aeroplane in the **sky**.

sleep [sliːp] **sleeping, slept**
睡觉 [shuì jiào]

You feel fresh after a good night's **sleep**.

slice [slaɪs] 片 [piàn]

Sandra takes a **slice** of bread.

slide [slaɪd] 滑梯 [huá tī]

Dick likes to play on the **slide**.

slide [slaɪd] **sliding, slid**
滑 [huá]

You may **slide** on slippery ground.

slip [slɪp] **slipping, slipped**
滑倒 [huá dǎo]

It is easy to **slip** on a wet floor.

slippery [slɪpərɪ]
滑的 [huá de]

Wet soap is **slippery**.

slow [sləʊ] 慢的 [màn de]

My sister is **slow**. We have to wait for her.

small [smɔːl] 小的 [xiǎo de]

This shirt is too **small** for Norman.

smell [smel] 气味 [qì wèi]

I can **smell** the cakes. They have a lovely **smell**.

smile [smaɪl] 微笑 [wēi xiào]

All the boys have a **smile** on their face.

smoke [sməʊk] **smoking, smoked**
烟 [yān]

There is **smoke** coming from the fire.

smooth [smuːð]
平滑的 [píng huá de]

A sheet of glass is **smooth**.

snail [sneɪl] 蜗牛 [wō niú]

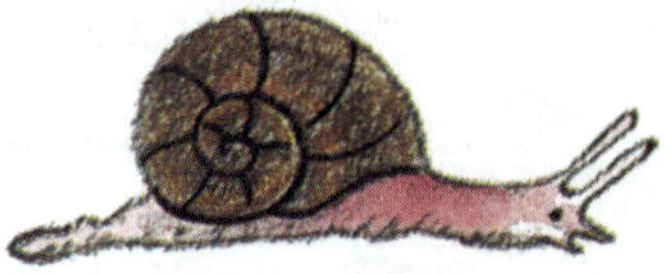

A **snail** moves very slowly. It has a shell on its back.

snake [sneɪk] 蛇 [shé]

A **snake** slides along the ground.

snow [snəʊ] 雪 [xuě]

Snow falls when it is very cold.

soap [səʊp] 肥皂 [féi zào]

Mrs. Lee washes her hands with **soap**.

sock [sɒk] 袜子 [wà zǐ]

There is a hole in one of my **socks**.

soft [sɒft] 柔软的 [róu ruǎn de]

The fur of a rabbit feels **soft**. Voices and music can be **soft** too.

soldier [ˈsəʊldʒə]
士兵 [shì bīng]

He is a **soldier** in the army. An army has many **soldiers**.

some [sʌm] 一些 [yī xiē]

Norman has **some** bread, **some** biscuits and **some** milk.

sometimes [ˈsʌmtaɪmz]
有时 [yǒu shí]

Mother **sometimes** gives me sweets. She does not give me sweets all the time.

song [sɒŋ] 歌 [gē]

We sing a **song** at Polly's party.

sore [sɔ:] 痛的 [tòng de]

My thumb feels **sore**. I cut it when I fell.

sorry [ˈsɒrɪ] 抱歉 [bào qiàn]

Dick broke Uncle Bob's window. He is **sorry**.

sound [saʊnd]
声音 [shēng yīn]

Grandmother hears a loud **sound**.

soup [su:p] 汤 [tāng]

Soup is made from meat or vegetables. I like to eat bread with my **soup**.

sour [ˈsaʊə] 酸 [suān]

A lemon tastes very **sour**. It is not sweet.

space [speɪs]
太空、空间 [tài kōng, kōng jiān]

Stars are in **space**. There is **space** for another person on this bench.

spaceship [ˈspeɪsʃɪp]
太空船 [tài kōng chuán]

A **spaceship** travels through space.

spade [speɪd] 铲 [chǎn]

Toby is digging with a **spade**.

speak [spi:k] **speaking, spoke**
说话 [shuō huà]

Do not **speak**. Grandfather is asleep.

spider [ˈspaɪdə] 蜘蛛 [zhī zhū]

A **spider** is a small animal that catches insects in its web.

spinach [ˈspɪnɪdʒ] 菠菜 [bō cài]

Spinach is a vegetable. It has green leaves.

splash [splæʃ] **splashing, splashed**
溅湿 [jiàn shī]

Sally makes a big **splash** in the water.

spoon [spuːn] 匙 [chí]

I am eating with a **spoon**.

spots [spɒts] 斑点 [bān diǎn]

This dog has black **spots** all over its body.

square [skweə]
正方形 [zhèng fāng xíng]

A **square** has four sides. All the sides are the same length.

squeeze [skwiːz] **squeezing squeezed** 挤 [jǐ]

I **squeezed** toothpaste onto my toothbrush.

squirrel [ˈskwɪrl]
松鼠 [sōng shǔ]

A **squirrel** has a bushy tail. **Squirrels** love to eat nuts.

stadium [ˈsteɪdɪəm]
体育馆 [tǐ yù guǎn]

There are many people in the **stadium**. They have come to watch a soccer match.

stairs [steə] 楼梯 [lóu tī]

Sally and Patrick climb the **stairs** to reach the top.

stamp [stæmp] **stamping, stamped**
邮票 [yóu piào]

We use **stamps** to send letters and cards in the mail.

stamp [stæmp] **stamping, stamped**
踩、跺 [cǎi, duò]

We are **stamping** our feet. What a noise!

stand [stænd] **standing, stood**
站 [zhàn]

The baby can **stand** up by himself now.

stars [stɑ:z] 星星 [xīng xīng]

The sky is full of **stars** tonight.

start [stɑ:t] **starting, started**
开始 [kāi shǐ]

We line up at the **start** of the race.

stay [steɪ] **staying, stayed**
留在 [liú zài]

Sandra will **stay** at home. Her brother is going out.

steal [sti:l] **stealing, stole**
偷 [tōu]

The thief **steals** Mrs. Lee's bag. He takes something that does not belong to him.

steel [sti:l] 钢 [gāng]

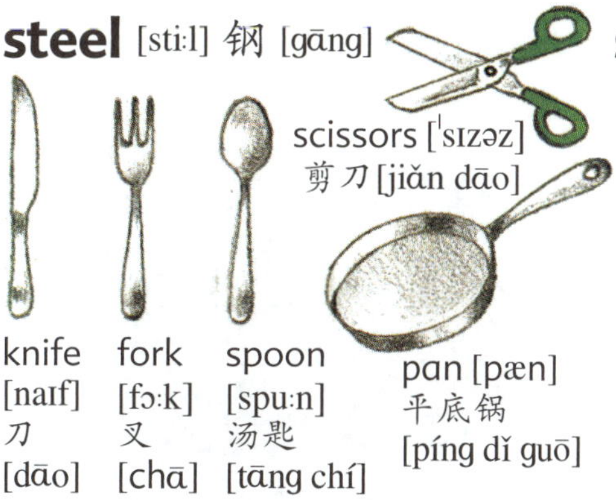

Steel is a hard metal. All these things are made of **steel**.

stem [stem] 茎 [jīng]

The **stem** of the plant has grown out of the ground. It has leaves and flowers on it.

step [step] 步 [bù]

Harry takes a large **step** over the water.

stick [stɪk] 树枝 [shù zhī]

I have a **stick** to put on the fire.

stick [stɪk] **sticking, stuck**
黏贴 [zhān tiē]

Polly will **stick** the picture into her book.

still [stɪl] 静止的 [jìng zhǐ de]

Stand **still**. Do not move.

stomach [ˈstʌmək] 胃 [wèi]

The food you eat goes into your **stomach**.

stomachache [ˈstʌməkeɪk]
肚痛 [dù tòng]

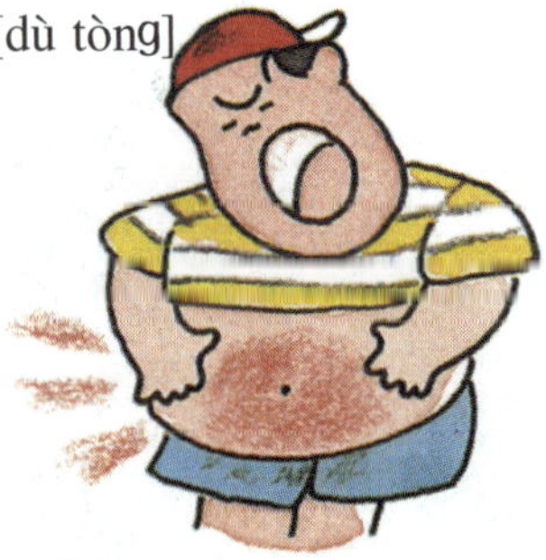

Norman has a **stomachache**.
His stomach is sore.

stone [stəʊn] 石头 [shí tou]

A **stone** is a piece of rock. I found this **stone** on the beach.

stop [stɒp] **stopping, stopped**
停 [tíng]

The light is red. Mother **stops** the car.

storm [stɔːm]
暴风雨 [bào fēng yǔ]

During a **storm** the sky is dark and the wind blows hard. It rains and there may be thunder and lightning.

storeroom [ˈstɔːruːm]
储藏室 [chǔ cáng shì]

Mrs Lee keeps many things in her **storeroom**.

story [ˈstɔːrɪ] **stories**
故事 [gù shì]

Grandfather is telling us a **story**. He knows many good **stories**.

stove [stəʊv] 炉 [lú]

Mother cooks food on a **stove**.

straight [streɪt] 直的 [zhí de]

I can draw a **straight** line. Sally's line is not **straight**.

straw [strɔː] 吸管 [xī guǎn]

Jimmy likes to drink through a **straw**.

strawberry [ˈstrɔːbərɪ]
strawberries 草莓 [cǎo méi]

A **strawberry** is a small red fruit.

street [striːt] 街道 [jiē dào]

A **street** is a road in town with houses along it.

string [strɪŋ] 绳 [shéng]

I tie up the parcel with **string**.

stripe [straɪp] 条纹 [tiáo wén]

A **stripe** is a long narrow mark. These things and animals have **stripes**.

strong [strɒŋ]

强壮的 [qiǎng zhuàng de]

Father is **strong**. He can carry the heavy box.

submarine [sʌbməˈri:n]

潜水艇 [qián shuǐ tǐng]

A **submarine** is a ship that travels under water.

subtract [səbˈtrækt]

subtracting, subtracted

减去 [jiǎn qù]

If I take away two apples, I have one left. I have **subtracted** two apples.

suck [sʌk] **sucking, sucked**

吮 [shǔn]

A baby likes to **suck** his thumb. Do you like to **suck** candies?

sugar [ˈʃʊgə] 糖 [táng]

Sugar makes food and drinks taste sweet.

sun [sʌn] 太阳 [tài yáng]

The **sun** gives us light during the day.

sunburn [ˈsʌnbɜ:n]

晒伤 [shài shāng]

Toby has a **sunburn**. He was in the sun for too long.

sunflower [ˈsʌnflaʊə]

向日葵 [xiàng rì kuí]

A **sunflower** is a large yellow flower. It is a tall plant.

supermarket [ˈsu:pəma:kɪt]

超级市场 [chāo jí shì chǎng]

We can buy all kinds of food in the **supermarket**.

supper [ˈsʌpə]
晚餐 [wǎn cān]

Before Sandra goes to bed she eats **supper**.

surprise [səˈpraɪz]
惊喜 [jīng xǐ]

We have a nice **surprise** for mother. We are giving her some flowers.

swallow [ˈswɒləʊ]
燕子 [yàn zi]

A **swallow** is a small bird. It has long wings and eats insects.

swan [swɒn] 天鹅 [tiān é]

A **swan** is a white or black bird with a long neck.

sweep [swiːp] **sweeping, swept**
扫 [sǎo]

Rita must **sweep** the floor. It is dirty.

sweets [swiːt]
糖果 [táng guǒ]

Sweets are made from sugar. You should not eat too many **sweets**.

sweet potato [swiːt pəˈteɪtəʊ] **sweet potatoes** 蕃薯 [fān shǔ]

A sweet potato is a vegetable. **Sweet potatoes** grow under the ground.

swim [swɪm] **swimming, swam**
游泳 [yóu yǒng]

I went for a **swim** in the sea.

swimming pool [swɪmɪŋ puːl]
游泳池 [yóu yǒng chí]

The children swim in the **swimming pool**.

swing [swɪŋ] **swinging, swung**
荡 [dàng]

Sally is **swinging** high on the **swing**.

sword [sɔːd] 剑 [jiàn]

Toby and I each have a **sword**.

syrup [ˈsɪrəp] 糖浆 [táng jiāng]

Syrup is made from sugar and water. It is sweet and thick.

tail [teɪl] 尾 [wěi]

The monkey is hanging by its **tail**.

tame [teɪm] 驯的 [xùn de]

These animals are **tame**. They are not wild.

T-shirt [ˈtiːʃɜːt] 汗衫 [hàn shān]

I do not know which **T-shirt** to buy.

take [teɪk] **taking, took**
拿 [ná]

Sandra **takes** the letter to her mother.

tank [tæŋk] 箱子 [xiāng zi]

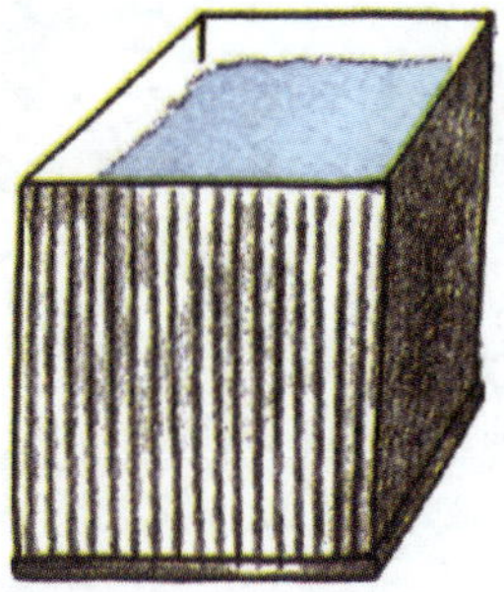

A **tank** holds a lot of water, oil or petrol. This is a water **tank**.

table [ˈteɪbl] 桌子 [zhuō zi]

A **table** is a place for eating, writing, playing a game and other things.

talk [tɔːk] **talking, talked**
谈话 [tán huà]

Mother likes to **talk** with her friend.

tap [tæp] 水龙头 [shuǐ lóng tóu]

Toby is turning on the **tap**.

tadpole [ˈtædpəʊl]
蝌蚪 [kē dǒu]

A **tadpole** grows into a frog.

tall [tɔːl]
高的 [gāo de]

Tim is **tall**. Harry is not **tall**.

taste [teɪst] 味道 [wèi dao]

I do not like the **taste** of lemons.

taxi [ˈtæksɪ]
计程车 [jì chéng chē]

A taxi is a car. We have to pay to ride in a **taxi**.

tea [ti:] 茶 [chá]

My parents drink **tea** in the afternoon.

teach [ti:tʃ] **teaching, taught**
教授 [jiào shòu]

Uncle Bill is showing me how to swim. He is **teaching** me.

teacher [ˈti:tʃə]
教师 [jiào shī]

Our **teacher** will teach us numbers today.

tear [tɪə] **tearing, tore**
眼泪、撕破 [yǎn lèi], [sī pò]

Sally is crying. A **tear** is rolling down her face.

I will **tear** the paper before I throw it away.

telephone [ˈtelɪfəʊn]
电话 [diàn huà]

Patrick talks to his friend on the **telephone**.

television [ˈtelɪvɪʒn]
电视机 [diàn shì jī]

Uncle Bob is repairing the **television** set. TV is short for **television**.

tell [tel] **telling, told**
告诉 [gào sù]

Can you **tell** me the way to the train station?

temperature [ˈtemprətʃə]
发烧 [fā shāo]

I have a **temperature**.

temple [ˈtempl]
庙宇 [miào yǔ]

Mrs. Lee is praying in the **temple**.

tent [tent] 帐篷 [zhàng peng]

It is fun to sleep in a **tent**.

term [tɜrm] 学期 [xué qī]

Our school **term** starts today. Our vacation has ended.

theatre [θɪətə] 剧院 [jù yuàn]

We are watching a play at the **theatre**.

they [ðeɪ] **them, their**
他们 [tā men]

They are doing **their** sewing. The teacher showed **them** how to sew.

thank [θæŋk] **thanking, thanked**
多谢 [duō xiè]

"**Thank** you for the present," said Sandra to her brother.

their [ðeər] 他们的 [tā men de]

That house belongs to the Thompsons. It is **their** house.

thick [θɪk] 厚的 [hòu de]

The red book is **thick**. It has many pages.

that [ðæt] **those**
这、那 [zhè, nà]

I would like **that** bag over there. **Those** are all too big.

there [ðeər] 那里 [nà lǐ]

The bicycle over **there** is mine.

thief [θiːf] **thieves**
小偷 [xiǎo tōu]

A **thief** has stolen our television set.

the [ðə] 这、那 [zhè , nà]

Toby is climbing a tree. **The** tree is tall.

thermometer [θəˈmɒmɪtə]
体温计 [tǐ wēn jì]

Mother uses a **thermometer** to take my temperature.

thin [θɪn]
瘦的、薄的
[shòu de], [báo de]

This book is **thin**. It has only ten pages. Tim is very **thin**. He is not fat.

think [θɪŋk] **thinking, thought**
想 [xiǎng]

Patrick will **think** about a present for his mother. What can he buy for her?

thirsty [ˈθɜːstɪ] 渴的 [kě de]

When I am **thirsty**, I have a drink.

this [ðɪs] **these**
这 [zhè]

This boy is my son.
These boys are playing.

thorn [θɔːn] 刺 [cì]

Some plants have **thorns**.
Thorns are sharp.

thread [θred] 线 [xiàn]

Sally has some blue **thread**.

through [θruː]
穿过 [chuān guò]

The dog walks **through** the big pipe.

throw [θrəʊ] **throwing, threw**
抛 [pāo]

Harry will **throw** the ball to you.

thumb [θʌm] 拇指 [mǔ zhǐ]

You have a **thumb** on each hand.

thunder [ˈθʌndə] 雷 [léi]

Thunder is a loud noise. It comes with lightning.

tick [tɪk] 对号 [duì hào]

Put a **tick** by the right answers.

ticket [ˈtɪkɪt] 票 [piào]

I must buy a **ticket** before I get onto the train.

tidy [ˈtaɪdɪ]
整齐的 [zhěng qí de]

Harry's room is not **tidy**. It is very messy.

tie [taɪ] 领带 [lǐng dài]

Father wears a **tie** to go to work.

tiger [ˈtaɪgə] 老虎 [lǎo hǔ]

A **tiger** is a large wild cat. It has stripes on its body.

time [taɪm] 时间 [shí jiān]

Do you know what **time** it is?
It is one o'clock.

tin [tɪn] 罐、锡 [guàn], [xī]

There is milk in this **tin**.
These things are made of **tin**.

tiny [ˈtaɪnɪ] 细小的 [xì xiǎo de]

Tiny means very small.
The elephant thinks the spider is **tiny**.

tired [ˈtaɪəd] 累的 [lèi de]

Father is **tired** after working all day. He is trying to sleep.

to [tuː] 去 [qù]

Sandra runs **to** the slide. She is going **to** go down the slide. Her mother is talking **to** her friend.

toast [təʊst]
烤面包 [kǎo miàn bāo]

Toast is bread cooked till the outside is hard.

today [təˈdeɪ] 今天 [jīn tiān]

Today is Monday.

toe [təʊ] 脚趾 [jiǎo zhǐ]

I have a sore **toe**.

together [təˈgeðə]
一起 [yī qǐ]

Three cats are eating **together**.
One cat is eating by himself.

toilet [ˈtɔɪlɪt] 厕所 [cè suǒ]

We need to go to the **toilet** many times every day.

tomorrow [təˈmɒrəʊ] 明天 [míng tiān]

Tomorrow is Tuesday.
Tomorrow is the day after today.

tongue [tʌŋ] 舌头 [shé tou]

You taste food and speak with your **tongue**.

tonight [təˈnaɪt] 今晚 [jīn wǎn]

Tonight is the evening of today.
My mother and father have gone out **tonight**.

tool [tuːl] 工具 [gōng jù]

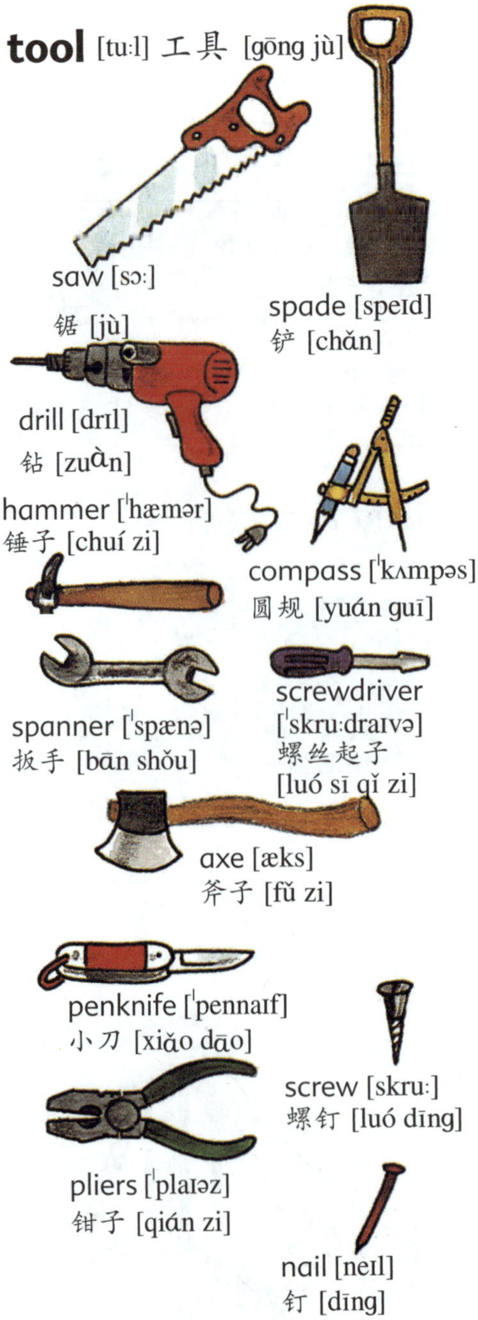

A **tool** helps us to work. These are Uncle Bill's **tools**.

tooth [tuːθ] **teeth** 牙齿 [yá chǐ]

The baby has one **tooth** now. Soon he will have more **teeth**.

toothbrush [ˈtuθbrʌʃ] **toothbrushes** 牙刷 [yá shuā]

We use a **toothbrush** to clean our teeth.

top [tɒp] 顶、陀螺 [dǐng], [tuó luó]

Polly is at the **top** of the ladder.
Ali is playing with a **top**.

torch [tɔ:tʃ] **torches**
电筒 [diàn tǒng]

Patrick uses a **torch** to help him see in the dark.

tortoise [ˈtɔ:təs] 龟 [guī]

A **tortoise** has a hard shell. It moves very slowly.

touch [tʌtʃ] **touching, touched**
摸 [mō]

Sally **touches** the flower with her hand.

towel [ˈtaʊəl] 毛巾 [máo jīn]

I dry myself with a **towel** after my bath.

town [taʊn] 市镇 [shì zhèn]

A **town** has many streets and houses. It also has shops, offices, schools and supermarkets.

toy [tɔɪ] 玩具 [wán jù]

Harry has a **toy** to play with.

traffic [ˈtræfɪk]
交通 [jiāo tōng]

There is a lot of **traffic** on the road.

train [treɪn] 火车 [huǒ chē]

The **train** is arriving at the railway station.

trap [træp] 陷阱 [xiàn jǐng]

We want to catch a mouse in this **trap**.

tray [treɪ] 托盘 [tuō pán]

Polly is carrying the glasses on a **tray**.

treasure [ˈtreʒə]
宝藏 [bǎo zàng]

They found the **treasure** when they were digging. What a lot of jewels and money!

tree [triː] 树 [shù]

A **tree** is a big plant. Here are some **trees**.

pine
[paɪn]
松 [sōng]

mango [ˈmæŋgəʊ]
芒果 [máng guǒ]

palm [pɑːm]
棕 [zōng]

willow [ˈwɪləʊ]
柳 [liǔ]

triangle [ˈtraɪæŋgl]
三角形 [sān jiǎo xíng]

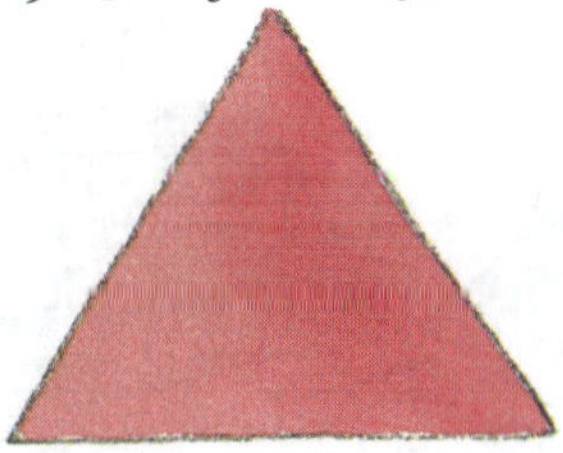

A **triangle** is a shape with three sides.

tricycle [ˈtraɪsɪkl]
三轮车 [sān lún chē]

A **tricycle** has three wheels. Sandra is riding a **tricycle**.

trousers [ˈtraʊzəz] 裤 [kù]

His **trousers** are too long.

truck [trʌk]
大卡车 [dà kǎ chē]

A **truck** carries heavy loads. This **truck** is full of sand.

true [truː] 真实的 [zhēn shí de]

A **true** story tells about things that really happened.

trumpet [ˈtrʌmpɪt]
喇叭 [lǎ ba]

Toby is learning to play the **trumpet**.

trunk [trʌŋk] 树干 [shù gàn]

The **trunk** is the thickest part of a tree. The elephant's nose is called a **trunk**.

try [traɪ] **trying, tried**
尝试 [cháng shì]

Omar will **try** to reach the book.

tube [tjuːb] 管 [guǎn]

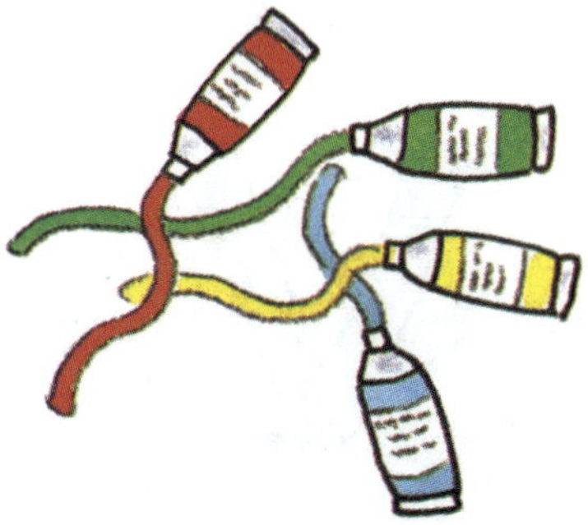

Rita has bought some **tubes** of paint.

tuck shop [tʌk ʃɒp] 小卖部 [xiǎo mài bù]

During recess, I buy food from the **tuck shop** in my school.

turkey [ˈtɜːkɪ] 火鸡 [huǒ jī]

A **turkey** is a large bird. **Turkey** is good to eat.

turn [tɜːn] **turning, turned** 转动 [zhuǎn dòng]

I **turn** the handle to open the door.

turtle [ˈtɜːtl] 海龟 [hǎi guī]

A **turtle** has a hard shell. Most **turtles** live in the sea.

twinkle [ˈtwɪŋkl]
twinkling, twinkled
闪烁 [shǎn shuò]

Can you see the stars **twinkle** at night?

tyre [ˈtaɪə] 轮胎 [lún tāi]

Father is changing the car **tyre**.

ugly [ˈʌglɪ] 丑陋的 [chǒu lòu de]

The witch is very **ugly**. I do not like to look at her.

umbrella [ʌmˈbrelə] 雨伞 [yǔ sǎn]

An **umbrella** keeps you dry when it is raining.

uncle [ˈʌŋkl] 叔、伯、舅 [shū, bó, jiù]

Your **uncle** is the brother of your father or mother.

under [ˈʌndə] 下面 [xià mian]

Dick is hiding **under** the table.

uniform [ˈjuːnɪfɔːm]

制服 [zhì fú]

A policeman wears a **uniform**. A soldier wears a **uniform**, too.

unkind [ʌnˈkaɪnd]

残忍的 [cán rěn de]

It is **unkind** to pull a dog's tail.

untidy [ʌnˈtaɪdɪ]

凌乱的 [líng luàn de]

My room looks very **untidy**. I must put everything away.

up [ʌp]

上 [shàng]

Harry is walking **up** the hill.

upside down [ˈʌpsaɪd ˈdaʊn]

上下翻转 [shàng xià fān zhuǎn]

Mrs. Lee is reading the book **upside down**.

upstairs [ˈʌpˈsteəz]

楼上 [lóu shang]

I can see many things from the window **upstairs**. We are going **upstairs**.

use [juːz] **using, used**

用 [yòng]

We will **use** a knife to cut the cake.

vacuum cleaner

[ˈvækjʊəm ˈkliːnə]

吸尘机 [xī chén jī]

Mrs. Lee uses a **vacuum cleaner** to clean the carpet.

van [væn] 客货车 [kè huò chē]

The men brought the cupboard in a **van**.

vase [vɑːz]

花瓶 [huā píng]

I will put these flowers in a **vase**.

vegetable [ˈvedʒtəbl]
蔬菜 [shū cài]

potato [pəˈteɪtəʊ]
马铃薯 [mǎ líng shǔ]

cabbage [ˈkæbɪdʒ]
卷心菜
[juǎn xīn cài]

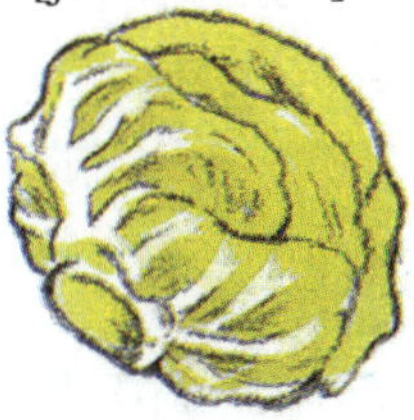
chilli [ˈtʃɪlɪ]
辣椒 [là jiāo]

green pepper
[griːn ˈpepə]
青椒 [qīng jiāo]

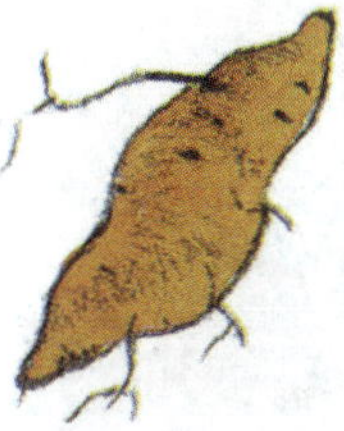
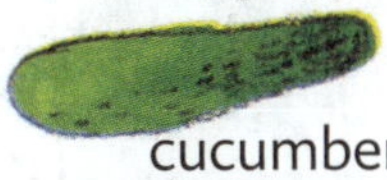
cucumber
[ˈkjuːkʌmbə]
黄瓜 [huáng gua]

sweet potato
[swiːt pəˈteɪtəʊ]
甘薯 [gān shǔ]

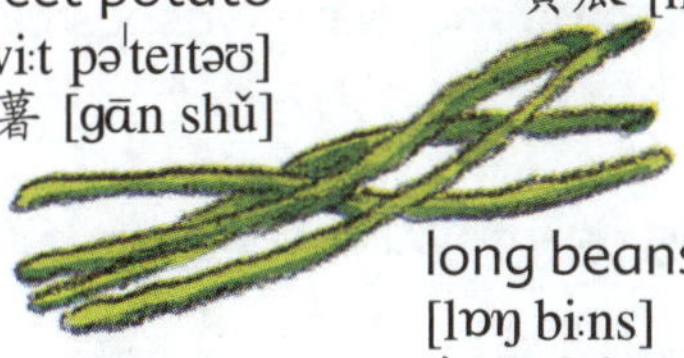
long beans
[lɒŋ biːns]
长豆 [cháng dòu]

onion [ˈʌnjən]
洋葱 [yáng cōng]

peas [piː]
豌豆 [wān dòu]

Which **vegetables** do you like to eat?

very [ˈverɪ] 很 [hěn]

I am wet. My sister is **very** wet.

vet [vet] 兽医 [shòu yī]

A **vet** looks after animals when they are sick.

village [ˈvɪlɪdʒ]
村庄 [cūn zhuāng]

A **village** is a small town.

violin [ˌvaɪəˈlɪn]
小提琴 [xiǎo tí qín]

Patrick is playing a **violin.**

visit [ˈvɪzɪt] **visiting, visited**
探望 [tàn wàng]

We **visit** our grandmother every week. We go to her house.

voice [vɔɪs] 声音 [shēng yīn]

I can hear my father's **voice**. He is calling me.

volcano [vɒlˈkeɪnəʊ] **volcanoes**
火山 [huǒ shān]

Hot rocks, fire and smoke sometimes come out of a **volcano**.

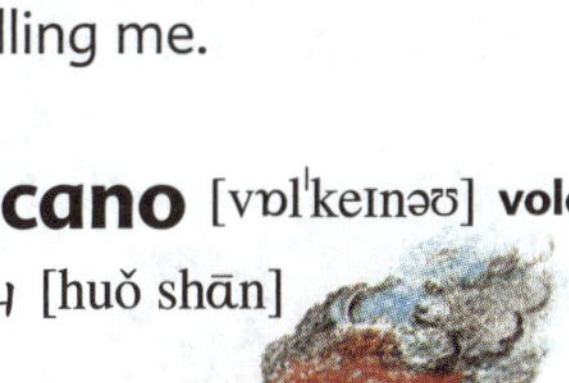

wait [weɪt] **waiting, waited**
等 [děng]

Don't go yet. Please **wait** for me.

wake [weɪk] **waking, woke**
叫醒 [jiào xǐng]

Sandra will **wake** up her grandfather. He must get up.

walk [wɔ:k] **walking, walked**
走 [zǒu]

We **walk** on two feet. A cat **walks** on four feet.

wall [wɔ:l]
墙壁 [qiáng bì]

Toby will hang this picture on the **wall**.

wand [wɒnd] 棒 [bàng]

The fairy waved her magic **wand** and the frog changed into a prince.

want [wɒnt] **wanting, wanted**
要 [yào]

We are thirsty. We **want** a drink.

warm [wɔ:m] 热的 [rè de]

It is **warm** when the sun shines.

wash [wɒʃ] 洗 [xǐ]

Dick needs a **wash**. He is very dirty.

washing machine
[ˈwɒʃɪŋ məˌʃi:n] 洗衣机 [xǐ yī jī]

A **washing machine** washes clothes for us.

waste [weɪst] **wasting, wasted**
浪费 [làng fèi]

Do not **waste** water. Turn off the tap when you have washed your hands.

watch [wɒtʃ]
手表 [shǒu biǎo]

I look at my **watch** to see what time it is.

water [ˈwɔ:tə] 水 [shuǐ]

Water is for drinking and washing. **Water** makes plants grow.

watermelon [ˈwɔ:təˈmelən]
西瓜 [xī guā]

A **watermelon** is a large fruit. It tastes sweet.

wave [weɪv] 浪 [làng]

The **waves** are splashing against the rock.

way [weɪ] 路 [lù]

This is the **way** to the zoo.

we [wi:] **us, our**
我们 [wǒ men]

Father and I cannot see the dog, so **we** call it. The dog comes to **us**. It is **our** dog.

weak [wi:k] 虚弱的 [xū ruò de]

Tim is **weak**. He is not strong enough to lift the box.

wear [weə] **wearing, wore**
穿 [chuān]

I like to **wear** dresses. My brother **wears** shorts.

weather [ˈweðə]
天气 [tiān qì]

In some countries the **weather** is hot. In other countries it is cold.

web [web] 网 [wǎng]

The spider traps insects in its **web**.

weed [wi:d] 杂草 [zá cǎo]

Weeds are plants that grow where we do not want them.

week [wi:k] 星期 [xīng qī]

There are seven days in one **week**.

weekend [ˌwi:kˈend]
周末 [zhōu mò]

Saturday and Sunday are the **weekend**.

weigh [weɪ] **weighing, weighed**
称重量 [chèng zhòng liàng]

Norman is **weighing** himself.

welcome [ˈwelkəm]
欢迎 [huān yíng]

"**Welcome**," says Sally. She is glad to see her friend.

well [wel]
井、很好 [jǐng], [hěn hǎo]

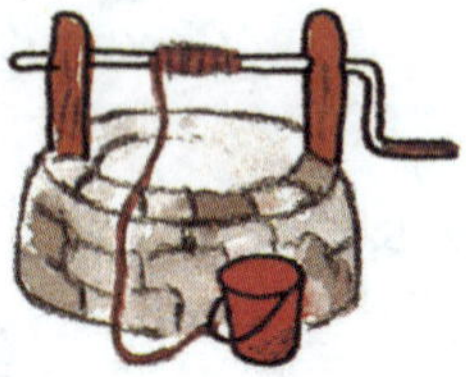

You can get water from the **well**. Rita sings **well**. People like to hear her sing. Betty has done good work. "**Well** done," says the teacher.

wet [wet] 湿的 [shī de]

Sandra is **wet**. She fell into the pool.

whale [weɪl] 鲸鱼 [jīng yú]

A **whale** is a large animal. **Whales** live in the sea.

what [wɒt] 什么 [shén me]

"**What** is that?" asks Mrs. Lee.

wheel [wi:l] 轮子 [lún zi]

That is Jimmy's bicycle **wheel**.

when [wen]
什么时候 [shén me shí hou]

When do you go to sleep? I go to sleep at eight o'clock.

where [weə] 哪里 [nǎ li]

Where is Toby?
He is behind the bush.

which [wɪtʃ] 哪 [nǎ]

Which dress shall I choose?

whisker [ˈwɪskə] 胡子 [hú zi]

A cat has **whiskers** on its face.

whisper [ˈwɪspə]
whispering, whispered
耳语 [ěr yǔ]

Polly **whispers** to Sally. Nobody else can hear what she says.

whistle [ˈwɪsl]
哨子 [shào zi]

The guard blows the **whistle** before the train leaves.

whistle [ˈwɪsl] **whistling, whistled**
吹口哨 [chuī kǒu shào]

Harry **whistles** to his dog.

white [waɪt] 白色 [bái sè]

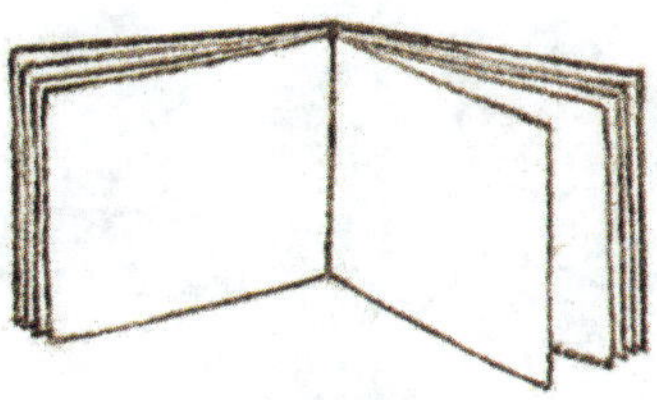

White is a colour. The pages of this book are **white**.

who [hu:] 谁 [shuí]

Who is he? He is my grandfather.

why [waɪ]
为什么 [wèi shén me]

Why is Patrick running? He is running because he is late.

wicked [ˈwɪkɪd]
邪恶的 [xié è de]

A **wicked** person likes to hurt people and be bad.

wide [waɪd] 宽的 [kuān de]

The door is not **wide** enough. The elephant cannot go through it.

wild [waɪld]
野生的 [yě shēng de]

A **wild** animal finds its own food. These are **wild** animals.

wild boar [waɪld bɔ:]
野猪 [yě zhū]

A **wild boar** is a wild pig. It has small horns by its mouth.

win [wɪn] **winning, won**
胜出 [shèng chū]

The first person to finish will **win** the race.

wind [wɪnd] 风 [fēng]

The **wind** has blown her hat away.

wire [ˈwaɪə]
金属线 [jīn shǔ xiàn]

Wire is made of metal. It can be thin or thick.

woman [ˈwʊmən] **women**
妇人 [fù rén]

Your mother is a **woman**. A girl grows up into a **woman**.

window [ˈwɪndəʊ] 窗 [chuāng]

I must close the **window**. It is raining.

wish [wɪʃ] 希望 [xī wàng]

Toby is making a **wish**. He wants to be able to fly.

wood [wʊd] 木柴 [mù chái]

Wood comes from trees.
Mr. Smiley is chopping some **wood**.

wing [wɪŋ] 翅膀 [chì bǎng]

A bird has two **wings**.
An aeroplane has two **wings**, too.

witch [wɪtʃ] **witches**
女巫 [nǚ wū]

The **witch** in this fairy tale is wicked.

wool [wʊl] 羊毛 [yáng máo]

Wool comes from sheep. **Wool** is used for making warm clothes.

wipe [waɪp] **wiping, wiped**
擦 [cā]

Dick **wipes** his wet hands on a towel to dry them.

wolf [wʊlf] **wolves**
狼 [láng]

A **wolf** is a wild dog. **Wolves** hunt for food.

work [wɜːk] 工作 [gōng zuò]

These people have a lot of **work** to do.

worker [ˈwɜːkə]
工人 [gōng rén]

These **workers** are helping to build the house.

world [wɜːld] 世界 [shì jiè]

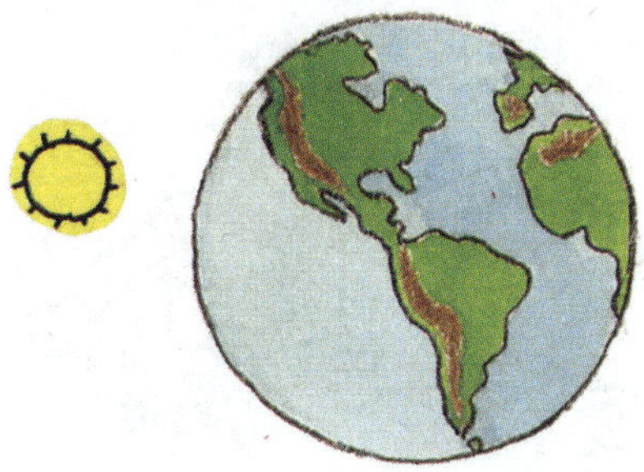

The **world** is another name for the Earth.

worm [wɜːm] 蚯蚓 [qiū yǐn]

A **worm** is long and soft. It lives in the ground.

worry [ˈwʌrɪ] **worrying, worried**
担心 [dān xīn]

Don't **worry**. I will help you with the work.

wrap [ræp] **wrapping, wrapped**
包起来 [bāo qǐ lái]

Polly **wraps** the box with blue paper.

wrist [rɪst] 手腕 [shǒu wàn]

Toby wears a big watch on his **wrist**.

write [raɪt] **writing, wrote**
写 [xiě]

Sandra can **write** her name.

wrong [rɒŋ] 错的 [cuò de]

That is the **wrong** piece. It does not look right.

X-ray [ˈeks reɪ]
X射线 [X shè xiàn]

An **X-ray** shows the inside of your body.

xylophone [ˈzaɪləfəʊn]
木琴 [mù qín]

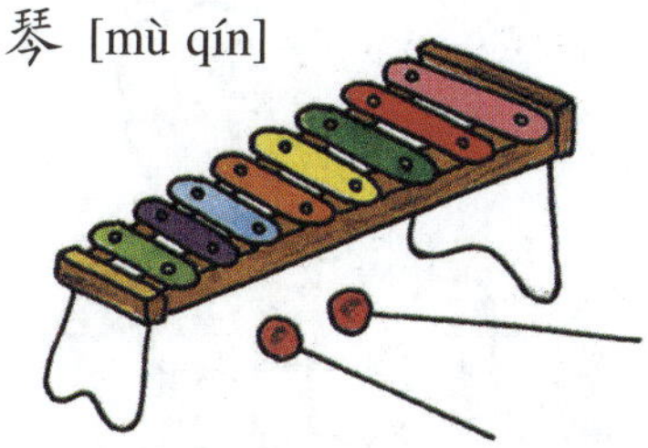

A **xylophone** makes music. You use little hammers to play a **xylophone**.

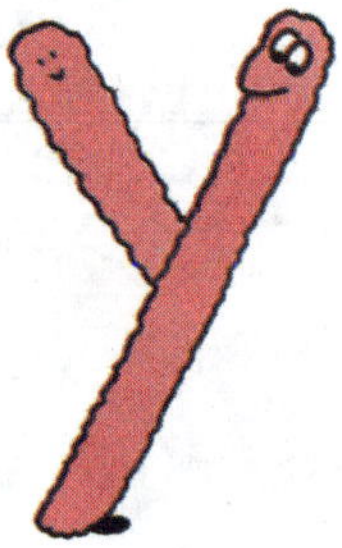

yell [jel] 喊叫 [hǎn jiào]

Patrick gave a **yell** when he stepped on a nail.

you [juː] **you, your**
你 [nǐ]

You have a new watch. Father gave it to **you**. It is **your** watch.

yacht [jɒt]
帆船 [fān chuán]

We go sailing in our **yacht**.

yellow [ˈjeləʊ]
黄色 [huáng sè]

Yellow is a colour. My raincoat is **yellow**.

young [jʌŋ]
年青的 [nián qīng de]

The boy is **young**. He is only ten years old. A puppy is a **young** dog.

yawn [jɔːn]
呵欠 [hē qiàn]

What a big **yawn**!

yesterday [ˈjestədɪ]
昨天 [zuó tiān]

Yesterday Father started to paint the fence. Today he has finished painting.

yo-yo [ˈjəʊ jəʊ]
摇摇 [yáo yao]

A **yo-yo** is a small toy. It goes up and down on a string.

year [jɪə] 岁、年 [suì], [nián]

The baby is one **year** old. There are 365 days in one **year**.

yolk [jəʊk] 蛋黄 [dàn huáng]

The **yolk** is the yellow part of an egg.

zebra [ˈzebrə] 斑马 [bān mǎ]

A **zebra** has black and white stripes.

zero [ˈzɪərəʊ] 零 [líng]

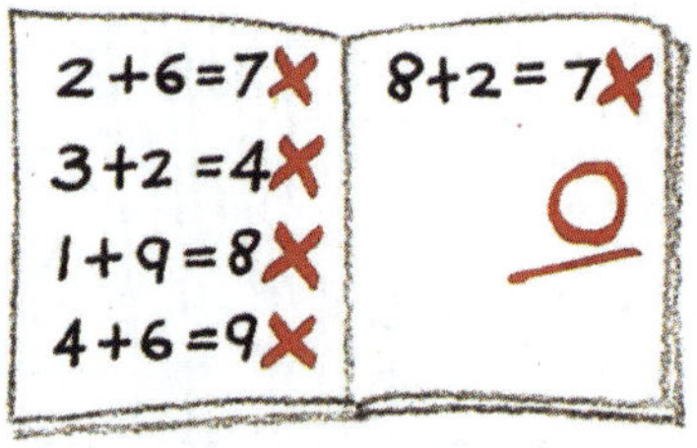

Zero means none at all.

zip [zɪp] 拉链 [lā liàn]

I have pulled up my **zip**.

zoom [zu:m] **zooming, zoomed**
急速移动 [jí sù yí dòng]

The cars **zoom** around the corner.

zoo [zu:]
动物园 [dòng wù yuán]

You can see many animals at the **zoo**.

• The Calendar

日历

DECEMBER [dɪˈsembə] 十二月 [shí èr yuè]

NOVEMBER [nəʊˈvembə] 十一月 [shí yī yuè]

OCTOBER [ɒkˈtəʊbə] 十月 [shí yuè]

SEPTEMBER [səpˈtembə] 九月 [jiǔ yuè]

AUGUST [ˈɔːgəst] 八月 [bā yuè]

JULY [dʒuːˈlaɪ] 七月 [qī yuè]

JUNE [dʒuːn] 六月 [liù yuè]

MAY [meɪ] 五月 [wǔ yuè]

APRIL [ˈeɪprl] 四月 [sì yuè]

MARCH [mɑːtʃ] 三月 [sān yuè]

FEBRUARY [ˈfebrʊərɪ] 二月 [èr yuè]

JANUARY [ˈdʒænjʊərɪ] 一月 [yī yuè]

SUNDAY [ˈsʌnd] 星期日 [xīng qī rì]	MONDAY [ˈmʌndɪ] 星期一 [xīng qī yī]	TUESDAY [ˈtjuːzdɪ] 星期二 [xīng qī èr]	WEDNESDAY [ˈwenzdɪ] 星期三 [xīng qī sān]	THURSDAY [ˈθɜːzdɪ] 星期四 [xīng qī sì]	FRIDAY [ˈfraɪdɪ] 星期五 [xīng qī wǔ]	SATURDAY [ˈsætədɪ] 星期六 [xīng qī liù]
			1 	2 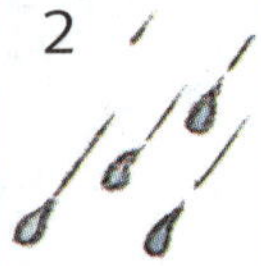	3 	4 
5	6	7	8	9	10	11
12	13	14	15	16	17	18
19	20	21	22	23	24	25
26	27	28	29	30	31	

There are seven days in a **week**.
There are four weeks in a **month**.
There are twelve months in a **year**.

The Family Tree
家谱

This is Harry's family tree.

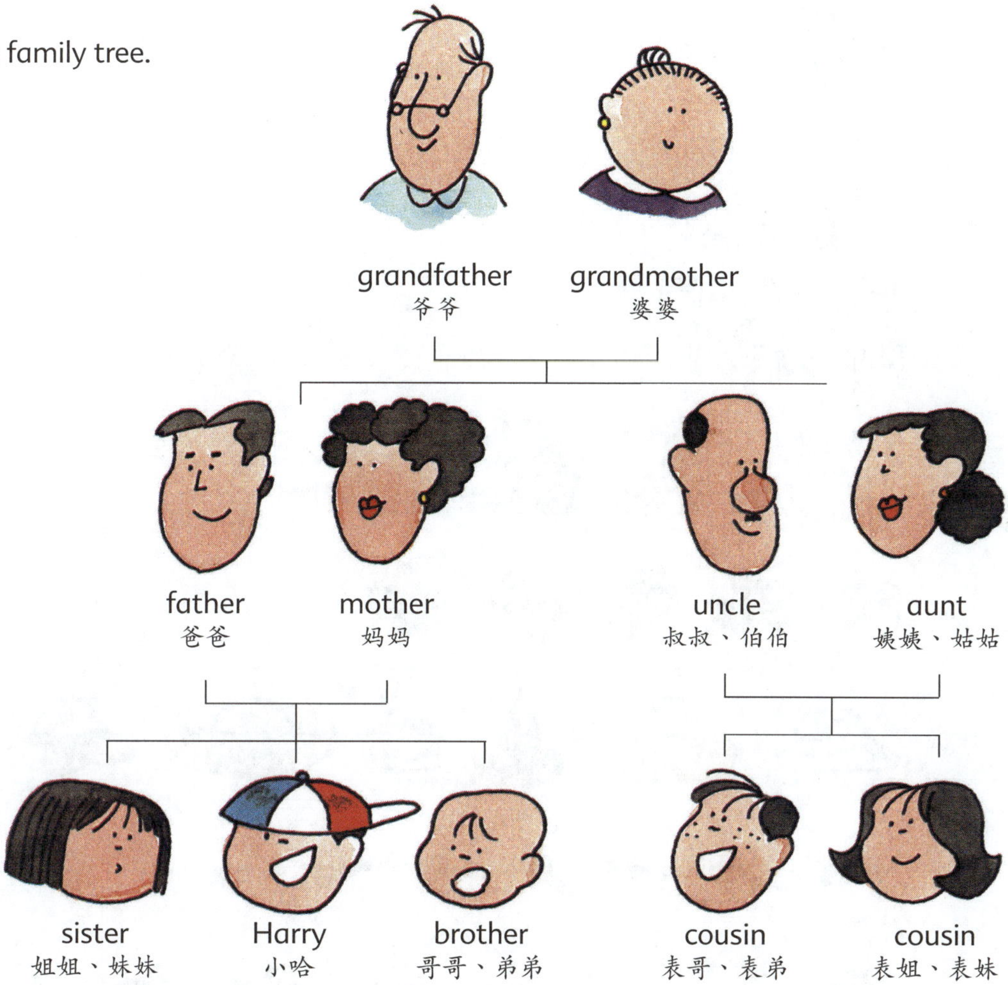

Festivals
节日

Christmas
圣诞节

Chinese New Year
农历新年

Numbers
数字

1 monster
一只妖怪

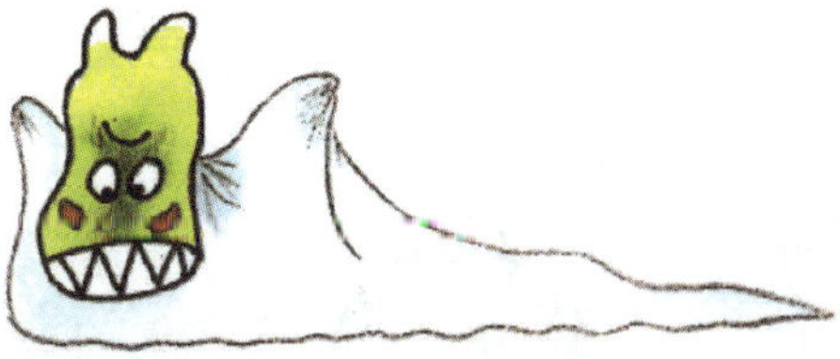

2 windows
两扇窗

3 chairs
三张椅子

4 cats
四只猫

5 cups
五个杯

6 hats
六个帽子

7 tadpoles
七只蝌蚪

8 frogs
八只青蛙

9 buttons
九枚钮扣

10 feathers
十条羽毛

11 bones
十一块骨头

12 apples
十二个苹果

13 worms
十三条蚯蚓

14 snails
十四只蜗牛

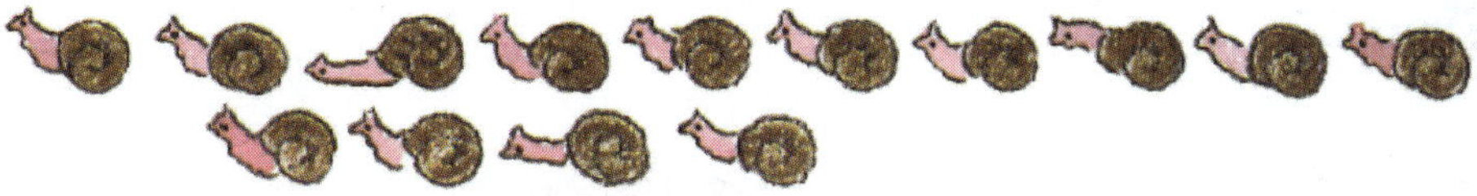

15 leaves
十五片叶子

16 crayons
十六支蜡笔

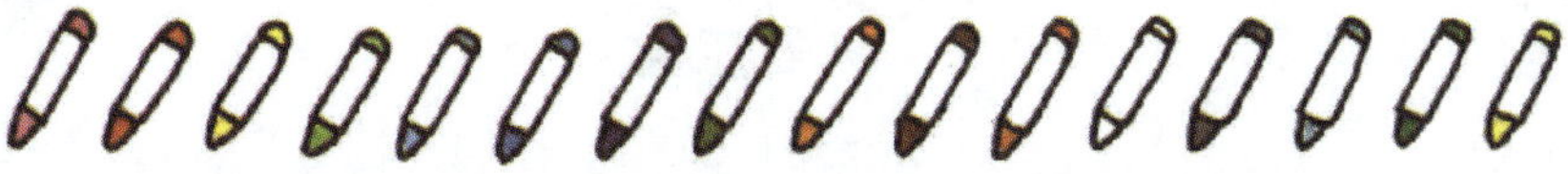

17 mangosteens
十七个山竹

18 biscuits
十八块饼干

19 eggs
十九只鸡蛋

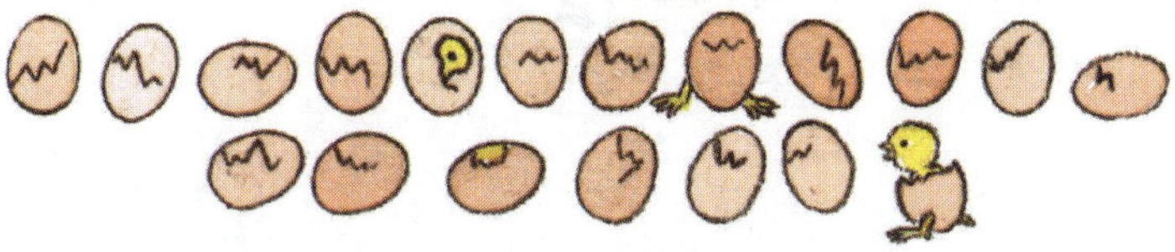

20 beads
二十颗弹珠

100
一百

1000
一千

• Time
时间

One o'clock
一点

Three o'clock
三点

Six o'clock
六点

Eight o'clock
八点

Ten o'clock
十点

Twelve o'clock
十二点

Half past six
6.30 am
上午六点半

Quarter past ten
10.15 am
上午十点一刻

Quarter to three
2.45 pm
两点三刻

Half past six
6.30 pm
傍晚六点半

Quarter past ten
10.15 pm
下午十点一刻

TIMES 1000 ACTION WORDS

Illustrated by

May Kong

Edited by Valerie Barth

A Note to Parents

This section of the book is designed to introduce to students 1000 of the more common action words in the English language. Action words are verbs, and they form an important part of a student's vocabulary.

In this section we have included both single-word verbs, e.g. call, and phrasal verbs, e.g. call off. Please note, however, that the verbs have not been listed in strict alphabetical order. While the words have been grouped according to their initial letters, within each group they have been arranged in a context which is more logical or more visually appealing than a strict alphabetical listing would allow.

Each entry is accompanied by a sentence which demonstrates the way in which the action word is typically used in the context of everyday speech. The lively and amusing illustrations will certainly appeal to students and make the learning of new action words an enjoyable experience.

给家长的话

本部分的目的是介绍给学生一千个常见的英文动词。有关动作的词叫动词，在儿童词汇占一重要部分。

在这部分，我们包括了简单的动词，如 **call** 和短语动词，如 **call off**。不过，请注意，动词没有严格按字母表顺序排列。 词依照起首的字母排列，但组内则由于情理和视觉效果而根据内容排列。

每个动词都附有一句造句，显示如何在日常生活用语中应用有关的动词。生动有趣的插图对学生充满吸引力，并为他们在学习新动词时增加不少乐趣。

Aa

answer [ˈɑːnsə]
answering, answered
接听 [jiē tīng]
Helen is **answering** the telephone.

accept [əkˈsept] **accepting, accepted**
接受 [jiē shòu]
Kathy **accepts** a gift from her father.

add [æd]
adding, added
加 [jiā]
Mother is **adding** some milk to her coffee.

attend [əˈtend] **attending, attended**
参加 [cān jiā]
We are **attending** Jane's birthday party.

add up [æd ʌp]
加起来 [jiā qǐ lái]
Teacher asked me to **add up** these numbers.

act [ækt] **acting, acted**
扮演 [bàn yǎn]
Jimmy **acted** as a wolf in the school play.

awake [əˈweɪk] **awaking, awoke**
弄醒 [nòng xǐng]
The alarm clock **awoke** me at seven o'clock.

admire [ədˈmaɪə] **admiring, admired**
羡慕 [xiàn mù]
Jane's friends **admire** her beautiful new doll.

arrive [əˈraɪv] **arriving, arrived**
到达 [dào dá]

We **arrived** at the station too late. The train had left without us.

agree [əˈgriː]
agreeing, agreed
同意 [tóng yì]

Peter **agreed** to help me with my bags.

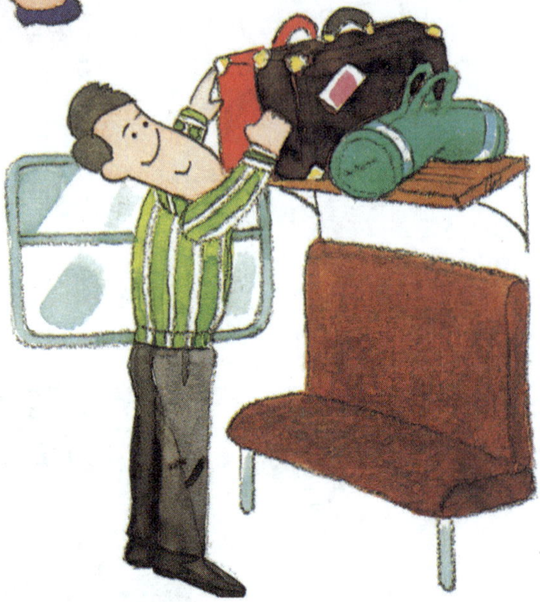

aim [eɪm]
aiming, aimed
瞄准 [miáo zhǔn]

Andy **aims** carefully at the apple.

arrange [əˈreɪndʒ] **arranging, arranged**
安排 [ān pǎi]

Father is **arranging** the bags on the shelf.

advise [ədˈvaɪs] **advising, advised**
劝告 [quàn gào]

The policeman **advised** us to cross the road carefully.

allow [əˈlaʊ] **allowing, allowed**
准许 [zhǔn xǔ]

Dogs are not **allowed** in this station.

appear [əˈpɪə] **appearing, appeared**
出现 [chū xiàn]
A bright star **appeared** suddenly in the sky.

attack [əˈtæk]
attacking, attacked
攻击 [gōng jī]
The fierce dog **attacked** the burglar.

announce
[əˈnaʊns]
announcing, announced
宣布 [xuān bù]
The station master **announces** the arrival of the train.

amuse [əˈmjuːz]
amusing, amused 娱乐 [yú lè]
The clown **amused** us with his tricks.

ache [eɪk] **aching, ached**
疼痛 [téng tòng]
Willy's stomach **aches** because he has eaten too much.

annoy [əˈnɔɪ] **annoying, annoyed**
弄 ...... 生气 [nòng ...... shēng qì]
Kathy's brother **annoyed** her by spilling coffee over her favourite dress.

ask [ɑːsk] **asking, asked**
问 [wèn]
I **asked** mother for another slice of cake.

Bb

bleed [bliːd] **bleeding, bled**
流血 [liú xuè]
Jimmy's arm is **bleeding**.

bandage [ˈbændɪdʒ] **bandaging, bandaged**
包扎 [bāo zhā]
The nurse is **bandaging** Jimmy's arm.

bake [beɪk] **baking, baked**
烤、烘 [kǎo, hōng]
Mother is **baking** a cake for Kathy's birthday.

belong [bɪˈlɒŋ] **belonging, belonged**
属于 [shǔ yú]
This book **belongs** to Jane.

barbecue [ˈbɑːbɪkjuː]
barbecuing, barbecued
烧烤 [shāo kǎo]
Father is **barbecuing** in the backyard.

bark [bɑːk] **barking, barked**
吠 [fèi]
The dogs are **barking** loudly at the cat.

bathe [beɪð] **bathing, bathed**
洗澡 [xǐ zǎo]
Mother **bathes** the baby in warm water.

beat [biːt] **beating, beat**
打、敲、击败 [dǎ], [qiāo], [jī bài]
Mandy is **beating** an egg.

Jimmy is **beating** the drum.

Helen **beats** Willy in the race.

break [breɪk]
breaking, broke
折断 [zhé duàn]

Willy **broke** the stick into two pieces.

break down [breɪk daʊn] 坏了 [huài le]
Father's car **broke down** on his way to work.

blush [blʌʃ] **blushing, blushed**
脸红 [liǎn hóng]

Linda **blushed** when Jimmy gave her a kiss.

bend [bend] **bending, bent**
弯曲 [wān qū]
Willy is **bending** a stick.

Benny **bent** down to pick up a coin.

block [blɒk] **blocking, blocked**
拦阻 [lán zǔ]
The fallen tree is **blocking** the road.

box [bɒks] **boxing, boxed**
拳击 [quán jī]
That big boy **boxed** Andy on the chin.

bounce [ˈbaʊns]
bouncing, bounced
使…… 弹回[shǐ …… tán huí]
Andy is **bouncing** a ball.

bow [bəʊ] **bowing, bowed**
鞠躬 [jū gōng]
The magician is **bowing** to the audience.

button [ˈbʌtn]
buttoning, buttoned
扣上[kòu shang]
Helen is **buttoning** her jacket.

bring [brɪŋ] **bringing, brought**
拿 [ná]
Mother is **bringing** us some food.

beg [beg] **begging, begged**
乞讨 [qǐ tǎo]
The clever dog **begs** for a bone.

borrow [ˈbɒrəʊ] **borrowing, borrowed**
借 [jiè]
Helen is **borrowing** some books from the library.

boil [bɔɪl] **boiling, boiled**
滚 [gǔn]
The water is **boiling**.

balance [ˈbæləns] **balancing, balanced**
平衡 [píng héng]
Andy is **balancing** a ball on his forehead.

Uncle Roy is **blowing** his nose.

blow [bləʊ] **blowing, blew**
吹 [chuī]
The wind is **blowing** through the trees.

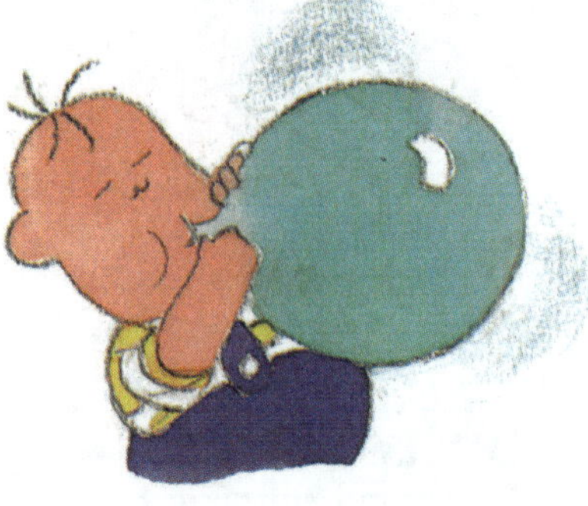

blow up [bləʊ ʌp]
吹起 [chuī qǐ]
Andy is **blowing up** a balloon.

blow out [bləʊ aʊt]
吹熄 [chuī xī]
Jane **blows out** the candles on her birthday cake.

bite [baɪt] **biting, bit**
咬 [yǎo]
The dog is **biting** a bone.

bury [ˈberɪ] **burying, buried**
埋藏 [mái cáng]
The dog is **burying** a bone.

burn [bɜːn] **burning, burned or burnt**
烧 [shāo]
Father is **burning** some leaves.

brush [brʌʃ] **brushing, brushed**
刷、梳 [shuā], [shū]
Jimmy is **brushing** his teeth.
Kathy is **brushing** her hair.

breathe [briːð] **breathing, breathed**
呼吸 [hū xī]
We **breathe** through our noses.

bump [bʌmp] **bumping, bumped**
撞 [zhuàng]
Willy **bumped** into a lamp post.

burst [bɜːst] **bursting, burst**
胀破 [zhàng pò]
The balloon **burst** with a loud bang.

build [bɪld] **building, built**
建造 [jiàn zào]
Peter is **building** a spaceship.

bully [ˈbʊlɪ] **bullying, bullied**
欺负 [qī fu]
That big boy is **bullying** the little children.

buy [baɪ] **buying, bought**
买 [mǎi]
Mandy is **buying** some flowers.

Cc

camp [kæmp] **camping, camped**
露营 [lù yíng]
The scouts **camped** at the beach.

call [kɔːl] **calling, called**
呼叫 [hū jiào]
Call the firemen to put out the fire.

call for [kɔːl fə] 呼救 [hū jiù]
Willy **called for** help when he got into trouble while swimming.

call off [kɔːl ɒf] 取消 [qǔ xiāo]
The teacher had to **call off** the picnic because it was raining.

care [keər] **caring, cared**
照顾 [zhào gu]
Simon **cares** for his pet rabbit. He feeds it and cleans its cage every day.

catch [katʃ] **catching, caught**
接住 [jiē zhù]
Jimmy held out both hands to **catch** the ball.

change [tʃeɪndʒ] **changing, changed**
换 [huàn]
Willy **changed** out of his wet clothes into dry ones.

catch up [katʃ ʌp]
赶上 [gǎn shang]
The snail cannot **catch up** with the rabbit. He is too slow.

cause [kɔːz] **causing, caused**
引起、造成 [yǐn qǐ, zào chéng]
Willy's sneeze **caused** the glass of water to fall over.

carry [ˈkærɪ] **carrying, carried**
抱 [bào]
Mother is **carrying** the baby.

cheat [tʃiːt] **cheating, cheated**
作弊 [zuò bì]
Jimmy **cheated** at cards.

chase [tʃeɪs]
chasing, chased
追赶 [zhuī gǎn]
The dog **chased** the cat up a tree.

carry on [ˈkærɪ ɒn] 继续 [jì xù]
Grandmother let me **carry on** watching television although it was past my bedtime.

choose [tʃuːz]
choosing, chose
挑选 [tiāo xuǎn]
It is hard to **choose** which sweets to buy when they all look so nice.

carve [kaːv] **carving, carved**
刻上 [kè shang]
Peter is **carving** a piece of wood into a boat.

celebrate [ˈselɪbreɪt]
celebrating, celebrated
庆祝 [qìng zhù]
Jane is **celebrating** her birthday by having a party.

chat [tʃæt]
chatting, chatted
聊天 [liáo tiān]
Kathy is **chatting** with her friends.

chip [tʃɪp] **chipping, chipped**
打碎 [dǎ suì]
Andy dropped a plate and **chipped** it.

7 + 8 = ?
(a) 5 (b) 10 (c) 15

circle [ˈsɜːkl]
circling, circled 打圈 [dǎ quān]
Helen is **circling** the right answer to the addition.

check [tʃek] **checking, checked**
检查、查看 [jiǎn chá], [chá kàn]

Linda is counting her school books to **check** if she has them all.

check in [tʃek ɪn] 登记 [dēng jì]

We **checked in** to the hotel at the start of our holiday.

check out [tʃek aʊt]
退房 [tùi fáng]

We were sad to **check out** of the hotel at the end of our vacation.

cling [klɪŋ] **clinging, clung**
依偎着 [yī wēi zhe]

The baby koala **clings** tightly to its mother.

We are going to see a movie tonight. Simon is **checking** the times of the shows.

chop [tʃɒp] **chopping, chopped**
砍 [kǎn]

Uncle Roy **chopped** down the tree.

charge [tʃɑːdʒ]
charging, charged
冲向 [chōng xiàng]

The rhinoceros **charged** at the fence.

cheer [tʃɪə] **cheering, cheered**
欢呼、打气 [huān hū, dǎ qì]

The girls are **cheering** for their team at the race.

cheer up [tʃɪə ʌp]
使 ...... 开心 [shǐ ...... kāi xīn]

The show **cheered up** the children and made them laugh.

clap [klæp] **clapping, clapped**
拍 [pāi]

When the show ended, they **clapped** their hands.

clean up [kliːn ʌp] 收拾 [shōu shi]

Mother told Jimmy to **clean up** his room.

clean [kliːn] **cleaning, cleaned**

清洗 [qīng xǐ]

Father **cleans** the car on Sundays.

chew [tʃuː] **chewing, chewed**

咀嚼 [jǔ jué]

The dog is **chewing** a bone.

clear [klɪə] **clearing, cleared**

清除 [qīng chú]

I am **clearing** the desk so that I have room to do my homework.

clear away [klɪə əˈweɪ]

收拾整齐 [shōu shi zhěng qí]

Kathy helps her father **clear away** the dishes after dinner.

clear up [klɪə ʌp]

清理 [qīng lǐ]

The children are **clearing up** the mess after the fun-fair.

clear off [klɪə ɒf] 溜走 [liū zǒu]

The thief **cleared off** when he saw a policeman coming.

cluck [klʌk] **clucking, clucked**

咯咯地叫 [gē gē de jiào]

A hen **clucks** loudly after laying an egg.

clear out [klɪə aʊt]

清理 [qīng lǐ]

Dad is **clearing out** the garage.

climb [klaɪm] **climbing, climbed**

爬 [pá]

The baby **climbed** up a chair.

complain [kəmˈpleɪn] **complaining, complained**
投诉 [tóu sù]
Kathy **complained** to her mother that Andy had torn her book.

clip [klɪp] **clipping, clipped**
夹 [jiā]
Mandy is **clipping** the papers together so that they will not get lost.

collect [kəˈlekt] **collecting, collected**
收集 [shōu jí]
Peter **collects** stamps from around the world.

colour [ˈkʌlə] **colouring, coloured**
填色 [tián sè]
Andy is **colouring** a picture of a lion.

comb [kəʊm] **combing, combed**
梳 [shū]
Jane is **combing** her long hair.

coach [kəʊtʃ] **coaching, coached**
训练 [xùn liàn]
Mr. Thomson **coaches** the football team. He shows them how to kick the ball.

congratulate [kənˈgrætʃʊleɪt] **congratulating, congratulated**
祝贺 [zhù hè]
Everyone **congratulated** the winner.

close [kləʊz] **closing, closed**
关上 [guān shang]
Mother is **closing** the door.

coil [kɔɪl] **coiling, coiled**
卷起 [juǎn qǐ]
Father **coiled** the garden hose after he had watered the plants.

collapse [kəˈlæps] **collapsing, collapsed**
倒下来 [dǎo xià lai]
The tent **collapsed** in the strong wind.

confuse [kənˈfjuːz] **confusing, confused**
弄糊涂 [nòng hú tu]
The signs **confused** the driver.

collide [kəˈlaɪd] **colliding, collided**
撞上 [zhuàng shang]
The car **collided** with a van.

compare [kəmˈpeər]
comparing, compared
比较 [bǐ jiào]
Benny is tall **compared** with Helen.

come [kʌm] **coming, came**
来 [lái]
Come with me. I'll show you the way.

come off [kʌm ɒf]
脱落 [tuō luò]
A button **came off** Kathy's coat.

come apart [kʌm əˈpɑːt]
裂开 [liè kāi]
The shirt was too small and **came apart** at the seam when Willy put it on.

come out [kʌm aʊt] 出来 [chū lai]
The moon and stars **come out** at night.

come across [kʌm əˈkrɒs]
发现 [fā xiàn]
Andy **came across** a gold chain while looking for his lost marble.

come back [kʌm bæk]
回来 [huí lái]
Boomerangs always **come back** when thrown.

come on [kʌm ɒn]
出场 [chū chǎng]
The magician **came on** the stage wearing a long black cape.

consider [kənˈsɪdə] **considering, considered**
考虑 [kǎo lǜ]
Mother and Father are **considering** what to get for Kathy for her birthday.

consist [kənˈsɪst]
consisting, consisted
由...... 组成 [yóu ...... zǔ ahéng]
This gift set **consists** of two storybooks and two tapes.

connect [kəˈnekt] **connecting, connected**
连接 [lián jiē]
Uncle Roy **connected** the aerial to the television.

construct [kənˈstrʌkt]
constructing, constructed
建造 [jiàn zào]
Peter **constructed** a spaceship from clothes pins.

control [kənˈtrəʊl]
controlling, controlled
控制 [kòng zhì]
Andy **controls** the robot by remote control.

continue [kənˈtɪnjuː]
continuing, continued
继续 [jì xù]
"Mother, don't stop now. Please **continue** reading the story," the children asked.

cool [kuːl] **cooling, cooled**
使凉快 [shǐ liáng kuai]
Mandy is **cooling** her feet in the stream.

cool off [kuːl ɒf]
降温 [jiàng wēn]
The children felt hot, so they jumped into the water to **cool off**.

cool down [kuːl daʊn]
变凉 [biàn liáng]
The porridge was hot, so the three bears let it **cool down**.

contain [kənˈteɪn] **containing, contained**
盛着 [chéng zhe]
This bottle **contains** ink.

cover [ˈkʌvə] **covering, covered**
掩 [yǎn]
Kathy **covered** her face with her hands.

cover up [ˈkʌvə ʌp] 盖起来 [gài qǐ lái]
Andy **covered up** the ink stain so his mother would not see it.

copy [ˈkɒpɪ] **copying, copied**
抄写 [chāo xiě]
Linda **copied** the arithmetic from the blackboard.

contribute [kənˈtrɪbjuːt] **contributing, contributed**
献出 [xiàn chū]
The children **contributed** some money to buy a present for their mother.

cook [kʊk] **cooking, cooked**
煮 [zhǔ]
Mother **cooked** a delicious roast chicken.

cost [kɒst] **costing, cost**
价钱为 [jià qián wéi]
This hamburger **costs** $4.50.

count [kaʊnt] **counting, counted**
计算 [jì suàn]
The rich man is **counting** his money.

cough [kɒf] **coughing, coughed**
咳嗽 [ké sou]
Willy **coughed** because he had a sore throat.

crack [kræk] **cracking, cracked**
裂开 [liè kāi]
The vase **cracked** when it was dropped.

crash [kræʃ] **crashing, crashed**
撞 [zhuàng]

The car **crashed** into the wall.

create [kriː'eɪt] **creating, created**
创造 [chuàng zào]

The magician **created** a monster with his spells.

crawl [krɔːl] **crawling, crawled**
爬行 [pá xíng]

The baby is **crawling** across the room.

crouch [kraʊtʃ] **crouching, crounched**
蹲伏 [dūn fú]

Kathy **crouched** behind a chair to hide from Willy.

creep [kriːp] **creeping, crept**
轻轻地走 [qīng qīng de zǒu]

Jimmy **crept** up behind Linda to frighten her.

cross [krɒs] **crossing, crossed**
穿过 [chuān guò]

We looked left and right before **crossing** the street.

croak [krəʊk] **croaking, croaked**
呱呱叫 [guā guā jiào]

The frogs are **croaking** away.

cry [kraɪ] **crying, cried**
哭 [kū]

Jane **cried** when she fell down and hurt her knee.

cross out [krɒs aʊt]
删去 [shān qù]

Peter **crossed out** a mistake in his book.

crumple [ˈkrʌmpl]
crumpling, crumpled
揉皱 [róu zhòu]
Andy **crumpled** the drawing.

cuddle [ˈkʌdl]
cuddling, cuddled
抱着 [bào zhe]
The baby is **cuddling** a teddy bear.

crumble [ˈkrʌmbl] **crumbling, crumbled**
弄碎 [nòng suì]
Mother is **crumbling** the biscuit into a bowl.

crow [krəʊ] **crowing, crowed**
啼 [tí]
The rooster **crows** loudly in the early morning.

cycle [ˈsaɪkl] **cycling, cycled**
骑自行车 [qí zì xíng chē]
Bobby **cycles** home from school.

crush [krʌʃ] **crushing, crushed**
压坏 [yā huài]
The football was **crushed** by the steamroller.

curtsy [ˈkɜːtsɪ] **curtsying, curtsied**
屈膝行礼 [qū xī xíng lǐ]
Cinderella **curtsied** to the queen.

curl [kɜːl] **curling, curled**
蜷缩 [quán suō]
The cat **curled** up on the cushion.

crowd [kraʊd] **crowding, crowded**
围着 [wéi zhe]
The children are **crowding** around the friendly chimpanzee.

Dd

cut [kʌt] **cutting, cut**
切 [qiē]
Aunt Molly is **cutting** the cake into slices.

cut down [kʌt daʊn]
砍倒 [kǎn dǎo]
Father **cut down** a tree in the garden.

cut off [kʌt ɒf]
剪下 [jiǎn xià]
Bobby is **cutting off** the sleeves from his T-shirt.

cut out [kʌt aʊt] 剪出来 [jiǎn chū lái]
Linda is **cutting out** pictures from a magazine.

cut up [kʌt ʌp]
切碎 [qiē suì]
Kathy **cuts up** the vegetables to make a salad.

damage [ˈdæmɪdʒ] **damaging, damaged**
毁坏 [huǐ huài]
The ship was **damaged** when it hit the rocks.

dance [dɑːns] **dancing, danced**
跳舞 [tiào wǔ]
The children are **dancing** happily round the Christmas tree.

dare [deə] **daring, dared**
敢 [gǎn]
Andy didn't **dare** touch the snake.

darn [dɑːn] **darning, darned**
缝补 [féng bǔ]
Mother is **darning** a hole in Jimmy's sock.

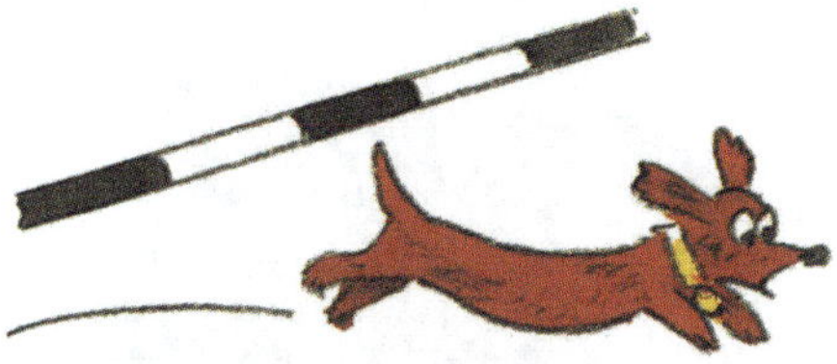

dash [dæʃ]
dashing, dashed
猛冲 [měng chōng]

The dog **dashed** across the street.

describe [dɪˈskraɪb]
describing, described
形容 [xíng róng]

Jimmy is **describing** to the policeman the dog that he has lost.

demand [dɪˈmɑːnd]
demanding, demanded
要求 [yāo qiú]

Andy **demanded** the biggest ice cream cone.

decorate [ˈdekəreɪt]
decorating, decorated
布置 [bù zhì]

Mandy is **decorating** the hall.

delight [dɪˈlaɪt]
delighting, delighted
喜欢 [xǐ huan]

Jane was **delighted** with her new puppy.

deliver [dɪˈlɪvə]
delivering, delivered
传送 [chuán sòng]

The mailman **delivered** a parcel to Linda's house.

decide [dɪˈsaɪd] **deciding, decided**
决定 [jué dìng]

Helen could not **decide** whether to wear shorts or a dress.

deal [diːl] **dealing, dealt**
发 [fā]

You **deal** all the cards to play this game.

deserve [dɪˈzɜːv]
deserving, deserved
应得 [yīng dé]

Bobby practised hard for the swimming contest and **deserved** first prize.

defend [dɪˈfend] **defending, defended**
保卫 [bǎo wèi]

The soldiers are **defending** their country from attack.

die [daɪ] **dying, died**
死 [sǐ]

The bear **died** after the hunter shot it.

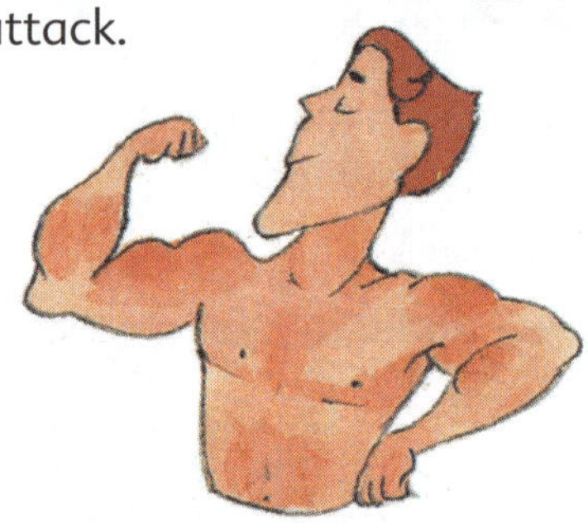

develop [dɪˈveləp]
delveloping, developed
锻炼 [duàn liàn]

The bodybuilder **developed** huge muscles.

die down [daɪ daʊn]
逐渐熄灭 [zhú jiàn xī miè]

We let the fire **die down** after the barbecue.

die away [daɪ əˈweɪ]
变弱 [biàn ruò]

The music **died away** at the end of the song.

destroy [dɪˈstrɔɪ] **destroying, destroyed**
摧毁、破坏 [cuī huǐ, pò huài]

The big boy **destroyed** Andy's sand castle.

dig [dɪg] **digging, dug**
挖 [wā]

Uncle Roy is **digging** a hole to plant the tree.

dial [ˈdaɪəl] **dialling, dialled**
打电话 [dǎ diàn huà]

Helen **dialed** 999 to call the police.

design [dɪˈzaɪn] **designing, designed**
设计 [shè jì]

Aunt Molly is **designing** a party dress for Kathy.

demonstrate [ˈdemənstreɪt]
demonstrating, demonstrated
示范 [shì fàn]

The fireman **demonstrated** how to put out the fire.

disguise [dɪsˈgaɪz]
disguising, disguised
假扮 [jiǎ bàn]

The thief **disguised** himself as an old lady.

direct [dɪˈrekt] **directing, directed**
指挥 [zhǐ huī]

The policeman is **directing** the traffic at the crossroads.

dismiss [dɪsˈmɪs]
dismissing, dismissed
解散 [jiě sàn]

At the end of the day the children are **dismissed** from class.

disappear [ˌdɪsəˈpɪə]
disappearing, disappeared
消失 [xiāo shī]

The wizard **disappeared** in a puff of smoke.

display [dɪˈspleɪ]
displaying, displayed
陈列 [chén liè]

The new books are **displayed** in the shop window.

dip [dɪp] **dipping, dipped**
浸 [jìn]

The cat **dipped** its paw into the fish tank to try to catch a fish.

discover [dɪsˈkʌvə]
discovering, discovered
发现 [fā xiàn]

The scientist **discovered** a new plant in the forest.

disturb [dɪˈstɜːb]
disturbing, disturbed
打扰 [dǎ rǎo]

Do not **disturb** Dad. He is sleeping.

discuss [dɪˈskʌs]
discussing, discussed
讨论 [tǎo lùn]

Willy, Linda and Jimmy **discussed** where they wanted to go for a picnic.

do [duː] **doing, did**
做 [zuò]
Jimmy must **do** his homework. He cannot play with Andy now.

do away with [duː əˈweɪ wɪð]
除掉 [chú diào]
Jack **did away with** the giant.

do up [duː ʌp]
修理 [xiū lǐ]
Bobby **did up** an old bike. Now it looks like new.

dream [driːm]
dreaming, dreamed or dreamt
梦想 [mèng xiǎng]
Helen **dreams** of being a pilot.

dress [dres] **dressing, dressed**
打扮 [dǎ ban]
Linda **dressed** as a witch for Halloween.

donate [dəʊˈneɪt]
donating, donated 捐出 [juān chū]
Mandy **donated** her savings to the old people's home.

dock [dɒk] **docking, docked**
停靠 [tíng kào]
The ship **docked** at the wharf to unload its cargo.

divide [dɪˈvaɪd] **dividing, divided**
分 [fēn]
Jimmy is **dividing** the candies into two equal piles.

dislike [dɪsˈlaɪk]
disliking, disliked
不喜欢 [bù xǐ huan]
Andy **dislikes** vegetables.

dive [daɪv] **diving, dove**
跳水 [tiào shuǐ]
Bobby is **diving** into the pool.

drag [dræg] **dragging, dragged**
拖 [tuō]

The men are **dragging** the boat up onto the beach.

drift [drɪft] **drifting, drifted**
漂 [piāo]

There was no wind and the boat **drifted** on the sea.

drown [draʊn]
drowning, drowned
遇溺 [yù nì]

The lifeguard rescued Willy when he was **drowning**.

drill [drɪl] **drilling, drilled**
钻洞 [zuān dòng]

Uncle Roy is **drilling** a hole in the wall.

draw [drɔː] **drawing, drew**
画 [huà]

Andy is **drawing** a rabbit.

doze [dəʊz] **dozing, dozed**
打瞌睡 [dǎ kē shuì]

Dogs love to **doze** in the sun.

drive [draɪv] **driving, drove**
开车 [kāi chē]

Father **drives** the car to work each morning.

drip [drɪp] **dripping, dripped**
漏 [lòu]
Water is **dripping** from the ceiling onto the floor.

doodle [ˈduːdl]
doodling, doodled
乱画、涂鸦 [luàn huà, tú yā]

Helen is **doodling** on a piece of paper.

drain [dreɪn] **draining, drained**
滴乾 [dī gān]

Kathy let the dishes **drain** after she washed them.

drink [drɪŋk] **drinking, drank**
喝 [hē]

Willy **drank** a glass of milk during breakfast.

drink up [drɪŋk ʌp]
吸乾 [xī gān]

The elephant **drank up** all the water in the bucket.

dry [draɪ] **drying, dried**
擦乾 [cā gān]

After a bath you **dry** yourself well with a towel.

dust [dʌst]
dusting, dusted
拂去灰尘 [fú qù huī chén]

Mother is **dusting** the furniture.

dry out [draɪ aʊt]
乾涸 [gān hé]

The puddle **dried out** in the hot sun.

duck [dʌk] **ducking, ducked**
低下头 [dī xià tóu]

The giant **ducked** his head to get through the door.

dump [dʌmp] **dumping, dumped**
倒掉 [dào diào]

The truck **dumped** the garbage in a heap.

drop off [drɒp ɒf]
让 …… 下车 [ràng …… xià chē]

Mother **dropped** Kathy **off** at school.

drop [drɒp] **dropping, dropped**
掉了 [diào le]

Linda **dropped** an egg onto the floor.

drop in [drɒp ɪn]
顺便探访 [shùn biàn tàn fǎng]

Andy **dropped in** to see his grandmother.

Ee

edge [edʒ] **edging, edged**
慢慢地移动 [màn man de yí dòng]

The clown **edged** his way carefully along the narrow plank.

eat [iːt] **eating, ate**
吃 [chī]

Elephants **eat** a lot.

eat up [iːt ʌp] 吃光 [chī guāng]
The mouse **ate up** all the cheese.

elect [ɪˈlekt] **electing, elected**
推选 [tuī xuǎn]
The team **elected** a new captain.

emerge [ɪˈmɜːdʒ] **emerging, emerged**
冒出来 [mào chū lái]

Suddenly a shark **emerged** from the water.

embrace [ɪmˈbreɪs]
embracing, embraced
拥抱 [yōng bào]

Father **embraced** Mother lovingly.

embarrass [ɪmˈbærəs]
embarrassing, embarrassed
使 ...... 难为情 [shǐ ...... nán wèi qíng]

Andy **embarrassed** his father by being rude in front of Aunt Molly.

earn [ɜːn] **earning, earned**
赚取 [zhuàn qǔ]
Bobby **earns** pocket money by washing cars.

escape [ɪˈskeɪp] **escaping, escaped**
逃走 [táo zǒu]

The monkey **escaped** from the cage.

engrave [ɪnˈgreɪv]
engraving, engraved
刻上 [kè shang]

Andy is **engraving** his name on the tree trunk.

entertain [ˌentəˈteɪn]
entertaining, entertained
娱乐 [yú lè]

The clown **entertained** us with his funny tricks.

enjoy [ɪnˈdʒɔɪ] **enjoying, enjoyed**
喜欢 [xǐ huan]

Mandy **enjoys** watching television.

enter [ˈentə] **entering, entered**
进入 [jìn rù]

The burglar is **entering** the house by the window.

employ [ɪmˈplɔɪ]
employing, employed
雇用 [gù yòng]

Sam is **employed** to clean windows.

empty [ˈemptɪ] **emptying, emptied**
弄空 [nòng kōng]

The baby **emptied** the box of blocks onto the floor.

1 + 1 = 2

equal [ˈiːkwəl] **equalling, equalled**
等于 [děng yú]

One plus one **equals** two.

end [end] **ending, ended**
结束 [jié shù]

The road **ends** at the cliff edge.

erase [ɪˈreɪz] **erasing, erased**
擦掉 [cā diào]

It is easy to **erase** mistakes with an eraser.

explain [ɪkˈspleɪn]
explaining, explained
解释 [jiě shì]
The teacher **explained** to the children how to jump over the hurdles.

examine [ɪgˈzæmɪn]
examining, examined
检查 [jiǎn chá]
The doctor is **examining** the sick boy.

excite [ɪkˈsaɪt] **exciting, excited**
兴奋 [xīng fèn]
Mandy was **excited** when she saw the gold cup.

excuse [ɪkˈskjuːz] **excusing, excused**
免除 [miǎn chú]
Jane is **excused** from sports because she has hurt her ankle.

exercise [ˈeksəsaɪz]
exercising, exercised
做运动 [zuò yùn dòng]
Bobby **exercises** every day to keep fit.

expect [ɪkˈspekt]
expecting, expected
预计 [yù jì]
I **expect** it will rain today. There are a lot of dark clouds in the sky.

expand [ɪkˈspænd]
expanding, expanded
膨胀 [péng zhàng]
A balloon **expands** when you blow it up.

explore [ɪkˈsplɔː]
exploring, explored
仔细查看 [zǐ xì chá kān]
Kathy is **exploring** the rock pools looking for crabs.

exchange [ɪksˈtʃeɪndʒ]
exchanging, exchanged
交换 [jiāo huàn]
Willy is **exchanging** shorts with Peter.

Ff

face up [feɪs ʌp] 面对 [miàn duì]

It is hard to **face up** to your teacher when you have not done your homework.

fade [feɪd] **fading, faded**

褪色 [tùn sè]

The curtains have **faded**.

face [feɪs] **facing, faced**

面向 [miàn xiàng]

Linda **faced** the clock to see what time it was.

fall [fɔːl] **falling, fell**

跌倒 [diē dǎo]

Willy tripped over a stone and **fell** on his hands and knees.

fall off [fɔːl ɒf]

跌下 [diē xià]

Andy **fell off** his chair in fright.

faint [feɪnt] **fainting, fainted**

晕倒 [yūn dǎo]

Mandy saw a ghost and **fainted**.

fake [feɪk] **faking, faked**

假装 [jiǎ zhuāng]

Andy **faked** a stomach ache because he did not want to go to school.

fan [fæn] **fanning, fanned**

扇凉 [shàn liáng]

Aunt Molly **fanned** herself to keep cool.

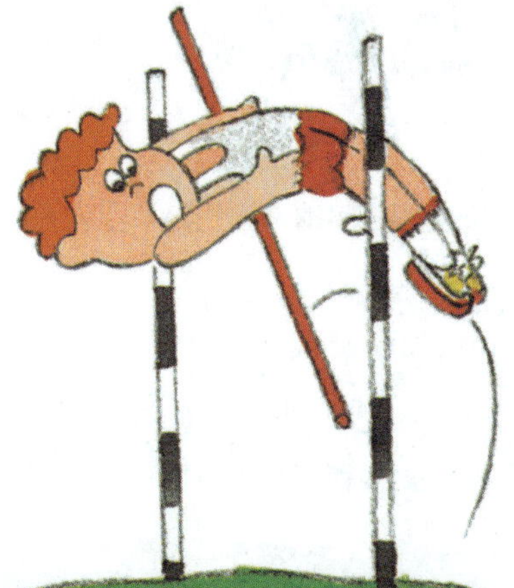

fail [feɪl] **failing, failed**

未能 [wèi néng]

Bobby **failed** to clear the high jump.

fast [fɑːst] **fasting, fasted**
斋戒 [zhāi jiè]
The holy man is **fasting**. He is not eating any food.

farm [fɑːm] **farming, farmed**
耕种 [gēng zhòng]
Uncle Roy **farms** a small piece of land behind the house.

feed [fiːd] **feeding, fed**
喂 [weì]
Simon **feeds** his pet rabbit carrots and lettuce.

fear [fɪə] **fearing, feared**
害怕 [hài pà]
Kathy **fears** snakes.

feel [fiːl] **feeling, felt**
给人 ...... 感觉 [gěi rén ...... gǎn jué]
Rabbits **feel** soft and cuddly.

fetch [fetʃ] **fetching, fetched**
衔回 [xián huí]
The dog **fetches** the stick for Jimmy.

feel like [fiːl laɪk]
想要 [xiǎng yào]
On a hot day we **feel like** a cold drink.

fasten [ˈfɑːsn]
fastening, fastened
扣上 [kòu shang]
Willy is **fastening** his seat belt.

find [faɪnd] **finding, found**
找到 [zhǎo dào]
Mandy **found** a coin on the footpath.

find out [faɪnd aʊt]
找出 [zhǎo chū]
Jimmy looked in the phone book to **find out** Peter's phone number.

fit [fɪt] **fitting, fit**
合适 [hé shì]

Cinderalla's foot **fit** the shoe perfectly.

fit in [fɪt ɪn]
容得下 [róng de xià]

Only five people could **fit in** the car.

finish [ˈfɪnɪʃ] **finishing, finished**
完成 [wán chéng]

The rabbit **finished** first in the race.

finish with [ˈfɪnɪʃ wɪð]
完成 [wán chéng]

Helen had **finished with** the book, so she returned it to the library.

fill [fɪl] **filling, filled**
注满 [zhú mǎn]

Andy is **filling** the pool with water.

fill up [fɪl ʌp]
装满 [zhuāng mǎn]

Jane **filled up** the bucket with sand.

fence [fens] **fencing, fenced**
围起来 [wéi qǐ lái]

Uncle Roy is **fencing** the tree with wire.

fight [faɪt] **fighting, fought**
打架 [dǎ jià]

Bobby and Jimmy are **fighting**.

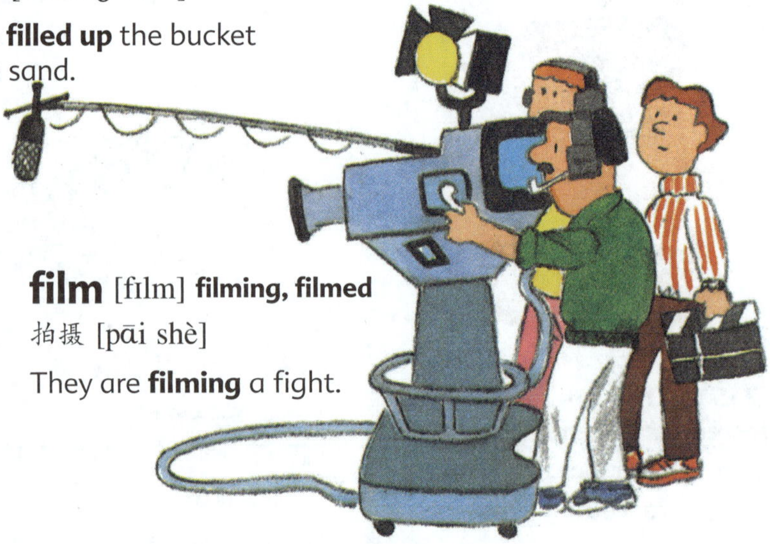

film [fɪlm] **filming, filmed**
拍摄 [pāi shè]

They are **filming** a fight.

flap [flæp] **flapping, flapped**
飘 [piāo]

The washing is **flapping** in the wind.

flash [flæʃ] **flashing, flashed**
闪亮 [shǎn liàng]

The light from the lighthouse **flashed** across the sea.

flag [flæg] **flagging, flagged**
挥手拦截 [huī shǒu lán jié]

We **flag** down a taxi.

flow [fləʊ] **flowing, flowed**
流 [liú]

The river **flows** down to the sea.

float [fləʊt] **floating, floated**
漂浮 [piāo fú]

Kathy can **float** on her back.

flood [flʌd] **flooding, flooded**
溢出 [yì chū]

Andy left the water running and **flooded** the floor.

flush [flʌʃ] **flushing, flushed**
冲洗 [chōng xǐ]

Jane is **flushing** the toilet.

fizz [fɪz] **fizzing, fizzed**
发出嘶嘶声 [fā chū sī sī shēng]
This drink **fizzes** for a while when I pour it out.

flatten [ˈflætn]
flattening, flattened
弄平 [nòng píng]
Willy **flattened** the plasticine.

fold [fəʊld] **folding, folded**
摺 [zhé]
Andy **folded** a piece of paper to make a dart.

flip [flɪp] **flipping, flipped**
捻 [niǎn]
I can **flip** a coin in the air.

fix [fɪks] **fixing, fixed**
准备 [zhǔn bèi]
Helen is **fixing** lunch.

freeze [friːz] **freezing, froze**
结冰 [jié bīng]
When water **freezes**, it becomes ice.

fling [flɪŋ] **flinging, flung**
扔 [rēng]
The lazy boy **flung** his clothes on the floor.

foam [fəʊm] **foaming, foamed**
起泡 [qǐ pào]
The beer **foams** over the glass.

form [fɔːm] **forming, formed**
构成 [guò chéng]
Jimmy **forms** a K with his body.

forget [fəˈget] **forgetting, forgot**
忘记 [wàng jì]
Poor Willy cannot write. He has **forgotten** to bring his pencil.

frown [fraʊn] **frowning, frowned**
皱眉 [zhòu méi]
Bobby **frowns** when he is worried.

fire [ˈfaɪə] **firing, fired**
开枪 [kāi qiāng]
The hunter is **firing** at the birds.

fly [flaɪ] **flying, flew**
飞 [fēi]
Birds **fly** in the sky.

fish [fɪʃ] **fishing, fished**
钓鱼 [diào yú]
Jimmy likes to **fish** with his father.

flick [flɪk] **flicking, flicked**
轻打 [qīng dǎ]
The cow is **flicking** the flies with its tail.

fluff [flʌf] **fluffing, fluffed**
抖开 [dǒu kāi]
The hen is **fluffing** its feathers.

flit [flɪt] **flitting, flitted**
飞来飞去 [fēi lái fēi qù]
The butterfly **flits** from flower to flower.

flee [fliː] **fleeing, fled**
逃跑 [táo pǎo]
The animals are **fleeing** from the burning forest.

free [friː] **freeing, freed**
放走 [fàng zǒu]
Linda is **freeing** the bird from its cage.

follow [ˈfɒləʊ] **following, followed**
跟随 [gēn suí]
The dog **followed** Jimmy home from school.

frighten [ˈfraɪtn]
frightening, frightened
吓唬 [xià hu]
Little Miss Muffet was **frightened** by the spider.

fry [fraɪ] **frying, fried**
炸 [zhá]
Mother is **frying** an egg for Andy.

furnish [ˈfɜːnɪʃ] **furnishing, furnished**
布置 [bù zhì]
Aunt Molly **furnished** her room with a bed, dressing table and chair.

Gg

gallop [ˈgæləp]
galloping, galloped
奔驰 [bēn chí]
Jimmy was afraid when his horse **galloped** down the hill.

gamble [ˈgæmbl]
gambling, gambled
赌博 [dǔ bó]
These men are **gambling**.

garden [ˈgaːdn]
gardening, gardened
从事园艺 [cóng shì yuán yì]
Father is **gardening**. He is planting roses.

gather [ˈgæðə] **gathering, gathered**
采集 [cǎi jí]
Grandfather **gathered** fruit from the trees.

gasp [gaːsp] **gasping, gasped**
喘气 [chuǎn qì]
The water was so cold, Bobby **gasped** with shock.

gaze [geɪz] **gazing, gazed**
注视 [zhù shì]
Kathy is **gazing** at the stars.

give [ɡɪv] **giving, gave**
给 [gěi]

Mother **gave** Andy a bag.

give away [ɡɪv əˈweɪ]
送掉 [sòng diào]

Jimmy didn't want his pencils, so he **gave** them **away**.

give up [ɡɪv ʌp] 自首 [zì shǒu]

The robber **gave** himself **up** to the police.

give back [ɡɪv bæk] 还 [huán]

The teacher is **giving back** the exercise books.

give out [ɡɪv aʊt] 颁发 [bān fā]

The headmaster is **giving out** prizes to the best pupils.

give off [ɡɪv ɒf]
冒出 [mào chū]

A fire **gives off** smoke.

glue [ɡluː] **gluing, glued**
粘贴 [zhān tīe]

Kathy **glued** a picture into the book.

glare [ɡleə] **glaring, glared**
盯 [dīng]

The two boys have stopped fighting, but they are still **glaring**.

glow [ɡləʊ]
glowing, glowed
发光 [fā guāng]

The cat's eyes **glow** in the dark.

get [get] **getting, got**
取 [qǔ]

Jimmy **got** a pail of water from the river.

get down [get daʊn]
下来 [xià lai]

Simon climbed a tree and could not **get down**.

get away [get əˈweɪ] 离开 [lí kāi]
Get away from the fire! You might get hurt.

get on [get ɒn]
骑上 [qí shàng]

Linda **got on** the horse without any help.

get at [get ət]
接近 [jiē jìn]

Andy cannot **get at** the bird.

get back [get bæk] 回来 [huí lai]
The runners were tired when they **got back** from the cross-country run.

get across [get əˈkrɒs]
通过 [tōng guò]

Jimmy **got across** the river on a bridge.

get over [get ˈəʊvə] 爬过 [pá guò]
Peter could not **get over** the wall.

get off [get ɒf] 下车 [xià chē]

Bobby **got off** the bus at the swimming pool.

get around [get əˈraʊnd] 往来 [wǎng lái]

Pilots **get around** a lot. They visit many countries.

get up [get ʌp] 起床 [qǐ chuáng]

Andy **gets up** at seven o'clock.

get in [get ɪn] 进去 [jìn qù]

Ali Baba **got in** a jar to hide from the thieves.

get dressed [get ˈdrest]
穿衣 [chuān yī]

It is late. You must **get dressed** at once.

giggle [ˈgɪgl] **giggling, giggled**
咯咯地笑 [gē gē de xiào]

The playful puppy made Kathy **giggle**.

get into [get ˈɪntə]
进入 [jìn rù]

Father **got into** the car and drove off.

get along [get əˈlɒŋ]
融合地相处 [róng hé de xiāng chǔ]

Helen is a sweet girl who **gets along** with all her classmates.

go [ɡəʊ] **going, went**
去 [qù]
Andy **goes** for a drive in his toy car.

glide [ɡlaɪd] **gliding, glided**
滑翔 [huá xiáng]
A paper aeroplane **glides** through the air.

go back [ɡəʊ bæk]
回去 [huí qù]
Linda forgot her umbrella, so she **went back** home for it.

go out [ɡəʊ aʊt] 出外 [chū wài]
Mr. and Mrs. Brown are **going out** to a party.

go away [ɡəʊ əˈweɪ]
走开 [zǒu kāi]
"**Go away**!" said Jane. "I want to be alone."

go on [ɡəʊ ɒn] 继续 [jì xù]
The roller coaster **went on** and on.

go without [ɡəʊ wɪˈðaʊt]
没有 [méi yǒu]
Andy was naughty and had to **go without** dinner.

grill [ɡrɪl] **grilling, grilled**
烤 [kǎo]
Father is **grilling** some sausages.

grip [ɡrɪp] **gripping, gripped**
紧握 [jǐn wò]
Kathy **gripped** her mother's arm when they were on the ferris wheel.

grin [ɡrɪn] **grinning, grinned**
咧嘴笑 [liě zuǐ xiào]
Willy is **grinning** because his mother has given him a toy.

grind [ɡraɪnd]
grinding, ground
磨 [mó]
The cook is **grinding** nuts.

grab [græb] **grabbing, grabbed**
抢夺 [qiǎng duó]
The thief **grabbed** Aunt Molly's handbag.

growl [graʊl] **growling, growled**
吠 [fèi]
The guard dog **growled** at the stranger.

grow [grəʊ]
growing, grew
生长 [shēng zhǎng]
Potatoes **grow** under the ground.

grunt [grʌnt] **grunting, grunted**
咕哝 [gū nong]
When pigs are hungry, they **grunt**.

group [gruːp] **grouping, grouped**
分类 [fēn lèi]
Simon **grouped** the toy animals into pets and wild animals.

greet [griːt] **greeting, greeted**
迎接 [yíng jiē]
We **greeted** Grandmother with a bunch of flowers.

guard [gɑːd] **guarding, guarded**
看守 [kān shǒu]
The soldiers **guard** the jewels from thieves.

guide [gaɪd] **guiding, guided**
带领 [dài lǐng]
The boy scout **guided** the blind man across the street.

gush [gʌʃ] **gushing, gushed**
喷出 [pēn chū]
Look! The water is **gushing** out of the broken pipe.

guess [ges] **guessing, guessed**
猜 [cāi]
Close your eyes and **guess** what your present is.

gum [gʌm] **gumming, gummed**
粘 [zhān]
Linda **gummed** the two cards together to make a thicker card.

Hh

hack [hæk] **hacking, hacked**
劈 [pī]

The fireman **hacked** the door with an axe.

halt [hɔːlt] **halting, halted**
站住 [zhàn zhù]

"**Halt**!" said the fireman. "You cannot enter."

halve [hɑːv] **halving, halved**
分成两半 [fēn chéng liǎng bàn]

Mandy **halved** the orange before squeezing out the juice.

handle [ˈhændl] **handling, handled**
拿 [ná]

Linda **handled** the glasses with great care.

hail [heɪl] **hailing, hailed**
呼叫 [hū jiào]

Aunt Molly **hailed** a taxi to take her home.

handcuff [ˈhændkʌf]
handcuffing, handcuffed
上手铐 [shàng shǒu kào]

The policeman **handcuffed** the thief.

hand out [hænd aʊt]
分发 [fēn fā]

Mother is **handing out** sweets to the children.

hammer [ˈhæmə]
hammering, hammered
锤 [chuí]

Jimmy **hammered** a nail into the wood.

hand [hænd] **handing, handed**
交给 [jiāo gěi]

The mailman **handed** the letter to Kathy.

hang [hæŋ] **hanging, hung**
挂起 [guà qǐ]
Andy **hung** his shirt in the cupboard.

have [hæv]
having, had
有 [yǒu]
Jimmy **has** a blue cap.

have got
[hæv gɒt]
患上 [huàn shang]
Willy **has got** chickenpox.

have to [hæv tuː]
必须 [bì xū]
We **have to** drink water every day.

harvest [ˈhɑːvɪst] **harvesting, harvested**
收割 [shōu gē]
The farmer is **harvesting** the crop.

hatch [hætʃ] **hatching, hatched**
孵出 [fū chū]
The chicks **hatched** out of the eggs.

hate [heɪt] **hating, hated**
讨厌 [tǎo yàn]
Willy **hates** to wake up early on cold mornings.

heal [hiːl] **healing, healed**
康复 [kāng fù]
The cut on my arm has **healed**.
I can take off the plaster.

harm [hɑːm] **harming, harmed**
伤害 [shāng hài]
Is the big bad wolf going to **harm** Little Red Riding Hood?

haul [hɔːl] **hauling, hauled**
拖拉 [tuō lā]
The fishermen **hauled** their net onto the boat.

heat [hiːt] **heating, heated**

加热 [jiā rè]

The fire **heats** the soup to the boiling point.

hear [hɪə] **hearing, heard**

听见 [tīng jiàn]

Mother **heard** the baby cry.

hiccup [ˈhɪkʌp]
hiccuping, hiccuped or hiccupped

打嗝 [dǎ gé]

Poor Andy is **hiccuping**. How can he stop it?

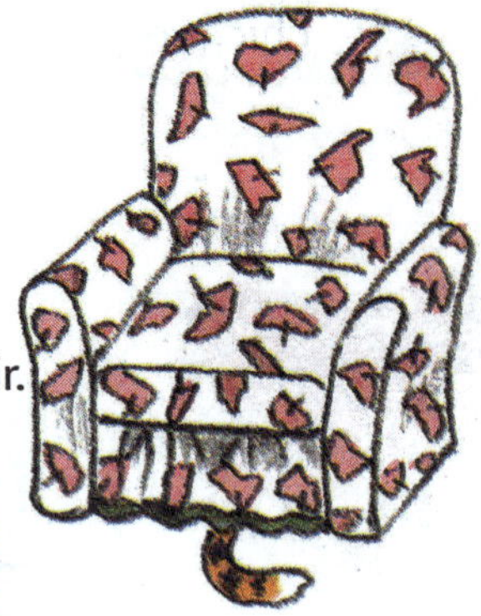

hide [haɪd] **hiding, hid**

躲藏 [duǒ cáng]

The cat is **hiding** under a chair.

heap [hiːp]
heaping, heaped

堆 [duī]

Kathy **heaped** her clothes on the floor.

help [help] **helping, helped**

帮助 [bāng zhù]

Kathy **helps** her mother make the bed.

head
[hed] **heading, headed**

用头顶、向 …… 走去

[yòng tóu dǐng], [xiàng …… zǒu qù]

Jimmy is **heading** the ball into the goal.

The last time I saw Bobby, he was **heading** for home.

hiss [hɪs] **hissing, hissed**

嘶嘶声 [sī sī shēng]

The snake **hissed** when Andy stepped on it.

hit [hɪt] **hitting, hit**

击 [jī]

Willy **hit** the ball with the baseball bat.

hike [haɪk]
远足 [yuǎn zú]

We **hiked** round the lake the whole day.

hire [ˈhaɪə] **hiring, hired**
租 [zū]

The tourist **hired** a car for $2000 a week.

hoist [hɔɪst] **hoisting, hoisted**
升起 [shēng qǐ]

Look! Bobby is **hoisting** the school flag.

hold [həʊld] **holding, held**
握住 [wò zhù]

Andy is **holding** a baby orangutan's hand.

hold on [həʊld ɒn] 抓紧 [zhuā jǐn]

Kathy **held on** tightly as her father carried her on his back.

hold out [həʊld aʊt]
伸出 [shēn chū]

Willy **held out** his hand. He wanted to shake Mandy's hand.

hold up [həʊld ʌp]
抢劫 [qiǎng jié]

Two masked men **held up** the cashier and took all the money.

hope [həʊp] **hoping, hoped**
希望 [xī wàng]

Linda **hoped** the postman would bring her a letter.

hoot [huːt] **hooting, hooted**
猫头鹰叫声 [māo tóu yīng jiào shēng]
Owls **hoot** at night.

hook [hʊk] **hooking, hooked**
钩住 [gōu zhù]
Jimmy has **hooked** a big fish.

honk [hɒŋk] **honking, honked**
鹅叫声 [é jiào shēng]
Geese **honk** at strangers.

hum [hʌm] **humming, hummed**
哼曲子 [hēng qǔ zi]
Willy is **humming** as he walks to the park.

hop [hɒp] **hopping, hopped**
跳来跳去 [tiào lái tiào qù]
The children are **hopping** around the playground.

hurl [hɜːl] **hurling, hurled**
用力地抛 [yòng lì de pāo]
Jimmy **hurled** the ball as far as he could.

hurt [hɜːt] **hurting, hurt**
受伤 [shòu shāng]
Simon **hurt** his toe on a rock.

huff [hʌf] **huffing, huffed**
喘气 [chuǎn qì]
The children **huffed** and puffed after the run.

huddle [ˈhʌdl] **huddling, huddled**
挤作一团 [jǐ zuò yī tuán]
The chicks are **huddling** together to keep warm.

hose [həʊz] **hosing, hosed**
用软管喷洗 [yòng ruǎn guǎn pēn xǐ]
Father is **hosing** the car down.

howl [haʊl] **howling, howled**
大声哭 [dà shēng kū]
The baby **howled** when he fell out of his crib.

hurry up [ˈhʌrɪ ʌp]
赶快 [gǎn kuài]
Hurry up if you want to get to school on time!

hurry [ˈhʌrɪ] **hurrying, hurried**
赶紧 [gǎn jǐn]
Jimmy got up late and **hurried** to get dressed.

hunt [hʌnt] **hunting, hunted**
找 [zhǎo]
Grandmother is **hunting** for her glasses.

hug [hʌg] 紧抱 [jǐn bào]
Mother **hugs** me when I come home from school.

Ii

imitate [ˈɪmɪteɪt]
imitating, imitated
模仿 [mó fǎng]

Willy can **imitate** Superman very well.

inspect [ɪnˈspekt] **inspecting, inspected**
检查 [jiǎn chá]

Bobby **inspected** his kite to make sure it was all right.

injure [ˈɪndʒə]
injuring, injured
受伤 [shòu shāng]

Simon fell down and **injured** his arm.

inform [ɪnˈfɔːm] **informing, informed**
通知 [tōng zhī]

The teacher **informed** the children where to go to fly their kites.

itch [ɪtʃ]
itching, itched
发痒 [fā yǎng]

Peter's arm **itches** because a mosquito bit him there.

invent [ɪnˈvent] **inventing, invented**
发明 [fā míng]

The scientist **invented** a machine to walk a dog.

imagine [ɪˈmædʒɪn]
imagining, imagined
想像 [xiǎng xiàng]

Kathy **imagined** she was a film star.

interrupt [ˌɪntəˈrʌpt]

interrupting, interrupted

打断 [dǎ duàn]

Andy **interrupted** his teacher who was talking to the others children.

instruct [ɪnˈstrʌkt]

instructing, instructed

指导 [zhǐ dǎo]

The teacher is **instructing** the children how to fly a kite.

install [ɪnˈstɔːl]

installing, installed

安装 [ān zhuāng]

The workers are **installing** a new pole.

introduce [ˌɪntrəˈdjuːs]

introducing, introduced

介绍 [jiè shào]

Mandy **introduced** Terry to Jimmy.

increase [ɪnˈkriːs]

increasing, increased

增加 [zēng jiā]

If you blow more air into the balloon, its size will **increase**.

interview [ˈɪntəvjuː]

interviewing, interviewed

访问 [fǎng wèn]

The reporter **interviewed** Bobby about the party.

invite [ɪnˈvaɪt]

inviting, invited

邀请 [yāo qǐng]

Bobby was **invited** to a masquerade party.

iron [ˈaɪən] ironing, ironed

熨 [yùn]

Father is **ironing** his shirt.

Jj

judge [dʒʌdʒ] **judging, judged**
裁定 [cái dìng]

Kathy's dog was **judged** the best dog in the show.

join [dʒɔɪn] **joining, joined**
结合 [jié hé]

Willy can **join** two pieces of string with a knot.

jingle [ˈdʒɪŋgl] **jingling, jingled**
叮当响 [dīng dāng xiǎng]

There are bells on the dog's collar. They **jingle** when it moves.

jack up [dʒæk ʌp] **jacking, jacked**
顶高 [dǐng gāo]

Father **jacked up** the car to change the tyre.

jump [dʒʌmp] **jumping, jumped**
跳 [tiào]

The cat **jumped** over the sleeping dog.

jump at [dʒʌmp ət]
扑向 [pū xiàng]

The dog **jumped at** the man passing by.

jump up [dʒʌmp ʌp]
跳上 [tiào shàng]

A cat **jumped up** onto Andy's lap.

jerk [dʒɜːk] **jerking, jerked**
震动 [zhèn dòng]
The car **jerked** a few times and then stopped suddenly.

joke [dʒəʊk] **joking, joked**
开玩笑 [kāi wán xiào]
The children are **joking** with one another. They are telling funny stories.

jumble [ˈdʒʌmbl] **jumbling, jumbled**
弄乱 [nòng luàn]
The naughty girl **jumbled** her clothes.

jam [dʒæm] **jamming, jammed**
塞进 [sāi jìn]
Andy **jammed** the clothes into the suitcase.

juggle [ˈdʒʌgl] **juggling, juggled**
耍弄 [shuǎ nòng]
The clown is **juggling** six balls.

jog [dʒɒg] **jogging, jogged**
慢跑 [màn pǎo]
Bobby **jogged** around the track.

jot [dʒɒt] **jotting, jotted**
速记 [sù jì]
Peter **jotted** down my phone number on a piece of paper.

Kk

kick [kɪk] **kicking, kicked**
踢 [tī]

Terry **kicked** the ball over the fence.

keep [kiːp] **keeping, kept**
放 [fàng]

Helen **keeps** her pet snake in a basket.

keep up [kiːp ʌp] 跟上 [gēn shàng]
Bobby can run faster than Willy. Willy can't **keep up** with him.

keep away [kiːp əˈweɪ]
不要靠近 [bú yào kào jìn]

Keep away from the dog. It bites!

keep off [kiːp ɒf]
远离 [yuǎn lí]

Keep off the grass!

knock [nɒk] **knocking, knocked**
敲 [qiāo]

The mailman is **knocking** on the door. He has a parcel to deliver.

kill [kɪl] **killing, killed**
杀死 [shā sǐ]

The prince became a hero when he **killed** a dragon.

kneel [niːl] **kneeling, knelt**
跪下 [guì xià]
Jimmy **kneels** down to pray.

kiss [kɪs] **kissing, kissed**
吻 [wěn]
Mother **kissed** Kathy on her cheek.

knit [nɪt] **knitting, knitted**
编织 [biān zhī]
Grandmother is **knitting** a jumper.

knot [nɒt]
knotting, knotted
打结 [dǎ jié]
Mandy is **knotting** a scarf round her neck.

know [nəʊ] **knowing, knew**
懂得 [dǒng de]
Peter **knows** the answer to the sum.

Ll

ladle [ˈleɪdl] **ladling, ladled**
舀 [yǎo]
The old woman is **ladling** soup into the children's bowls.

leap [liːp]
leaping, leaped or leapt
跳 [tiào]
Helen opened the box and a frog **leapt** out.

laugh [lɑːf] **laughing, laughed**
笑 [xiào]
The children are **laughing** at the clown's tricks.

lead up to [liːd ʌp tuː]
通向 [tōng xiàng]
The winding path **leads up to** the haunted house.

lead [liːd] **leading, led**
带领 [dài lǐng]
Andy is **leading** his dog up the winding path.

last [lɑːst] **lasting, lasted**
持续 [chí xù]
I wonder how long the rain will **last**.

lay [leɪ] **laying, laid**
摆放、生蛋 [bǎi fàng, shēng dàn]
Kathy is **laying** the table for dinner.

leak [liːk] **leaking, leaked**
漏 [lòu]
The roof is **leaking**.

lean [liːn] **leaning, leaned**
斜靠 [xié kào]
The ladder **leans** against the wall.

Our hen **lays** two eggs every day.

land [lænd] **landing, landed**
降落 [jiàng luò]
Bobby's ball **landed** in Aunt Molly's soup.

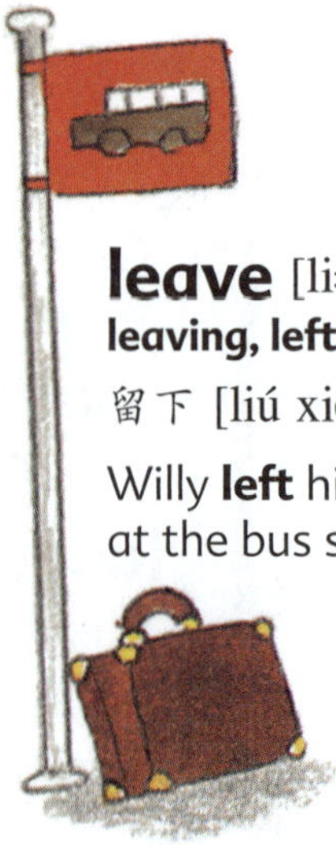

leave [liːv]
leaving, left
留下 [liú xià]
Willy **left** his school bag at the bus stop.

leave out [liːv aʊt] 不理会 [bù lǐ huì]
The boys were playing marbles, and Linda was **left out**.

learn [lɜːn] **learning, learned**
学习 [xué xí]

Jane is **learning** to play the piano.

let [let] **letting, let**
让 [ràng]

The teacher **let** Andy play the guitar.

lend [lend] **lending, lent**
借 [jiè]

Mandy **lent** Linda her music book.

let down [let daʊn]
放下 [fàng xià]

Rapunzel **let down** her long hair.

let go [let gəʊ]
放开 [fàng kāi]

Bobby **let go** of the balloon, and it floated away.

like [laɪk]
liking, liked
喜欢 [xǐ huan]

Jimmy **likes** the trumpet.

listen [ˈlɪsn] **listening, listened**
听 [tīng]

Andy is **listening** to the radio.

let in [let ɪn]
让 ...... 进来 [ràng ...... jìn lai]

Open the door and **let** Simon **in**.

let out [let aʊt]
放出 [fàng chū]

Willy **let out** a cry of pain when he hit his finger.

lie [laɪ] **lying, lied or lay**

说谎、平躺 [shuō huǎng], [píng tǎng]

Andy is **lying**.

The cat is **lying** in the basket.

lie down [laɪ daʊn]

躺下 [tǎng xià]

Grandmother **lay down** on the sofa.

link [lɪŋk] **linking, linked**

连接 [lián jiē]

The new road **links** the two towns.

light [laɪt] **lighting, lit**

点燃 [diǎn rán]

Grandfather is very careful when he **lights** the candle.

lose [lu:z] **losing, lost**

丢失 [diū shī]

Jimmy dropped $10 and **lost** it.

list [lɪst] **listing, listed**

编列出来 [biān liè chū lai]

Aunt Molly is **listing** the things she needs to buy.

limp [lɪmp] **limping, limped**

一拐一拐地走 [yī guǎi yī guǎi de zǒu]

The dog has a sore paw and is **limping**.

lift [lɪft] **lifting, lifted**

举起 [jǔ qǐ]

Willy **lifted** Jimmy above his head.

lick [lɪk] **licking, licked**

舔 [tiǎn]

Andy is **licking** a lollipop.

litter [ˈlɪtə] **littering, littered**

乱丢 [luàn diū]

Andy had **littered** the floor with sweet wrappers.

long [lɒŋ] **longing, longed**

渴望 [kě wàng]

Andy is **longing** for chocolate. It is his favourite food.

line [laɪn] **lining, lined**

铺 [pū]

Kathy is **lining** the shelf with paper.

line up [laɪn ʌp]

排好 [pái hǎo]

Mandy **lined up** the chairs for the concert.

live [lɪv] **living, lived**

住 [zhù]

There was an old woman who **lived** in a shoe.

live on [lɪv ɒn]

以 ...... 为主食 [yǐ ...... wèi zhǔ shí]

Monkeys **live on** fruit and nuts.

look [lʊk] **looking, looked**
看 [kàn]
Look at the aeroplane flying upside down!

look out [lʊk aʊt]
当心 [dāng xīn]
Look out! A branch is falling down.

look after [lʊk ˈɑːftə]
照顾 [zhào gù]
Mother **looks after** the baby all day.

look for [lʊk fə]
寻找 [xún zhǎo]
The children are **looking for** the lost ball.

lock up [lɒk ʌp]
锁进 [suǒ jìn]
Aunt Molly **locks up** her jewels in a safe.

look up [lʊk ʌp]
翻查 [fān chá]
Helen is **looking up** a word in the dictionary.

lock [lɒk] **locking, locked**
锁 [suǒ]
Every night father **locks** the door.

load [ləʊd] **loading, loaded**
装载 [zhuāng zài]
The men are **loading** the van with sacks of flour.

loop [luːp] **looping, looped**
扣住 [kòu zhù]
The cowboy **loops** the rope round the bull.

love [lʌv] **loving, loved**
爱 [ài]
I **love** my grandmother.

lunch [lʌntʃ] **lunching, lunched**
吃午餐 [chī wǔ cān]
Andy is **lunching** with his aunt.

Mm

mark [mɑːk] **marking, marked**
批改 [pī gǎi]
The teacher is **marking** the exercise books.

mount [maʊnt] **mounting, mounted**
骑上 [qí shang]
Bobby is **mounting** his bicycle.

mow [məʊ] **mowing, mowed**
割 [gē]
Father is **mowing** the lawn.

mash [mæʃ]
mashing, mashed
捣碎 [dǎo suì]
Jimmy is **mashing** the potatoes.

measure [ˈmeʒə]
measuring, measured
量度 [liáng duó]
Andy is **measuring** the flour with a cup.

melt [melt]
melting, melted
融化 [róng huà]
Ice **melts** when you take it out of the freezer.

make [meɪk]
making, made
做 [zuò]
Willy is **making** a sandwich for himself.

make off with [meɪk ɒf wɪð]
离开 [lí kāi]
The thief **made off with** a big cake.

make out [meɪk aʊt]
认出 [rèn chū]
The stranger wore a mask, so Helen could not **make out** who he was.

make for [meɪk fə]
冲向 [chōng xiàng]
Jimmy **made for** the door when Linda ran after him with a rolling pin.

mince [mɪns] **mincing, minced**

绞碎 [jiǎo suì]

Simon is **mincing** the meat to make pies.

mix [mɪks] **mixing, mixed**

混合 [hùn hé]

Willy **mixed** flour and water to make dough.

mend [mend] **mending, mended**

修理 [xiū lǐ]

Bobby is **mending** the broken toaster.

mistake [mɪˈsteɪk]
mistaking, mistook

弄错 [nòng cuò]

Andy **mistook** pepper for salt.

mess up [mes ʌp]

弄乱 [nòng luàn]

The wind **messed up** Kathy's hair.

mew [mjuː]
mewing, mewed

咪咪叫 [mī mī jiào]

The cat is **mewing**. It wants some food.

mop [mɒp]
mopping, mopped

抹 [mǒ]

Peter is **mopping** the floor to clean off his dirty footprints.

mime [maɪm] **miming, mimed**

比划、比手势 [bǐ huà, bǐ shǒu shì]

Andy is **miming** that he wants a drink.

model [ˈmɒdl]
modelling, modelled
当模特儿 [dāng mó tèr]

Kathy is **modelling** a party dress.

marry [ˈmærɪ] **marrying, married**
结婚 [jié hūn]

Aunt Jane **married** a soldier.

match [mætʃ]
matching, matched
相配 [xiāng pèi]

Jimmy's socks do not **match**.

miss out [mɪs aʊt] 漏掉 [lòu diào]
When the teacher was giving children crayons, he **missed out** Willy.

miss [mɪs] **missing, missed**
没打中目标 [méi dǎ zhòng mù biāo]

The paper aeroplane just **missed** Linda's head.

meet [miːt]
meeting, met
遇见 [yù jiàn]

Bobby **met** Mandy outside the post office.

march [mɑːtʃ]
marching, marched
步操走 [bù cāo zǒu]

The band **marched** down the street playing music.

moo [muː] **mooing, mooed**
哞哞 [mōu mōu]

Cows **moo**.

milk [mɪlk] **milking, milked**
挤奶 [jǐ nǎi]

The farmer is **milking** the cow.

mine [maɪn] **mining, mined**
开矿 [kāi kuàng]

The miners are **mining** coal from under the ground.

move [muːv] **moving, moved**
移、搬 [yí, bān]

Jimmy **moved** his books to another desk.

move in [muːv ɪn]
搬进新家 [bān jìn xīn jiā]

Mr. and Mrs. Sharp are **moving in** next door.

move out [muːv aʊt]
搬出 [bān chū]

Bobby is **moving out** of the haunted house.

Nn

nap [næp] **napping, napped**
打盹 [dǎ dǔn]

Willy is **napping** in the garden.

nail [neɪl] **nailing, nailed** 钉 [dīng]
The workman is **nailing** a sign to the fence.

nod [nɒd] **nodding, nodded**
点头 [diǎn tóu]

Uncle Roy is **nodding** his head to show that he wants the coffee.

nudge [nʌdʒ] **nudging, nudged**
用肘轻轻推 [yòng zhǒu qīng qīng tuī]

Uncle Roy is **nudging** a workman who has fallen asleep.

nip [nɪp] **nipping, nipped**
咬 [yǎo]

The dog is **nipping** the man on the leg.

need [niːd] **needing, needed**
需要 [xū yào]

This workman **needs** a new pair of shoes.

neigh [neɪ] **neighing, neighed**
嘶叫 [sī jiào]

Horses **neigh**.

notice [ˈnəʊtɪs] **noticing, noticed**
注意到 [zhù yì dào]

Mr. Trump **noticed** a man sneaking out through the back gate.

nibble [ˈnɪbl] **nibbling, nibbled**
啃 [kěn]

The mouse is **nibbling** the bread.

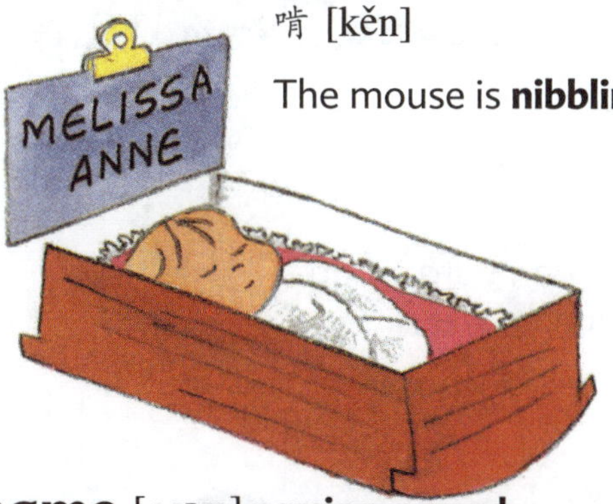

name [neɪm] **naming, named**
取名 [qǔ míng]

The baby was **named** Melissa Anne.

net [net] **netting, netted**
网住 [wǎng zhù]

Jimmy has **netted** a big fish.

nurse [nɜːs] **nursing, nursed**
照料 [zhào liào]

Mother **nursed** Andy when he had measles.

Oo

overturn [ˌəʊvəˈtɜːn] **overturning, overturned**
打翻 [dǎ fān]

The boat **overturned** in the storm.

owe [əʊ] **owing, owed**
欠 [qiàn]

Peter borrows $1 from Jimmy. He **owes** Jimmy $1.

open [ˈəʊpən]
opening, opened
打开 [dǎ kāi]

Linda is **opening** her birthday presents.

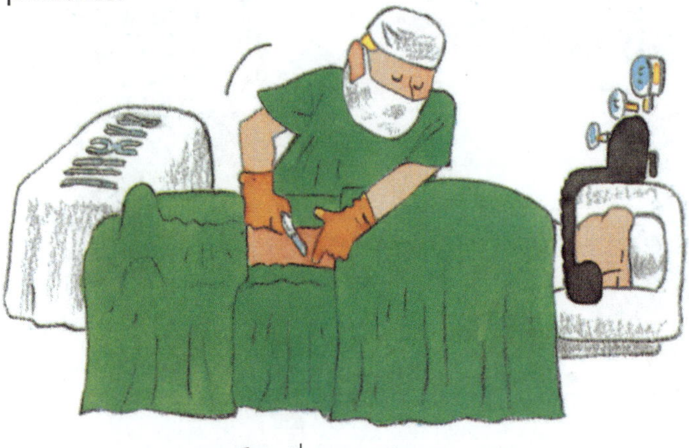

operate [ˈɒpəreɪt] **operating, operated**
动手术 [dòng shǒu shù]

The surgeon is **operating** on a man who has broken his leg.

overtake [ˌəʊvəˈteɪk]
overtaking, overtook 超越 [chāo yuè]
Our car is **overtaking** the truck.

order [ˈɔːdə] **ordering, ordered**
点菜 [diǎn cài]
Kathy **ordered** a hamburger and French fries for lunch.

oil [ɔɪl] **oiling, oiled**
涂油 [tú yóu]

Andy **oiled** the wheels of his toy car.

offer [ˈɒfə] **offering, offered**
提出 [tí chū]

Bobby **offered** to help Helen repair her bicycle.

own [əʊn] **owning, owned**
拥有 [yōng yǒu]

Mandy saved up her money, and she now **owns** a new bicycle.

obey [əˈbeɪ] **obeying, obeyed**
听从 [tīng cóng]

Mother said, "Go to bed", and I had to **obey**.

occupy [ˈɒkjʊpaɪ] **occupying, occupied**
占用 [zhàn yòng]

Peter wanted to use the bathroom, but it was **occupied**.

Pp

pierce [pɪəs] **piercing, pierced**
刺穿 [cī chuān]

The arrow **pierced** the apple.

paddle [ˈpædl] **paddling, paddled**
划 [huá]

Bobby is **paddling** the canoe down the river.

pack [pæk] **packing, packed**
装入 [zhuāng rù]

Kathy is **packing** food for a picnic.

picnic [ˈpɪknɪk] **picnicking, picnicked**
野餐 [yě cān]

The children are **picnicking** by the river.

pack up [pæk ʌp]
收拾 [shōu shí]

The picnic is over. The children are **packing up** the things.

peel [piːl]
peeling, peeled
剥皮 [bō pí]

Linda is **peeling** an orange.

peck [pek] **pecking, pecked**
啄 [zhuó]

The little bird is **pecking** the apple.

poke [pəʊk] **poking, poked**
插、戳 [chā, lù]

Andy is **poking** a stick into the sand.

pluck [plʌk] **plucking, plucked**
摘 [zhāi]

Jimmy is **plucking** apples from the tree.

parachute [ˈpærəʃuːt]
parachuting, parachuted
跳伞 [tiào sǎn]

Linda is **parachuting** into the forest.

pedal [ˈpedl] **pedaling, pedaled**
踩踏板 [cǎi tà bǎn]

Bobby is **pedaling** his new bicycle up the hill.

peep [piːp]
peeping, peeped
偷看 [tōu kàn]

Mandy is **peeping** through the window.

photograph [ˈfəʊtəgrɑːf]
photographing, photographed
拍照 [pāi zhào]

Jimmy is **photographing** the playful kitten.

pose [pəʊz] **posing, posed**
摆姿势 [bǎi zī shì]

Andy is **posing** for a photograph.

pant [pænt] **panting, panted**
喘气 [chuǎn qì]

The dog is **panting** after running up the steep slope.

pat [pæt] **patting, patted**
轻拍 [qīng pāi]

Linda is **patting** the dog on the head.

paw [pɔː] **pawing, pawed**
抓 [zhuā]

The dog is **pawing** the rubber bone.

perform [pəˈfɔːm]
performing, performed
表演 [biǎo yǎn]

The magician is **performing** a trick.

park [pɑːk] **parking, parked**
停车 [tíng chē]

Mother **parked** the car next to a van.

patch [pætʃ]
patching, patched
缝补 [féng bǔ]

Mother is **patching** the knee of Andy's jeans.

plant [plɑːnt] **planting, planted**
栽种 [zāi zhòng]

Mother is **planting** some daisy seeds in the garden.

pay [peɪ] **paying, paid**
付钱 [fù qián]

Father is **paying** for the groceries at the checkout counter.

pay back [peɪ bæk]
付还 [fù huán]

Jimmy is **paying back** the ten dollars Peter lent him.

prepare [prɪˈpeə]
preparing, prepared
准备 [zhǔn bèi]

Father is **preparing** the fruit for dinner.

peg [peg] **pegging, pegged**
夹衣服 [jiā yī fu]

Mother is **pegging** her washing to the clothesline.

present [prezənt] **presenting, presented**
送 [sòng]

Andy is **presenting** his mother with a bunch of roses.

place [pleɪs] **placing, placed**
放置 [fàng zhì]

Mother **placed** the antique vase on the mantelpiece.

paint [peɪnt] **painting, painted**
画 [huà]

Andy is **painting** a picture of his family.

paste [peɪst] **pasting, pasted**
粘贴 [zhān tiē]

Bobby is **pasting** a poster on the wall.

pin [pɪn] **pinning, pinned**
钉 [dīng]

Our teacher **pinned** a notice on the noticeboard.

pair [peə] **pairing, paired**
配对 [pèi duì]

The socks are all mixed up. Can you **pair** them again?

part [pɑːt]
分 [fēn]

He always **parts** his hair on the left.

praise [preɪz] **praising, praised**
称赞 [chēng zàn]

The teacher is **praising** Peter for his schoolwork.

play [pleɪ] **playing, played**
玩 [wán]

Mandy and Kathy are **playing** hopscotch in the playground.

pretend [prɪˈtend]
pretending, pretended
假装 [jiǎ zhuāng]

Willy is **pretending** to be a ghost.

punish [ˈpʌnɪʃ]
punishing, punished
惩罚 [chéng fá]

Andy was **punished** for being naughty.

pound [ˈpaʊnd]
pounding, pounded
槌打 [chuí dǎ]

Mother is **pounding** the meat to make it tender.

pass [pɑːs] **passing, passed**
传、递 [chuán, dì]

Jimmy is **passing** the salt to Linda.

powder [ˈpaʊdə]
powdering, powdered
拍粉 [pāi fěn]

Aunt Molly is **powdering** her face.

pinch [pɪntʃ]
pinching, pinched
拧 [níng]

A monster sneaked up and **pinched** my arm.

pick [pɪk] **picking, picked**
采摘 [cǎi zhāi]

Jimmy is **picking** mangoes from a tree in his garden.

pick out [pɪk aʊt]
拣出 [jiǎn chū]

Mandy has **picked out** all the black jelly beans.

patrol [pəˈtrəʊl] **patrolling, patrolled**
巡逻 [xún luó]

Two policemen are **patrolling** our street.

pick up [pɪk ʌp]
捡起 [jiǎn qǐ]

Willy is **picking up** the pieces of broken glass.

polish [ˈpɒlɪʃ] **polishing, polished**
擦亮 [cā liàng]

Father is **polishing** the car.

plough [ˈplaʊ]
ploughing, ploughed
犁 [lí]

The farmer **ploughs** his field before planting corn.

protect [prəˈtekt]
protecting, protected
保护 [bǎo hù]

The shell of the snail **protects** it from harm.

pave [peɪv] **paving, paved**
铺设 [pū shè]

The workmen are **paving** the road.

press [pres]
pressing, pressed
按 [àn]

Press this button to start the machine.

prick [prɪk] **pricking, pricked**
刺 [cì]

A thorn **pricked** Helen's finger when she was cutting the roses.

pull [pʊl] **pulling, pulled**
拉 [lā]

The elephant is **pulling** the log out of the forest.

pull down [pʊl daʊn]
拉倒、拆 [lā dǎo, chāi]

The workman is **pulling down** the house.

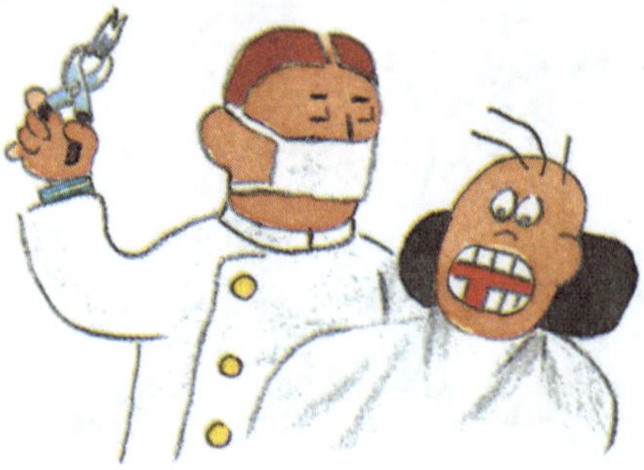

pull out [pʊl aʊt]
拔出 [bá chū]

Andy's tooth was loose, so the dentist **pulled** it **out**.

pour [pɔː] **pouring, poured**
倒 [dǎo]

Aunt Molly is **pouring** the tea into the cups.

pounce [paʊns] **pouncing, pounced**
扑过去 [pū guò qù]

The cat **pounced** on the mouse.

purr [pɜː] **purring, purred**
呜呜地叫 [wū wū de jiào]

Our cat **purrs** when you pat it.

promise [ˈprɒmɪs] **promising, promised**
答应 [dā ying]

"I **promise** to look after it well," said Simon.

point [pɔɪnt] **pointing, pointed**
指向 [zhǐ xiàng]

Andy is **pointing** at the puppies that chewed his father's slippers.

point out [pɔɪnt aʊt]
指出 [zhǐ chū]

The guide **pointed out** the old tower to the tourists.

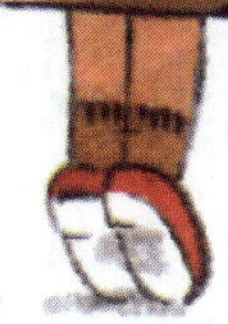

post [pəʊst] **posting, posted**
邮寄 [yóu jì]

Kathy **posted** a letter to her French penfriend.

pump [pʌmp] **pumping, pumped**
泵气 [bèng qì]

Every Saturday Bobby **pumps** up his bicycle tyre.

push [pʊʃ] **pushing, pushed**
推 [tuī]

Jimmy is **pushing** the box up the hill.

practise [ˈpræktɪs] **practising, practised**
练习 [liàn xí]

Kathy **practises** hard for a ballet performance.

put away [pʊt əˈweɪ]
收好 [shōu hǎo]

Helen **puts away** her toys after playing with them.

put [pʊt] **putting, put**
放 [fàng]

Peter is **putting** his coins into his money box.

print [prɪnt] **printing, printed**
印 [yìn]

The machine **prints** posters.

puzzle [ˈpʌzl] **puzzling, puzzled**
弄糊涂 [nòng hú tu]

The men **puzzled** over the huge footprint in the snow.

Qq

quack [kwæk] **quacking, quacked**
嘎嘎叫 [gā gā jiào]

The ducks **quack** when the farmer comes to feed them.

question [ˈkwestʃən]
questioning, questioned
盘问 [pán wèn]

The policeman **questioned** Jimmy about the accident.

quarter [ˈkwɔːtə]
quartering, quartered
分成四份 [fēn chéng sì fèn]

Aunt Molly **quartered** the cake.

quarrel [ˈkwɒrəl]
quarrelling, quarrelled
吵架 [chǎo jià]

Mandy and Helen are **quarrelling** over the torn storybook.

Rr

reach [riːtʃ] **reaching, reached**
触到、拿到 [chù dào, ná dào]

Linda can't **reach** the book on top of the bookcase.

queue up [kjuː ʌp] **queuing, queued**
排队 [pái duì]

The children are **queuing up** to return their library books.

renew [rɪˈnjuː]
renewing, renewed
更新 [gēng xīn]

Willy had not finished his book, so he took it to the library and **renewed** it.

read [riːd] **reading, read**
阅读 [yuè dú]

Andy is **reading** Treasure Island.

raise [reɪz] **raising, raised**
举起 [jǔ qǐ]

Peter **raised** his hand, because he knew the answer to the question.

relate [rɪˈleɪt] **relating, related**
讲述 [jiǎng shù]

Grandfather **related** the story of his childhood.

record [rɪˈkɔːd] **recording, recorded**
记录 [jì lù]

Kathy **recorded** the day's events in her diary.

rush [rʌʃ] **rushing, rushed**
急送 [jí sòng]

The ambulance is **rushing** a very sick man to hospital.

rain [reɪn] **raining, rained**
下雨 [xià yǔ]

It is **raining** very heavily so we cannot go outside.

report [rɪˈpɔːt] **reporting, reported**
报告 [bào gào]

Uncle Roy **reported** to the police that his truck was stolen.

reverse [rɪˈvɜːs]
reversing, reversed
倒退 [daò tuì]

Mother is **reversing** the car. Get out of the way!

ram [ræm] **ramming, rammed**
猛击 [měng jī]

A bus **rammed** Uncle Roy's truck.

replace [rɪˈpleɪs] **replacing, replaced**
放回 [fàng huí]

The mechanic **replaced** the wrench after he had used it. He put it back into the tool box.

repair [rɪˈpeə] **repairing, repaired**
修理 [xiū lǐ]

Our car would not start, so the mechanic is **repairing** it.

run [rʌn] **running, ran**
跑 [pǎo]

Rusty can **run** very fast.

run out of [rʌn aʊt əv]
用完 [yòng wán]

The car **ran out of** gas in the middle of the road.

run over [rʌn ˈəʊvə]
辗过 [zhǎn guò]

The car **ran over** a watermelon and squashed it.

run into [rʌn ˈɪntə]
撞 [zhuàng]

The car **ran into** a lamp-post.

run away [rʌn əˈweɪ]
逃 [táo]

The thief is **running away** with the jewels.

run after [rʌn ˈɑːftə]
追捕 [zhuī bǔ]

Bobby **ran after** the thief, trying to catch him.

request [rɪˈkwest] **requesting, requested**
要求 [yāo qiú]

Hospital visitors are **requested** to leave by nine o'clock in the evening.

refuse [rɪˈfjuːz] **refusing, refused**
拒绝 [jù jué]

The camel **refuses** to stand up.

remind [rɪˈmaɪnd] **reminding, reminded**
联想起 [lián xiǎng qǐ]

The tall thin man **reminds** Mandy of a giraffe.

race [reɪs] **racing, raced**
比赛 [bǐ sài]

The hare and the tortoise are **racing** against each other.

ride [raɪd] **riding, rode**
骑 [qí]

Jimmy is **riding** on a horse.

release [rɪˈliːs]
releasing, released
放走 [fàng zǒu]

Linda is **releasing** the rabbit from the cage.

roar [rɔː]
roaring, roared
吼 [hǒu]

The lion is **roaring** because it is angry.

repeat [rɪˈpiːt]
repeating, repeated
重复 [chóng fù]

The parrot is **repeating** the same word over and over again.

receive [rɪˈsiːv] **receiving, received**
收到 [shōu dào]

Andy **received** many presents on his birthday.

remove [rɪˈmuːv] **removing, removed**
脱掉 [tuō diào]

Peter is **removing** his dirty boots.

rake [reɪk] **raking, raked**
耙 [pá]

Grandfather is **raking** the leaves into a pile.

reflect [rɪˈflekt]
reflecting, reflected
倒映 [dào yìng]

The moon is **reflected** in the lake.

regret [rɪˈgret]
regretting, regretted
后悔 [hòu huǐ]

Andy **regrets** that he cannot go to the picnic.

reserve [rɪˈzɜːv] **reserving, reserved**
保留 [bǎo liú]

This table is **reserved** for the Brown family.

rescue [ˈreskjuː]
rescuing, rescued
拯救 [zhěng jiù]

The fireman **rescued** Jane from the fire.

ruffle [ˈrʌfl]
ruffling, ruffled
弄乱 [nòng luàn]

Uncle Roy is **ruffling** Jimmy's hair.

reveal [rɪˈviːl] **revealing, revealed**
显露 [xiǎn lù]

The artist removed the sheet and **revealed** the statue.

respect [rɪˈspekt]
respecting, respected
尊敬 [zūn jìng]

Jimmy **respects** old people and gives them his seat on the bus.

ruin [ˈruːɪn] **ruining, ruined**
毁坏 [huǐ huài]

The painting that was left out in the rain was **ruined**.

reply [rɪˈplaɪ] **replying, replied**
回答 [huí dá]

"What's your name?" asked the robot. "Andy," I **replied**.

remain [rɪˈmeɪn]
remaining, remained
剩下 [shèng xià]

Willy had four sweets. He has eaten three. One **remains**.

remember [rɪˈmembə]
remembering, remembered
记得 [jì de]

Father **remembered** it was Mother's birthday today.

row [rəʊ] **rowing, rowed**
划 [huá]

Jimmy is **rowing** the boat across the lake.

roller-skate [ˈrəʊlə skeɪt]
roller-skating, roller-skated
滚轴溜冰 [gǔn zhóu liū bīng]

Bobby is **roller-skating** down the path.

rest [rest] **resting, rested**
休息 [xiū xi]

After hiking all day, Linda is **resting** her feet.

rub [rʌb] **rubbing, rubbed**
擦 [cā]

Willy **rubs** himself dry after his shower.

result [rɪˈzʌlt] **resulting, resulted**
结果 [jié guǒ]

The race **resulted** in a tie. Bobby and Terry shared the first prize.

rip [rɪp] **ripping, ripped**
扯 [chě]

The naughty dog is **ripping** the curtain to pieces.

rub out [rʌb aʊt]
擦掉 [cā diào]

Mandy made a mistake and she **rubbed** it **out**.

rise [raɪz] **rising, rose**
升起 [shēng qǐ]

The smoke is **rising** from the chimney.

return [rɪˈtɜːn] **returning, returned**
返回 [fǎn huí]

Father **returns** from work at 5:30 pm.

roast [rəʊst] **roasting, roasted**
烘烧 [hōng shāo]

Mother is **roasting** chestnuts over the fire.

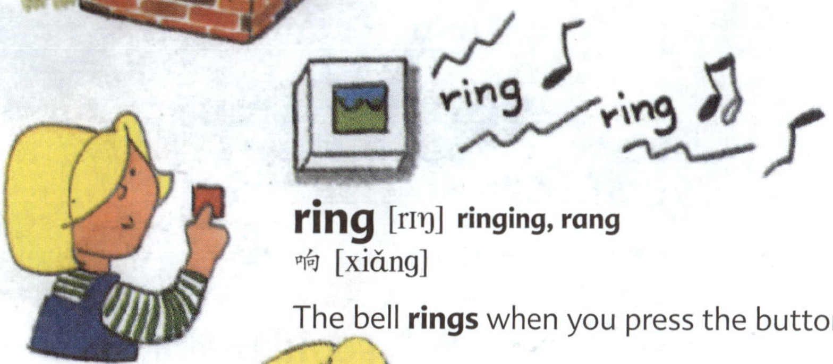

ring [rɪŋ] **ringing, rang**
响 [xiǎng]

The bell **rings** when you press the button.

rock [rɒk]
rocking, rocked
摇 [yáo]

Kathy is **rocking** the baby in its cradle.

roll [rəʊl] **rolling, rolled**
滚 [gǔn]

The ball is **rolling** down the hill.

ring up [rɪŋ ʌp]
打电话 [dǎ diàn huà]

Kathy is **ringing up** her best friend to have a chat.

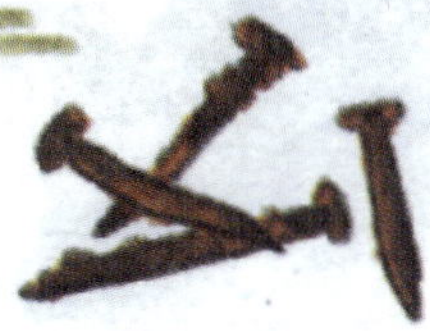

roll up [rəʊl ʌp]
卷起 [juǎn qǐ]

Father is **rolling up** the carpet. He wants to vacuum under it.

rust [rʌst] **rusting, rusted**
生锈 [shēng xiù]

Some of the nails have **rusted**.

ring off [rɪŋ ɒf]
挂断电话 [guà duàn diàn huà]
Kathy is **ringing off** because her mother is calling her.

roam [rəʊm] **roaming, roamed**
漫步 [màn bù]

The girls are **roaming** the park, looking at the flowers.

rule [ru:l] **ruling, ruled**
统治 [tǒng zhì]

The king **rules** his country wisely.

Ss

rob [rɒb] **robbing, robbed**
抢劫 [qiǎng jié]

The thieves are **robbing** the man of his money.

sag [sæg] **sagging, sagged**
下陷 [xià xiàn]

The top shelf **sags** because the books are too heavy.

scold [skəʊld] **scolding, scolded**
骂 [mà]

The teacher is **scolding** Jimmy because he has not done his homework.

scream [skri:m]
screaming, screamed
尖叫 [jiān jiào]

Mandy **screamed** when a bee landed on her arm.

scrub [skrʌb]
scrubbing, scrubbed
擦洗 [cā xǐ]

We **scrub** the floors to get them clean.

shape [ʃeɪp] **shaping, shaped**
塑造 [sù zào]

The potter is **shaping** the clay to make a pot.

screw [skru:]
screwing, screwed
拧紧 [nǐng jǐn]

Uncle Roy is **screwing** the shelf to the wall.

salute [səˈluːt] **saluting, saluted**
致敬 [zhì jìng]

The children are **saluting** the flag.

save [seɪv] **saving, saved**
省下 [shěng xià]

Terry **saves** ten dollars from his pocket money every day.

save up [seɪv ʌp]
储蓄 [chǔ xù]

He wants to **save up** enough money to buy a pair of roller skates.

score [skɔː] **scoring, scored**
得分 [dé fēn]

Bobby **scored** a goal for his team.

scratch [skrætʃ]
scratching, scratched
抓 [zhuā]

The cat is **scratching** the flag pole to sharpen its claws.

scrape [skreɪp] **scraping, scraped**
擦伤 [cā shāng]

Jimmy fell down and **scraped** his knee.

scratch out [skrætʃ aʊt]
擦掉 [cā diào]

Kathy is **scratching out** the words so that no one can read them.

search [sɜːtʃ] **searching, searched**
寻找 [xún zhǎo]

Linda is **searching** everywhere to find the lost crayon.

select [sɪˈlekt]
selecting, selected
选出 [xuǎn chū]

The judge **selected** the best painting in the show.

sail [seɪl] **sailing, sailed**
航行 [háng xíng]

Father is **sailing** his yacht around the buoy.

sink [sɪŋk] **sinking, sank**
沉没 [chén mò]

The boat **sank** in the storm.

scoop [skuːp]
scooping, scooped
挖出 [wā chū]

Jane **scooped** a bucketful of sand.

suck [sʌk] **sucking, sucked**
吸 [xī]

Terry is **sucking** the juice through a straw.

swim [swɪm] **swimming, swam**
游泳 [yóu yǒng]

Terry is **swimming** in the sea.

shout [ʃaʊt] **shouting, shouted**
喊叫 [hǎn jiào]

Willy is **shouting** for help. He cannot swim.

scoop up [skuːp ʌp]
捞起 [lāo qǐ]

Jimmy **scooped up** the kitten from the water.

scoop out [skuːp aʊt]
舀出 [yǎo chū]

Mother is **scooping out** ice cream for the boys.

splash [splæʃ] **splashing, splashed**
泼 [pō]

Andy is **splashing** water on Helen's face.

say [seɪ] **saying, said**
说 [shuō]

Linda **says**, "I'm going for a swim."

sun [sʌn] **sunning, sunned**

晒 [shài]

Willy is **sunning** himself on the beach.

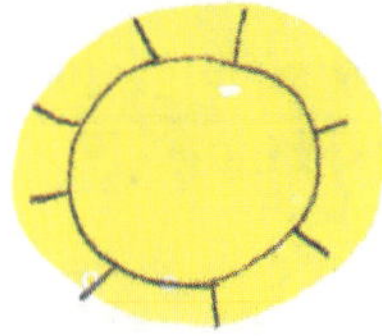

strike [straɪk] **striking, struck**

打 [dǎ]

Bobby **struck** the ball with his hand.

shade [ʃeɪd] **shading, shaded**

遮 [zhē]

The umbrella is **shading** Kathy from the sun.

smoke [sməʊk] **smoking, smoked**

吸烟 [xī yān]

Grandfather is **smoking** a pipe.

skip [skɪp] **skipping, skipped**

跳 [tiào]

Linda is **skipping** with her skipping rope.

spread [spred] **spreading, spread**

摊开 [tān kāi]

Father is **spreading** the cloth on the ground for the picnic.

share [ʃeə] **sharing, shared**

分享 [fēn xiǎng]

Mandy and Helen are **sharing** the sweets.

sob [sɒb] **sobbing, sobbed**

哭泣 [kū qì]

Jane is **sobbing** because her sand castle is ruined.

scare [ˈskeə] **scaring, scared**

吓怕 [xià pà]

Our fierce dog **scares** Simon.

send back [send bæk]
送回 [sòng huí]
Rusty followed Kathy to school, so she **sent** him **back** home.

send [send]
sending, sent
派…去 [pài…qù]
Mother **sent** Andy to buy some sugar.

send off [send ɒf]
罚离场 [fá lí chǎng]
The soccer player was **sent off** the field for kicking another player.

sell [sel] **selling, sold**
卖 [mài]
Simon helped his father **sell** oranges.

set [set] **setting, set**
摆放 [bǎi fàng]
Andy is **setting** the table for dinner.

sell out [sel aʊt]
卖完 [mài wán]
The oranges **sold out** in an hour.

set about [set əˈbaʊt]
开始 [kāi shǐ]
Andy **set about** his homework right after dinner.

set off [set ɒf]
出发 [chū fā]
The boys **set off** on their hike at daybreak.

shear [ʃɪə] **shearing, sheared**
剪毛 [jiǎn máo]
The farmer is **shearing** a sheep.

shine [ʃaɪn] **shining, shined**
擦亮 [cā liàng]
Jimmy **shines** his shoes every morning before school.

shock [ʃɒk] **shocking, shocked**
吓 [xià]
The news **shocked** Mandy. She didn't expect such a terrible thing to happen.

seal [siːl] **sealing, sealed**
糊住 [hú zhù]
Peter put the letter in the envelope and **sealed** it.

sign [saɪn] **signing, signed**
签名 [qiān míng]
Peter **signed** his name at the bottom of the letter.

show [ʃəʊ] **showing, showed**
给 ...... 看 [gěi ...... kān]
The salesman is **showing** Kathy some shoes.

shop [ʃɒp] **shopping, shopped**
选购 [xuǎn guò]
Linda is **shopping** for a pair of sunglasses.

show off [ʃəʊ ɒf]
炫耀 [xuàn yào]
Kathy is **showing off** her new shoes.

show up [ʃəʊ ʌp]
出现 [chū xiàn]
Jimmy **showed up** after Helen had waited for him for an hour.

shake [ʃeɪk] **shaking, shook**
摇动 [yáo dòng]

Andy is **shaking** the bottle to mix the medicine.

shake off [ʃeɪk ɒf]
抖落 [dǒu luò]

A spider landed on Mandy's hand, but she **shook** it **off**.

separate [ˈseprət]
separating, separated
分开 [fēn kāi]

Mother is **separating** the egg yolk from the egg white.

serve [sɜːv] **serving, served**
奉上 [fèng shɑng]

Kathy is **serving** drinks to her guests.

sharpen [ˈʃɑːpən]
sharpening, sharpened
磨利 [mó lì]

Father is **sharpening** the carving knife.

sew [səʊ] **sewing, sewed**
缝 [féng]

Grandmother **sewed** the button on my jacket.

sit [sɪt] **sitting, sat**
坐 [zuò]

Andy is **sitting** on the beanbag.

sit down [sɪt daʊn]
坐下 [zuò xiɑ]

Jimmy **sat down** and watched television.

sit up [sɪt ʌp]
坐正、坐好 [zuò zhèng, zuò hɑ̀o]

The teacher told Andy to **sit up** and pay attention.

sit back [sɪt bæk]
休息 [xiū xi]

Grandfather **sits back** while Kathy does the work.

shift [ʃɪft] **shifting, shifted**
搬 [bān]

Willy is **shifting** the armchair closer to the fireplace.

soak [səʊk] **soaking, soaked**
泡 [pào]

Bobby is **soaking** his feet in a bucket of hot water.

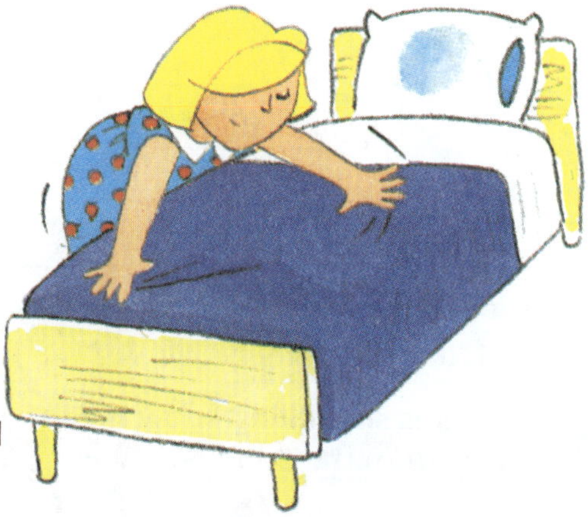

smooth [smuːð]
smoothing, smoothed
弄平 [nòng píng]

Kathy is **smoothing** out the wrinkles on the bed.

shower [ˈʃaʊə]
showering, showered
洗澡 [xǐ zǎo]

You are dirty! Go and **shower**.

sing [sɪŋ] **singing, sang**
唱歌 [chàng gē]

Andy likes to **sing** in the shower.

shell [ʃel] **shelling, shelled**
剥壳 [bō ké]

Linda is **shelling** the nuts for the fruitcake.

shut [ʃʌt] **shutting, shut**
关上 [guān shang]

Kathy is **shutting** the window because the rain is coming in.

shut up [ʃʌt ʌp]
住口 [zhù kǒu]

Andy has been talking for an hour. His brother tells him to **shut up**.

snore [snɔː] **snoring, snored**
打鼾 [dǎ hān]

Grandfather **snores** when he sleeps.

ski [skiː] **skiing, skied**
滑雪 [huá xuě]

Jimmy learned to **ski** during his holiday in Switzerland.

shovel [ˈʃʌvl]
shovelling, shovelled
铲 [chǎn]

Father is **shovelling** snow away from the door.

shiver [ˈʃɪvə]
shivering, shivered
发抖 [fā dǒu]

It is so cold that Simon is **shivering**.

skate [skeɪt] **skating, skated**
溜冰 [liū bīng]

The children are **skating** on a frozen pond.

slap [slæp] **slapping, slapped**
拍打 [pāi dǎ]

Jimmy **slapped** his friend on the back.

shrink [ʃrɪŋk]
shrinking, shrank
缩小 [suō xiǎo]

Willy's sweater **shrank** in the wash.

stamp [stæmp]
stamping, stamped
跺脚 [duò jiǎo]

Helen is **stamping** her feet to keep warm.

step [step] **stepping, stepped**
跨 [kuà]

Mandy is **stepping** over the fallen log.

slope [sləʊp] **sloping, sloped**
斜 [xié]

The path is **sloping** up the hill.

spin [spɪn] **spinning, spun**
旋转 [xuán zhuǎn]

Can you **spin** on a frozen pond?

slide [slaɪd] **sliding, slid**
滑动 [huá dòng]

Bobby is **sliding** down the hill on a tyre.

sniff [snɪf] **sniffing, sniffed**
嗅 [xiù]

The dog **sniffed** the rabbit.

surprise [səˈpraɪz]
surprising, surprised
使惊奇 [shǐ jīng qí]

Andy **surprised** Mandy when he jumped out from behind the snowman.

snow [snəʊ] **snowing, snowed**
下雪 [xià xuě]

It **snows** in winter, and you can make a snowman.

sneeze [sniːz]
sneezing, sneezed
打喷嚏 [dǎ pēn tì]

Willy **sneezes** because he has a cold.

support [səˈpɔːt] **supporting, supported**
支撑 [zhī chēng]

We **supported** Willy and helped him off the snow.

stare [steə] **staring, stared**
盯着 [dīng zhe]

Linda is **staring** at the chick in amazement.

shoot [ʃuːt] **shooting, shot**
射 [shè]

Bobby **shoots** at the target twice.

shelter [ˈʃeltə] **sheltering, sheltered**
躲避 [duǒ bì]

The sheep **found shelter** from the rain under the tree.

stink [stɪŋk] **stinking, stank**
发臭 [fā chòu]

The rotting fish **stinks**.

slip [slɪp]
slipping, slipped
滑倒 [huá dǎo]

The clown **slipped** on the banana skin.

slip off [slɪp ɒf]
脱下 [tuō xià]

Jimmy **slipped** his shoes **off** before entering the house.

spell [spel] **spelling, spelled**
拼读 [pīn dú]

Linda can **spell** her name.

smash [smæʃ] **smashing, smashed**
打碎 [dǎ suì]

Willy dropped a glass and it **smashed** into pieces.

snatch [snætʃ]
snatching, snatched
抢走 [qiǎng zǒu]

Andy **snatched** the toy from his sister.

slice [slaɪs] **slicing, sliced**
切片 [qiē piān]

Aunt Molly is **slicing** some bread for lunch.

sow [səʊ] **sowing, sowed**
播种 [bō zhǒng]

Andy **sows** the seeds in the garden.

spray [spreɪ] **spraying, sprayed**
浇洒 [jiāo sǎ]

Grandfather is **spraying** water on the plants.

sweep [swiːp]
sweeping, swept
扫 [sǎo]

Jimmy is **sweeping** the leaves from the path.

sprinkle [ˈsprɪŋkl] **sprinkling, sprinkled**
轻洒 [qīng sǎ]

Kathy is **sprinkling** water on the flowers.

see [siː] **seeing, saw**
看见 [kàn jiàn]

Willy **sees** a caterpillar on the leaf.

spot [spɒt] **spotting, spotted**
发现 [fā xiàn]

Simon **spotted** a bug on another leaf.

swallow [ˈswɒləʊ]
swallowing, swallowed
吞下 [tūn xià]

The snake **swallowed** a whole chicken.

sting [stɪŋ] **stinging, stung**
叮 [dīng]

A bee **stung** Mandy on the finger.

smell [smel] **smelling, smelled**
嗅 [xiù]

Smell this and tell me what it is.

swell [swel] **swelling, swelled**
肿 [zhǒng]

Mandy's finger **swelled** up after a bee stung her there.

spill [spɪl] **spilling, spilled**
洒落 [sǎ luò]

The baby knocked his plate over and the food **spilled** onto the floor.

spoon [spu:n] **spooning, spooned**
舀 [yǎo]

Mother is **spooning** food into the baby's mouth.

spring [sprɪŋ] **springing, sprang**
弹起 [tán qǐ]

The jack-in-the-box lid **sprang** open, making the baby laugh.

speak [spi:k] **speaking, spoke**
说话 [shuō huà]

Speak softly! Baby is sleeping.

stuff [stʌf] **stuffing, stuffed**
塞满 [sāi mǎn]

Mother is **stuffing** the pillow with feathers.

sleep [sli:p] **sleeping, slept**
睡 [shuì]

Babies look sweet when they are **sleeping**.

smile [smaɪl] **smiling, smiled**
微笑 [wēi xiào]

The baby **smiled** when it saw its father.

spit [spɪt] **spitting, spat**
吐 [tǔ]

The food tasted awful so Andy **spat** it out.

spank [spæŋk] **spanking, spanked**
打屁股 [dǎ pì gǔ]

Father **spanked** Andy for tearing the book.

speed [spi:d] **speeding, sped**
加速前进 [jiā sù qián jìn]

Uncle Roy is **speeding** around the race track on his motorbike. See how fast he goes.

spend [spend] **spending, spent**
用 [yòng]

Jimmy has **spent** all his money. He has no money left.

split [splɪt] **splitting, split**
劈开 [pī kāi]

Father **split** the wood with an axe.

split up [splɪt ʌp]
分开 [fēn kāi]

Terry and Andy talked in class so the teacher **split** them **up**.

stack [stæk] **stacking, stacked**
堆 [duī]

Mandy is **stacking** her building blocks.

squat [skwɒt] **squatting, squatted**
蹲下 [dūn xià]

The policeman **squats** down to talk to the little lost girl.

steer [stɪə] **steering, steered**
驾驭 [jià yù]

You **steer** a horse with the reins.

squash [skwɒʃ] **squashing, squashed**
压扁 [yā biǎn]

Andy's car ran over the ball and **squashed** it.

spoil [spɔɪl] **spoilling, spoiled**
溺爱 [nì ài]

Willy's parents **spoil** him. They put the television and video recorder in his room.

store [stɔː] **storing, stored**
储藏、收藏 [chǔ cáng, shōu cáng]

The boxes are **stored** in the attic.

shave [ʃeɪv] **shaving, shaved**
剃 [tì]

Father **shaves** every morning.

squeeze [skwiːz]
squeezing, squeezed 挤 [jǐ]

Willy is **squeezing** some toothpaste onto his toothbrush.

shampoo [ʃæmˈpuː]
shampooing, shampooed
洗发 [xǐ fà]

Kathy is **shampooing** her hair.

stay [steɪ] **staying, stayed**
住 [zhù]

Grandfather has come to **stay** with us for the weekend.

stay up [steɪ ʌp]
熬夜 [áo yè]

Andy **stayed up** till midnight to finish the ghost story.

stay in [steɪ ɪn]
留堂 [líu táng]

Helen had to **stay in** after school to do her homework.

stay out [steɪ aʊt]
在外面 [zài wài miàn]

The boys **stayed out** in the garden all night.

stay away [steɪ əˈweɪ] 离开、别靠近 [lí kāi, bié kào jìn]
"**Stay away** from the fire," said Aunt Molly. "You might get burned."

steal [stiːl] **stealing, stole**
偷 [tōu]

The burglar is **stealing** the silver.

start [stɑːt]
starting, started
开始 [kāi shǐ]

Grandmother has **started** knitting a jumper, but she hasn't finished it yet.

stretch [stretʃ] **stretching, stretched**
伸展 [shēn zhǎn]

Willy gets out of bed and **stretches** himself.

stick [stɪk] **sticking, stuck**
贴 [tiē]

Kathy is **sticking** a stamp on the envelope.

stoop [stuːp] **stooping, stooped**
弯腰 [wān yāo]

Andy **stoops** to pick up the pencil.

stir [stɜː] **stirring, stirred**
搅拌 [jiǎo bàn]

Kathy is **stirring** the soup in the saucepan.

stick up [stɪk ʌp]
举起 [jǔ qǐ]

"**Stick up** your hands!" said the robber.

stick out [stɪk aʊt]
伸出 [shēn chū]

Andy is **sticking out** his tongue at his friend.

stick together [stɪk təˈgeðə]
黏在一起 [nián zài yī qǐ]

The pieces of the broken vase have been **stuck together** with glue.

stand for [stænd fə]
代表 [dài biǎo]

What colour **stands for** danger?

stand [stænd] **standing, stood**
站 [zhàn]

Andy **stands** on the stool to reach the cookie jar.

stand back [stænd bæk]
退后 [tuì hòu]
The police officer told everyone to **stand back** from the monster.

stitch [stɪtʃ]
stitching, stitched
缝缀 [féng zhuì]

Grandmother **stitched** a pretty bow on the collar of the dress.

stand up [stænd ʌp]
站起来 [zhàn qǐ lái]

Stand up and give your seat to the old gentleman.

stitch up [stɪtʃ ʌp]
缝好 [féng hǎo]

My hem came undone, so I **stitched** it **up**.

stop [stɒp] **stopping, stopped**
停止 [tíng zhǐ]

Our car **stopped** at the red light.

stop up [stɒp ʌp]
塞住 [sài zhù]

Bobby **stopped up** the hole in the wall with cardboard.

string [strɪŋ] **stringing, strung**
串起 [chuàn qǐ]

Linda is **stringing** the beads to make a necklace.

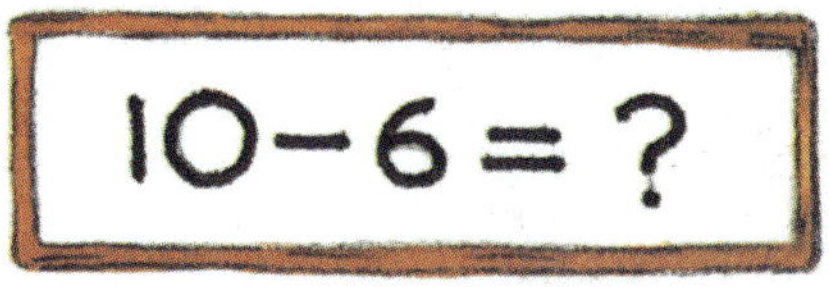

subtract [səbˈtrækt]
subtracting, subtracted 减 [jiǎn]

Can you **subtract** six from ten?

surround [səˈraʊnd] **surrounding, surrounded**
包围 [bāo wéi]

Sharks **surrounded** the boat.

study [ˈstʌdɪ] **studying, studied**
学习 [xué xí]

Every night Peter **studies** for his exam.

succeed [səkˈsiːd] **succeeding, succeeded**
成功 [chéng gōng]

Peter **succeeded** in passing his exam.

suit [suːt] **suiting, suited**
适合 [shì hé]

This dress doesn't **suit** Aunt Molly. It makes her look fat.

sweat [swet] **sweating, sweated**
出汗 [chū hàn]

The runners are **sweating**.

swing [swɪŋ] **swinging, swung**
荡 [dàng]

The monkey is **swinging** from one bar to another.

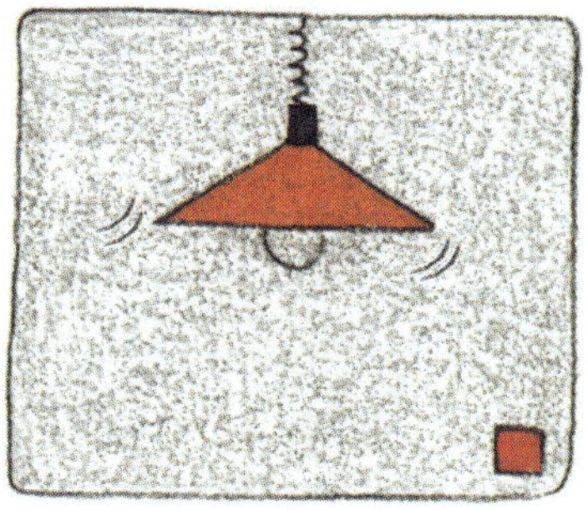

switch [swɪtʃ] **switching, switched**
调换 [diào huàn]

The clowns **switched** their hats, making the people laugh.

switch off [swɪtʃ ɒf]
关 [guān]

Mother **switched off** the light before leaving the room.

switch on [swɪtʃ ɒn]
开 [kāi]

Jimmy **switched on** the television.

Tt

teach [tiːtʃ] **teaching, taught**
教 [jiào]

Grandmother is **teaching** Kathy how to knit.

thread [θred] **threading, threaded**
穿针线 [chuān zhēn xiàn]

Aunt Molly **threaded** the needle to do some sewing.

tap [tæp] **tapping, tapped**
轻拍 [qīng pāi]

Linda **tapped** Andy on his shoulder to get his attention.

telephone [ˈtelɪfəʊn]
telephoning, telephoned
打电话 [dǎ diàn huà]

The house is on fire! **Telephone** the fire station.

tick [tɪk] **ticking, ticked**
给 ...... 标记号 [gěi ...... biāo jì hao]

The teacher **ticked** all the sums that were correct.

test [test] **testing, tested**
检验 [jiǎn yàn]

The doctor is **testing** Bobby's eyes to see if he needs glasses.

tidy [ˈtaɪdɪ] **tidying, tidied**
整理 [zhěng lǐ]

The desk was a mess, so Kathy **tidied** it up.

tick off [tɪk ɒf]
剔除 [tī chú]

Benny **ticked off** the things on the list that he has got for the camp.

throw [θrəʊ]
throwing, threw
投掷 [tóu zhì]

Jimmy **threw** the ball to Rusty.

throw away [θrəʊ əˈweɪ]
扔掉 [rēng diào]

The radio was broken, so Andy **threw** it **away**.

tie [taɪ] **tying, tied**
打结 [dǎ jié]

Scouts learn to **tie** different knots.

tie up [taɪ ʌp]
捆绑 [kǔn bǎng]

We are playing cops and robbers. We are **tying up** the robber so he can't escape.

tighten [ˈtaɪtn] **tightening, tightened**
绑紧 [bǎng jǐn]

Willy **tightens** the knot to make sure that the rope will not slip down the tree.

tour [tʊə] **touring, toured**
旅行 [lǚ xíng]

Mandy is **touring** France with a friend.

touch [tʌtʃ] **touching, touched**
触摸 [chù mō]

Bend down and **touch** your toes.

touch down [tʌtʃ daʊn]
降落 [jiàng luò]

Our aeroplane **touched down** at the airport on time.

time [taɪm] **timing, timed**
计时 [jì shí]

Jimmy is running round the field. Father is **timing** him.

tip [tɪp] **tipping, tipped**
给小费 [gěi xiǎo fèi]

Father **tipped** the waiter for being helpful.

tip over [tɪp ˈəʊvə]
翻倒 [fān dǎo]

The bottle **tipped over** and the ketchup spilled on the carpet.

toast [təʊst] **toasting, toasted**
烘烤 [hōng kǎo]

Linda is **toasting** bread for breakfast.

thank [θæŋk] **thanking, thanked**
感谢 [gǎn xiè]
Jane **thanked** Peter for the birthday present.

tear [teə] **tearing, tore**
扯破 [chě pò]
Jimmy **tore** his coat on a nail.

tear up [teə ʌp]
撕毁 [sī huǐ]
Linda didn't like her drawing, so she **tore** it **up**.

tear out [teə aʊt]
撕下 [sī xià]
Bobby **tore out** a photograph from the newspaper.

trick [trɪk] **tricking, tricked**
戏弄 [xì nòng]
Andy **tricked** Linda with a plastic spider.

talk [tɔːk] **talking, talked**
讲话 [jiǎng huà]
The parrot can **talk**.

take off [teɪk ɒf]
脱下 [tuō xià]
Kathy is **taking off** her coat.

take [teɪk] **taking, took**
拿 [ná]
Willy is **taking** a cookie from the jar.

take up [teɪk ʌp]
开始学习 [kāi shǐ xué xí]
Mandy wants to **take up** ballet.

think [θɪŋk] **thinking, thought**
想 [xiǎng]

Terry **thought** of what he wanted for his birthday.

think up [θɪŋk ʌp]
设计 [shè jì]

Mandy **thought up** a good costume for the fancy-dress party.

try on [traɪ ɒn] 试穿 [shì chuān]

Kathy is **trying on** a beautiful party dress.

toss [tɒs]
tossing, tossed
抛 [pāo]

Willy and Helen are **tossing** the ball to each other.

try [traɪ] **trying, tried**
尝试 [cháng shì]

Benny is **trying** to lift the weights, but he cannot.

tickle [ˈtɪkl] **tickling, tickled**
搔痒 [sāo yǎng]

Bobby **tickled** Andy's feet to make him laugh.

taste [teɪst] **tasting, tasted**
品尝 [pǐn cháng]

Lemons **taste** sour.

twist [twɪst] **twisting, twisted**
拧 [nǐng]

Willy **twisted** the cap to open the bottle.

tell [tel] **telling, told**
告诉 [gào su]

Simon is **telling** Kathy about his trip to Switzerland.

turn [tɜːn] **turning, turned**
转动 [zhuǎn dòng]

Mandy is blowing the windmill. See how it **turns**!

turn back [tɜːn bæk]
往回走 [wǎng huí zǒu]

The path is blocked, so Jimmy has to **turn back**.

turn down [tɜːn daʊn]
关小 [guān xiǎo]

Father asked Andy to **turn down** the radio because it was too loud.

turn on [tɜːn ɒn]
扭开 [niǔ kāi]

Mother **turned on** the television to watch the news.

turn off [tɜːn ɒf]
关上 [guān shang]

Turn off the bath water before it overflows!

turn up [tɜːn ʌp]
露面 [lòu miàn]

Jimmy **turned up** late for the party.

turn round [tɜːn raʊnd]
转身 [zhuǎn shēn]

The ballet dancer is **turning round** and round.

tremble [ˈtrembl]
trembling, trembled
发抖 [fā dǒu]

Andy **trembled** when he saw a monster coming towards him.

twinkle [ˈtwɪŋkl]
twinkling, twinkled
闪烁 [shǎn shuò]

The stars **twinkle** in the clear sky.

train [treɪn] **training, trained**
训练 [xùn liàn]

The man is **training** the elephant to stand on its back legs.

trap [træp] **trapping, trapped**
设陷阱捕捉 [shè xiàn jǐng bǔ zhuō]

The fox is **trapped**.

trip [trɪp] **tripping, tripped**
绊倒 [bàn dǎo]

Andy **tripped** over a stone.

tiptoe [ˈtɪptəʊ] **tiptoeing, tiptoed**
踮起脚走 [diǎn qǐ jiǎo zǒu]

The burglar is **tiptoeing** down the hall.

treat [triːt] **treating, treated**
对待 [duì dài]

Linda **treats** her pet rabbit very well. She feeds it and cleans its cage every day.

trim [trɪm] **trimming, trimmed**
修剪 [xiū jiǎn]

Grandfather is **trimming** the hedge.

travel [ˈtrævl] **travelling, travelled**
去 [qù]

Kathy **travels** to school by bus.

trace [treɪs] **tracing, traced**
描画 [miáo huà]

Andy is **tracing** a picture of a dinosaur.

type [taɪp] **typing, typed**
打字 [dǎ zì]

The secretary is **typing** a letter.

tuck [tʌk] **tucking, tucked**
盖好 [gài hǎo]

Mother is **tucking** the blanket in around the baby.

Uu

understand [ˌʌndəˈstænd]
understanding, understood
明白 [míng bɑi]

Bobby doesn't **understand** why the television won't work.

underline [ˌʌndəˈlaɪn]
underlining, underlined
在 ...... 下面画线
[zài ...... xià mian huà xiàn]

Kathy is **underlining** all the important words.

unload [ˌʌnˈləʊd] **unloading, unloaded**
卸下 [xiè xià]

The strong men are **unloading** the piano from the truck.

upset [ˌʌpˈset] **upsetting, upset**
弄翻 [nòng fān]

The cat **upset** the bowl of fish.

urge [ɜːdʒ] **urging, urged**
催促 [cuī cù]

Jimmy **urged** the dog to jump into the water.

unfasten [ˌʌnˈfɑːsn]
unfastening, unfastened
解开 [jiě kāi]

When the car stops, you can **unfasten** the safety belt.

unlock [ˌʌnˈlɒk]
unlocking, unlocked
开锁 [kāi suǒ]

Father is **unlocking** the door.

untie [ˌʌnˈtaɪ]
untying, untied
松开 [sōng kāi]

Untie your shoelaces before you take your shoes off.

undress [ˌʌnˈdres]
undressing, undressed 脱衣服 [tuō yī fu]

Kathy got **undressed** and ready for her bath.

unpack [ˌʌnˈpæk] **unpacking, unpacked**
打开 …… 取出东西
[dǎ kāi …… qǔ chū dōng xi]

Mandy **unpacks** her suitcase after her trip.

unwrap [ˌʌnˈræp]
unwrapping, unwrapped
打开 [dǎ kāi]

Linda is **unwrapping** her Christmas present.

use [juːz] **using, used**
用 [yòng]

Andy is **using** a blue crayon to colour the car.

unroll [ˌʌnˈrəʊl] **unrolling, unrolled**
铺开 [pū kāi]

Andy is **unrolling** his painting.

use up [juːz ʌp]
用光 [yòng guāng]

The milk is **used up**. We must buy some more.

Vv

vacuum [ˈvækjʊəm]
vacuuming, vacuumed
吸尘 [xī chén]

Aunt Molly is **vacuuming** the room.

visit [ˈvɪzɪt] **visiting, visited**
探望 [tàn wàng]

We **visited** Grandma at the hospital this afternoon.

vanish [ˈvænɪʃ] **vanishing, vanished**
消失 [xiāo shī]

The magician waved his wand and the rabbit **vanished**.

Ww

waddle [ˈwɒdl]
waddling, waddled
摇摇摆摆地走
[yáo yáo bǎi bǎi de zǒu]
A duck **waddles**.

wag [wæɡ]
wagging, wagged
摇动 [yáo dòng]
The puppy is **wagging** its tail happily.

wade [weɪd] **wading, waded**
涉水 [shè shuǐ]
Jimmy is **wading** through the water.

walk [wɔːm] **walking, walked**
散步 [sàn bù]
Grandfather is **walking** in the park.

walk off with
[wɔːk ɒf wɪð]
轻易赢得 [qīng yì yíng dé]
Andy **walked off with** the first prize in the painting contest.

wake [weɪk] **waking, woke**
弄醒 [nòng xǐng]
Be quiet! Don't **wake** the baby.

wake up [weɪk ʌp]
醒来 [xǐng lái]
The baby **woke up** because Andy was making a lot of noise.

wait [weɪt] **waiting, waited**
等候 [děng hòu]
Bobby is **waiting** at the bus stop.

wander [ˈwɒndə] **wandering, wandered**
徘徊 [pái huái]
Simon and Linda are **wandering** through the woods. They are lost.

warm [wɔːm] **warming, warmed**
取暖 [qǔ nuǎn]
We are **warming** ourselves round the fire.

warn [wɔːn] **warning, warned**
警告 [jǐng gào]

The red light **warns** you when the machine gets too hot.

wash [wɒʃ] **washing, washed**
洗 [xǐ]

Linda **washed** her hands after playing with the clay.

wash up [wɒʃ ʌp]
洗碗碟 [xǐ wǎn dié]

Kathy **washed up** the dishes after dinner.

waste [weɪst] **wasting, wasted**
浪费 [làng fèi]

Turn off the lights so you don't **waste** electricity.

weep [wiːp] **weeping, wept**
哭泣 [kū qì]

Jane is **weeping** over her broken doll.

water [ˈwɔːtə] **watering, watered**
浇水 [jiāo shuǐ]

Mandy **waters** her plants every day.

watch [wɒtʃ] **watching, watched**
观看 [guān kàn]

Bobby is **watching** a football game on television.

watch over [wɒtʃ əʊvə]
看守 [kān shǒu]

The mother hen **watches over** her chicks to make sure they are safe.

watch out [wɒtʃ aʊt]
注意 [zhù yì]

You must **watch out** for cars when you cross the road.

wave [weɪv] **waving, waved**
挥手 [huī shǒu]

Kathy is **waving** goodbye to her friend.

wear [weə] **wearing, worn**
穿 [chuān]

Kathy is **wearing** her mother's shoes.

wear out [weə aʊt]
穿破 [chuān pò]

Jimmy's shoes have holes in them. They are **worn out**.

wheel [wiːl]
wheeling, wheeled
推 [tuī]

The nurse is **wheeling** Willy down the corridor.

whip [wɪp] **whipping, whipped**
搅拌 [jiǎo bàn]

Linda is **whipping** the cream for the apple pie.

wet [wet] **wetting, wetted or wet**
弄湿 [nòng shī]

Bobby **wet** his shoes when he stepped into a puddle.

weigh [weɪ] **weighing, weighed**
秤 [chèng]

The butcher is **weighing** the meat.

whistle [ˈwɪsl] **whistling, whistled**
吹口哨 [chuī kǒu shào]

Jimmy is **whistling** his dog back.

whisper [ˈwɪspə] **whispering, whispered**
耳语 [ěr yǔ]

Whisper the secret so only I can hear you.

win [wɪn] **winning, won**
赢得 [yíng dé]

My pet dog **won** first prize at the dog show.

weave [wiːv]
weaving, wove
编织 [biān zhī]

Mandy is **weaving** a basket.

welcome [ˈwelkəm]
welcoming, welcomed
欢迎 [huān yíng]

Kathy **welcomes** her aunt with flowers.

wind [wɪnd] **winding, wound**
绕 [rào]

The road **winds** around the hill.

wind up [wɪnd ʌp]
给 ...... 上发条 [gěi ...... shàng fā tiáo]

Father **winds up** grandfather's clock once a week.

wink [wɪŋk] **winking, winked**
眨眼 [zhǎ yǎn]

Willy **winked** at me.

wish [wɪʃ] **wishing, wished**
希望 [xī wàng]

Andy **wished** that he had never gone for a ride with Uncle Roy.

work [wɜːk] **working, worked**
从事 [cóng chì]

Mr. Hart **works** as train driver.

work out [wɜːk aʊt]
算出 [suàn chū]

The teacher is **working out** the answer on the blackboard.

wriggle [ˈrɪgl] **wriggling, wriggled**
蠕动 [rú dòng]

The worms **wriggled** in the jar.

wipe [waɪp] **wiping, wiped**
擦 [cā]

Andy is **wiping** his hands on the cloth.

wring [rɪŋ] **wringing, wrung**
拧 [níng]

Mother is **wringing** the water out of the cloth.

wound [wuːnd] **wounding, wounded**
受伤 [shòu shāng]

The soldier was **wounded** in the shoulder.

worry [ˈwʌrɪ] **worrying, worried**
担心 [dān xīn]

Andy is **worrying** about his sick grandmother.

wrap [ræp] **wrapping, wrapped**
包 [bāo]

Mandy is **wrapping** up the birthday present.

wrinkle [ˈrɪŋkl]
wrinkling, wrinkled
皱起来 [zhòu qǐ lái]

When Uncle Tom frowns, he **wrinkles** his forehead.

wonder [ˈwʌndə]
wondering, wondered
很想知道 [hěn xiǎng zhī dao]

Simon cannot find his cat. He **wonders** where it is.

write [raɪt] **writing, wrote**
写 [xiě]

Linda is **writing** a letter to her cousin.

write down [raɪt daʊn]
记下 [jì xià]

Aunt Molly is **writing down** all the things she needs to buy.

Yy

yawn [jɔːn] **yawning, yawned**
打呵欠 [dǎ hē qiàn]

When you are tired, you **yawn**.

yell [jel] **yelling, yelled**
喊叫 [hǎn jiào]

The baby is **yelling** for her mother.

Zz

zip [zɪp] **zipping, zipped**
拉上拉链 [lā shàng lā liàn]

Jimmy carefully **zipped** his jacket.

zoom [zuːm] **zooming, zoomed**
飞驰而过 [fēi chí ér guò]

The car **zoomed** past us.

Published by Marshall Cavendish Education
Marshall Cavendish Education is an imprint of Times Publishing Limited.

Times Publishing (Hong Kong) Limited
10/F, Block C, Seaview Estate,
2-8 Watson Road, North Point, Hong Kong
Tel: (852) 2481 1930 Fax: (852) 2481 3379
Email: genoffice@marshallcavendish.com.hk
Website: www.marshallcavendish.com.hk

Other Marshall Cavendish Offices:
Marshall Cavendish Corporation. 99 White Plains Road, Tarrytown NY 10591-9001, USA · Marshall Cavendish International (Singapore) Pte Ltd., Times Centre, 1 New Industrial Road, Singapore 536196 · Marshall Cavendish International (Thailand) Co Ltd. 253 Asoke, 12th Flr, Sukhumvit 21 Road, Klongtoey Nua, Wattana, Bangkok 10110, Thailand · Marshall Cavendish (Malaysia) Sdn Bhd, Times Subang, Lot 46, Subang Hi-Tech Industrial Park, Batu Tiga, 40000 Shah Alam, Selangor Darul Ehsan, Malaysia

Exclusive distributor for China:
SINO-COMMERCIAL TRADING CORP. International Book Services
Email: b.marketing@sino-commercial.com
Online-shop: zhswts.tmall.com

ISBN 978-988-226-269-0

First published 2013

P01-0813EB